Praise for M

Moving to L

This is kind of a funny book for me to be re~~~~~~~ter, but a lot of people ask me about this~~~~~~~columnist for *Linux Journal*, and in Movi~~~~~~~ he's prepared a step-by-step guide to converting a Windows PC to Linux—or just trying it! The book includes a bootable CD with a version of Linux that you can poke around in without touching or changing anything about your Windows installation. If your boss is asking, "What's with this Linux stuff?", "Moving to Linux" is a great way to show that you know what you're talking about.

— Brian Livingston, `Briansbuzz.com`

Pros: Too many to list in the available space. We liked the book from the very first page right through to the end. Gagné has done a solid job of exposing Linux and all its components in a way that is both inviting, useful and easy to understand…We really liked this book—highly recommended.

— Howard Carson, *Kickstart News*

Marcel walks the user through each technique in a very chatty and comfortable style: in fact, when I put the book down, I had a momentary impression that I'd just finished watching a good cooking show with an entertaining chef. (Australian readers may understand if I say that it felt like having just watched Ian Parmenter do an episode of 'Consuming Passions.')

— Jenn Vesperman, `Linuxchix.org`

As I read Marcel Gagné's "Moving to Linux" I was conflicted. In many ways I was envious because this is the book I wish I had written. On the other hand I wished I could add a little more detail here and there. However, without a doubt this is an excellent resource for the uninitiated Linux desktop user. I enjoy Marcel's conversational style and subtle humor, which make this book more interesting than the many Linux books that aim to supplement readers' existing Linux knowledge rather than start them on their journey into the Linux desktop.

— Mark R. Hinkle, *LinuxWorld Magazine*

Marcel Gagné, true to form, has written another excellent book. What's more, its release couldn't have been timed better and the formula he proposes for Linux migration is just what we need right now. With his book you have the possibility of trying Linux with no pain and no strings attached. If you like what you see, you can get yourself some Red Hat or Mandrake CDs and then, using this book as your guide, you'll be "Moving to Linux" and handing the hat to viruses and lost productivity and of course, kissing the blue screen of death goodbye.

— Michael Jordan, `Linux.org`

More Praise for Marcel Gagne's *Moving to Linux*

Gagné's "Moving to Linux" is a straightforward exposition of just how a non-hacker PC user can get rid of "The Blue Screen of Death". If you have a friend, a co-worker, a significant other, or a relative who periodically screams, sighs, bursts into tears, or asks for help, here's the simple solution. It comes with a bootable CD of Knoppix, Klaus Knopper's variant of Debian.

— Peter H. Salus, writing in *;login:, the Usenix magazine.*

If you are a Windows user, and you would like to know how Linux can benefit you, without all the technical jargon that could put an insomniac asleep? This is the book you have been waiting for…All in all, the book is great, and I would recommend it to anyone interested in trying Linux. If you want a no nonsense, non confusing and all around easy to read and understand book about Linux, this is it.

— *SJ LUG Book Reviews*

This is a book aimed not at you, dear developer/techie/guru, but at your friends, acquaintances and family who are lowly users of Windows. Yes, such people do exist even in the tightest of families. Fear not, however, because salvation is at hand should any of them decide that this Linux thing might be worth investigating. No longer will you be faced with the unenviable task of walking them through the process of switching OS. "Moving to Linux: Kiss the Blue Screen of Death Goodbye!" is a big, bold and friendly guide to help them along. The emphasis is firmly on using Linux as a desktop system—this isn't a book about Linux as a file, print or web server.

— *Tech Book Reports*

Moving to Linux is definitely a beginner's book. It's a big fluffy puppy of a book that will help ease new users into Linux without scaring them with tons of commands to know. In fact, the book is almost wholly devoted to life at the GUI, which means that Windows and Mac users should feel fairly comfortable with the switch…One problem that many Linux books for beginners face is trying to cover all of the various window managers that users might run into. Gagnè avoids this by sticking with KDE throughout the book. Some might quibble that this doesn't give users the full spectrum of possibilities with Linux—but I like Gagnè's approach.

— Joe "Zonker" Brockmeier, `UnixReview.com`

Moving to the
Linux Business Desktop

Moving to the Linux Business Desktop

Marcel Gagné

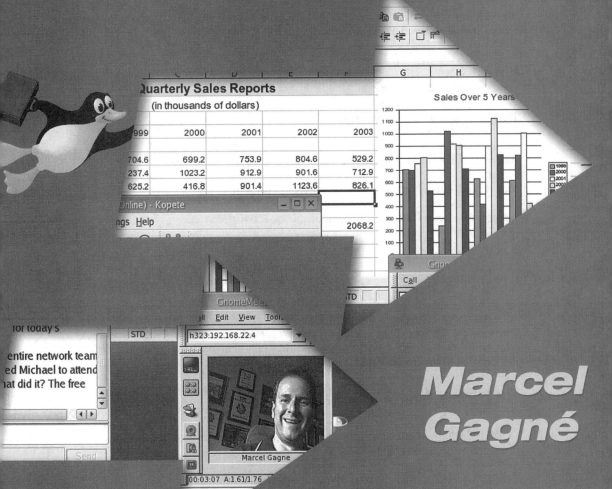

Quarterly Sales Reports
(in thousands of dollars)

	999	2000	2001	2002	2003
	704.6	699.2	753.9	804.6	529.2
	237.4	1023.2	912.9	901.6	712.9
	625.2	416.8	901.4	1123.6	826.1
					2068.2

Sales Over 5 Years

Marcel Gagne

✦ Addison-Wesley

Boston • San Francisco • New York • Toronto • Montreal
London • Munich • Paris • Madrid
Capetown • Sydney • Tokyo • Singapore • Mexico City

05

The publisher offers discounts on this book when ordered in quantity for bulk purchases and special sales. For more information, please contact:

U.S. Corporate and Government Sales
(800) 382-3419
corpsales@pearsontechgroup.com

For sales outside of the U.S., please contact:

International Sales
international@pearsontechgroup.com

Visit Addison-Wesley on the Web: www.awprofessional.com

Library of Congress Cataloging-in-Publication Data: 2004107955

ISBN 0-131-42192-1

Pearson Education, Inc.
Rights and Contracts Department
75 Arlington Street, Suite 300
Boston, MA 02116
Fax: (617) 848-7047

ISBN: 0-131-42192-1
Text printed on recycled paper
2   3   4   5   6   7
First printing, [August 2004]

This book is dedicated to
Christine,
Guylaine,
Lynda,
and Michael,
the best siblings a brother could ask for!

Contents

Part 2

Chapter 11
Web-based Administration   **239**

Chapter 27
Word Processing (It Was a Dark and Stormy Night...)　509

Acknowledgements

The book you hold in your hands is my third, and as such, a kind of milestone for me. Having been born in Québec, I am French-Canadian and, as with all cultures, there are these little phrases or sayings that follow you through life. Some call them truisms, others superstitions. Some, like me, just find that these little phrases form a kind of indelible program written in a kind of personal ROM. The saying in question is *"Jamais deux sans trois,"* which translates to "never two without three." In this case, I'm thrilled to see it come true.

This book, as with all books, was both amazingly hard work, but exciting and rewarding at the same time, a feeling that I hope will echo in the words and pages that follow. No book is ever the product of one individual, and while writers basically spend a lot of time locked away by themselves, putting words to paper, this is not something you do on your own. My wife, Sally, as well as my friends and family—all have played a part in the creation of this book. Their confidence, support, and love helped to keep me going. I'd like to take a moment to recognize some of these people.

First and foremost, I have to thank my beautiful wife, Sally Tomasevic, first reviewer of everything I write. She is my love, my life, my inspiration, and my strength.

Many thanks to Mark Taub, my editor, and to everyone at my publisher, Addison-Wesley. Also, many thanks to Richard Curtis, my agent.

Sincere thanks to those people who reviewed my book along the way. They are (in alphabetical order by last name) Scott Dier, Jim McQuillan,

Jordan Rosen, Sally Tomasevic, and Aaron Weber. The process of reviewing is hard work and I truly appreciate their efforts, sharp eyes, and suggestions.

Finally, I would like to recognize and thank the Linux community: the developers and software designers, the members of Linux user groups (including my own WFTL-LUG), the many who share their experiences on Usenet, and all those unnamed folks who give free advice under pseudonyms in IRC groups.

I thank you all.

part
1
Getting to Know Linux

1

Introduction

Welcome to the Linux universe and your new, all-powerful Linux desktop!

Very recently, city council in Munich, Germany, decided to switch its 14,000 computer systems running Windows over to Linux. As I write this, Paris, France, is looking at converting 17,000 workstations and 400 servers to Linux. The region of Extremadura in Spain deployed 80,000 Linux desktops for its schools. A little further east, Rome, Italy, is looking to deploy Linux desktops to some 9,500 employees. On a smaller scale, and closer to my part of the world, Legal Aid Manitoba converted its 150 workstations and its servers to Linux for a conservatively estimated taxpayer savings of $350,000. In its report, "The Linux Tipping Point" (March 2003), Forrester Research stated that 72% of the interviewed IT executives from $1 billion companies expected to use more Linux in 2004. Of that group, 26% were replacing Windows servers, and 13 of the 50 consulted said they would be using Linux on the desktop.

My Linux use goes back some ten years. Although in those early years I concentrated on server applications, I was already wondering about running my desktop on Linux. As I write this in 2004, I'm marking six years of running my system entirely Microsoft-free. The operating system for my desktop computer currently is Mandrake Linux; however, I have run many other Linux distributions as well. In all those years, I can honestly say that I never missed running Windows. In particular, I don't miss the constant crashes, "illegal operations," or virus-of-the-week problems. I read and send my email, communicate with others, write my documents, and indulge in the occasional bit of light entertainment. I am writing this book using OpenOffice 1.1, a full-featured and free alternative to Microsoft Office. With it, I can write documents in Word format, edit spreadsheets in Excel format, and create presentations in PowerPoint format, and I don't need Microsoft Office.

Many businesses, governments, and schools are discovering that, like me, they don't need Microsoft Windows to run their businesses. In return, they save thousands to millions of dollars. Amazon.com, Toyota, Largo City, Florida, and numerous other companies and government agencies around the world are making the switch to Linux on the desktop. Their reasons are the same as mine:

- Cost savings
- Freedom from proprietary licensing issues
- Stability and reliability
- Security
- An open source model that admits to and corrects problems
  rather than hiding them.

Open source means no secrets, which is particularly important to governments and security-conscious organizations that demand to know what their computers are really doing.

The numbers of people, companies, and organizations looking for an alternative to Microsoft are growing, but moving to Linux requires a roadmap. How will they continue to read and write the hundreds of Word documents, Excel spreadsheets, and email messages on their systems? How can they pick up where they left off and continue on with their new Linux desktops? The systems administrators in charge of these deployments need an understanding of the process, the potential problems, and the issues surrounding such a move.

Answering these questions and dealing with these challenges is precisely what this book is about. It is a real-world look at moving from Windows to Linux. I wrote this book with the corporate systems administrator in mind, but I have made a few assumptions. The first is that you are probably coming from the Windows world. That means I'll start with the basics and build in complexity as you make your way through the various sections of the book. The second is that you aren't necessarily coming from a large business. The information in this book applies just as easily to a company of one or two people as it does to an organization of two or three thousand.

My final assumption is that you might be reading this book strictly for yourself, looking to learn about Linux and the Linux desktop. Rest assured that there is also a great deal of focus on the end user experience.

Today, Linux stands ready to provide the first serious competition to the Microsoft empire and its virtual monopoly in office servers and desktop systems. The new licensing costs, the constant security issues, the virus of the day—all of these issues are very real to people in the business world. In that alone, the importance and potential of the Linux operating system is undeniable. In the cash-strapped world of the early twenty-first century, Linux makes great business sense. Linux is no longer simply about providing server services. It is about the desktop as well.

What Is Linux?

Linux has finally hit the mainstream; so much so that the first question I get from people these days is no longer, "What is Linux?" but rather, "What do I have to do to get Linux on my system?" Nevertheless, allow me a moment to introduce your new operating system.

Linux is a fully multitasking operating system based on UNIX, although technically, Linux is the kernel, the master program that makes running a Linux system possible. That kernel, by the way, was written by a young Finnish student named Linus Torvalds. On August 25, 1991, Torvalds posted the following now-famous and perhaps legendary message to the Usenet group `comp.os.minix`. The last paragraph is especially interesting when you consider where we are today in the Linux world.

```
From: torvalds@klaava.Helsinki.FI (Linus Benedict Torvalds)
        Newsgroups: comp.os.minix
        Subject: What would you like to see most in minix?
        Summary: small poll for my new operating system
        Message-ID: <1991Aug25.205708.9541@klaava.Helsinki.FI>
        Date: 25 Aug 91 20:57:08 GMT
        Organization: University of Helsinki
```

```
Hello everybody out there using minix -
    I'm doing a (free) operating system (just a hobby, won't be
big and professional like gnu) for 386(486) AT clones. This has
been brewing since april, and is starting to get ready. I'd like
any feedback on things people like/dislike in minix, as my OS
resembles it somewhat (same physical layout of the file-system
(due to practical reasons) among other things).
    I've currently ported bash(1.08) and gcc(1.40), and things
seem to work. This implies that I'll get something practical
within a few months, and I'd like to know what features most
people would want. Any suggestions are welcome, but I won't
promise I'll implement them :-)
            Linus (torvalds@kruuna.helsinki.fi)
    PS. Yes - it's free of any minix code, and it has a multi-
threaded fs. It is NOT protable (uses 386 task switching etc), and
it probably never will support anything other than AT-hard disks,
as that's all I have :-(.
```

Much has happened since then. Linus somehow captured the imagination of scores of talented programmers around the world. Joined together through the magic of the Internet, they collaborated, coded, tweaked, and gave birth to the operating system that is now revolutionizing the world of computing.

These days, Linux is a powerful, rock-solid, reliable, expandable, flexible, configurable, multiuser, multitasking, and completely free operating system that runs on many different platforms, including Intel PCs, DEC Alphas, Macintosh systems, PowerPCs, and a growing number of embedded processors. You can find Linux in PDA organizers, digital watches, golf carts, and cell phones. In fact, Linux has a greater support base in terms of platforms than just about any other operating system in the world.

What we call the Linux operating system is not the work of just one man alone. Linus Torvalds is the original architect of Linux—its father, if you will—but his is not the only effort behind it. Perhaps Linus Torvalds' greatest genius lay in knowing when to share the load. For no other pay but satisfaction, he employed people around the world, delegated to them, worked with them, and asked for and accepted feedback in a next generation of the model that began with the *GNU project*.

GNU is a recursive acronym that stands for GNU's Not UNIX, a project of the Free Software Foundation. This project was started in 1984 with the intention of creating a free, UNIX-like operating system. Over the years, many GNU tools were written and widely used by many commercial UNIX vendors and, of course, system administrators trying to get a job done. The appearance of Linus Torvalds' Linux kernel has made the GNU dream of a completely free, UNIX-like operating system a reality at last.

Is Linux Really Free?

When the discussion of what *free* means in relation to software, you'll often see the expressions "free as in speech" or "free as in beer." Free, in this case, isn't a question of cost, although you can get a free copy (as in *free beer*) of Linux and install it on your system without breaking any laws. As Robert A. Heinlein would have said, there ain't no such thing as a free lunch. A free download will still cost you connection time on the Internet, disk space, time to burn the CDs, and so on.

Walk into a computer software store and you'll see copies of Mandrake, SUSE, and Red Hat on the shelves, so this free software can also cost you money. On the other hand, the boxed sets come with documentation, support, and CDs, the latter saving you time and energy downloading and burning discs. Furthermore, some distributors offer boxed sets at multiple price points, such as Red Hat's personal and professional editions. The differences between these editions may be additional software, documentation, or support.

Linux is distributed under the GNU General Public License (GPL), which, in essence, says that anyone may copy, distribute, and even sell the program, so long as changes to the source are reintroduced back to the community and the terms of the license remain unaltered. Free means that you are free to modify Linux and create your own version. Free means that you are not at the mercy of a single vendor who forces you into a kind of corporate servitude by making sure that it is extremely costly to convert to another environment. If you are unhappy with your Linux vendor or the support you are getting, you can move to the next vendor without forfeiting your investment in Linux.

In other words, free as in speech—or freedom.

The GPL

The GNU GPL permits a distributor to "charge a fee for the physical act of transferring a copy," and, if the distributor desires, to "offer warranty protection in exchange for a fee." This is further qualified by the statement that the distributor must release "for a charge no more than your cost of physically performing source distribution, a complete machine-readable copy of the corresponding source code." In other words, the GPL ensures that such programs as Linux will at best be free of charge. At worst, you may be asked to pay for the cost of a copy.

You should take some time to read the GNU GPL, which is reprinted in Appendix A, "The GNU General Public License."

So What Do I Gain?

No operating system is perfect, and nothing comes without some hassles, but as time goes on, Linux just keeps on getting better. These days, Linux is even easier to install than your old operating system, and you don't have to reboot time and again as you load driver disk after driver disk. I won't bore you with everything that I consider an advantage, but I will give you a few of the more important points.

Security

Say goodbye to your virus checker, and stop worrying. Although Linux is not 100% immune to viruses, it comes pretty close. In fact, to date, most so-called Linux viruses do not exist *in the wild;* they live only under tightly controlled environments in *proof-of-concept* labs. The design model behind it means that Linux is built with security in mind. Consequently, viruses are virtually nonexistent in the Linux world, and the Linux community deals with security issues quickly and efficiently. Security flaws are well-advertised. It isn't unusual for a security hole to be discovered and a fix created within a few short hours of the discovery. If something does present a risk, you won't have to wait for the next release of your operating system to come along.

Stability

The stability of Linux is almost legendary. Living in a world where people are used to rebooting their PCs one or more times a day, Linux users talk about running weeks, months, and even *years* without a reboot. "Illegal operations" and the "Blue Screen of Death" are not part of the Linux experience. Sure, programs occasionally crash here as well, but they don't generally take down your whole system with them.

Power

Linux is a multitasking, multiuser operating system. In this book, I concentrate on the desktop features of Linux, but under the hood, Linux is a system designed to provide all of the power and flexibility of an enterprise-class server. Linux-powered web site servers and electronic mail gateways move information along on the Internet and run small to large businesses. Under the friendly face of your graphical desktop, that power is still there.

Money

It is possible to do everything you need to do on a computer without spending any money on software—that means new software and upgrades alike. In fact, free software for Linux is almost an embarrassment of riches. In Chapter 7, "Installing New Applications," I'll show you how to install additional software on your Linux system.

Freedom from Legal Hassles

When you run Linux, you don't have to worry about whether you've kept a copy of your operating system license. The GNU GPL means you are legally entitled to copy and can legally redistribute your Linux CDs if you wish.

Keep in mind, however, that although Linux itself can be freely distributed, *not all software* that runs on Linux is covered by the same license. If you buy or download software for your system, you should still pay attention to the license that covers that software.

 Quick Tip I would be remiss if I didn't address one wrinkle in the world of free software. In March 2003, SCO (formerly Caldera), with boss Darl McBride at the helm, launched an incredible $1 billion USD lawsuit against IBM. The company later upped the suit to $3 billion, then again increased it to $5 billion. This suit and SCO's allegations are largely seen as unfounded and an effort by a failed company to generate income through litigation. At the time of this writing, the case was ongoing and unresolved.

What Do I Lose?

Nothing ever seems to be perfect. By moving to Linux you gain a great deal, but I would be doing a disservice if I did not mention the disadvantages.

Hardware and Peripheral Support

The hardware support for Linux is, quite honestly, among the best there is. In fact, when you consider all of the platforms that run Linux, its hardware and peripheral support is better than that of the Windows system you are leaving behind. Unfortunately, there are some consumer devices designed with Windows specifically in mind. Consequently, certain printers or scanners may have limited support under Linux, because the manufacturer is slow in providing drivers.

On the upside, Linux automatically recognizes and supports an amazing number of peripherals without you having to do anything extra or hunt down a driver disk, unlike in your old OS. Furthermore, the Linux community is vibrant in a way that few businesses can ever hope to be. If you have your eye on a hot new piece of hardware, you can almost bet that some Linux developer somewhere has an eye on exactly the same thing. Chances are it won't be long before your dream device is part of standard Linux.

I'll talk about devices and device drivers later in the book.

Software Packages

There is a huge amount of software available for the Linux operating system, with much of it noncommercial. On the one hand, you can download *thousands* of programs to run on your system—Internet and office applications, tools, and even games. Much of it will cost you nothing more than download time.

On the other hand, commercial, shrink-wrapped software, including those hot new 3D games at your local computer store, are still hard to come by. As Linux grows in popularity, particularly on the desktop, this is starting to change.

On the other hand, software that enables you to run Windows applications is available for Linux. I'll talk more about that in the next chapter.

A Step into the Unknown

Let's face it. For some, moving to Linux is a step into the unknown. Things won't be exactly as they were with your old operating system, and for the most part, this is a good thing. You will have to do a little relearning and get used to a different way of doing things.

Even so, if you are used to working in your Windows graphical environment and you are comfortable with basic mousing skills, writing the occasional email, surfing the Web, or composing a memo in your word processor, moving to Linux won't be a big deal. Your Linux desktop is a modern graphical environment, and much of what you have learned in your old operating system can be taken with you into this new world.

Some Tips on Using this Book

My intention in creating this book was to simplify the move from your old OS to Linux. I'll cover such aspects as installation shortly, but the majority of the book has to do with working in your new Linux environment. I want to show you how to do the things you have grown used to doing: surfing the Net, writing emails, printing, communicating via instant messaging, burning CDs, and so on. Furthermore, I am going to tell you how to start using your collected Word documents, Excel spreadsheets, and other files with Linux. In short, my plan is to have you move as effortlessly as possible from Windows to Linux.

Working your way through the chapters, you'll notice that I constantly invite you to try things. That's because I believe the best way to learn anything is by doing. Yes, you're going to learn to work with a new operating system, but that doesn't mean you can't have fun.

Quick Tips and Shelling Out

Throughout the book, I will provide you with two kinds of boxed asides called Quick Tip and Shell Out. Quick Tip boxes will contain little reminders or simpler ways to do things. I intend to concentrate on working with graphical tools in a graphical way when discussing the end user tools, as well as those geared to the systems administrator. Still, much of the power of Linux comes from working with the command line, or the *shell*. The Shell Out asides will guide you in working with the shell.

Learning to wield the command line is akin to getting a black belt in martial arts or earning a first aid certificate. It doesn't mean that you are going to run out and take on all comers or that you are going to be facing daily crisis situations. Working with the shell does give you the means and the confidence to step outside the confines of the graphical environment. For systems administrators, the shell can be the quickest way of getting the job done, leaving graphical tools in the dust. This is particularly true when you have to perform some administrative task over a slow modem or network connection.

The shell is power, and it is always there for you, so you should not fear it. After a nice desktop introduction, I'll cover the shell in detail in Chapter 10, "Becoming One with the Shell."

Meet Your Desktop

Modern Linux distributions come with powerful, easy-to-use graphical environments—that's the friendly desktop from which you launch your programs, write emails, or create documents. There are many such environments, and in time, you will learn about them. Part of that freedom I spoke about is the freedom to do things *your* way, and that extends to the type of graphical environment you may want to work in. The most popular desktop environments today are the K Desktop Environment (KDE) and GNOME (pronounced *gee-nome*), but WindowMaker, IceWM, and others have quite a following as well. My personal choice is KDE, but I often switch to other desktops when the mood takes me.

Although much of what you do with GNOME or KDE is pretty interchangeable, it makes sense in a book like this to pick one and run with it. Consequently, I will concentrate on the KDE desktop, primarily version 3.2 (although much of what I cover is very similar to what you would see in release 3.1).

KDE comes with most major distributions, including SUSE, Red Hat, Debian, Xandros, Mandrake, and others. I recommend KDE, because I think it is more mature, more beautiful, and better developed than the alternatives. It sports a clean, consistent, and integrated set of tools, widgets, and menus. Because of all these things, KDE is also much easier and friendlier to work with. In fact, many Linux companies install KDE as the default.

When you become comfortable with KDE and Linux, I invite you to experiment with other desktop environments. *Exercise your freedom to be yourself.*

Help Me!

Once you are done working with this book, I am confident that Linux will be your operating system of choice in the foreseeable future. That doesn't mean, however, you won't have questions that aren't answered in this book. When they come up, consult my web site at www.marcelgagne.com.

The site has links to a number of other resources, including many articles I have written on using and administering Linux, links to other information sites, and much more. Click on the MTLBD (Moving To the Linux Business Desktop) link, and you'll be transported to the support pages for this book.

I also run a few mailing lists for readers, which you'll find under the WFTL (Writer and Free Thinker at Large) heading. One of those lists is the WFTL-LUG (a LUG is a Linux user group), an online discussion group where readers can share information, ask questions, and help each other out with their various Linux adventures. I invite you to join any of the lists I offer there. There is *no cost*, and you can unsubscribe at any time.

If you check under the Linux Links menu of my web site, you'll find a useful list of additional links to Linux information sources. One of these is the Linux Documentation Project (LDP).

The Linux Documentation Project

The LDP is a dynamic community resource. On your Linux distribution CD, you probably have a collection of documents known in the Linux world as *HOWTOs*. These are user- or developer-contributed documents that are maintained and updated by one or more individuals. You can find the latest version of these documents at the LDP site (www.tldp.org).

Essentially, the mandate of the LDP is to provide a comprehensive base of documentation for all things Linux. If you've been looking high and low for information on installing that bleeding-edge FTL radio card on your PC and still haven't found what you are looking for, try the LDP. The LDP also makes a point of offering the latest versions of the man pages, as well as user guides that tend to cover more ground than standard HOWTOs.

Note Man pages are online help provided with your Linux installation. They are called man pages because the command used to read this documentation is man.

Linux User Groups

A few paragraphs back, I made passing reference to Linux user groups, or LUGs. Put technology aside for a moment to consider something else you may have heard about: the Linux community. Yes, there really is a Linux community. All around the world, you will find groups of enthusiastic Linux users gathering for regular meetings, chatting over beer and pizza, and sharing information. This sharing of information is part of what makes Linux so friendly.

LUGs tend to run electronic mailing lists where informal exchanges of information take place as I do with my online LUG. New users are welcomed, and their questions are happily answered. These users range from newbies getting their feet wet to seasoned kernel developers. Should you find yourself stuck with nowhere to turn, seek out your local LUG and sign on to the mailing list. Today, someone helps you. As you grow more knowledgeable in administering your Linux system, maybe you will return the favor.

Locating a LUG in your community is as simple as surfing over to the Linux Online web site (www.linux.org). Once there, click the User Groups button, and you are on your way. The list is organized by country, then by state or province, and so on.

About the CD

Included with this book is a full-featured Linux distribution called Knoppix.

Knoppix is a Debian-based Linux distribution that runs entirely from your PC's CD-ROM drive. That's right. You can run Linux on your system without having to change your system or uninstall Windows. Furthermore, this particular CD has the Linux Terminal Server Project files included so you can run a thin client network from it. (I'll cover thin clients in detail later on.)

 Note The version of Knoppix included with this book is *not* the official version, but one that I have slightly modified. I wish to express my admiration and thanks to Klaus Knopper, the creator of Knoppix, for his fine work, but any questions regarding the included disk should be directed to me (or subscribe to the WFTL-LUG).

This CD is full of great software, some of which I will be covering in this book. You'll have access to email applications, Web browsers, word processors, spreadsheets, games, and more. In fact, you should be able to follow along with this book and do many—*though not all*—of the things I talk about without having to install Linux. The bootable CD is a fantastic introduction, but it has limitations.

The first limitation is that the CD runs *much slower* than a hard-disk Linux install, so keep in mind that the performance you experience from the CD is not indicative of the performance you will experience from a Linux hard-disk install. At their fastest, CD-ROM drives are no match for even the slowest hard drive. Furthermore, because this bootable Linux does not install itself on your hard drive, you are limited to the packages on the CD. In other words, you can't add or install any new software. If you are truly ready to make the move to Linux, consider installing a full distribution, a topic I will cover in the next two chapters.

Want to Try Linux Right Now?

Loading Knoppix is easy.

Insert your CD into your CD-ROM drive. Shut down Windows, and select Restart. Make sure your PC is set to boot from the CD. Knoppix boots up to a nice, graphical screen with a simple boot prompt, from which you can simply press <Enter> and let Knoppix do the rest; this is an amazingly simple *install*.

Quick Tip Many systems are set to boot directly from the CD-ROM drive if a bootable CD is found there. If your system does not, you may have to change the BIOS settings on your PC. This is generally done by pressing <Delete> or <F2> to enter Setup as the system is booting. (You will usually see such a message before the operating system starts to load.) Because the menus vary, it is impossible for me to cover them all, but look for a menu option that specifies the boot order. You'll see something like A: first, then C: (in other words, your floppy drive, then the hard disk). Change the boot order so that it looks to the CD first, save your changes, then restart your system.

The boot process is all text, but it is certainly colorful because Knoppix identifies devices, disks, sound cards, and so on in different colors. At some point, the screen will go dark as your video card is configured and X, the Linux graphical user interface, is started. If the screen doesn't respond instantly, don't panic. Give it a few seconds. If nothing has happened even after you've waited a while, it is possible that your video card is one of the rare ones not included in the distribution. Never fear; most, if not all, modern cards support VESA. Reboot and type the following at the boot prompt:

```
knoppix xmodule=vesa
```

Once the system has booted, you can start playing with Knoppix. You can speed things up a bit right off the bat by letting Knoppix create a *swap file* in your Windows partition. This won't hurt anything on your system. All it does is allow Linux to use some of your disk space as though it were real memory, to dedicate it as *swap space*. Doing this is easy. Click on KDE's program launcher (the big K in the lower-left corner), and move your cursor up to the KNOPPIX entry in the menu. There are four submenus here, one of them being Configure; under that menu, you'll see an entry labeled SWAP File Configuration. Click this option, and you'll get a nice little warning that you are about to create a file named knoppix.swp on your existing DOS (Windows) partition. Click Yes. You'll be asked for the size of your swap file in megabytes. What qualifies as a good size depends on how much real memory you already have, but taking the default is probably a good bet.

While you are looking at the Configure menu, notice that you can configure a printer and sound card as well (both local and network connected).

Before I move on, I'd like to point out one final item on this KNOPPIX menu; Save KNOPPIX Configuration. As you go along, you'll be making some changes, such as configuring printers or setting up your network. Using this menu option, you can save all of these configuration details to a disk. The next time you boot Knoppix, make sure the diskette is in your drive, and enter this command at the boot prompt:

```
knoppix floppyconf
```

One of the other items under the KNOPPIX menu is Network/Internet. From here, you can setup an ADSL/PPPOE connection for your local phone company's high-speed service, a dial-up modem, a network card, and so on. For network access, simply choose whatever makes sense for your setup, and answer the questions that follow. I will be covering Internet access and network tools later in the book.

I'm going to leave the discussion of Knoppix right here. Using the bootable Linux and this book, you should be able to get a pretty good handle on Linux without sacrificing your system, but at some point, you will want to go further. In the first few chapters, I'll discuss where and how to get a copy of Linux, Linux desktop options, distributions, and installation.

It's My Philosophy

I have a philosophy. All right, I have many, and this is just one of them.

Every once in a while, people tell me that desktop Linux is just crazy, that it is just too complicated for the majority of people.

I don't know about you, but I am tired of being told that people can't learn to use something that is both good and powerful. With a certain amount of training and proper guidance, *anyone who is familiar with a computer can learn to use Linux*.

That isn't to say that working with Linux is difficult (it's not), but as you go along, you will be learning new things. This book is meant for users at every level of experience. It is meant to be read for fun, as well as for reference. And because I'll ask you to try things throughout this book, it's a training guide as well.

I'm delighted and thrilled that you've decided to join me in deploying Linux and *Moving to the Linux Business Desktop*.

Resources

Linux Documentation Project

www.tldp.org

Linux.org List of LUGs

www.linux.org/groups/index.html

Linux User Groups Worldwide

http://lugww.counter.li.org/groups.cms

Marcel (Writer and Free Thinker at Large) Gagné's Web Site

www.marcelgagne.com

2

Overview of Deployment Options

Your Linux adventure is about to begin.

To really get going, though, you need to deal with two major things. First and foremost, you need to get a copy of Linux. You may have chosen to try things out using the included bootable Knoppix CD, but at some point, you may want to do a proper hard-disk install.

The second thing you will need to take care of is important only if you have Windows on your system and you need to preserve and migrate data. Start with the first step.

Getting Linux

This one is actually the easy part.

One way to get Linux is to buy a copy. Head down to your local computer software store and ask for your favorite distribution. Alternatively, go online to find your favorite vendor, whether it is Mandrake, SUSE, Red Hat, or any of the many distributions listed on the DistroWatch (www.distrowatch.com). Incidentally, DistroWatch also lists the top ten major distributions at any given time.

Which distribution should you get? Well, every Linux vendor does things a little differently. If you think of this in terms of cars, it starts to make sense. Every single car out there is basically an engine on wheels with seats and some kind of steering mechanism so that drivers can get to where they want to go. What kind of car you buy depends on what else you expect from a car—comfort, style, the vendor's reputation, and so on.

Recommendation You *really* want me to suggest something? Let me start by saying that I think it is a wonderful thing that so many Linux distributions exist. Aside from creating a rich OS landscape, it furthers creativity and fosters innovation in software design. This can only be a good thing.

If you *push* me for a suggestion, however, and you are *just getting started* with desktop Linux, I suggest that you look at either Mandrake or SUSE.

Both are excellent, well-engineered, and beginner-friendly Linux distributions. An immediate advantage of Mandrake is that you can download ISOs from the Internet and burn your own CDs. SUSE does provide a download version, but it is just a jumpstart CD. The whole SUSE installation takes place online via FTP, which can take a while. If you are going to purchase your Linux distribution, SUSE (now owned by Novell) has a very business-friendly look and feel whereas Mandrake is perhaps a little more home user-friendly.

If you can get a free copy of Linux, why would you want to pay for one? As it turns out, there is more than one answer to that question. First, buying a boxed set usually gets you some amount of technical support from the vendor, which is reassuring if you are feeling nervous about your first Linux installation. Furthermore, working with a vendor may offer other advantages, such as certification of certain enterprise applications (Oracle and PeopleSoft, for example) to run with your specific platform. You'll often see messages stating that this database or that CRM system is certified to work on a particular version of Red Hat or SUSE.

Second, the boxed set usually contains some kind of manual or manuals *specific* to that version of Linux. That will inevitably lead to another question as to what makes this Linux different from that one. Finally, in purchasing a boxed set, you are supporting the company that put leather on the seats or tinted the windows. It's a way of saying thanks for all the hard work.

Because it is possible to get a free copy of Linux, you don't have to shell out the dollars if you don't want to. At most, you'll need a fast Internet connection, a CD burner, and some blank CDs—or a helpful friend who has these.

Getting a Free Copy of Linux

The idea of free software—a free operating system in particular—takes some getting used to, but it happens fast. When you are working with other operating systems, getting and trying new releases involves some kind of cash outlay. In the case of Linux, the most you need is a spare machine on which to play. Consequently, you can load one version of Linux, take it for a spin, then load another and see whether that feels any better to you.

If you have a high-speed Internet connection (and a CD burner), you can visit any of the vendors' sites listed at the end of this chapter and download their latest and greatest. Remember, though, that although you may download their latest Linux free of charge, technical support may still be an extra cost.

If you don't like the idea of visiting each and every one of those sites, a visit to LinuxIso.org (`www.linuxiso.org`) may be in order. This site provides you with a one-stop shop for the more popular Linux distributions with ISOs (CD-ROM images) available for download.

Package Managers and Updates

Package managers often have a great deal to do with what people end up choosing in terms of a distribution. In this book, I'll be talking about installing software using RPM, and every distribution I mentioned above uses RPM as the package manager, so the information you take with you will work with any of these releases. I have also developed a great respect for the power and simplicity of Debian's apt-get program. In fact, you now get apt-get for RPM-based systems.

The method of update is also worthy of consideration. Many vendors now provide an option for updating and patching your system online. As long as you have a fast Internet connection, you are all set. Finally, here's the great disclaimer of the decade: Linux, like all dynamic, living things, is evolving and changing. It is a moving target and, consequently, the details of a specific distribution will change over time. In the next chapter, I'll cover three major distributions and their installation procedures to give you an idea of what you can expect to see. For now, let's talk about what you are going to need in preparation for getting Linux on your system.

Quick Tip This is as good a time as any to start stressing the importance of keeping your system up to date. Linux vendors usually offer update and patch systems specific to their distribution in an effort to provide the customer with the simplest method for applying updates. Red Hat offers up2date, SUSE has its Online Update (part of YaST), Mandrake has drakrpm-update (part of the Mandrake Control Center), and so on. Some of these may be free services, and others may offer such premium services as longer support, faster downloads, and so on. For a distribution agnostic service, consider Ximian's Red Carpet system.

For bug fixes alone, keeping your system up to date just makes sense, but add security considerations and it becomes extremely important that you stay on top of updates.

Dual Booting

As much as I would like to think that each and every one of you is more than ready to say goodbye forever to your old operating system and hello to Linux, I know that for many this is a *very* big jump. If you are still feeling a little insecure about simply breaking free and running Linux, I'm here to tell you that you can get the best of both worlds. It is called *dual booting*.

Dual booting is the technique of making a home for both operating systems on your machine. When you start your computer, a small program called a *boot loader* offers you a menu of choices from which you can decide to boot Linux or whatever other operating system you have installed. That boot loader, for the most part, is called Grand Unified Bootloader (GRUB). A second and still very common boot loader is called LILO, the Linux Loader.

When you load Linux on a system that already has Windows installed, your new system is smart enough to recognize the existence of this other operating system. You'll find that entries for both of your operating systems will magically appear in your boot loader menu.

Preserving Your Data

When you've been using a computer for a long time, you amass a lot of data. Forget software. The *data* is the *most important thing* on your system, and you need to get it backed up. Whether you dual boot or not, I want to stress that you are going to be doing some major changes to your hard disk. Please don't take any chances with your data. Make a backup.

Because Windows backup programs aren't necessarily going to be helpful in getting your data onto a Linux system, you should copy the various word processing documents, spreadsheets, graphics (all those pictures you took with your digital camera), music files, and anything else that you will want later onto some kind of media, whether it is a ZIP disk, floppy diskette, or CD.

If you have large amounts of data, it might make sense to keep a Windows partition around long enough to copy from one to the other. Most of the major Linux distributions not only notice the existence of your Windows partition, but also provide you with an icon on your desktop so that you can easily access that data. Although this may seem like a great way to avoid backing up your data, *please* don't ignore this step. In fact, if you haven't been backing up your system, your system has been living on borrowed time. *If in doubt, back up*.

A Linux-Only System

This is by far the easiest alternative, because you don't have to worry about keeping an intact copy of something else on the system. This represents quite the leap, because there is no going back aside from reinstalling from scratch. If you go down this road, you have access to all your disk space, and Linux uses disk space more efficiently. You can also kiss goodbye those proprietary licensing issues, not to mention the "Blue Screen of Death."

When you are ready to install, simply choose the option that will overwrite the entire system. The installation process will take care of the rest for you. It's that simple.

Windows on Linux

Under Linux, it is possible to run a number of Windows applications without having Windows installed at all. This is done with Wine. I'm not talking about the fermented beverage some of us are quite fond of, but a package that runs on Linux. Allow me to paraphrase from the Wine web site: *Wine Is Not an Emulator*. Wine is a compatibility layer, a set of APIs that enable some Windows applications to operate on a Linux system running the X window system (the Linux graphical environment).

Wine will not run every Windows application, but the number of applications it is capable of running is increasing all the time. Some commercial vendors have ported certain Windows applications to Linux by making some of the code run in Wine. This has sped up the normal production cycle and made it possible for them to get their programs to Linux users faster.

 Quick Tip When it comes to Wine (the software), younger is most definitely better. A well-aged Wine (the software) will not be as good at running your Windows software as a brand new Wine. As for wine (the beverage), aging is certainly a good thing, but there are limits. As a rule, reds can age longer than whites, but it all depends on the variety. Consult your local wine vendor, or pick up a good book on the subject.

Many Linux distributions include a version of Wine on the CDs, and some let you select Windows compatibility applications as part of the installation procedure. Keep in mind that the newer your Wine, the better. For the latest and greatest on Wine development, visit the Wine web site at www.winehq.com. A great deal of Wine development is being done at CodeWeavers (www.codeweavers.com). Its version provides an installation wizard to guide you through the installation and configuration process for Wine. It makes the whole process extremely simple.

VMware

The Wine project has done some impressive work, but it will not run all Windows applications. Sometimes you just need to run the whole shebang, and that means a *full* copy of Windows. Because you don't want to boot back and forth between Linux and Windows, it would be great if you could run Windows entirely on your Linux machine. This is the philosophy behind VMware—and it doesn't stop there.

VMware enables you to create virtual machines on your computer. Complete with boot-up BIOS and memory checks, VMware virtualizes your entire hardware configuration, making the PC inside the PC as real as the one you are running. Furthermore, VMware enables you to run, not emulate, Windows 95, 98, 2000, NT, FreeBSD, or other Linuxes. For the developer or support person who needs to work or write code on different platforms, this is an incredible package. Yes, you can even run another Linux on your Linux, making it possible to test or play with different releases without reinstalling on a separate machine. VMware knows enough to share your printers, network cards, and so on. You can even network between the "real" machine and the virtual machine as though they were two separate systems.

All this capability comes at a price, however. Aside from the dollars that you spend on this package (and it can be well worth it), there is a considerable price in performance. VMware is a hungry beast. The more processor power and memory you have, the better. A Pentium III with 96 or more megabytes should be your starting point. Unlike with Wine, for VMware you do need a licensed copy of Windows (or whatever OS you are installing) to run.

VMware comes in a variety of packages and price points. Visit the VMware Web site at www.vmware.com for details.

Win4Lin

Still another alternative is Win4Lin from Netraverse (www.netraverse.com). This package is designed to let you run Windows on your system, but unlike VMware, *only* Windows (95, 98, and ME at this writing). It is, however, somewhat less expensive than VMware. Once again, remember that because you aren't *emulating* Windows but actually running a copy, you still need that licensed copy of Windows.

Win4Lin's magic is performed at the kernel level. Consequently, this requires that you download a patched kernel equivalent to what you are currently running or that you patch and rebuild your own. If you have compiled custom drivers into your kernel, you are going to have to go through the process again to get Win4Lin going.

What I have found interesting is that Windows installs and loads much faster under Linux than in native mode. Win4Lin works very well indeed and requires surprisingly little in terms of resources. I have run it on a Pentium 233 notebook with 64MB of RAM and found that it was reasonably peppy. You do take a performance hit, but it feels minor and should not distract you under most circumstances.

Desktop Considerations

This isn't about the desktop environment, namely KDE or GNOME, but rather about what you might want to consider in terms of user desktops and the users' needs. That means finding out where Linux desktops are a good fit, and furthermore, what kind of Linux desktops. I'll get to that in a moment, but let me start by suggesting that you take an inventory. Look around at the various PCs you have in your business, and make a list of what software runs on which PC. You are likely to find that PC users fit into a small handful of categories.

Power users, engineers, and technical users of all kinds are the first group I'll mention, partly because this group is probably already dabbling in desktop Linux. Look around your office and talk to these workers. You may find that their desktop already dual boots between Linux and Windows, or that they are already running Linux exclusively. The unique skills and demands of these power users mean that Linux is precisely what they have needed all along. Being technologically savvy, they may have already made the move or set up a Linux workstation to help them be as productive as possible.

The second group is composed of lightweight users in that their application needs center around basic office tools: word processors, spreadsheets, web browsers, and email. They may also use a terminal emulator to communicate with a central server. Their desktop needs can be met easily and exceeded by the offerings of Linux desktops. These people generally constitute the majority of users in an organization. Focusing on this group for Linux desktop deployment can provide the greatest rewards both from a financial and administrative viewpoint.

The third group is a little more difficult. In addition to basic core applications of the last group, they may also have bought into Windows-only proprietary applications that can't be easily provided by Linux desktops. They may require a little more work and time before they can successfully be converted to Linux desktop. Options exist—Win4Lin, VMware, and so on—but some of these users may have to stay with Windows, at least for now. As Linux continues to increase in popularity, alternatives to almost every application are making their way into the Linux world.

The best thing to do is to start with a small pilot project. I guarantee that you will find people in your organization who would love to give Linux a try. Give them the opportunity to take a Linux desktop out for a spin. You'll gain insight into the needs of your people, and you'll also be training those who can later train others.

Making The Switch...Easy!

Installing Linux and providing users with a powerful desktop isn't difficult. Most modern Linux distributions are often easier to install than Windows; what makes Windows easy is that most PCs come with Windows pre-installed. Still, you can run Linux on dozens, hundreds, or even thousands of PCs without having to install each and every one.

One of the easiest and most cost-effective ways to deploy Linux desktops in the enterprise is by setting up Linux thin clients. Linux thin clients are typically PCs booting from an Ethernet card with a chip that asks for an address from a large central server running Linux. The thin-client workstations book and run desktop Linux entirely from the network. In fact, thin-client PCs don't even need a hard drive to provide a user with all the functions they need.

Linux thin clients are an excellent idea, and I can't stress enough how useful, energy efficient, cost efficient, and downright easy to administer they are. That's why I'm devoting two chapters to help you get a thin-client network up and running. Chapters 20 and 21 are dedicated to setting up Linux thin clients.

With Linux thin clients, you get centralized backup, upgrade, and administration. Because workstations have no disks, and software is under the control of the administrator, support becomes that much simpler. Close your eyes and imagine doing away with the endless hours spent fixing individual workstation problems.

Unfortunately, thin clients may not be the answer for your entire enterprise. Some users need a full-blown distribution loaded on their PCs. Notebooks are perfect examples. Because thin clients require a fast, local network connection to the server, your road warriors will need their own Linux desktops installed on their notebooks. Your technical people and power users may also need their own Linux desktop. Running high-performance, graphical applications across a network may not be the best solution. Keep an open mind, and you'll find a Linux solution for almost every application and every user.

Transitional Applications

Change is difficult for people. That's just the way we are built. Such expressions as "the devil you know" attest to our reluctance to choose new directions if it means drastic change. So it is with moving from Windows desktops to Linux desktops. Moving to Linux isn't terribly difficult, and most people will find themselves at home very quickly, but sometimes it helps to pave the way by introducing some Linux familiarity to the Windows desktop—and saving yourself a small fortune in the process. If you can't see yourself switching immediately, or you have some reluctant users, this can be a wonderful way to ease the transition when the time comes.

For starters, consider loading up the OpenOffice.org office suite, an excellent and powerful replacement for Microsoft Office. It provides a word processor that can read and write Word documents, an Excel-compatible spreadsheet package, and a PowerPoint-compatible presentation graphics package. I will cover these three applications in Chapters 27, 28, and 29. OpenOffice.org is free for the price of a download. Simply using OpenOffice.org can save a medium-sized office thousands of dollars.

The second transactional application I would like you to consider is Mozilla, a web browser that is already far superior to Internet Explorer. Mozilla is a free, open-source browser that is also available for Windows. It comes with an email package, IRC client, and an HTML editor. With tabbed browsing and a pop-up ad blocker, Mozilla should already be part of every desktop—Linux or otherwise. Chapter 26, "Surfing the Net," covers Mozilla in depth.

I'll give you one last package to consider. An increasingly common tool in the modern office is the instant messaging (IM) client. IM is no longer strictly the playground of teenagers or friends and family looking to keep in touch across the networked world. It is rapidly becoming a serious tool for business as well. Nothing beats being in constant touch with employees and team members, even if those people are scattered in offices around the globe. GAIM is a powerful, multiprotocol, IM client that makes it unnecessary to run a package for every service you use. It supports Yahoo!, MSN, Jabber, ICQ, AOL, and others. GAIM, a free, open-source application is also available for Windows. Chapter 31, "Instant Messaging," covers GAIM in detail.

Once you get used to the idea that you can live without Microsoft, the Linux desktop is not far away.

Breaking Free!

You may not need to go through any of these hoops to preserve your old operating system. As you go through this book, you may find that all of your needs are met just running Linux. There are plenty of applications as slick and as capable as anything in the Windows world.

Why go back and forth when you can just go forward? On that note, turn the page to Chapter 3, and get Linux installed on your system.

Resources

CodeWeavers

www.codeweavers.com

Debian

www.debian.org

DistroWatch (for a great distribution roundup)

www.distrowatch.com

Linux.org

www.linux.org

Mandrake

www.mandrakelinux.com

Red Hat Software

www.redhat.com

Slackware Linux

www.slackware.org

SUSE Linux

www.suse.com

VMware

www.vmware.com
Win4Linwww.netraverse.com

WINE Project

www.winehq.com

chapter

3

Installation

For this book, I will be basing a great deal of the desktop on KDE version 3.2. (KDE 3.1 is very similar, too.) From the Linux installation perspective, this implies that you are planning to run a modern Linux distribution and not some disks you've had lying around for the last three years. An up-to-date release of your favorite distribution, whether it is Fedora, SUSE, Mandrake, or something else, is essential.

A modern Linux installation is easy. I will go so far as to say that it is even easier than installing Windows. For the most part, you boot from your CD-ROM drive, click Next a few times, and you are running Linux. Okay, perhaps there is a bit more to it than that, but not much. Linux will, for the most part, auto-detect nearly all devices on your machine and automatically configure them optimally.

Getting Ready for Your Installation

If your machine has Windows already installed and you have documents, spreadsheets, pictures, or music files that you wish to keep, now is a good time to back them up, either on diskette or burned to a CD-ROM. Even if you plan on preserving your Windows installation for a dual-boot system, it's always prudent to have a good backup if you are going to be doing major work on your hard disk. You might also want to take advantage of all that hard work that was done in pre-installing Windows and make notes on all the hardware in your machine—the type of network and video cards and anything else you can think of. You do that by clicking the Start button, selecting Settings>Control Panel, then double-clicking the System icon. Now, walk through the hardware profiles, and take some notes. Odds are you won't need it at all, but you can never have too much information.

The average Linux installation takes about 30 to 60 minutes, although I have seen it take as little as 5 minutes on a really fast system. That's a fully network-ready, configured, all-set-to-work machine with no rebooting every few minutes to load another driver. It doesn't get much easier than this.

That said, unless you are feeling particularly adventurous, I would highly recommend that you read through this chapter once before actually starting.

Hardware Considerations

Before moving on, let's talk hardware. The sad truth is that not every device will work with Linux. You should not think of this as being strange or as somehow representing a weakness in Linux. After all, Linux is not unique in this. In fact, Linux may be fairly unique when it comes to the sheer number of devices and platforms that it does support. Linux runs on Intel-based systems as well as Alpha, RISC, and Macintosh systems. IBM's entire line of computers, from small desktop PCs to such large mainframe systems as the S/390, run Linux. Then there are MIPS, SPARC, and StrongARM. You can also find Linux embedded in microchips, running on portable MP3 players, PDAs, cell phones, and even digital watches. That's incredible hardware support!

From the perspective of your computer, it is highly unlikely that Linux won't install and run well. If something is going to be unsupported, it will have to do with some Windows-only modems, printers, or scanners. To find out whether or not your computer and its associated devices will work with your Linux installation, first check your Linux vendor's web site. Another great hardware resource is the Hardware HOWTO. You can always find the latest version by surfing on over to the LDP's Linux Hardware Compatibility HOWTO page at www.tldp/HOWTO/Hardware-HOWTO.

As Linux gains in popularity, you'll find that hardware vendors are increasingly interested in tapping into this ever-growing market. I remember being on site, adding hardware to a customer's system (Ethernet cards come immediately to mind) and finding that the system did not have the drivers. When I quickly visited the Ethernet card manufacturer's web site, I found precompiled drivers ready and waiting for me. With the incredible growth of Linux, it won't be long before these issues are a thing of the past.

Dual Booting Revisited

In the last chapter, I mentioned dual booting, a means by which you can run both Linux and Windows on one machine. At boot time, a menu lets you start one *or* the other. Pretend for a moment that you still want to run Windows from time to time. Perhaps you want the comfort of knowing that you can go back to your old operating system to do certain things. This is where dual booting comes into play. Please note, however, that dual booting requires a little more up-front work.

One dual-boot scenario involves a completely separate disk that you can dedicate to a Linux installation. Although this is an ideal situation, most people have a single disk with Windows already loaded. If you have a large disk, there is a good chance that it already has two partitions: the C: drive and the D: drive. Erase the D: drive, and use it for Linux instead. If you are going to follow this route, make sure you back up any documents or copy them into folders on your C: drive.

Unfortunately, Windows is just as likely to be taking up the entire partition table. The trick is to *shrink* the existing Windows partition, thereby creating some space on which to install Linux. To do this, you must defragment your disk in Windows before resizing your partitions. Click the Start button, and then select Programs>Accessories>System Tools>Disk Defragmenter.

Resizing the partition is your next step. Once again, there are two ways of doing this. Some recent distributions, such as Mandrake and SUSE, automatically detect a Windows-only disk and offer to shrink the partition for you. Alternatively, you can do this with a little DOS program called FIPS, which you can find on your Linux distribution CD. On Debian, check the tools directory. On Red Hat or SUSE, check the dosutils directory.

In most cases, there will probably be a directory called FIPS or FIPS20 with a number of files inside, including the FIPS.EXE program itself.

A Sample FIPS Session

 Quick Tip When doing anything this drastic with your drives, *always* make a backup. In fact, no matter what you do with your system, always make regular backups.

Say you've already run your defragmenter and you have plenty of space on your hard drive. Start by creating a DOS/Windows boot diskette. This is generally done by typing the following command from the DOS/Windows command prompt (after inserting a blank diskette into the diskette drive):

```
FORMAT A: /S
```

The /S tells DOS/Windows to transfer the system to the boot diskette. You will also want to have a second boot diskette handy, so do this a second time. You'll need it to back up your boot sector. I'll explain why in a moment. Next, copy the FIPS.EXE utility and its associated files from the CD-ROM drive to the first diskette:

```
COPY D:\DOSUTILS\FIPS20\*.* A:
```

Remember that the path to the FIPS20 directory may vary depending on your distribution CD. Now, shut down Windows, and boot from the FIPS diskette. When the boot completes, you should be at a DOS prompt. This is where the split occurs. Now, run the FIPS command:

```
FIPS
```

FIPS displays a partition table showing you how the disk space has been allocated and asks which partition you want to split. Because you have only one partition in this example, the answer is easy. Enter the partition number, and press <Enter>. As a precaution, FIPS will ask you whether you want to make a copy of your boot sector on the remote chance that disaster strikes. You probably want to answer Y (yes) to the question. This requires a second, pre-formatted diskette. Put in your second diskette, and answer Y to the next question: Do you have a bootable floppy disk in drive A: as described in the documentation (y/n)? Because you just inserted the diskette, press <Enter>.

Now the fun begins. FIPS displays your partition table again. Using the Left and Right Arrow keys, change the size of the partition. You'll see the numbers changing each time you press the keys. When you are happy with your changes, press <Enter>. FIPS asks you to confirm the changes. You can still change your mind at this time. If everything looks good, press the <c> key to continue, then answer Y when asked if you are ready to write the new partition scheme to disk.

When FIPS completes, reboot your system. You might want to reboot into Windows first just to make sure that things are working properly. If everything looks as you want it to, pop in your Linux installation CD, shut down Windows, and reboot the system.

Windows XP Considerations Although the install tools included on the distribution CDs are very good at determining the presence of a Windows 95, 98, or ME partition and shrinking it for you, not every distribution can shrink a Windows XP NTFS partition. Of the distributions covered in this chapter, SUSE 9.0 and Mandrake 10.0 can both do the job. Fedora cannot.

What that means, unfortunately, is that FIPS and the magical tools included as part of the Linux install CD won't work here. Once again, there are two possibilities. One is to get your hands on a product called PartitionMagic (www.partitionmagic.com), an alternative to using FIPS. It's a nice, friendly, commercial package that enables you to modify partitions on the fly, including NTFS partitions, such as those found on Windows XP systems.

The second option is to back up your data, reformat your hard drive, and reinstall Windows XP from scratch, this time making sure that only half (or a third or a quarter) of your disk is allocated to Windows. Please be sure that you are completely comfortable with the idea of reinstalling XP before you proceed.

There is a third option, of course: Install Linux and forget about XP.

An Installation Comparison

Modern installations offer a nice, graphical process, and for the most part, installing Linux today is a point-and-click experience with help every step of the way. Of course, a graphical installation makes a lot of assumptions that might not necessarily be what you want. Should all else fail, try the text-based installation. Most distributions still provide one, and I don't see that changing anytime soon.

A Very Generic Install

Every installation is similar in many ways, though the order of the steps may vary slightly. After booting, you get a nice welcome screen usually followed by a request for the language you want to install in. Hot on the heels of this is some kind of basic peripheral selection, namely for your keyboard and mouse. You're also asked for your time zone. Somewhere near here, every installation asks you for options on partitioning and formatting your drive. For most users, the defaults are fine, and your Windows partition (if you opted for a dual-boot system) is detected and set aside. This is also the point where you are asked to select a boot loader and to confirm the operating systems you want to be able to launch at boot time. Once again, this is particularly important if you are setting up a dual-boot system.

After all of these preliminary steps, it is time to load your software. Some kind of default collection is offered (workstation, server, and so on), at which point your system starts to load. There may be one or more CDs to load, depending on how much you asked for. Once this is over, it is time to configure your network connection, followed by the graphical window setup, also known as the X window system.

That's when you get your first introduction to Linux security. The installer asks you for an administrative user (*root*) password and provides you with the opportunity to create one or more additional users for day-to-day use. Under normal circumstances, the root user should not be used except to install software or to update and administer your system in some fashion. The separation of administrative from *regular* users is one of the ways Linux protects your system from accidental or malicious damage.

Usually, that is pretty much it. The system reboots, and you're running Linux.

Note Installers tend to make fairly intelligent choices along the way. Nevertheless, you should still check to make sure that what is selected is indeed correct.

Another source of information is the distribution itself. Most Linux distribution CDs have extensive installation information on the CD, in the box (if you purchased it), or on the distribution's web site. If you are feeling less than adventurous, print out a copy before you begin your installation.

Remember that until you have actually formatted your drives, you can still change your mind about many of the decisions you make along the way. Just click the Back button or use the Tab key to move to it, and reenter the information the way you intended.

Of course, my generic install is just that: generic. To give you an idea of just what you can expect when you go through the real thing, I will walk you through *three different installations* using some of the more popular Linux distributions.

Note As of this writing, Mandrake 10.0 was just released, Fedora Core 1 was out with version 2 in test, and SUSE 9.1 was the also a new kid on the block. I mention this release information because the screens you see may not be precisely as I describe here—probably nothing major, but some things may be a bit different. That's why I want you to look at these install examples *as* examples. They are meant to prepare you for what you will experience during an installation.

Warning Almost any modern PC can boot from a CD-ROM, and this is the easiest way to install. If your system cannot boot from the CD, you can create a boot diskette. If this is a problem for you, put your first Linux CD into the drive and use Windows Explorer (the file manager) to look for a directory called boot on the CD. There will be a boot disk image there (the name may vary) and instructions on how to create the diskette.

A Mandrake Linux Install

For this Mandrake install, I used version 10.0.

Reboot your system with the installation CD in the drive. Mandrake boots with a graphical screen with two options. Pressing <F1> enables you to choose between text and low-resolution install modes; the default is the standard graphical install. Press <Enter> and you are on your way.

Basic hardware detection takes place at this time, and the installer is loaded into memory. In a few seconds, you'll be at the main install screen. On the left side of the screen, there's a set of steps, each with a light beside the label to let you know roughly where you are in the installation process. The first of these steps involves selecting your preferred language for installation; there are many, and they are organized by continent to help you narrow things down. Select your language of choice, or click OK to accept the English (American) default and continue. On the next screen, read the license agreement to learn about the GPL and related licenses, click the Accept radio button, then click Next.

The next screen deals with security. Mandrake's default install lets you choose among four security levels. What each level allows or denies is documented on the page. Take a moment to read it, and choose the level that works for you. Most people choose the default of Standard.

Mandrake's install then automatically detects your hard drive, which means it is time to set up your file systems. The options here involve erasing the entire disk, doing your own custom disk partitioning, or using the free space on the Windows partition. This is quite *interesting*, because it enables you to automatically resize the Windows partition, making use of the free space in order to install Mandrake. Remember, the only caveat is that the Windows disk must be defragmented first.

The default option is Use Free Space, and that is probably what you should choose. Click OK to continue. The partitions are created and formatted, and a list of available packages is pulled from the install disk. Now, it is time to decide what kind of a system you want. You will be looking at the Package Group Selection screen. A standard Mandrake install is a Workstation install, and that's where the emphasis is placed with the defaults. Office Workstation is automatically selected, as is Internet Station. That means you get your word processors and spreadsheets, as well as email clients and web browsers. If you want to play games and music, you should click on Game Station and Multimedia Station.

Once again, if you want to be able to compile programs—those bleeding-edge new programs—you should also click on Development. In addition,

I recommend Configuration and Console Tools to help with system configuration. Network Computer (client) provides the SSH client. In an office situation, you will most certainly want that as well.

Before you move on, look over on the right. If this computer will be a server, you may wish to add web, FTP, email, and database servers. Pause your mouse pointer over the choices to see a tool tip containing a short description of what each server offers. Finally, look under Graphical Environment where the KDE environment is selected by default. You may, however, want to choose GNOME here as well. Furthermore, if you would like to experiment with even more desktop environments at some future time, consider checking on Other Graphical Desktops. This loads WindowMaker, IceWM, and others. At the bottom of the screen, there's a check box labeled Individual Package Selection, which enables you review your choices and add or remove items as you see fit.

Click Next, and the package installation begins. You'll be treated to a little slide show telling you about Open Source software, Mandrake products, joining the Mandrake Club, and information about the various things that come with your Mandrake system. In short, the show tells you why you are going to love working with Mandrake Linux. Depending on the choices you made, you may need to switch the CD at some point.

When the installation completes, you are asked to choose a root password, after which you have the opportunity to create one or more normal users. You need to create only one at this time. Notice that the Mandrake install lets you choose a representative icon for your users. Just click on the icon, and select one that suits you. I particularly like the cat myself. After entering your information, click Accept User, then click Next (unless you are adding multiple users, of course).

Mandrake then asks you to choose your default Window manager. KDE is displayed as the default, and that will do nicely. You can also choose to have the system automatically log in a single user on boot. Although this is fine for a home user who is the only user on the system, I highly recommend that others, particularly those in office environments, make sure this check box is off.

Click Next to continue and view a summary screen of various hardware options, such as printer, sound card, network, and so on. Some of these will be configured already, but others may need to be set up (the Network/LAN option, for instance). Click the Configure button to make changes. In most cases, a wizard will take you through the various choices available. The installer is very good at autodetection of printers, network connections, and graphical interfaces, so if you aren't sure, take the defaults. When you are happy with all your choices, click Next.

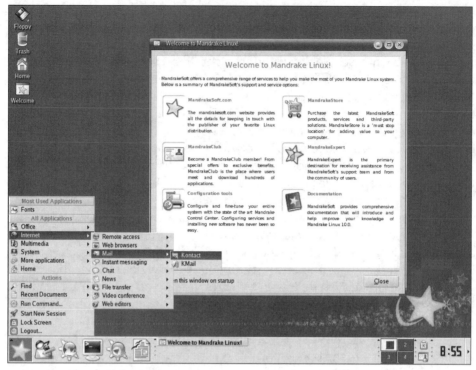

FIGURE 3-1   Your Mandrake 10 desktop, ready for use.

You're almost done! Ideally, you should have a live Internet connection at this point and high-speed access, because the packages can be *substantial*. Downloading the updates can take a long time if your only connection is a dial-up modem. What Mandrake does here is provide you with a chance to load and install any updates and security fixes that may have been released since the OS first came out. Select Yes, then click Next to start the update, but remember what I said about high-speed access.

That's it. Click Reboot to reboot, and make sure that you take the CD out of the drive when it is ejected. Take a look at Figure 3-1 for a look at a Mandrake 10 desktop.

Putting On the Fedora

The version I used for this install was Fedora Core 2. I should point out that I was using the Beta release, but that the official Fedora Core 2 will be out by the time you read this book. In terms of installation, there were virtually no differences at all between Red Hat 9.0, Fedora Core 1, and Fedora Core 2.

Start by putting in the CD-ROM and rebooting your system. The boot menu appears, giving you the option of choosing either a graphical or text install. For almost every system out there, the graphical install is just fine. All you need to do is click or press Install, and the system will start booting. The system identifies devices, and you see a number of messages scroll by.

A few seconds later, you'll see an interesting message. Fedora's install has a Media Check option. Here's the idea: You have your installation CDs, but you don't know for sure whether the disk is free from surface defects that will make installation impossible. Isn't it better to find out before you start all the work? The choice is yours. You can choose to test each CD in your set before you proceed, or you can simply skip the step.

After the media check, the graphical install screen appears. This is just a welcome screen; click Next to continue on. On the following screen, select the language you would like to use for the installation. I selected English and clicked Next again. The keyboard selection screen follows. Once again, I selected the default of U.S. English and clicked Next, which brought up the mouse selection screen.

On the mouse selection screen, the installer does an autodetect and makes a selection. Make sure that the mouse selected is more or less what you have. Notice the Emulate 3 Buttons option at the bottom of the screen. Unless you already have a three-button mouse, select this, because the Linux graphical X window system makes use of all three buttons. Clicking the left and right button simultaneously is the same as clicking the middle button on a three-button mouse. Hot on the heels of mouse selection, it's time for the monitor configuration, another screen where you can pretty much just accept the default unless, of course, you can tell that the autodetection is way off from what you own.

The next screen is for installation type. The default option is Personal Desktop, which Fedora suggests is "perfect for personal computers or laptops." Most people will want to accept the default and click Next.

On the next screen, you can accept the default, which is to allow the install to automatically partition your disk. After clicking Next, you get some choices on Automatic Partitioning, which is to decide how the installer will make use of the available space. The default is Remove All Linux Partitions on This System, and this is probably the right choice. If you want to double check the decisions made by the installer, make sure that you check off the option Review (and Modify if Needed) the Partitions Created.

A warning box appears, letting you know that all data will be erased. Click OK. Depending on the size of your hard drive, you may get a warning, such as

"Boot partition/boot may not meet booting constraints for your architecture. Creation of a boot disk is highly encouraged." I'll talk about a boot disk later.

The Boot Loader Configuration is next. Red Hat installs the GRUB boot loader by default, but you can change it to LILO. Both work very well, and in the end, it is your choice. I have grown to like GRUB quite a bit, but I still use LILO on other systems without a care. At this point, you also have the option of setting a password on the boot loader. Home users don't have to worry about this, but some network installations may want the additional security of having to enter a password when the system is booted. Before you move on, you may want to have a look at the labels the installer assigns. I mention this because if you are setting up a dual-boot system, it will be identified as DOS. When you are happy with your choices, click Next.

The following screen is for network configuration. If you do not have a network card installed, you can skip to the next step. If your Internet connection is through a DSL or cable modem connection, that will likely be the case. The default is to boot and pull an address via DHCP, and this is what you would choose. If your PC is on a home or corporate network with fixed addresses, click Edit, check off Configure Using DHCP, and enter your address information. If you are in an office, check with your systems administrator for this information. Otherwise, enter your IP address and netmask, then click OK. Enter your hostname, gateway, and DNS information, then click Next.

The next section, the Firewall Configuration screen, is very important. There are many options here, and you should take the time to read what each one offers. Network security is extremely important, because the incidence of cyber-attacks continues to rise all the time. Linux PCs aren't as susceptible to viruses, particularly if you don't run as the root or administrative user, but that doesn't mean you should let your guard down. If you are a single user on a home PC that is connected to the Internet, choose Enable Firewall, leave the various services checked off, and click Next.

What follows is yet another language selection screen: Additional Language Support. That's because the OS can support multiple languages, and you can change that default at a later time. Unless you have another language at your disposal, leave the choice as it is and click Next. On the next screen, you will be asked to enter your time zone (in my case, America/Montreal). When you are done, click Next.

When you arrive at the next screen, you will get your first taste of Linux's multiuser nature with the Account Configuration. This is where you set your root password (root is the administrator login). After the installation completes, you have the opportunity to create other nonroot (regular user) accounts. It's early, but I'll stress it now: You should create at least one nonroot account from which to work on a day-to-day basis.

This brings you to the screen with the goodies: Package Selection. The packages selected for the Personal Desktop are:

- Desktop shell (GNOME)
- Office Suite (OpenOffice)
- Web browser (Mozilla)
- Email (Evolution)
- Instant messaging
- Sound and video applications
- Games

Because I will be concentrating on KDE as the desktop, click Customize the Set of Packages to Be Installed. Click Next, and you will be on the Package Group Selection screen. You'll notice that packages are ordered into categories such as Desktops, Applications, and so on. Check off the KDE Desktop Environment under Desktops. Then, click Details and make sure that *all* KDE packages have been selected before you click OK.

 Note For the most part, you can leave everything else as is, but there is one other thing you may want to consider here. Despite the fact that most *desktop users* will not want to compile packages, I think that the lure of trying out something that is leading-edge or unusual will be more than even home users will be able to resist as they get familiar with their systems. That's why you might want to choose to install such development tools as gcc, perl, python, and more, as well as X Software Development, GNOME Software Development, and KDE Software Development.

When you're done here, click Next. This is the last step before the installation takes off on its own. You receive a final opportunity to change your mind before committing to this installation. Click Next, and a pop up window informs you of which other CDs you will need. For mine, I needed CD 1 and CD 2. Click Continue, and you are on your way.

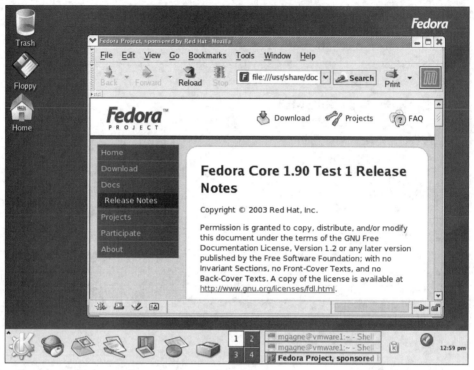

FIGURE 3-2   Fedora Core 2 (beta) desktop.

As your partitions are formatted, a progress bar keeps track of where you are in the installation. As the installation progresses, you are treated to some information about the Fedora project and some of the included products. Incidentally, this is usually a good time to take a break and grab something to drink. From time to time, you'll need to change CDs; you may need all three. When the installation completes, you have the opportunity to create an emergency boot diskette. Follow the instructions to do so, and label the diskette "Linux emergency boot diskette."

Note Make sure you take out the CD-ROM before the system reboots.

When the diskette creation is done, click Next. The system reboots to a graphical Welcome screen. From here, you go through a few final configuration details. Accept the license agreement and click Next (Figure 3-2). If the date and time are incorrect, you can adjust them here. On the next screen, you'll have an opportunity to fine-tune the display based on your monitor type and the number of colors you want displayed.

Click Next, and come to one of the more important parts of the process: user account creation. You must create at least one nonroot user for the system, and this is the time to do so. After clicking Next, the system lets you test your sound card and install additional CDs if you have them, after which you are done. The graphical login manager starts up, and you can log in as your nonroot user.

A SUSE Install

For my SUSE install, I used exactly the same machine and started from the same place. I used SUSE 9.0, which comes with both multiple CDs and a single DVD. The advantage of the DVD is that you do not have to swap disks.

Reboot your system with the CD or DVD in the drive. You now have the option of selecting various install modes. For a fresh installation, simply press <Enter> or wait, and the system will begin the installation.

The next screen you see after this is the Welcome screen, which is also where you select a language. The default is English, but you can certainly choose something else. Click Accept, and the install process begins analyzing your system for peripherals. All of these choices are shown to you on a single page; the keyboard, mouse, partitioning, software install, booting, and time zone information are all there on one screen. Notice the blue underline on each setting, much like on a web page. Check the suggested settings to make sure that things look right. If you need to change something, click the blue link. For instance, to change your time zone from the default of US/Pacific, click Time Zone, select from the list, and click Accept.

Be sure to look at Partitioning and Software. If you do have a Windows partition, you should see it listed as /windows/C. This is its mount point, unless you would like a different name. The software choices are the KDE Desktop Environment, Office Applications (this is OpenOffice.org), Help & Support Documentation, and Graphical Base System (the X window system).

Again, the lure of playing with some leading-edge software might be overwhelming at some point. You can prepare for that here by clicking on the blue Software link. On the screen that follows, click the Detailed Selection button. On the left side of the next screen, you'll see a number of categories for additional software. If you do want to compile your own programs, select C/C++ Compiler and Tools. I'm also pretty sure you'll want the Games and Multimedia packages. If I am right, choose those as well.

Finally, there's the GNOME desktop environment. Even though I am concentrating this book on KDE, it is a good thing to experiment with another desktop environment. In the end, you might like GNOME better than KDE. In the Linux world, you have a choice. Furthermore, it doesn't hurt anything to load it at the same time; you just use up some disk space. When you are done, click Accept to go back to your Installation Settings screen. Have a final look, and click Accept. You'll be given a final warning regarding installation. If you are ready to start, click Yes, Install.

Your drive will be formatted, your Linux system will load, and you'll see a progress bar at the top right. After a little while, the basic installation completes, and you see a message to that effect. Remove the CD, and press <Enter>.

This is where the SUSE installation is different. If you are installing from CD, you are asked for additional CDs to complete the package installation. If, on the other hand, you were using the DVD to install, you immediately jump to final configuration. The first of these steps is account creation, starting with the setting of the root password. The root account is used for such administrative functions as installing software. You do not want to run as root under normal circumstances, because root is essentially *all-powerful*.

After selecting a root password, click Next and create at least one user login. The SUSE install is interesting here in that it allows you to redirect all of root's mail directly to a user account. Check off the box that says Receive System Mail when you are creating your personal user ID. There's also a check box for Auto Login, which logs in this particular user without a password automatically at boot time. This is probably fine if you are running this system at home and are the only user, but in an office environment or with multiple users, you don't want to check this box. You can choose to create additional users at this time, or simply click Next to continue.

After a brief interlude describing some of the changes in SUSE 9.0, you get to the X window graphical configuration to lock in your video settings. The dialog here may vary depending on what kind of video hardware you have or whether your card is 3D accelerated. Just *make sure* that you test out the final settings before moving on. Even if the information looks right, click the Change button for an opportunity to test your settings. Video settings work perfectly 99.99% of the time. It's just good to be sure beforehand. When you are done here, click Accept.

The SUSE installer writes these settings to disk, then does some final hardware settings, starting with your printer configuration. Make sure that your printer is plugged in and turned on, then click Yes when asked whether you want YaST (the SUSE system administration tool) to detect your printer.

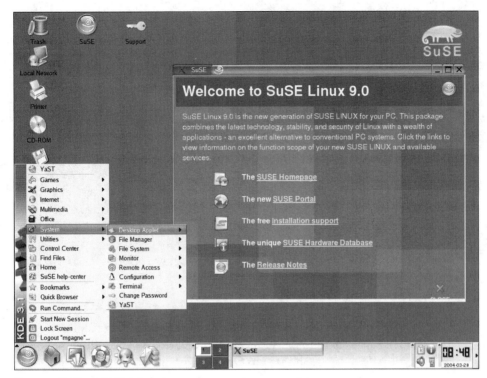

FIGURE 3-3   SUSE 9.0 desktop.

After a few seconds, YaST returns you to the Installation Settings screen for your connected peripherals and hardware. This includes Ethernet cards, printers, modems, sound cards, and so on. Make sure that things are as you expect them to be and change them if necessary. For instance, if your network card is connected to a cable modem, the DHCP settings are probably exactly as you want them to be. If you are on an existing network, however, you will probably want to change your interface to reflect your network's addressing scheme.

When you are happy with the changes, click Next. YaST finishes writing all of these settings to disk and finishes bringing the system up. Seconds later, you'll be at your login screen and ready to go. For a sneak peek at a SUSE Linux desktop, check out Figure 3-3.

Not So Tough Installs

As you can see, installing Linux isn't difficult, but it does vary from distribution to distribution. The thing to remember is that every distribution has similar steps such as language, keyboard, and mouse selection. All distributors ask you about dealing with disk partitions and offer to do it for you if you would rather keep it simple. For the most part, it's just a matter of accepting the defaults and clicking Next.

Starting and Stopping Linux

This sounds like such a simple thing that you might wonder why I am spending any time on it at all. After all, you turn on the power switch, sit back, and watch Linux come to life. Depending on the installation, you may have more than one boot option. The default will almost certainly be to take you into Linux. If you opted for a dual-boot system, you may have to select Linux from the boot menu.

The lesson here is simply this: Because you do have options, take the time to read what's on the menu and go with that.

 Warning Here is *rule number one* when it comes to shutting down your system: Never, ever simply power off the system. You must do a *proper* shutdown. Oh, and get an uninterruptible power supply (UPS) so that your system doesn't shut down accidentally. I should perhaps make it clear that you do not *need* a UPS to run Linux. If you don't want a random power fluctuation or a three-second power outage to take down your system, however, the added protection of a UPS makes sense.

Linux is a multiuser, multiprocessing operating system. Even when it appears that nothing is happening, there can be a great deal going on. Your system is maintaining disk space, memory, and files. All this time, it is busy making notes on what is happening in terms of security, email, errors, and so on. There may be open files or jobs running. A sudden stop as a result of pulling the plug can damage your file systems. A proper shutdown is essential. Even in the world of your old OS, you still had to do a proper shutdown. That doesn't change for Linux.

There are a few ways of shutting down your system. You start by logging off from your system. Make sure that you've closed all of your applications and saved anything you might have been working on. Now, right-click on the desktop, and select Logout from the pop-up menu. You should see something similar to Figure 3-4.

FIGURE 3-4   Available options when preparing to end a login session.

This particular logoff screen is from a SUSE system, but the types of options are similar regardless of which system you're on. At this point, select Turn Off Computer. There's rarely any need for choosing Restart Computer in the Linux world. When you shut down, it's usually because you intend to power off the system.

Shell Out   You can also log out from the command line, but it must be done from the root login. From a terminal window, switch to root with:

```
su - root
```

When you are prompted for the password, type:

```
shutdown -h now
```

When you call shutdown with the -h option, it is another way of saying, "Shut the system down and keep it down." On some systems and with proper hardware, this option powers off the system after it is down. Another choice is to type:

```
shutdown -r now
```

The -r option tells Linux to reboot immediately after a shutdown. A reboot option is usually used after a kernel rebuild.

And Now...Linux!

Congratulations! You have installed your Linux system, as well as learned how to bring it up and shut it down properly. Now you are ready to get to know your Linux system intimately, and as you turn to the next chapter, the fun really begins.

To paraphrase a line from *Casablanca*, one of my favorite movies, this will be the beginning of a beautiful friendship.

Resources

FIPS

www.igd.fhg.de/~aschaefe/fips/fips.html

Mandrake

www.mandrakelinux.com

PowerQuest (for Partition Magic)

www.partitionmagic.com

Fedora Linux

fedora.redhat.com

SUSE Linux

www.suse.com

chapter
4

Getting Your Hands Dirty

Welcome to the multiuser, multitasking, multieverything world. Linux is designed to run multiple users and processes concurrently. Therefore, your system is capable of doing many things even while it appears to be idle. This is the reason so many businesses and organizations use Linux as a web server, an email server, a file server, a print server...well, you get the idea.

From an individual user's perspective, this means that all users in your office or family can have desktop environments that are truly theirs and theirs alone. Your desktop can be configured and modified to let you work the way you want to, with different backgrounds, icons, colors, or themes, depending on your mood. It also protects your personal information from others, meaning that the kids can totally change their desktops and reorganize things, but you won't be in any way affected when you log in. That same philosophy applies to thin clients in an office environment, which I will discuss later in the book.

I'll have you logging in very shortly, but for the moment, I want to say a few words about your new desktop.

Getting to Know You...KDE

Linux is extremely flexible. Linux makes it possible to run in a number of different desktop environments. The plus side of this is that *you* decide how you want to work. Your system works the way you want it to and not the other way around. The down side is exactly the same. Let's face it; being told what to do is often easier, even if it means getting used to working in a way that you may not particularly like at first—not necessarily better, but easier.

On that note, at some time when you've gotten comfortable with your Linux system running the KDE desktop, I'm going to ask you to be brave and experiment with some of these other environments, whether it be GNOME, WindowMaker, IceWM, or one of the many other desktop environments available to the Linux user. You may find yourself totally taken with a different way of doing things. All of your programs will still work as they did, but the *feel* of your desktop—the *experience,* if you prefer—will be all yours. For now, I'll stick to KDE. That said, given the popularity of the GNOME desktop, I will end each chapter with suggestions on how you can do the same things in GNOME.

KDE is the most popular desktop environment in the Linux world, and deservedly so. It is beautiful, slick, mature, powerful, and easy to use. Plus, it is loaded with great applications for email, surfing the web, playing movies, burning CDs, writing documents, working with spreadsheets, and more. KDE also features a great collection of games to help keep you busy at the end of the workday.

A Few Words about X

In a few seconds when I start showing you around your desktop, what I am telling you now will fade into the background of your memory, but I still think you should know. KDE, that great-looking desktop system, is the friendly face that rides above your Linux system's real graphical engine. That engine is called the *X window system, XFree86,* or simply *X.* KDE, your desktop environment, provides control of windows, borders, decorations, colors, icons, and so on.

When you installed your system, you went through a graphical desktop configuration step of some kind. What you were setting up at that time wasn't KDE or GNOME, but X.

X is what the desktop and every graphical program *really* runs on.

Logging in

In most cases, your workstation will boot up to a graphical login screen. You will likely see the names of users you set up during the installation of your system, with a box for the username and another for the password. Remember that both the username and password are case-sensitive, so you must type both as they were created. You can always change the password at a later time. (I'll tell you about it just a little later in the chapter.)

This graphical login screen is known as the *login manager*. Depending on the installation, it may appear different from system to system. The KDE login screen looks something like the one shown in Figure 4-1, which comes from a Mandrake Linux system. Login managers, like so many things on your system, can be configured to take on different looks and styles. As a result, the companies that provide Linux distributions often customize them to suit their needs. What they all have in common is a place for your login name, your password, and an option for selecting your desktop environment (KDE, GNOME, or another).

FIGURE 4-1   Getting ready to log in.

Start by logging in with the nonroot user you created when you installed the system. For Session Type, make sure you choose KDE. If this is your first time logging in, you may be presented with the KDE personalizer (kpersonalizer). I say *may*, because some distributions log you into a default desktop with a look and feel that you can then change to suit your needs and tastes, something Chapter 5, "Customizing the Desktop," discusses in detail.

Quick Tip If you don't see the KDE personalizer after logging in, you should still take a few minutes to read through this section, as it does introduce you to some basic concepts. You can always run the KDE personalizer with the command `kpersonalizer`: Click the button in the bottom-left corner of your screen, select "Run Command", type `kpersonalizer`, and press <Enter>. Note that some distributions may not include the Kpersonalizer; instead, they provide a tour that lets you set some of the same items. Even so, all of these settings can be changed using the tools described in Chapter 5. The Kpersonalizer information applies to first-time logins only.

When kpersonalizer runs, it asks for your country and language of choice (Figure 4-2). Aside from the obvious usefulness of the language setting, this sets some intelligent defaults for you based on that decision, such as currency and date format.

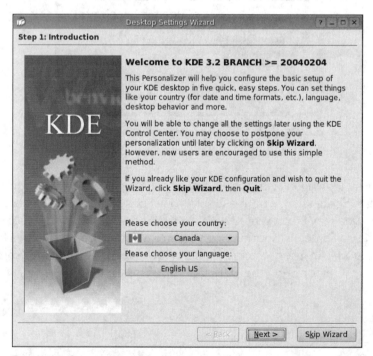

FIGURE 4-2   Setting your country and default language with Kpersonalizer.

The next screen, System Behavior, is particularly interesting (Figure 4-3). If you are coming from the Windows world, you are used to double-clicking on desktop icons to make things happen by now. Not so in the Linux world. Single-clicking on an icon activates your program. If you like double-clicking, choose Windows for System Behavior or stick with the single-click KDE default.

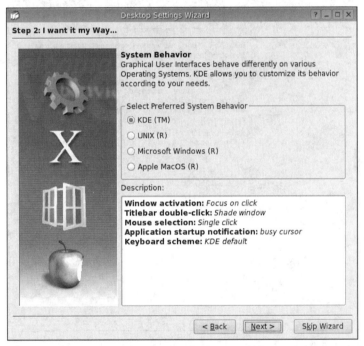

FIGURE 4-3 *System behavior affects mouse clicks and window behavior.*

Notice the Window activation item? This is sometimes referred to as *focus*. On a windowing system, it is possible to have many application windows on your screen at the same time. Sometimes they overlap. When you want to start using a particular window, you click on that window to bring it forward. That's *focus on click*. Aside from the KDE and Windows behaviors, you could also choose UNIX, which has an interesting method of focus. Simply moving your mouse cursor over the background window brings it forward. This is referred to as *focus follows mouse*. It takes some getting used to, but some people, particularly those with large monitors, may find it useful.

The next step brings up the Eyecandy-O-Meter (Figure 4-4). If you have a powerful, fast machine, you might want to just crank the slider to the maximum. What you will get are animated icons, sound themes, and special effects of various types. Click on the Show Details button to find out just what you get for your processor and memory buck.

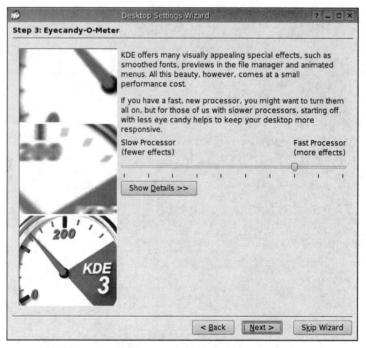

FIGURE 4-4   How much eyecandy do you need?

Hot on the heels of this screen is even more eyecandy, this time in the guise of a desktop theme (Figure 4-5). What kind of style would you like for your desktop? Pick one, click Next, and your desktop style changes automatically. If you don't like the choice, hit the Back button and try again. For the time being, I *highly recommend* that you pick the *KDE classic theme,* because the look and feel of the windows I'm going to describe are affected by the theme you choose. I will revisit this subject in the next chapter, at which point, you can go wild.

Finally, depending on your particular system, kpersonalizer may offer to load up your panel with some default settings and icons. For now, just accept the default, click Next, and you are done setting up your desktop.

FIGURE 4-5   Use Kpersonalizer to set your desktop theme.

Click Here! Click Here!

A quick note on clicking before continuing: Everything is pretty much launched by single-clicking the *left* mouse button. As I mentioned, you can change that to double-clicking if you prefer. For the moment, however, I suggest that you try to get used to single-clicking. I think you will like it.

Clicking the *right* mouse button almost anywhere brings up a menu of available options.

If you have one or have configured your two-button mouse to emulate a three-button mouse, the *middle* mouse button serves a number of purposes, based on the application. The best one, to me, is pasting text from one application to another.

Becoming One with the Desktop

The bar at the bottom of your screen is the panel, called *Kicker*. Among other things, notice the large *K* icon in the bottom-left corner. This is the

Application Starter, similar to the Start button on that other OS. Clicking the big K brings up a menu of menus, a list of installed applications that you can run with a single click.

Speaking of running things, Kicker also has a taskbar embedded in it. When you start an application, you'll see it listed in the taskbar. This not only shows you what you have running on your desktop, but it also provides a quick way to switch from process to process. Just click on the program in the taskbar. Alternatively, you can press <Alt+Tab> to switch from one running program to another. The taskbar can be configured to list all processes from all desktops, group similar processes together, or simply show you what is on your current virtual desktop.

Did he just say *virtual desktop*?

Yes, virtual desktop. This is one feature you are going to absolutely love! On the default installation, you'll also notice four little squares labeled 1 through 4. This is your desktop switcher, enabling you to switch between any of the four virtual desktops with a mouse click. Think of it as having a computer monitor that is four times as large as you already have, with each desktop running different things. You can leave each one the way you want it without having to minimize things when you want to use them. It gets better; you can have five, six, or even more virtual desktops if you find that four aren't enough (Figure 4-6).

 FIGURE 4-6   The desktop switcher with six virtual desktops.

Another way to switch virtual desktops is by pressing <Ctrl+Tab>.

Kicker also has a number of icons to the right of the big K. To find out what they are, move your mouse over each one and pause. Context-sensitive bubble help or *tool tips* appear, showing you each icon's purpose. Clicking on any of these icons launches the program it represents. One you might want to take note of right now is the life-preserver icon, which opens up your desktop documentation and help files. You can access these by clicking the big K and looking for Help as well.

Moving to Kicker's far right, you'll notice the embedded clock and smaller icons: clipboard, calendar, or speaker. These also represent programs: running programs. These applications have been *swallowed* by the panel and can be called up with a click. This mini-icon area is called the *system tray* (Figure 4-7).

 **FIGURE 4-7**   System tray icons.

Finally, notice the two little icons sitting together vertically. One looks like a lock and the other like a power button. On my desktop, the lock is blue and the power button is red. The lock button locks your desktop and activates the screensaver. (I'll cover screensavers in the next chapter.) To unlock the desktop, move the mouse or hit a key. The system then prompts you for your password. The power button logs you out and returns the system to the login manager so that you or someone else can log in.

Quick Tip The logout and lock buttons are an applet, which can be added or removed from the panel, and there are many other such applets. If you don't see the lock/logout applet, right-click on an empty part of the panel, select Add, then choose it from the list. If you wish, you can experiment with some of the other applets available for the panel. To remove a running applet, right-click the panel again, select Remove, then click the appropriate applet.

Your First Application

It's time to nail down some terminology and get you really working with the system. Starting a program or opening up an application is as simple as clicking on an icon. Give it a try with *the* great KDE application, *Konqueror*.

You'll be using Konqueror a lot. It is the KDE file manager that lets you work with files and folders. Konqueror makes it easy to create, copy, delete, and move folders, or *directories*, as they are known in the Linux world. To move folders and files around, just drag and drop them. Konqueror is also a web browser from which you can surf the Internet, as well as a universal file viewer so you can view and organize your photo collection, preview documents, and much, much more.

Quick Tip   This is a good time to let you in on a secret: Although you will find KDE under Red Hat, Mandrake, SUSE, and others, the menus may vary somewhat. Things on your menu may not be in *exactly* the same place as on my menu. For example, multimedia applications, such as the CD player, will be under a menu that sounds like multimedia, such as Enjoy Music & Video, whereas a web browser might be under a menu named Internet or Use the Internet. The *command's name*, however, will be consistent. For that reason, I will be telling you how to call a program by name throughout this book.

Down in your Kicker panel, notice the icon that looks like a folder with a little house in front of it (the icon may just be a house). The tool tip that pops up when you hover your mouse over it says Home. This opens Konqueror as a file manager in your home directory. Click it, and you should get something that looks like Figure 4-8.

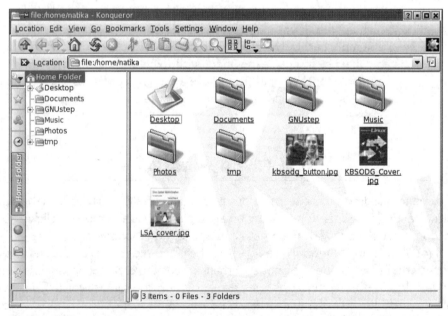

FIGURE 4-8   Introducing Konqueror, the all-purpose file manager and browser.

On the left, Konqueror shows a tree view of your home directory. This is the *navigation panel*. Pressing <F9> hides or brings forward the navigation panel. The tabs let you switch between a view of your home directory to bookmarks for the web, a history of places you've visited on the Internet, connected services (such as printers), FTP archives, and so on. On the right, the contents of the current location are displayed. If this is a directory, such as your home directory, the various directories appear as folder icons. Depending on how Konqueror is configured, images in your folders may appear as little thumbnails. Would you like to see the full-sized image? Just click on the thumbnail, and Konqueror does the rest.

Konqueror is flexible, powerful, and definitely worth your time to get to know. In fact, it will likely become your most used desktop application. I'm going to give Konqueror the focus and consideration it deserves in the next chapter. For the moment, leave Konqueror where it is and read on for a discussion of windows—and I don't mean the operating system.

Windows, Title Bars, and Menus, Oh My!

Each graphical program that runs on your desktop has certain common characteristics. Have a look at the top of your Konqueror window; it should be similar to Figure 4-9.

FIGURE 4-9   Most windows have a title bar, as well as a menu bar.

The Title Bar

The top bar on a running program is called the *title bar*. Depending on the application, it may display the name of a program name, the document you are working on, a location on the web, or it might show a nice description of what you are running. Left-clicking on the title bar and dragging it with the mouse moves the program window around on your desktop.

Quick Tip Most modern desktops assume a fairly sizeable monitor running at least 1024×768, and a number of applications assume this to be a universal truth. This plays havoc when your monitor is smaller, say 800×600, and the buttons you need to click are off screen. Clicking the title bar and dragging the window gets you only so far.

Don't despair. By pressing the <Alt> key and left-clicking on a window, you can drag it anywhere you wish, including beyond the boundaries of your desktop. This is particularly handy if you need to get at a hidden OK button.

Double-clicking on the title bar *shades* your program; the application appears to roll up like a window blind. Move your mouse pointer back to the title bar, and the application unrolls. Move off the application completely, and it rolls up again. Double-click on the title bar again, and the application *unrolls* and stays unrolled. Doing this with a number of running applications is an interesting phenomenon that takes some getting used to, kind of like someone reading your mind.

The title bar also has a number of small icons. Pause your mouse cursor over them for tool tips about their functions. Two icons of interest are in the left corner of the title bar. The far left one brings up a small drop-down menu that enables you to move the program to another virtual desktop and to minimize or maximize the application, among other things.

You *may* also have a push-pin (or stick-pin) icon beside the menu icon; this makes a window *sticky*. Clicking it again makes it *unsticky*. Try this. Click on one of your other three virtual desktops. If you haven't already excitedly opened dozens of other programs on each one, you should find yourself with a nice, clean desktop. Now go back to your first virtual desktop. Click the stick-pin icon. Now jump back to the second virtual desktop. Konqueror is there. Click on desktop number three, and it is there also. In fact, if you had ten virtual desktops, Konqueror would be waiting for you on all of them.

Quick Tip Some buttons, such as the push pin, are optional. To turn them on or off, right-click on the title bar and select Configure Window Behavior. Under the Buttons tab, click the check box for Use Custom Titlebar Button Positions.

Here's a cool bit of information: You are still running only *one* instance of Konqueror, but it is available to you on every desktop. Finally, if you stuck the window on virtual desktop one and you unstuck it on virtual desktop three, it would stay on desktop three.

Before moving on to other things, look at the buttons on the right side of the title bar. You use the icon that has a dot, or sometimes an underscore, in the center to minimize or iconize a window. Remember that you can pause over the top with your mouse button to get the tool tip. The icon with a square in the center maximizes a window, causing it to take up every bit of space on your desktop except for Kicker's panel. Finally, the X icon does pretty much what you would expect it to: It closes a running application.

On to the Menu Bar

Directly below the title bar is the *menu bar*. The menu bar generally has a number of labels, such as File, Edit, View, and so on, each grouping the various things you can do into some kind of sensible order.

Every program has a different set of menu options, depending on the nature of the application. Clicking on a menu label drops down a list of your options for that function, as shown in Figure 4-10.

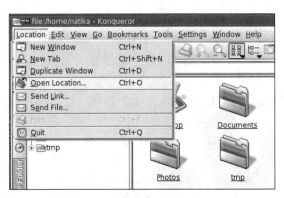

FIGURE 4-10   Drop-down menus.

Resizing Windows

The last thing you should know is that, for the most part, you aren't stuck with the default window size. By grabbing any of the corners of an application window, you can drag that corner and stretch the window to a size that is more comfortable for you. The same applies to the top, bottom, and sides of a program window.

As you position the cursor on a corner or a side, it changes to a double arrow. Just drag the side or corner to the desired position, and you are done.

Command Central

Sometimes if you know the command, it is just as easy to type that command and tell the program to run without having to work your way through all those menus. On your old system, you would have clicked that Start button, selected Run, and typed something in, usually setup because that is when you tended to use the Run option. On your Linux system, you can do the same thing by clicking the big K and selecting the Run command. You can also simply hold down the <Alt> key and press <F2> (<Alt+F2>). A nice dialogue box will appear, asking you to type the name of the program you want to run.

Are you wondering what those programs are called?

Let me give you a hint.

Click on the big K, select the Utilities menu, and start the scientific calcula-tor, which is a powerful calculator with trigonometric and statistical analysis functions. Now look at the title bar at the top of the player. See that it says Kcalc? That's the name of the program—almost. It's the name in mixed case. To run it, forget all those capital letters and just type the command in lower case; kcalc is the name of the program that runs the KDE scientific calculator.

To recap, pressing <Alt+F2>, typing kcalc in the dialog box, and pressing <Enter> is the same as going through the menus. Have a look at Figure 4-11 for an example.

FIGURE 4-11   Running a command with <Alt+F2>.

A Polite Introduction to the Command Line

In your line of Kicker icons, look in the lower-right corner for the screen with a shell or simply the computer screen. When you pause your mouse over it for a second, the tool tip tells you that the icon is for your terminal program;

in this case, the terminal program is called Konsole. This is your command prompt, similar to your DOS prompt in Windows-land.

There is a shell in front of the icon, because Konsole is your access to the Linux command line, known also as the *command shell*. There are many types of shells, each of which works similarly (enabling you to run commands, for example), but each may have different capabilities. The default on Linux is called bash, the GNU Bourne-Again Shell (yes, we do love acronyms in the Linux world).

The shell is powerful, and learning about its capabilities will make you a wizard of the Linux world. Become one with the shell, and nothing can stop you. The shell is the land of the Linux systems guru and the administrator. For the most part, you can do just about anything you need to do by staying and working with the X window system and your KDE desktop. Still, from time to time, I will ask you to do something from the shell prompt. As time goes on, you too will *feel the power* of the Linux shell.

Here's a polite introduction. Click the Konsole icon. Konsole will appear with a Tip of the Day window in front of it (Figure 4-12). Early on in your Linux experience, you might want to leave these tips on. You can even walk through them by clicking on the Next button. When you've had enough tips, you can banish them by turning off the Show Tips on Startup check box and clicking Close. If you find yourself missing the tips later on, click Help on the menu bar and select Tip of the Day.

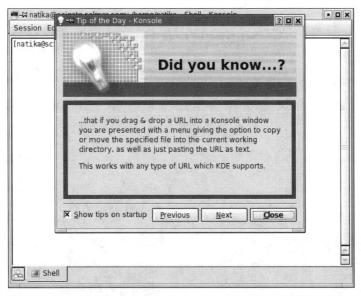

FIGURE 4-12   Konsole (shell) with Tip of the Day.

When you do click Close, you are left with an open Konsole and your cursor sitting beside a dollar sign prompt. This is the shell prompt. Whenever you find yourself at a shell prompt, the system is waiting for you to type in a command. Remember the calculator from earlier? You could type kcalc here and start it up just as easily. For now, type date at the shell prompt, then press the <Enter> key.

```
[marcel@mypc marcel]$  date
Sat May 15 12:31:57 EDT 2004
```

Aside from learning the date and time that I wrote this paragraph, you learn the current date and time when you try the command for yourself. That's what date is, a command that displays the date and time. You'll also find yourself back at the shell prompt as your system patiently awaits your next command. Type exit, and press the <Enter> key.

The Konsole disappears. That's it. You'll use the shell again as you go through this book, but for now, your polite introduction to the shell ends here.

 Give Me More This is just a sample of what you can do with the Linux command shell. Chapter 10, "Becoming One with the Shell," covers the shell in greater detail.

Changing Your Password

It is good security policy to change your password from time to time. Under your K menu, there's an option for changing your password; most likely it's under the Settings submenu. You can also run the command as in the scientific calculator example by using your <Alt+F2> run sequence and typing the command kdepasswd. Either way, a window appears (Figure 4-13), asking for your current password.

FIGURE 4-13   Using kdepasswd to change your password.

Notice that, like the login manager, your password is not visible. Instead, each key you press is echoed as an asterisk. When you have successfully entered your password, the system asks you for a new password. Then it asks for the password again, this time for confirmation. That's it. Be sure to remember your new password. You'll need it next time you log in.

Shell Out You can easily change your password from the command line as well. Just open a shell prompt, and type the command:

```
passwd
```

You will see the following:

```
[marcel@mysystem marcel]$ passwd
Changing password for user marcel.
(current) UNIX password:
New UNIX password:
Retype new UNIX password:
passwd: all authentication tokens updated
successfully.
```

chapter

5

Customizing the Desktop

After having taken the first steps into the Linux world, you are probably thinking it is pretty easy and wondering what the fuss was all about. For what it's worth, I'm thinking the very same thing. Now that the fear of dealing with a new operating system is gone, it's time to get really comfortable.

In this chapter, I'm going to show you how to make your system truly your own—how to change your background, your colors, your fonts, and anything else you'll need to create a desktop as individual as you are. Would you like some icons on your desktop? Perhaps some shortcuts to programs you use on a regular basis? No problem. I'll cover all of those things, too.

I Am Sovereign of All I Survey

As I've already mentioned, working in the Linux world is working in a *multiuser* world. What this means is that everyone who uses your computer can have a unique environment. Any changes you make to your desktop while you are logged in as yourself will have no effect on little Sarah when she logs in to play her video games. If she happens to delete all the icons on her desktop or changes everything to a garish purple and pink, it won't affect you, either.

The first thing most people want to change is their background. It's sort of like moving into a new house or apartment. The wallpaper or paint that someone else chose rarely fits into your idea of décor. The same goes for your computer's desktop. Let's get you something more to your liking.

Changing the Background

Start by right-clicking somewhere on the desktop; make sure you aren't clicking on an icon. From the menu that appears, choose Configure Desktop. From the configuration card (Figure 5-1) you can make a number of cosmetic and functional changes relating to your desktop. On the left side of the dialog, a row of icons specifies the various desktop changes you can make, starting with an item called Background. If it isn't selected by default, click on that, and you will be able to modify your background settings.

Over on the right side, a display shows you a preview of what your new desktop will look like for the specific settings. Look for a drop-down box labeled Setting for Desktop near the top; by default All Desktops is selected. This gives you the opportunity to change your settings for all of your virtual desktops or each individually. That way, if you are feeling *particularly* creative, you can play around with creating a unique identity for every virtual desktop. For now, leave the setting to All Desktops.

Below the virtual desktop setting are two additional sections: Background and Options. To change the background image, click on the radio button labeled Picture (in the Background section). Now select an image by clicking on the Wallpaper drop-down list. These are the default system wallpapers, and quite a few are installed already. Scroll down the list, highlighting titles as you go, and notice that a preview of your new wallpaper appears in the small monitor image. To find images in something other than the default directory, click the Browse button (the folder icon) to the right of the wallpaper name. A Konqueror-like file manager pops up, enabling you to navigate the disk in search of your personal images. When that file dialog opens, you can turn the image preview on and off by pressing <F11>. You'll definitely want it *on*. It makes looking for images a lot easier.

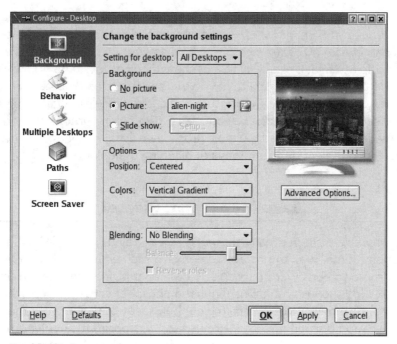

FIGURE 5-1   Wallpaper settings.

When you see something you like, click on either OK or Apply to make it official. OK exits the configuration program, whereas Apply changes your background but leaves the settings program running (the window does not go away as with OK). Try it both ways, and you'll see what I mean.

Another setting you might have noticed in the Options section is Position, which tells the system how to treat the image you select. Some images are only small graphic *tiles*, designed to be copied over and over until they fill your screen. For these, you would change the mode to Tiled. If the image you are using is a bit small for your screen, you might consider Centered Maxpect, which grows the image as much as possible while retaining the relative width and height. If you just want the image to fill your screen and you don't care what it looks like, go for Scaled. Play. Experiment. These are *your* walls.

It is also possible to configure multiple wallpapers. This provides you with a means of picking several wallpapers that will automatically switch at whatever interval you decide on; the default is 60 minutes. Back in the Background section, click on the Slide Show radio button. The Setup button at the bottom becomes active. Click it, and you'll be asked to select the time interval for the images to rotate and whether you want the rotation to be sequential or random.

I happen to like random. Now, click Add to access the Konqueror-like file manager and select the images you want to use in the random rotation. Select as many or as few as you like (remember to hold down the <Ctrl> key to select random, multiple images), click OK to exit the various dialogs, and you are done.

Incidentally, you don't *have* to have a wallpaper. You can create a nice, plain background by clicking the No Picture radio button. After that, look in the Options section, and you can select one or two colors, gradients, and some ready-made patterns. Click the Colors drop-down list for choices. The Blending button lets you select different ways of blending the colors.

Save My Screen, Please!

Okay, screensavers don't really do much screen saving these days. The idea, once upon a time, was to protect screens from phosphor burn-in. Old-style monochrome screens were particularly bad for this. In time, the letters from your text-only menus would burn into the phosphor screen. Even when you turned off the monitor, you could still see the ghostly outline of your most popular application burned into the screen itself. As programs evolved to color screens and graphics, that changed somewhat, but the problem continued to exist for some time, partly due to the static nature of the applications.

Time passes, and some bright light somewhere got the idea that if you constantly changed the image on the screen, that type of burn-in would not be as likely. What better way to achieve this than to have some kind of clever animation kick in when the user walked away from the screen for a few minutes or hours. Heck, it might even be fun to watch. The screensaver was born. Modern screens use scanning techniques that all but banish burn-in, but screensavers have not gone away. Those addictive fish, toasters, penguins, snow, spaceships, and so on have managed to keep us entertained, despite the march of technology. Let's face it; we are all hooked.

Depending on your distribution, your screensaver may or may not already be active by default. Getting to your screensaver setup involves the same first steps as changing your background. Right-click on a clear part of the desktop, and choose Configure Desktop. The desktop configuration card appears, saying "You can customize the desktop here." On the left side of that card, click on the item called Screen Saver.

As with the wallpaper manager, you get a nice little preview window over to the right that gives you an idea of what your screensaver will look like (Figure 5-2). Click the Start Screen Saver Automatically check box, assuming it isn't on already. Now pick a screensaver from the list and watch the results on the preview screen. To see the real thing in action, click the Test button. To go back to the configuration screen, press any key. Some screensavers can be modified, which is why you also have a Setup button. For instance, the Clock screensaver, which floats an old analog clock, can be modified to be larger or smaller, to use different colors, or to stay nicely centered on your screen.

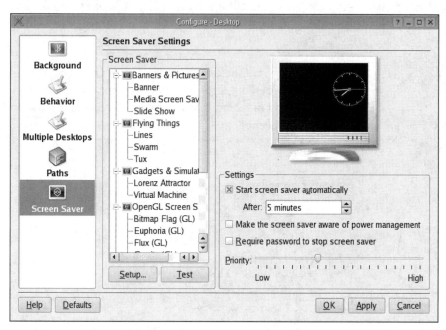

FIGURE 5-2   Selecting a screensaver.

Before you click OK, you may want to change the default time before your screensaver kicks in. Mine is set for five minutes. In an office environment or a busy household, you will probably want to password-protect your screen when you walk away. To do this, click on Require Password. After the screensaver starts, you will need to enter your login password to get back to your work. Always remember that your password is case-sensitive.

Moving Things Around

If you haven't already done this, click on an icon (hold the click) and drag it to some other spot on the desktop. Easy, isn't it? When you log out from your KDE session later on, make sure that you click Save session for future logins so that any changes you make here will follow you into the next session.

The taskbar is something else you may want to move. Just drag the panel and drop it to one of the four positions on the desktop (top, bottom, left, or right). The location, by the way, can also be changed by right-clicking on the taskbar, selecting Configure Panel (you can also right-click the program launcher, and select Panel menu), and choosing the location of the panel. On the card that appears (Figure 5-3), you can select the location, the size of the panel and its icons, and the length that you are willing to allow the panel on your desktop.

Note Technically, the taskbar is that portion of the *panel* that shows your open programs, letting you quickly click from one to the other. That said, you may find that people speak of the taskbar and the panel interchangeably.

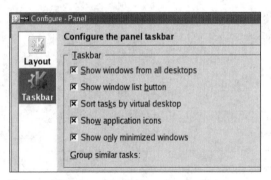

FIGURE 5-3   Panel and taskbar settings.

On that customization card, you can lock in on some taskbar-specific configurations. For instance, by default, your taskbar will show windows from all desktops or programs, regardless of which virtual desktop you opened them on. Some people like this feature, but I am not one of them. This is something I check off, because I want to see only the programs on the virtual desktop I am currently running. Remember, these settings are a personal thing.

The Show Window List Button option provides a small pop-up right next to the taskbar. This pop-up shows a quick list of all windows on all desktops; handy if, like me, you turned off the first option. Group Similar Tasks is another very personal option. Say that you opened up three Konsoles. If you have this option set, only one task group shows up in the taskbar; a small black arrow on the task lets you know that there are more like that. If you click on the Konsole task in the taskbar, you'll see all three.

The last two items aren't particularly exciting, but I will quickly mention them. The first lets you sort tasks by virtual desktop, and the other shows tiny icons next to the task name.

Finally, look just below these taskbar settings, and you will see three options dedicated to your mouse. These define what occurs when you click an item in the taskbar with your right, left, or middle mouse button.

Is That a Theme or a Motif?

Not a musical theme, but a desktop theme. A *theme* is a collection of buttons, decorations, colors, backgrounds, and so on, preselected and packaged to give your desktop a finished and coherent look. Some themes even incorporate sounds for startup, shutdown, opening and closing program windows, and so on. It can be a lot of fun.

Then there are *styles*, which are sort of like themes, but not as all-encompassing. Styles tend to concentrate on window decorations and behavior as well as *widgets*. Widgets are such elements as radio buttons, check boxes, combo boxes (drop-down lists), sliders, tabs, and so on. Some distributions include only styles and not themes, letting you deal separately with individual elements, such as sounds and colors.

Alright, I know you want to get to it and change your theme a time or two, but first I'm going to tell you something rather important. Most, if not all, of the things I've shown you so far on customizing your desktop can be done through the KDE Control Center. To find it, click on the big K and look for Control Center. If you are having trouble locating it, remember that you can bring it up by pressing <Alt+F2> and typing kcontrol, its program name.

Quick Tip   You may recall a friendly little warning I gave you earlier: Different Linux distributions arrange the menus in different ways. You may also find a Preferences menu or a Look and Feel menu in your program launcher menu (the big K). As you will hear again and again, *there's more than one way to do it.*

As soon as the KDE Control Center loads, it displays some capsule information about the system, its hostname, and the version of Linux running on it. Over on the left side, an index page covers a number of items that can be either viewed or modified on the system. I say either, because some of what you see here is just information and cannot be changed. One of these items is Look and Feel. Click the plus sign beside it, and you'll get a list of options for changing your desktop environment's look and feel (Figure 5-4).

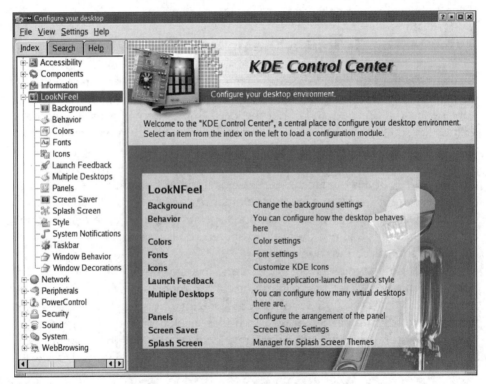

FIGURE 5-4   Changing the look and feel in KDE's control panel.

Almost everything you could possibly ever want to do to alter your desktop experience is here. Change the background, colors, fonts, icons, screensaver— you name it. It is all here! That includes your themes and styles. Go ahead. Click on Style, and select a style from the Widget Style list. As you click, the preview window shows you how it affects the overall look. If you just want to see it in action but you don't want to commit yet, click Apply. When you know you can live with the changes, click OK.

So, what are some of those LookNFeel changes, and how do they affect what you do and how you work?

Window Decorations

This is also your opportunity to undo something you changed in Chapter 4, "Getting Your Hands Dirty." When you ran Kpersonalizer, you selected the KDE Classic style so that we could all be on the same page (so to speak) in terms of what you see in your title bar. With the introduction of KDE 3.1, the default theme became Keramik, a slick, modern-looking theme that changes a number of things related to your desktop experience. KDE 3.2 followed up with Plastik, a somewhat lighter, more corporate-feeling window decoration and theme. Figures 5-5 through 5-7 show the Classic, Keramik, and Plastik window decorations, respectively.

If you would like to use something different, you can make that change now. Just remember that things may look a little different than what I show you in the book from here on in. With that little disclaimer in place, you may now express your individuality.

FIGURE 5-5   KDE 2 Classic window decoration.

FIGURE 5-6   KDE 3.1's default Keramik window decoration.

FIGURE 5-7   New with KDE 3.2 is the Plastik window decoration.

Themes and Styles

Themes and styles are essentially collections of look and feel changes. A style is a collection of definitions affecting primarily widgets, such as buttons, tabs, and so on (Figure 5-8).

A theme, on the other hand, might encompass changes in window decorations, wallpaper, colors, and icons to create a cohesive, integrated desktop experience, whereas a change in window decoration would affect only the window decoration itself.

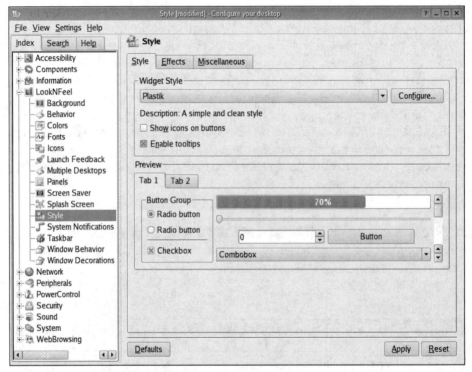

FIGURE 5-8   Changing styles are reflected in the KDE Control Center.

The theme manager (Figure 5-9) is similar. Although it is no longer present in KDE 3.2, it is in all releases prior. Under the Installer tab, it lists the installed themes and provides a preview window. The Contents tab is interesting, in that you can limit what changes the theme manager applies to your system. For instance, and I know this will sound like sacrilege to some, I hate sound themes. Honestly, I can't stand having little tunes play each time I start a program or minimize a window. That's why I personally turn off the Sound effects check box.

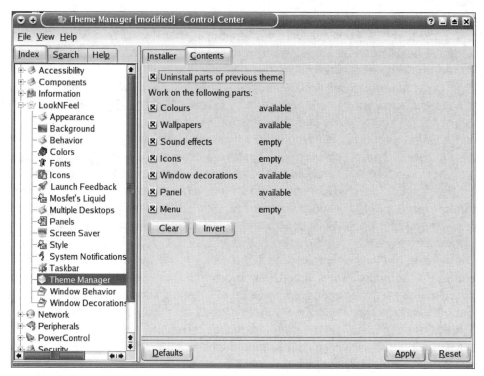

FIGURE 5-9   Theme manager options in the Control Center.

The fashion slaves among you will quickly grow tired of the themes and styles your system comes with. There are quite a few, but not nearly enough for those surfing the edges of what's hot today. That's why you should keep the web site www.kde-look.org in mind.

This little site has tons of themes, styles, alternative wallpapers, and icons, enough to keep you busy for a long, long time. Now, I know I haven't talked about getting on the Internet yet; there are still a few things to cover. If you just can't wait, you could jump over to Chapter 9, "Network and Internet Connections." Just make sure you come back here. You wouldn't want to miss anything.

Adding Icons and Shortcuts to Your Desktop

I covered this topic somewhat in the last chapter, but it is time to look at it in detail. While working with Konqueror, you might recall that you had a direc-tory called Desktop and that this directory actually *was* your desktop. If you wanted to get a file onto your desktop, you could just drag and drop (copy or link) a file there. A good reason for doing this is that it puts things you use on a regular basis, such as a business spreadsheet or a contact list, right where you can quickly get to them.

The single most useful icon you will want to add to your desktop is a link to a program on your system, something you might have called a *shortcut* under your old OS. Maybe you need to have your word processor or your CD player handy. Whatever it is, you would like it there in front of you.

The second most useful link is a Uniform Resource Locator (URL) to a regularly visited web site. This could also be a file (more on this in Chapter 6), because a URL can point to a file just as easily as a web site. Instead of the path to a file, simply type in the URL to your favorite site. I will cover surfing the Net in greater detail later in this book. Let's continue by adding a program to your desktop.

What you need to understand is that you won't really be putting the program there, but rather a link to it. Right-click on the desktop and move your mouse cursor over Create New, then File, then select Link to Application. The dialog box or card that opens has three tabs. The first, General, lets you choose a name for the program. Notice that the words "Link to Application" are highlighted. You can just type a name that makes sense to you here. To the left of the name is a square with a gear-like icon. Clicking this square brings up a large collection of icons from which you can select whatever happens to take your fancy (Figure 5-10).

FIGURE 5-10   *Selecting an icon for your new shortcut.*

Once you have chosen an icon, skip over to the third tab, Application. (In KDE 3.1, look for the Execute tab instead.) This is where you enter the program's real name. For example, if you wanted a link to the calculator, you would enter /usr/bin/kcalc in the Command field. Another way to get there is to click the Browse button and navigate your way to the application. You can also enter a description or comment about your shortcut if you wish, but this isn't necessary. The Permissions tab lets you decide whether others can see, modify, or execute the icon. (Remember that it is possible to create these links in other directories, including public directories.) If you are creating an icon for your personal home directory, you can pretty much ignore this.

When you are happy with your changes, click OK. Your new program link, which you can launch by single-clicking, should appear on your desktop.

Shell Out To create a shortcut icon for a command, you first have to know what and where the command is. To be honest, a command or program (such as the KDE calculator, kcalc) could be almost anywhere on the disk. For the most part, programs tend to be in one of the *bin* directories: /bin, /usr/bin, or /usr/local/bin. You can also use the whereis command to tell you exactly. For instance, to know where the kcalc program is, I would do the following at the bash shell prompt under Konsole (the $ sign):

```
[mgagne@mysystem mgagne]$ whereis kcalc
kcalc: /usr/bin/kcalc /usr/lib/kcalc.la
/usr/lib/kcalc.so
```

As you can see, there are other files associated with the kcalc program, but the actual executable kcalc (the one to use) is in /usr/bin. You can also use whereis with the -b switch to limit the search to binary or executable files, as in:

```
whereis -b kcalc
```

Miscellaneous Changes

Now that I have shown you how to find all of these things, I'm going to let you explore the LookNFeel menu on your own. Check out the Fonts dialog if you would like different desktop fonts than those set by default. You might find it interesting to note that there are different icon sets available than the ones you currently see. Click Icons, and go wild. If you do change the icons, just *be aware* that those I describe when pointing to the panel or to various applications may look a little different than what you now see.

Let me give you one final treat before I close this chapter. Still working from the KDE Control Center, look for Keyboard Shortcuts (under Regional and Accessibility), and you'll discover lots of interesting keyboard shortcuts to do such things as switching from one application to the other, switching from one desktop to the other, opening and closing windows, getting help, taking a desktop screenshot (in case you want to share your fashion sense with others), and so on. A minor word of warning, though: You may have to scroll down through the list to see everything.

Resources

KDE Look

www.kde-look.org

6

Using Konqueror for File Management

Anyone who has ever had a system crash without a handy backup of their files knows that nothing is more important than data. Computers are about storing and dealing with information. That's why getting a good hang of working with that data—moving, copying, renaming, and deleting it—is vitally important to getting comfortable in your Linux world.

That means it is time to revisit your old friend, Konqueror.

Files, Directories, and the Root of All Things

As Ken Thompson, the developer of UNIX, once said, everything is a file. That includes directories. Directories are just files with files inside them. All of these files and directories are organized into a hierarchical file system, starting from the root directory and branching out.

> *Note* Folders and directories are the same thing. The terms can be used interchangeably, but I will be calling them directories. If you are more comfortable thinking of them as folders, don't worry. Depending on the application, you'll see both terms used.

The root directory, referred to as *slash* or /, is actually aptly named. If you consider your file system as a tree's root system spreading out below the surface, you start to get an idea of just what things look like.

Under the root directory, you'll find directories called usr, bin, etc, tmp, and so on. Use the program launcher to open up Konqueror, or click on the taskbar icon that looks like a house or a house in front of a folder. Konqueror opens in file manager mode; remember, it is also a web browser. If your navigation panel isn't up on the left side, press <F9> to open it (Figure 6-1). To either the right or left of the navigation panel (this is all configurable), you'll see a row of tabs. Click on the root directory tab, the one that looks like a small folder. Here's a hint: If you move your mouse over the tabs and pause, a tool tip pops up to let you know you are in the right place. When the file system tree appears on the left side, click on the top folder, Root Directory, then look at the names of those folders.

These are all system directories, and they contain all of the programs that make your Linux system run, including documentation, devices, and device drivers. For the most part, you aren't going to be touching these files. Accidentally changing things around in this part of your system probably isn't a good thing, which is why everyone logs in with their own accounts. The administrator account, called *root*, should be used only as needed.

One of the directories under the root is called home, and inside that directory, you'll discover other directories, one for each login name on your system. These are the individual home directories and where you'll find your *personal* files and directories. If you want to store personal documents, music files, or pictures, this is the place. Once in Konqueror, you can jump to your home directory by clicking the house icon on the left panel or clicking Go on the menu bar and selecting Home URL. This is your $HOME.

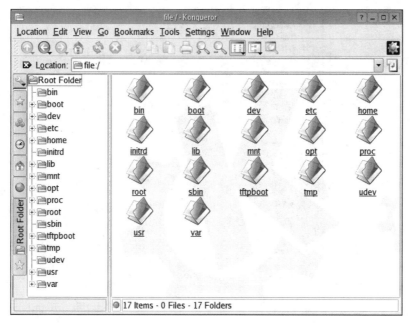

FIGURE 6-1   Konqueror's file manager view with navigation panel (left) open.

Quick Tip My use of $HOME isn't just to be silly. The system can recognize some things based on environment variables, symbolic names that can refer to text, numbers, or even commands. In the DOS/Windows world, you had similar variables; for instance, the PATH in your autoexec.bat file. $HOME is an environment variable assigned to every person who logs in. It represents a person's home directory. If you want to see all of the environment variables assigned to your session, shell out and type the env command.

Try this. Over on the left side of the tree view, you'll see a little plus sign beside the home directory. Click on the plus sign, and the tree view expands to show your own personal directory. Notice that the plus sign has become a minus sign; click it to collapse the directory view. With the home directory expanded, click on your personal directory. You should see a few items appear in the right side view, including one icon labeled Desktop (Figure 6-2). On the left side, /dev is expanded, and the right side view shows the same directory collapsed.

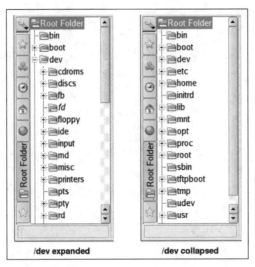

/dev expanded   /dev collapsed

FIGURE 6-2   Expanding and collapsing
directories.

Before you do anything else, I want you to look down in your taskbar at the bottom of the screen. Do you see the desktop icon there, just to the right of the program launcher (the big K)? It looks like a desktop blotter with a lamp above it. When you move your mouse cursor over it, the tool tip displays Show Desktop. Click it, and your desktop appears, free of windows. Click it again, and everything returns to normal.

Quick Tip If the Show Desktop icon isn't there, you can easily add it. Right-click on the big K, select Panel Menu>Add>Special Button>Desktop Access. The button will appear in your taskbar.

The reason I am having you do this is that I want you to take note of what icons are on your desktop. Now, go back to your Konqueror session, and click on the Desktop icon in the right (or main) window. All of the icons on your desktop show up there. Why is that, you ask? Because even those icons on your desktop are files or directories. Cool? Let's move on.

Shell Out Open a Konsole by clicking the terminal icon in
your panel (the one with the shell). At the shell prompt, type:

```
ls Desktop
```

The `ls` command lists the contents of your Desktop directory.
Compare what you see there with the icons currently on your
graphical desktop. Do the names look familiar? When you are done,
type `exit` to close the Konsole.

Directories (and subdirectories) usually show up as folders, although this isn't
a hard and fast rule, because you can customize this. Nevertheless, some directories have different icons right from the start; the Desktop icon you just visited
and the Trashcan are two notable examples.

Wherever You Go...

To move from directory to directory, you can simply click on an icon, whether
in the right tree view or in the left expanded view. You can also move the directory tree around by using your Arrow keys. You'll see the highlight bar move
from directory to directory. To see the contents in the main window, move to
a folder and press <Enter>. To go up a level in the directory tree (rather than
folder by folder), press <Alt+Up Arrow>. Substituting the <Down Arrow>
for the <Up Arrow> takes you to the other directory.

   There's another way, as well. If you look up at the menu bar, you'll see an
up arrow, a left-pointing arrow, and a right-pointing arrow (Figure 6-3). Right
next to that is an icon of a house. Clicking that house icon always takes you back
to your personal home directory. Clicking the up arrow moves you up the directory tree, and the left arrow takes you back to whatever directory you were
last visiting.

FIGURE 6-3   Konqueror's main navigation toolbar.

The quickest way to navigate your file system is simply to type a directory name in the location bar, assuming you know the directory you want. Clicking that little *X* on the black arrow to the left of the location bar (where it says Location) clears the field. That saves you having to select the text and erase it. Now, just type in wherever you want to go, such as /home/marcel.

Navigating the Navigation Panel

You should spend a couple of minutes looking at that navigation panel (the left side panel you open and close with <F9>), because it is quite important. You've already seen how to use it to navigate your file system, but wait—there's more (as they say on television). Look at those tabs on the right side of the navigation panel. Move your mouse over them to identify them with tool tips. This is an important step, because the icons may vary from those in Figure 6-2. Click on them to switch to whatever view they offer. Click on them again, and the navigation panel slams shut, leaving only the tabs behind and giving you more viewing space in the main Konqueror window.

Now, about those tabs. The first is a *Bookmark tab* (mine has an image of a star on it, but the icon could be different). When you experiment with using Konqueror as a web browser later in the book, you'll be using the bookmark feature a lot. For now, you should probably know that you can bookmark locations on disk. If you use a particular directory a lot, such as your music collection, you can bookmark that for easy access. You can also get to the bookmarks or add them by clicking Bookmarks on the menu bar.

After the Bookmark tab, you'll see the Devices tab, which provides access to your folders on CD-ROMs, floppy disks, hard disks, or other attached storage devices. Clicking the History tab shows you a tree view listing various files and directories on your disk or sites you've visited recently.

The tab with a house on it is a direct link to your personal home directory. Next to it is the KDE Media Player tab, which you'll recognize by the image of a little blue speaker with "music" pouring out. I'll cover that later when I talk about multimedia. Below that is an icon with a globe of the Earth. That's the Network tab. The Network tab provides you with a quick link to the KDE download areas (FTP sites) and web pages. For these to work, you must be connected to the Internet. Again, more on this later in the book.

The second-to-last tab accesses your system's root directory, as discussed earlier in this chapter. That leaves only one tab, the Services tab, which lets you zoom in on network services, such as printers or shared directories on other machines or your local network. There is a font browser as well. You can even access your CD-ROM device from here and play audio tracks. Once again, this is something I will discuss later in the book. For the moment, I just wanted you to get a feel for what's there when you open Konqueror.

Enhancing Konqueror

Konqueror is an amazingly powerful tool, and some of its features may be lying dormant and unconfigured. When you ran kpersonalizer, you had the opportunity to select your favored level of eyecandy. Keeping in mind that more toys means more demands on your system, some features that are fun, but CPU-intensive may have been turned off if you selected anything other than "give me the works."

One of these features has to do with file tips. Try this. In an open Konqueror session, move your mouse over a file or directory and pause there. If you don't see a tool tip pop up describing the file type, its size, and other properties, you can turn that feature on now.

Click Settings on Konqueror's menu bar, and select Configure Konqueror. Konqueror's configuration dialog will appear (Figure 6-4).

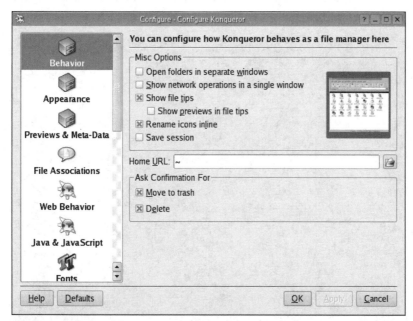

FIGURE 6-4   Configuring Konqueror's file tips.

To the left is a panel with the various setting groups that are available under Konqueror (File Associations, Fonts, and so on). For the time being, click on Behavior. There are two Behavior icons; the first is for the file system, and the second is for the web browser view. You want the first. Now, look to the right, under Misc Options. Check on the Show File Tips option, but leave the Show Previews in File Tips option off. Click Apply, then click OK to close the Settings dialog. You'll be using that file tips feature very shortly.

Quick Tip For a scaled-down version of tool tips, just look to the status bar at the bottom of your Konqueror window. As you move your mouse over files and directories, one-line information summaries on the files appear there.

In just a moment, I'm going to tell you all about selecting, copying, and moving files. Before moving on, however, I should tell you about another really cool Konqueror trick that makes this whole copying and moving process a whole lot easier. Click on Window in the menu bar, and select Split View Left/Right. Suddenly, Konqueror has two main windows instead of just one (Figure 6-5).

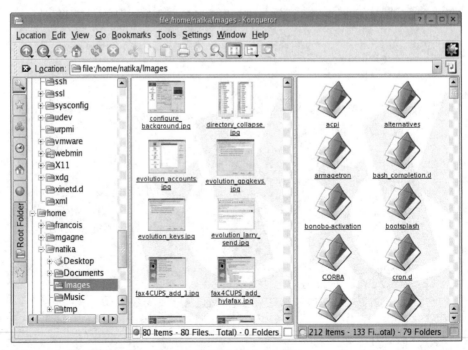

FIGURE 6-5   Konqueror with a two-panel split view.

The trick is in trying to remember which window you are working in at any given time. Look in the bottom-left corner of one of your split windows. Do you see that little *green light*? It indicates the *active* window, and its pathname will be in the location bar just under the menu bar. When you click on the other window, the green light jumps to that window. The location bar changes to that location also, which immediately makes you think, "Hey, I can just type in the pathname for the active window in the location bar, and my active window will take me there!" And you are right.

Uh, Roger, Copy That...

You can create, copy, move, rename, and delete files and directories by using Konqueror, but before you can do any of these things, you need to *select* a file or directory. Selecting files is something you will be doing a lot, so let's start with that. Place your mouse cursor just outside one of the icons of your choosing. Now drag the cursor across the icon and notice the dashed-line box appearing as you drag the pointer. You'll know a file is selected, because it becomes *highlighted*. Right-clicking also selects a file, but in a somewhat different way, bringing up a menu dialog that then asks you what you want to do with that file.

Don't forget your Arrow keys either. Moving left, right, up, or down highlights whatever file or directory you happen to be sitting on. You can then click on Edit in the menu bar (or press <Alt+E> to get to the Edit menu), and decide what it is you want to do with the file. I'll talk about those decisions in a moment.

Sometimes, one just isn't enough. You need to select *multiple files*. The easiest way is with the mouse. Left-click to the top and left of the icon you want to start with, then drag your cursor across a series of icons. Notice again the dotted-line box that surrounds the files and directories you select. Perhaps you just want a file here and a file there. How do you pick and choose multiple files? Simply hold down the <Ctrl> key and drag with the mouse. Say that you have selected a group of four files, and you want one further down in your directory. Let go of the mouse button but keep holding down the <Ctrl> key, position your mouse to the top and left of the next group of icons, and select away. As long as you continue to hold down the <Ctrl> key, you can pick up and select files here and there at will.

It is also possible to do all these things with the Arrow keys by simply moving your cursor over the file you want to start with, holding down the <Shift> key, and moving the cursor to the left (or whatever direction you like). As you do this, you'll notice file after file being selected. Try it for yourself. For nonsequential selection, use the <Ctrl> key as you did with the mouse. Select or deselect the files by pressing the <Spacebar>. When your cursor is sitting on the file you want, press the <Spacebar> to highlight the files.

Finally, and probably quite important for the future, you can also select by extension. Perhaps you want to select all the files with an .mp3 or .doc extension in your directory. Click Edit on the menu bar, then click Select. A small window pops up, asking you for an extension. If you want all the .mp3 files, you enter *.mp3. The .mp3 extension limits your selection to a certain type of file, and the asterisk requests everything that matches.

Creating New Directories

If you aren't already running Konqueror, start it up now and make sure you are in your personal home directory. In the main Konqueror window, right-click on any blank area and look at the menu that pops up. Move your mouse pointer over the top item (Create New), and you'll see a secondary menu appear. The first item is Folder, as in "create new folder." (Remember that the terms *folder* and *directory* are used interchangeably.) Click here, and the system prompts you for a directory name. This can be pretty much anything you like. If this directory will house your music files, perhaps its name should be Music.

Just remember that you can create directories inside directories, and you can start organizing things in a way that makes sense. For instance, you might want to create directories called Rock, Jazz, Hip Hop, and Classical in your Music directory.

"I've Changed My Mind," or Renaming Files

You created a folder called Classical, but you really meant Opera. You could delete the folder, or you could simply rename it. To rename a file or directory, select it and right-click to get the menu, then choose Rename. The name under the appropriate icon becomes highlighted; just type the new name, and press <Enter>. Alternatively, select it and choose Rename from the Edit menu in the menu bar. The easiest way of all is to press <F2> after you select the file or directory.

 Shell Out Open a Konsole and type ls to see your directories. Renaming a file or directory from the shell is easy. Type:

```
mv oldname newname
```

and press <Enter>. For instance, to change your Classical directory to Opera, you type:

```
mv Classical Opera
```

Copying Files and Directories (and Moving, Too!)

Ah! This is where you learn another great trick with Konqueror. An easy way to copy a file from one directory to another is to fire up two versions of Konqueror. In the first, you find the file or files you want to copy. In the second Konqueror window, you locate the directory to which you want those files copied. Simply drag the file from one window into the other. A little menu pops up, asking you whether you want to copy the file here or move it here (Figure 6-6).

FIGURE 6-6   Confirmation when moving or copying files.

An interesting question, isn't it? That's because copying and moving files is done in pretty much the same way. Both involve a copy. The difference is in what happens *after* the copy is done. In one case, you copy the file over and keep the original, thus giving you two copies of the same file, but in different places. A *move*, on the other hand, copies the file and deletes the original from where it was.

One easy trick is to select the file you want, right-click to get the menu, then click on Copy. Now go into the directory where you would like this file to appear, right-click somewhere on a blank space of Konqueror's main window, and click Paste from the pop-up menu. You can also specify the Copy and Paste options from the menu bar under Edit.

Shell Out The Linux command to copy is cp. If you want to copy a file called big_report to notsobig_report, you type:

```
cp big_report notsobig_report
```

Wait! What about Links?

If you're following along, you probably noticed that the pop-up menu for dragging and dropping a file offered a third option, Link Here. A Link is a kind of copy that doesn't take up much space. In the world of that other OS, you probably thought of them as *shortcuts*. Links let you create a pseudo-copy of a file or directory that doesn't take up the space of the original file. If you wanted a copy of a particularly large file to exist in several places on the disk, it makes more sense to point to the original and let the system deal with the link as though it *were* the original. It's important to remember that deleting a link doesn't remove the original file, just the link.

Speaking of links, if you know the pathname to something, you can create a link in any directory at any time. You might remember that I said your desktop itself was a directory; in fact, you saw it in Konqueror when I had you navigating your personal home directory. Anyhow, by right-clicking in Konqueror's active window, you can choose Create New (like you did to create a directory) and select Link to Location (URL) from the menu.

A pop-up window appears with the words "Enter Link to Location (URL)" and a blank box for you to enter a location. In this case, you have to know the name of the location that you are linking. For instance, your system comes with a number of sample wallpapers, which I will talk about in the next chapter. If for some reason I wanted to have a copy of one of these wallpapers in my home directory, I might link to it as Figure 6-7 shows. Enter the full pathname and press <Enter>. That's it.

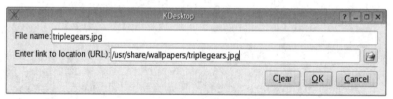

FIGURE 6-7   *Creating an icon link to a URL.*

When the icon shows up on your desktop, the full path to the file will be the name. If you would like to see something different, right-click on the link you just created and select Properties. A dialog box appears with three tabs: General, which is the link name; Permissions, which represents security-related information; and URL, the path to the file itself (Figure 6-8). Once it is created, you probably shouldn't need to change the URL.

On the General tab, you should see an icon next to the name of the file you are linking to. You can change that icon by clicking on it and selecting a new one from the list that pops up (you'll find hundreds). Furthermore, you can change the name of the link you just created to something that makes more sense to you. When you first open the Properties dialog, the filename is already highlighted. Just type the new name and press <Enter>.

The middle tab, Permissions, lets you change who gets access to a file or directory and what kind of access they get.

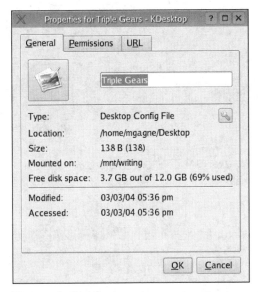

FIGURE 6-8   Desktop icon properties.

Which Brings Us to Permissions

This is your first look at Linux security, this time at the file or directory level. Under that Properties tab is a list of access permissions (Figure 6-9).

This is how you would go about changing permissions. There is, however, another way to identify file permissions that doesn't involve opening up a Properties dialog for every file. Remember those file tips I had you configure for Konqueror? Well, you are going to use those now.

Move your mouse pointer so that it hovers over any file. A file tip dialog pops up (Figure 6-10), telling you the type of file, the size, the last modification date, and the permissions.

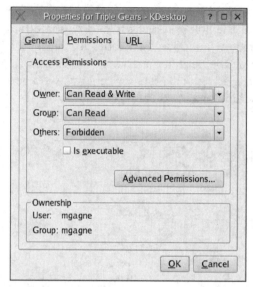

FIGURE 6-9   File permissions in the Properties dialog.

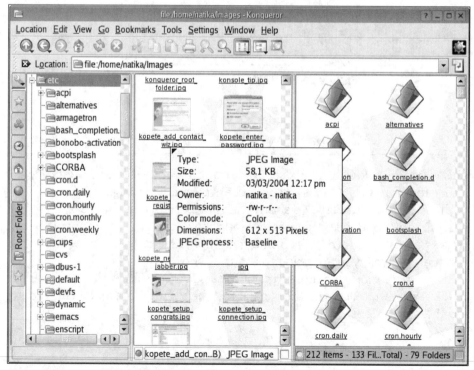

FIGURE 6-10   File tips displaying permissions in Konqueror.

There are actually ten columns describing permissions for a file. For the most part, you'll see either a hyphen or a d in the first column, which represents a directory. The next nine columns are actually three sets of three columns. Those other nine characters (characters two through ten) indicate permissions for the user or owner of the file (first group of three), the group (second three), and others or everyone else (last three). When you look at an image and see -rw-rw-r--, this means that the user and group have read and write permissions (an x indicates that the file has execute permission). All others have *read-only* permission, the same permission everyone else has.

Shell Out Want to see the permissions at the shell prompt? Simply add -l to the ls command, like this:

ls -l

From time to time during your Linux experience, you will have to change permissions, sometimes to give someone else access to your directories or files or to make a script or program executable. By using the Permissions tab, you can select read, write, or execute permissions for the owner (yourself), the group you belong to, and everyone else by checking off the permissions in the appropriate check boxes. I'll be covering permissions, as well as file ownership, in much more detail in Chapter 10, "Becoming One with the Shell."

Deleting Files and Directories

Every once in a while, some file or directory outlives its usefulness. It is time to be ruthless and do a little cleaning up on the old file system.

As you've no doubt come to expect, there are several ways to get rid of an offending file or directory. The friendliest and safest method is to drag the file from Konqueror to the Trashcan icon on your desktop. For the novice, this is a safer method, because items sent to the trash can be recovered—until you take out the trash, that is. Until that time, you can click on the Trashcan icon, and (you guessed it) a Konqueror window appears, showing you the items you have sent to the trash. These items can then be moved or copied back to wherever you need them. To remove files from the trash permanently, right-click on the Trashcan icon and click on Empty Trash Bin.

Note Once you empty the trash bin, the files it contained are gone forever.

I did say that there were other ways of deleting a file. From Konqueror, you can select a file or directory, right-click, and select Move to Trash. Notice that there is another option on the menu labeled simply Delete. If you are absolutely sure that you don't want a file hanging around even in the trash bin, select Delete from the menu or press <Shift+Delete>. The file will be gone for good.

Quick Tip To really and truly delete something, *shred* it. You do this by selecting a file and pressing <Ctrl+Shift+Delete>. This writes random bits of garbage over the file before deleting it.

My World, My Way

I'm hoping that you are walking away from this chapter impressed with some appreciation for the power and flexibility of the tools you have at your disposal. Konqueror may well become your most important application by the time you are finished reading this book. I've barely touched on the some of its capabilities. Never fear, you'll see more of Konqueror when you get to Chapter 26, "Surfing the Net."

Before we move on to the next chapter, I have a special treat for the power users among you. You know who you are, because you were getting excited every time I had you shell out. Click Window in Konqueror's menu bar, and select Show Terminal Emulator. Just like that, a shell prompt opens up at the bottom of your Konqueror window (Figure 6-11).

From there, you can type all your Linux commands. When you are done, simply type exit, and the window will close.

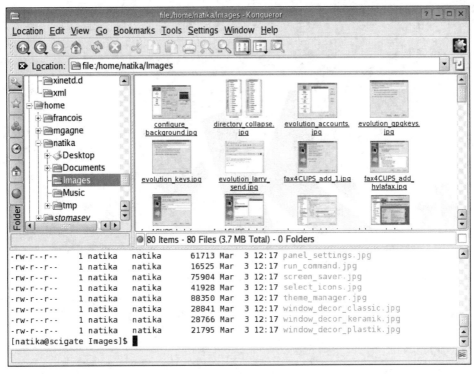

FIGURE 6-11   A command shell running inside Konqueror.

2

Administration and Deployment

chapter
7

Installing New Applications

The average Linux distribution CD comes with several gigabytes of software. SUSE, for one, delivers several CDs in a boxed set with enough software to keep you busy for weeks, maybe months. I'll tell you how to install that software easily and without fuss. Despite all that your distribution has to offer, sooner or later you will find yourself visiting various Internet sites, looking for new and updated software. Where will you find this stuff, and will installing it be the same as getting it from your CDs?

Before I get into finding, building, and installing software, I'd like to address a little myth. You have no doubt heard that installing software on Linux is difficult and that it is inferior to what you are used to in the Windows world. Nothing could be further from the truth. In fact, software installation under Linux is actually superior to what you are leaving behind in your old OS.

Note When you install software and software packages, you must often do so as the root, or administrative user. As root, you are all-powerful. Linux tends to be more secure and much safer than your old OS, but that doesn't mean disasters can't strike. Know where your software comes from and take the time to understand what it does. When you compile software, which I will cover later in this chapter, get into the habit of building as a nonroot user, then switching to root for the installation portion. Don't worry; I'll explain.

Linux and Security

When it comes to installing software, security is something I should talk about. I've already said that you should know where your software is coming from, but that is only part of the consideration. That's why I'm going to clear up some bad press Linux gets when it comes to installing software.

In the Windows world, it is frighteningly easy to infect your PC with a virus or a worm. All you have to do is click on an email attachment, and you could be in trouble. Some email packages under Windows do the clicking for you, and by their being so helpful, once again, you could be in trouble. You won't find many Linux packages provided as simple executables (.exe files and so on). *Security is the reason*. To install most packages, you also need root privileges, again, for security reasons. Linux demands that you be conscious of the fact that you might be doing something that could hurt your system. If an email attachment wants to install itself into the system, it will have to consult the root user first.

Package managers, such as rpm (the RPM Package Manager) or Debian's dselect and apt-get, perform checks to make sure that certain dependencies are met or that software doesn't accidentally overwrite other software. Those dependency checks take many things into consideration, such as what software already exists and how the new package will coexist. Many of you are probably familiar with what has been called *DLL hell*, where one piece of software just goes ahead and overwrites some other piece of code. It may even have happened to you. Blindly installing without these checks can be disastrous. At best, the result can be an unstable machine—at worst, it can be unusable.

Installing software under Linux may take a step or two, but it is for your own good.

Identifying Software Packages

What most major Linux distributions have in common is the concept of a *package*: a pre-built bundle of software ready to be installed on your system. Despite the numerous distributions out there, most use the same package management systems. They often have different ways of dealing with them, but the packaging system remains pretty consistent. With the exception of Slackware, pretty much all distributions use either the RPM format of packages or Debian. Before getting into installing packages, I'm going to show you how you can identify one type of package from another.

Assume that I am talking about a hypothetical package called ftl_transport. If I were looking for this package to run my Debian or Debian-like system (such as Xandros or Libranet), I would find it in this type of format:

```
ftl-transport_2.1-1_i386.deb
```

The first part is the package name itself. The numbers between the underscore and hyphen indicate the software version number. The number following the hyphen is the package release number. Following that is the architecture for which the package was compiled; in this case, i386. The final suffix, .deb, is a dead giveaway that this is a Debian package, sometimes referred to as a *deb*.

Those of you running Fedora, Mandrake, SUSE, or one of the other RPM-based distributions will find a similar format:

```
ftl_transport-2.1-1.i386.rpm
```

As you can see, the format is similar to that of the deb package, but with a couple of fairly important differences. For instance, hyphens denote both versions and release numbers. As you might have guessed, .rpm denotes an RPM package, and although that is an important distinction, the following is somewhat more interesting. The i386 portion of the package name tells you that it was compiled for a generic x86 processor family. You might also see i586 or i686 in here to denote that the package requires a Pentium class processor or better in order to run. Here are some other things you might see:

- For a DEC alpha-type processor: ftl_transport-2.1-1.ialpha.rpm
- For a Sun SPARC processor: ftl_transport-2.1-1.sparc.rpm
- For a Power PC chip: ftl_transport-2.1-1.ippc.rpm

You may also find packages listed as noarch. Using the example above, the name would be:

```
ftl_transport-2.1-1.noarch.rpm
```

These packages can safely be installed on any system and any processor type.

The Many Faces of Software Installation

Because most packages are either RPMs or debs, knowing how to install them primarily involves knowing how to deal with that particular type of package. In truth, it isn't that complicated, but there can be stumbles along the way, particularly when it comes to dependencies. Sometimes a package requires the presence of another package before it can be installed. Sometimes, it may require several packages. Going through a process of trial and error to get all your dependencies resolved can create quite the headache.

Every major Linux vendor wants to make the Linux experience as wonderful as possible, particularly when it comes to installing software packages. Consequently, almost all have software installation tools that they have tweaked to make the user experience as simple as possible, tools that deal with package dependencies easily. For instance, SUSE provides YaST2. Mandrake has RpmDrake (or the command-line urpmi). Linspire has its Click-N-Run service. The new Red Hat/Fedora distribution uses Yum. Slackware uses installpkg. Using the software installation tools provided by your vendor is almost always the easiest approach.

When you just can't get what you want through the vendor's packages, or if you can't find the appropriate package, sometimes going back to the source is your best approach. Yes, I'm talking about source code. Compiling from scratch really isn't all that difficult either, and I'll show you how at the end of this chapter.

First, let's start by looking at a couple of vendor-specific software installation tools starting with SUSE's YaST2 installer.

SUSE Software Package Installs

A SUSE boxed set comes with thousands of applications, so much so that you may not have to look anywhere else for some time. SUSE software installations, as well as software updates, are handled through the YaST interface (command name yast2). When the YaST control center comes up, select Install and Remove Software. A second window opens from which you can search for a particular package. Say you wanted to install a video conferencing application, but you didn't know what the application was called. Enter the word "video" in the search field, and all of the packages that have video in either their package name or description will appear in the window to the right. You can specify other search criteria on the page, too.

Click on a package name for a description of the software in the tabbed Description window in the lower-right of the screen (Figure 7-1). If this is the package you want, click on the check box next to the package name, then click the Accept button in the bottom-right corner. Should there be dependencies associated with the package you chose to install, a pop-up window appears informing you of this fact. Click Continue, and the installation proceeds. That's all there is to it.

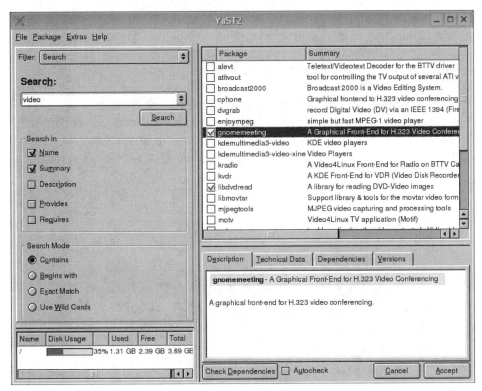

FIGURE 7-1   Installing a package from SUSE's YaST tool.

For those times when you know the package name, you can call the YaST installation module directly. For example, you want to install Kover, a package that makes creating CD jewel case covers easy. In a Konsole command shell, type:

```
/sbin/yast2 -i kover
```

Mandrake's urpmi

Installing software with Mandrake is done with the `urpmi` command. Like Debian's apt-get, which I will discuss shortly, `urpmi` takes care of all that nasty checking for prerequisite software. When installing an RPM package using `urpmi`, you will sometimes be told that other packages are needed and asked whether you want `urpmi` to automatically install them. The right answer is almost always yes. But I'm getting ahead of myself.

Most people running directly from the desktop will see `urpmi` through the Mandrake Control Center (command name `drakconf`). When the control center starts up, click on Software Management in the left sidebar. This gives you four choices: install software packages; remove packages; search for and install updates, which is very important for security and bug fixes; or add new software installation sources. When you choose to install or remove software, you are actually running another program called rpmdrake (command name `rpmdrake`).

When the rpmdrake window comes up (Figure 7-2) you'll be able to search for packages. At the top of the rpmdrake window, there's a small search field with the default search criteria set to In Names. The example in Figure 7-2 shows a search for word, which found, among other things, the Abiword package. You can also search more broadly by selecting In Descriptions. That may actually take a little longer, but it gives you a more flexible search, particularly if you don't know the package name.

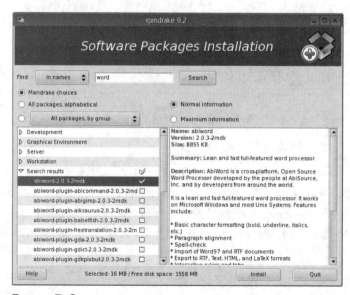

FIGURE 7-2   Searching for and installing packages from the Mandrake Control Center.

When you have found a piece of software that you are looking for, click the check box next to the name. If additional packages are required, rpmdrake informs you. When you have everything picked out that you want, click Install.

If you know which package you want to install, you can easily do it from the command line as root. To install Abiword, for example, you type:

```
urpmi abiword
```

Mandrake's urpmi Made Even Easier

Those of you running Mandrake know that adding a package is as easy as typing urpmi package_name and letting the program do the rest. The urpmi program (or rpmdrake if you go graphical) even goes out to the right place (an update site, for example) and downloads what you need. In doing so, it alerts you to any dependencies that need addressing. You may also even know that other sites offer Mandrake RPM repositories. So where are these sites, and how do you add urpmi repositories to your system?

Start by visiting the Easy URPMI site (http://plf.zarb.org/~nanardon) at the Penguin Liberation Front (more on them shortly). Once there, just fill in the form, identifying your Mandrake release level (10.0, 9.2, and so on), whether you are interested in regular distrib packages, updates, contribs, and the like. Upon processing, the form tells you what to type at the root prompt to get these sources added to your system. It's easy, and you'll be extending the number of available packages you can easily install on your system.

Ah yes, the PLF. Some packages may not be legal in your part of the world, most notably DVD decryption libraries in the United States. If you are in the U.S., you should not add the link to the PLF repository while on the page. If you do, you will be able to install packages that may not be legal in your jurisdiction, such as the aforementioned DVD decryption libraries.

Searching for Common Ground

As you can see from the examples of installing software under Mandrake, SUSE, Debian, and Fedora, there are many alternatives. I'd like to follow this up by trying to be as release-*agnostic* as possible and show you a tool that should be in almost any distribution running KDE. That tool is KDE's own package manager, *KPackage*. Depending on the distribution, you may have to install KPackage from your distribution CDs. (Remember what I said about a particular distribution preferring that you do it their way.) It is usually called kdeadmin-kpackage.

KPackage

KDE's package tool, KPackage, uses a graphical interface to allow for easy installation or removal of packages. You can quickly call KPackage by pressing <Alt+F2> and typing kpackage. When it first starts, you'll get a two-panel display with the installed packages on the left and an information window on the right. Click on an installed package (such as *tar* in Figure 7-3), and you'll get to know all about that package in the right window's Properties tab.

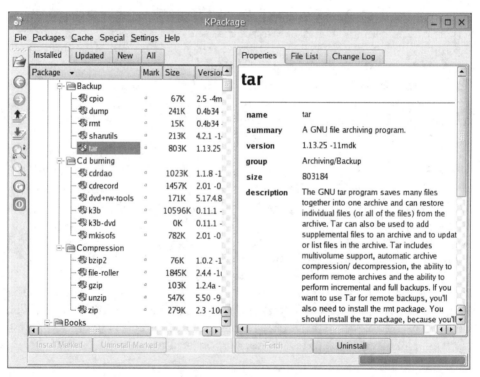

FIGURE 7-3   KPackage, the KDE package manager.

Click on the File List tab, and you'll get a listing of every file that makes up this package and where these files live on your system. This is actually a great way to get to know the packages installed on your system, and I would highly recommend walking through the list and getting a feel for what comprises your Linux system.

Notice as well that all of the packages in that tree view to the left are in a category hierarchy, based on what kind of package they are.

To remove, or uninstall, a package, just click on the Uninstall button at the bottom of the screen (Figure 7-4). A warning screen appears, listing the package you are looking to uninstall. If this is really what you want to do, click Uninstall. The right side information window provides a report of the uninstall process. (Speaking of warnings, I *do not* recommend that you uninstall tar. This is just an example of the process.)

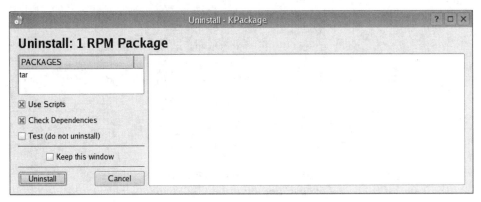

FIGURE 7-4   Using KPackage to uninstall software.

Installing Packages

To install a package, you first need to identify one, and there are many ways of doing this. Using Konqueror, you can surf over to your favorite software repository, such as RpmFind at `www.rpmfind.net`, and search for a package. When you find something compiled for your particular Linux distribution, click on the package file. Konqueror recognizes this as an RPM package and offers to bring up KPackage, the installation tool. You can also right-click on the package, click Open with from the menu, and select or type `kpackage`.

Another way to do this is to define package sources. These sources could be on a CD-ROM, on your hard drive, or a location somewhere on the Internet. To add a package source, click Settings on the menu bar and select Configure KPackage. From the resulting dialog, you can check off which package source you want to add (Figure 7-5)—Debian APT, RPM, Slackware, and others. For this example, I clicked the Location of Packages button for RPM.

FIGURE 7-5 Selecting sources for package installation.

In the case of each of these possible package types, you have a lot of room for entering data sources. Each of the seven tabs is an opportunity for entering six different package locations. Enter the path to the directory containing the RPM packages you wish to install from, then click the Use check box to the left of the path. If this is a network location, make sure you enter the path to the directory in proper URL format, such as `ftp://ftp.server.dom/path/to/packages`.

Quick Tip You'll see many different types of packages in these listings. Pay particular attention to the last two suffixes in the package name. For example, `.i386.rpm` implies a package built for the Intel x86 architecture. The suffixes `.i586.rpm` indicate a package that will not work on anything less than a Pentium architecture; no 486 for you. Another you may see is `.alpha.rpm`, which represents the Power PC architecture. If you see `.src.rpm`, expect a nonbinary source package that would have to be built on your system before you could use it (more on this a little further on).

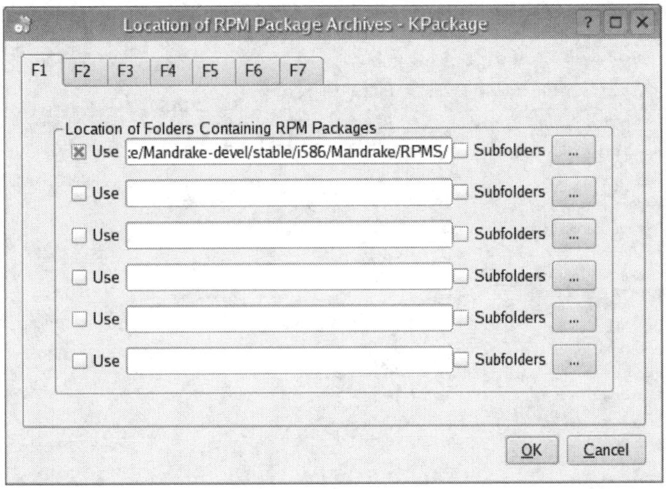

FIGURE 7-6   Selecting the path to a software installation source.

Dealing with Dependencies

Installing a single package without dependencies is easy. Select the package, then click Install Marked. If the package has dependencies, it requires additional steps. Say you want to install Gnumeric, a spreadsheet package that makes an excellent replacement for Excel. The first step is to find the package in the list from your new package archive. You can either scroll down the list until you find the package, or you can take a shortcut and search for it.

To search for a package, either click the Find Package icon on the left button bar or press <Ctrl+F> to bring up the Search dialog. With Gnumeric located, you can download the package by clicking the Fetch button on the bottom-right side (Figure 7-7).

After fetching the Gnumeric package, you are suddenly presented with quite a bit more information, including a list of unsatisfied dependencies. In this Gnumeric example, there are two packages missing: libgda2 and libgnome-db2. Over on the left side, you still have a listing of all the packages from your software repository.

One by one, fetch the remaining packages. By the way, it isn't necessary to wait until one package is downloaded before fetching the other. After you click Install Marked, the installation dialog appears (Figure 7-8) with a few last-minute options: Upgrade, Replace Files, Replace Packages, Check Dependencies, and Test (which doesn't actually do an installation).

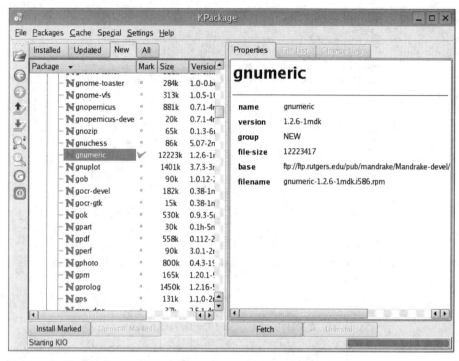

FIGURE 7-7   Searching for and fetching a package with KPackage.

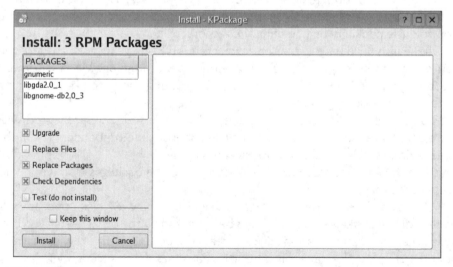

FIGURE 7-8   All set to launch the installation of multiple packages.

You can safely accept the default options, which are to upgrade, replacing old packages as well as checking dependencies. When you are ready to do the install, select your package, which is listed to the left, and click Install. When asked for the root password, enter it and press <Enter>.

After a few seconds, the package installation completes, and KPackage displays the status of the new package, along with its description.

Quick Tip There's another way to install using KPackage, and this is particularly good if you are installing more than one piece of software or if you are a big fan of drag-and-drop computing. After finding a package with Konqueror, simply drag the RPM package onto a running KPackage and follow the steps.

RPMs, the Shell Way

Would you like a very fast and easy way to install RPM packages? You may find this hard to believe, but at times, opening up a shell and typing commands can be much faster than going through all those graphical steps. I'll show you how it is done in this extended Shell Out session. Pretend that you have just downloaded some great package, and now the RPM file for it is sitting in one of your directories. Using a hypothetical package of my invention, I'll show you how to install that package with command-line rpm.

```
cd /directory_where/package_lives
rpm -ivh ftl-transport-2.1-1.i386.rpm
```

The only thing you need to be aware of here is that package installation needs to be done as the root user. The command that does all the work is called rpm. The flags that I am passing to it tell rpm to install the package (the -i flag), to be verbose (the -v flag), and to print out little hash marks while it does its work (the -h flag). Note that you do not have to have a dash before each letter option (-i -v -h); you can combine them instead (-ivh).

```
# rpm -ivh ftl-travel-2.1-1.i386.rpm
ftl-travel        ###############################################
```

If you want to know everything that is happening, drop the -h flag and add two more -v flags. The results are pretty wordy, but you do get to see what is happening during the various stages of the installation, as well as which files are being installed and where.

 Note Commands in the Linux world are case-sensitive. The hypothetical command makecoffee would be different than MakeCoffee. The same is true for command-line parameters such as in the RPM example above; options and flags such as -U mean different things than -u.

Upgrading an existing package is just as easy. As part of the process, older versions of files are replaced, and the package's default configuration files may be moved or renamed to preserve the originals. You will usually see appropriate messages if this occurs. Upgrading is more or less the same as installing, except that you use the -U flag on the command line instead of the -i flag. For example:

```
rpm -Uvh matter_transporter-1.2-1.i386.rpm
```

To erase a package, use the -e flag instead.

```
rpm -e matter_transporter
```

Notice that when I delete the package, I don't add the release number extensions (the -2.1-1.i386.rpm type of suffix).

A full-blown Linux installation will have a lot of packages installed. If you are curious, you can list every single package by typing:

```
rpm -qa | sort | more
```

This shell command is actually three in one. The rpm -qa portion tells rpm to *query* the RPM database and list *all* the packages. The bar that you see is called the *pipe* symbol. It literally means to pipe the output of the first command into the second command. In this case, the second command is sort. After the packages have been listed and sorted, you pipe that output one more time into the more command. In other words, you're saying, "Show me a screen full of information, then pause before showing me more." To see the next page, press the <Spacebar>. To quit the listing, type q by itself.

RPM can tell you a lot about the packages you have installed. To find out which version of the fileutils package you have on the system and what it is, use the -q flag along with the -i flag.

```
$ rpm -qi fileutils
Name        : fileutils     Relocations: (not relocateable)
Version     : 4.1.11        Vendor: MandrakeSoft
Release     : 5mdk          Build Date: Wed 28 Aug 2002 08:39:42 AM EDT
Install date: Sun 20 Oct 2002 10:00:04 AM EDT
Build Host  : ke.mandrakesoft.com
Group       : File tools    Source RPM: fileutils-4.1.11-5mdk.src.rpm
Size        : 2344533       License: GPL
Packager    : Thierry Vignaud <tvignaud@mandrakesoft.com>
URL         : ftp://alpha.gnu.org/gnu/fetish/
Summary     : The GNU versions of common file management utilities
Description :
The fileutils package includes a number of GNU versions of common and
popular file management utilities.  Fileutils includes the following
tools: chgrp (changes a file's group ownership), chown (changes a
file's ownership), chmod (changes a file's permissions), cp (copies
files), dd (copies and converts files), df (shows a filesystem's disk
usage), dir (gives a brief directory listing), dircolors (the setup
program for the color version of the ls command), du (shows disk
usage), install (copies files and sets permissions), ln (creates file
links), ls (lists directory contents), mkdir (creates directories),
mkfifo (creates FIFOs or named pipes), mknod (creates special files),
mv (renames files), rm (removes/deletes files), rmdir (removes empty
directories), sync (synchronizes memory and disk), touch (changes file
timestamps), and vdir (provides long directory listings).
```

Using -l instead of -i lists all of the files in the package. You can even do a sort of reverse file listing by asking rpm to look in its database to identify which package a particular file belongs to. To find out which package a file belongs to, use the -f flag. For example, in my /sbin directory, there is a file called sysctl. If I want to know where this file came from and what package it belonged to, I use this command:

```
# rpm -qf /sbin/sysctl
procps-2.0.7-14mdk
```

To discover all the things the rpm command can do for you, type man rpm, and you will be able to read the manual page related to that command. As you can see, it really isn't all that complicated to work from the command line.

If you prefer the graphical tools, then by all means use them. But don't be afraid of using the shell when you have the opportunity.

Rebuilding RPMs from Source

Sometimes you'll discover that there are updated packages for a particular piece of software. For instance, as I write this, I still have a server running Red Hat 7.2. Well, it's kind of hard to say that it's a Red Hat 7.2 system, because it has a custom web server, custom kernel, custom many things, and is continually updated. The point is that I never ran an update installation on the machine to make it officially something newer. When running custom applications, particularly on servers, it isn't always practical to upgrade at every new release.

Nevertheless, Red Hat no longer releases updated packages for a Red Hat 7.2 system. So, what can you do if your system is no longer supported but you need updated packages? One way is to build from source bundles, something I will cover shortly. The second is to pick up source RPMs and rebuild.

Here's an example. On my old quasi-Red Hat 7.2 system, I needed an updated MySQL package. No recent RPMs (binary or source) had been released and none would ever be. There were, however, source RPM packages available for Fedora Core 1, the new Red Hat-supported community Linux distribution. I downloaded the package and rebuilt it as follows:

```
rpm --rebuild mysql-3.23.58-4.src.rpm
```

This process took some time as the source was extracted and the code compiled. Once the build process completed, I was left with new, up-to-date RPMs of this particular package, built specifically for a Red Hat 7.2 architecture.

The beauty here is that you can also share those packages with other systems at that release. Furthermore, you can do a classic RPM upgrade using the new packages and a command in the form:

```
rpm -Uvh package_name.i386.rpm
```

Quick Tip It is still possible to get updated packages for old Red Hat releases by subscribing to an inexpensive service from Progeny (www.progeny.com). It provides constant updates and patches for Red Hat systems going back to release 7.2. This is a great option for admins who are running older Red Hat releases and who don't want, or find it inconvenient, to upgrade or switch.

Debs, The Shell Way

This doesn't have to be Debian specifically. Other Debian-based distributions, such as Lycoris, Xandros, or Linspire, work the same way. Keep in mind, of course, that their own package management systems may be the approach you choose to follow. The most basic method of installing a package, either off your distribution CD or downloaded, is with this format of the dpkg command:

```
dpkg --install ftl-transport_2.1-1.deb
```

The basic package installation tool for Debian systems is dpkg. To remove a package, use the format:

```
dpkg --remove ftl-transport
```

Note If it looks like I am saving keystrokes here, there is a reason. You need to indicate the package release number and subsequent extensions at installation time only. To remove a package, you need just the package name itself.

Be aware that there is another step to consider when removing a package. Although the program is now gone from your system, its configuration files remain, which can be a good idea. To get rid of those as well, you need to purge the package with this command:

```
dpkg --purge ftl-transport
```

That's the long way. If you are *sure* you are done with the package, you could start with a purge to both *remove* the package and *purge* the configuration files in one step.

Great, But Can You Tell Me What Is Already There?

Sure thing. If you want to get a list of every package on your system, use the —list option to dpkg. You might want to pipe that output to the more command as well, as in:

```
dpkg --list | more
```

If something in that list should prove interesting and you would like to know more about the package, try the `--print-avail` flag. In the following example, I try to discover something about the mysterious `mtools` package.

```
speedy:~# dpkg --print-avail mtools
Package: mtools
Priority: standard
Section: otherosfs
Installed-Size: 311
Maintainer: Mark W. Eichin <eichin@thok.org>
Architecture: i386
Version: 3.9.6-3.1
Depends: libc6 (>= 2.1.2), xlib6g (>= 3.3.5)
Size: 183456
Description: Tools for manipulating MSDOS files
  Mtools is a public domain collection of programs to allow
Unix systems to read, write, and manipulate files on an MSDOS
filesystem (typically a diskette).  Each program attempts to
emulate the MSDOS equivalent command as closely as practical.
```

Finding Out a Package's Current Release Level

To find out what version of a package is already installed on your system, use the `-1` flag. In the following example, I query the system to find out which version of bash (the Bourne Again Shell) I am working with.

```
# dpkg -l bash
Desired=Unknown/Install/Remove/Purge/Hold
| Status=Not/Installed/Config-files/Unpacked/Failed-config/
| Half-installed
|/ Err?=(none)/Hold/Reinst-required/X=both-problems
(Status,Err: uppercase=bad)
||/ Name           Version        Description
+++-=============-===============================================
ii  bash           2.03-6         The GNU Bourne Again Shell
```

What Is That Strange File?

Say that you are wondering what some file is doing on your system. For instance, there is something called hinotes in my /usr/bin directory, and I don't remember installing it. Furthermore, if I try to look it up in the man pages, I am told that there is no information on this file. Using the -S flag, I can have dpkg identify what package this file was a part of.

```
# dpkg -S /usr/bin/hinotes
pilot-link: /usr/bin/hinotes
```

Because I remember installing the pilot-link software to help me synchro-nize my Palm Pilot with my Linux system, I can rest a bit easier.

Using apt-get to Install or Update Software

People who use Debian distributions on a regular basis sometimes point to this wonderful little program as the reason why Debian is so great. Well, I certainly won't be the one to deny that apt-get is wonderful.

Note Both RPM and Deb are great package management systems, although you sometimes see *heated* arguments espousing the virtues of one over the other. The biggest of these arguments have to do with dependency problems. Some say that debs are better than RPMs, because they take care of dependencies for you, installing whatever packages are necessary and saving you a lot of time.

The truth is that debs don't save you from dependency problems, but apt *does*. In the RPM world, Mandrake offers the same kind of functionality with urpmi. Although apt traces its origins to Debian, it is no longer unique to Debian, and apt is available for many RPM-based distributions. Check out apt4rpm at http://apt4rpm.sourceforge.net.

If you want to install a package called xpilot, for example, this is how to do it:

```
speedy:~# apt-get install xpilot
Reading Package Lists... Done
Building Dependency Tree... Done
The following extra packages will be installed:
  xpilot-server
The following NEW packages will be installed:
  xpilot xpilot-server
0 packages upgraded, 2 newly installed, 0 to remove and 2 not
upgraded.
Need to get 317kB of archives. After unpacking 1017kB will be used.
Do you want to continue? [Y/n]
```

The great thing here is that you did not have to go to a variety of sites to hunt down and identify appropriate software. You called `apt-get` with the install parameter, and off you went. Notice as well that `apt-get` automatically picks up dependencies for a given package and installs them when needed. If you want to update to the latest version of xpilot, substitute the `install` parameter with `update`.

I don't want to confuse things here, but speaking of updates, one of the most important things an administrator must do is keep packages up to date. You can install upgrades to installed packages with this version of the `apt-get` command:

```
apt-get upgrade
```

Educating apt-get

Perhaps the most famous example of Debian's prowess is symbolized by the following command:

```
apt-get dist-upgrade
```

For a command that will do a complete upgrade of your system to the latest release, this is deceptively simple. It's like magic, but it isn't entirely magic. After all, `apt-get` has to get that information somewhere, right?

That somewhere is the `/etc/apt/sources.list` file. Ah! A list of sources for software. This is a simple text file that you can modify with your favorite editor. Each line has the format:

```
deb url_path distribution components
```

The first parameter, `deb`, may also be `deb-src` for source distribution lists.

```
# Use for a local mirror - remove the ftp1 http lines for the bits
# your mirror contains.
# deb file:/your/mirror/here/debian stable main contrib non-free
```

The following is from a Debian system here at the office:

```
deb ftp://ftp.ca.debian.org/debian potato main contrib non-free
```

The above line identifies a Debian mirror accessible by FTP. In this case, the stable release is identified as `potato`. Generally, this is something like `stable`, `unstable`, or `frozen` but, as you can see, it is possible to identify the specific distribution. The final section is the components section. It will be identified as `main`, `contrib`, `non-free`, or `non-us`.

From time to time, you should update your local `sources` database with the latest available package information. Use the command:

```
apt-get update
```

If you are installing Debian files on a regular basis from a development site, such as the Wine site, you might want to update your local sources file. Edit the file `/etc/apt/sources.list`, and add the site information.

In the case of the Wine development site, I added the following lines:

```
deb http://gluck.debian.org/~andreas/debian wine main
deb-src http://gluck.debian.org/~andreas/debian wine main
```

Note Remember, Wine is a package that enables you to run Windows applications on Linux.

Look, Use the Source

Once you've downloaded that new software, you'll no doubt be anxious to take things out for a spin. The truth is that there is an *amazing* amount of software available for Linux. If trying out new things is exciting for you, I can pretty much guarantee that you won't get bored anytime soon.

Much of this software is available as source—not surprising, because the GPL license, under which much of the Linux software out there is distributed, requires that you distribute source along with the programs. There are also open source projects that have no relation to the GNU projects that employ the license as a means of copyright. Then there are other open source projects that use BSD-style licensing, artistic licensing, postcard licensing, and many others; all distribute their programs in source format.

At first glance, this may appear to be nothing but a *nuisance*, yet source makes software *portable*. The number of platforms on which a single package can be compiled tends to be much higher, because the applications can be built using your system at your operating system level with your libraries. It means that if you are running VendorX 8.1, you don't need to go looking for the VendorX 8.1 package.

Here's another reason. It takes developers time to provide packages compiled and ready to run on multiple platforms—time they may not have, particularly if they are doing development without pay. Consequently, developers sometimes have source code available that is much more recent than the precompiled packages they offer. Why? Because they haven't found the time to build the packages for all those platforms. Here's a plus side you may not have considered: If at some point you decide that you want to try your hand at programming, open source means that *you too* can get into the game.

Note As crazy as it may sound, building from source is not all that complicated, and many of the steps required are common across most source distributions. At first it may sound difficult, but no more so than any of the myriad things you've learned how to do with your computer over the years. I admit that compiling from source isn't as straightforward as downloading an RPM package and installing it, but it does open up *thousands* of possibilities.

Here's an added bonus: If you can build one software package, you can pretty much build them all.

The Extract and Build Five-Step

The vast majority of source packages can be built using what I call the *extract and build five-step*. I suppose that step one could also involve the downloading of the software, but I'll pretend you've already found and downloaded something, a hypothetical little package called ftl-travel, and you are now anxious to take it for a ride. I'll give you the five steps, then I will discuss them in more detail.

```
tar -xzvf ftl-travel-2.1.tar.gz
cd ftl-travel-2.1
./configure
make
su -c "make install"
```

Easy, isn't it? From here, you can just type ftl-travel and be on your way. Those are the basics of a source package installation, now let me give you some details.

Step 1: Unpacking the Archive

Most program sources are distributed as *tarballs*, meaning that they have been stored using the tar archiving command. In the name above, ftl-travel-2.1.tar.gz, the ftl-travel part is the name of the program itself. The 2.1 represents the version number of the package, and tar.gz tells you that this package is archived using the tar command and compressed using the gzip command.

You can, therefore, extract the archive with the command:

```
tar -xzvf ftl-travel-2.1.tar.gz
```

The x means extract. The z tells the tar command to use the gunzip command to extract. The v says that tar should show a list of the files it is extracting; in other words, it should be verbose. Finally, the f identifies the file itself, the one you just downloaded.

Sometimes the extension .tar.gz is shortened to .tgz. There are a few other extensions in use out there. For instance, the package may have a .tar.z extension instead, meaning that the file has been compressed using the compress command. To extract the source from this tarball, you first uncompress the file using the uncompress command. Then you continue with your tar extract:

```
uncompress ftl-travel-2.1.tar.z
tar -xvf ftp-travel-2.1.tar
```

To make life even easier, you could also just shorten the whole thing to:

```
tar -xZvf filename.tar.Z
```

Every once in a while, if the package is very large, the extension is .bz2, otherwise known as a *bzip2 archive*. To open this one, you perform essentially the same steps you did with compress. Use the command:

```
bunzip2 ftl-drive-1.01.tar.bz2
```

to uncompress the file, then extract using the standard tar command.

Steps 2 through 5: Building Your Programs

Once you have extracted the program source from the tar archive, change directory to the software's distribution directory. That's Step 2. Using the current ftl-travel example, type:

```
cd ftl-travel-2.1
```

From there, build and install your software, like this:

```
./configure
make
su -c "make install"
```

 Quick Tip Most programmers include a configure script, but if it is missing, make sure you read the README and INSTALL files provided in the installation directory.

The `./configure` step builds what is called a *Makefile*. The Makefile is used by the next command, `make`. In building the Makefile, the configure step collects information about your system and determines what needs to be compiled or recompiled in order to build your software. This brings you to the next step, which is to type `make`. You'll see a lot of information going by on your screen as programs are compiled and linked. Usually, after a successful compile, you follow the `make` command by typing:

```
su -c "make install"
```

This copies the software into the directories defined in the Makefile.

 Quick Tip I have you type `su -c "make install"` because the final step of an installation usually needs to be done by the root user. Because, for security reasons, you don't want to be running as root on a regular basis, the `su -c` step lets you quickly jump into root user mode for one command (where you will be prompted for the root password) and just as quickly jump back out.

A number of programmers also provide a `make uninstall` option, should you decide that you do not want to keep the program around.

> *Note* If you are an open source programmer or plan to be one and you want to make people happy, *always* provide an uninstall option.

README, Please!

If you are like me, you tend to want to just install and run that software, which is partly why I jumped ahead a bit and skipped a very important step. You generally do not have to do this, because 95% of installs are the same, but just before you go ahead with your final three steps, you should consider pausing in the source directory and typing `ls` to list the files in the directory. What you would see are numerous files, something like this:

```
CHANGES     README      Makefile      Makefile.in   configure
INSTALL     ftl-travel.h   ftl-travel.c   engine.c     config.h
```

The first thing you want to do is read any README and INSTALL files. The next step is almost always going to be the `./configure` step I mentioned as part of my extract and build the five-step, but there may be details you want to know about in those files. There may also be some prerequisites that you should know about or some personal options that you may want to set. It takes only a few minutes, and it may be extremely useful.

Getting Your Hands on Software

Way back when, at the beginning of this chapter, I mentioned that there was plenty of software available for your Linux system. Finding it isn't difficult, and there are many ways to start your search. One way is to join a Linux user group or chat with other Linux enthusiasts or users. That's a sure-fire way of getting your hands on the latest, greatest, and coolest software.

Another way is to visit some of the more popular Linux software repositories. These include search engines for both packaged software (RPMs) and source (tarred and gzipped files). My favorites in this arena are Rpmfind and TuxFinder. (I'll list all of these in the resources section.) Take a moment as well to visit the monster archive at `ibiblio.org`. For Debian packages, you can also take a look at `packages.debian.org`.

You might also want to look at the project and review sites. My favorites in this group are Freshmeat, Sourceforge, and Linux TUCOWS.

At this rate, you'll never run out of software to try out!

Resources

apt4rpm

> http://apt4rpm.sourceforge.net

Debian Package Search

> http://packages.debian.org

Freshmeat

> www.freshmeat.net

Ibiblio.org

> www.ibiblio.org

Progeny

> www.progeny.com

Rpmfind

> www.rpmfind.net

Pbone.Net

> http://rpm.pbone.net/

SourceForge

> www.sourceforge.net

TUCOWS Linux

> http://linux.tucows.com

TuxFinder

> www.tuxfinder.org

8

Devices and Services

Ah, hardware...I hate hardware!

Part of the personal computer experience seems destined to be an eternal battle in getting your current system to talk to the latest and greatest devices. There's always a new, hyper-fantastic, 3D video card; mind-blowing stereo sound system; or hair-trigger game controller out there. Then there are more mundane things, such as modems, scanners, and printers. Getting all of these devices to work with your system is something that has caused us all grief over time, regardless of what operating system we were running.

We are used to assuming that anything works with Windows, but even that isn't true. From time to time, even Windows users must visit hardware vendors' web sites to download a driver. I personally spent several hours looking for and downloading an accelerated video driver for my little niece's Windows computer so she could run a Barbie ice-skating program. (She's my niece; I couldn't really let her down.)

In this chapter, I'm going to give you the tools you need to deal with common issues, as well as some tips on avoiding problems in the first place. The other things I intend to cover are system services, runlevels, and daemons. Devices are resources that your system provides and that you, in turn, provide to your users. Sometimes access to these resources must be turned on or off as needed via system services. This is particularly true when dealing with such shared resources as printers, scanners, and even network services.

Yes, It Runs with Linux!

Device support under Linux is excellent. No, really. The sheer number of things that work out of the box without you having to search for and install drivers is impressive and, quite frankly, beats your old OS. That doesn't mean all is rosy, however. Let me be *brutally* honest here. Some devices have been written to work with Windows and only Windows—or so it seems. One of the great things about this open source world is that developers are constantly working to write drivers to enable you to run that faster-than-light communications card.

That said, if you haven't already bought that new gadget, there are a couple of things that you should do. For starters, if you are in the store looking at that new printer, pull the salesperson aside and *ask* whether it runs with Linux. If the person doesn't know, which is sometimes a problem but less so as time goes on, take a few minutes to check out the excellent Hardware HOWTO document. You can always find the latest version by surfing on over to the LDP's Linux Hardware Compatibility HOWTO page at www.tldp.org/HOWTO/Hardware-HOWTO/index.html.

If you don't find what you are looking for there, check out the hardware compatibility guide on your Linux vendor's site.

 Quick Tip Red Hat's hardware compatibility guide is worth the visit (http://hardware.redhat.com/hcl), regardless of what version of Linux you are running. Keep in mind, however, that things do change on web sites. If you don't find it there, just go to the main Red Hat site at www.redhat.com and look for *hardware*. Once there, use the Quick Search option for a fast keyword search.

Although Linux is Linux, different releases of different vendors' products may be at different levels of development. Consequently, at one time or another,

Red Hat may have slightly more extensive support for hardware than the others, and a month later SUSE may have the widest range of support.

As Linux gains in popularity, you'll find that hardware vendors are increasingly interested in tapping into this ever-growing market.

Plug and Play

For the most part, adding a device to a Linux system is simply a matter of plugging it in. If you don't want to configure it manually, a reboot will force hardware detection, and the system should recognize the device and configure it. USB devices tend to be even easier because of their hot-plug nature. In other words, you don't need to reboot the system to have a USB device recognized, and you can unplug it while the system is running.

Getting a device recognized is only part of it, though. Just because your system knows about the device doesn't necessarily mean that it is configured for your applications.

Going back to the driver issue, you may still have to install a driver, as you sometimes had to do in the Windows world. I wouldn't be fair to you if I simply ignored this little tidbit, so I won't.

Getting Familiar with Your Hardware

Meeting new people isn't always easy. Sociologists tell us that a complex interplay takes place whenever we meet someone new, much of it subconscious. Although it is possible to meet someone and instantly like him or her, it is more likely that you become comfortable enough to develop a friendship only after having been around a person for some time—in other words, after you've gotten to know a person better.

Now, what the heck does this have to do with hardware and your Linux system?

Well, it's like this: For most, the computers we use are black (or beige) boxes with a few things plugged into them and some magic happening inside that makes it possible to surf the Internet. Anything that falls outside the small subset of applications we use makes us uneasy. That's why the notion of trying something new may be intimidating. The best way to get over that is to become comfortable with what you have.

The KDE Info Center (Figure 8-1) is the perfect place to start for getting to know what makes up your system. You'll find it by clicking on the big K and looking for Info Center, or you can click on the Kicker panel. If you are having trouble locating it, remember that you can bring it up by pressing <Alt+F2> and typing in `kinfocenter`, its program name.

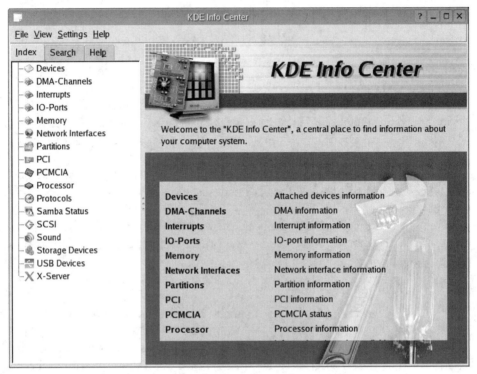

FIGURE 8-1　The KDE Info Center (`kinfocenter`).

As soon as the KDE Info Center loads up, it displays some capsule information about the various system features on which it can display information. The descriptions in the main window to the right correspond to the various categories in the bar on the left.

Would you like to know just how fast your processor really is? Click on Processor in the category list. You might be surprised. How about memory? Just click on Memory, and you'll know where every bit of RAM and swap is allocated. For a look at your X window configuration, click X-Server. There is a lot to it, isn't there? Take a few minutes to explore this hardware landscape. When you are ready to continue, I'll spend a little time on some specific areas, starting with PCI devices.

PCI Devices

Adding a PCI device definitely requires a reboot, because we are talking about internal devices. These are cards that fit in the slots inside your computer. When you reboot the machine, Linux should be able to scan for these cards and identify them without any problem. When you click on PCI in the Control Center Information category, you get a detailed list of every device known to the system (Figure 8-2).

Shell Out You can also run the command /sbin/lspci for a more succinct list.

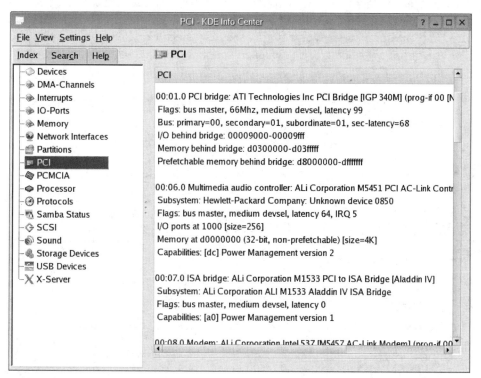

FIGURE 8-2 Using KDE Info Center to list PCI devices.

If the Linux kernel has the appropriate device drivers available as modules, the system automatically loads them, and nothing else needs to be done to make the device available. The reason that this information is useful has to do with those times when you do not have a driver handy or directly available. Being able to get the details on the troublesome device in this way is the first step toward getting it working.

A classic example of this is the *Winmodem*, so called because it was designed to work specifically with Windows. If you have one of these modems and it was not automatically configured by the system, never fear. I'll talk about Winmodems in more detail later in the chapter. For the moment, consider USB.

USB Devices

The whole idea behind USB (*Universal Serial Bus*) was eventually to replace all those different connectors on the back of a computer: serial ports, parallel ports, mouse connectors, and keyboard connectors. To get a list of USB devices, click on the USB Devices information category. All USB systems have at least one USB hub and whatever devices are attached. For example, Figure 8-3 shows a generic webcam and an Epson scanner connected to my system.

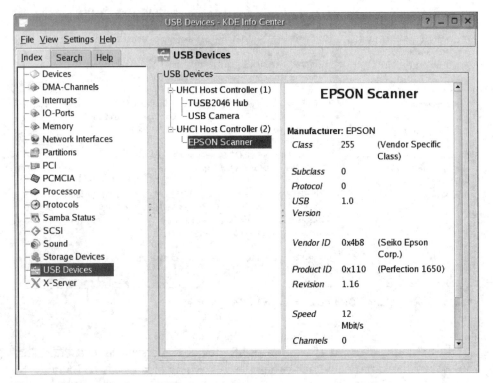

FIGURE 8-3   Info Center USB device list.

The sheer number of USB devices available is phenomenal, to say the least, and the list is growing. Many of these devices use a standard set of drivers, which means that a number of things can literally be plugged in and used. No need to mess with loading drivers, because it is all being done for you.

You noticed the word *many* in that last sentence, right? Keeping track of what works and what *doesn't* and providing access to drivers that aren't included in current distributions is the *raison d'être* of the Linux USB Device Overview web site (www.qbik.ch/usb/devices). If you find yourself looking at a new webcam and you aren't sure whether it is supported under Linux, look there first.

The site is organized into sections, depending on the device type: audio, video, mass storage, and so on. Each device is assigned a status identifying just how well a device is supported, from *works perfectly* to *works somewhat* to *don't bother*.

Note One of the most important classes of devices is printers. In fact, printers and printing take up an amazing amount of time and resources in this supposedly paperless society. For that reason, all of Chapter 14, "Printers and Printing," is dedicated to this particular class of device and how to get them working.

Modems versus Winmodems

As you recall, Winmodems, modems designed to work only with Windows, are one of the few minuses of running Linux. They are sometimes referred to as *software* or *controllerless* modems and tend to be less expensive than controller-based modems.

If you are running a Winmodem, all is not lost. The Linux community is nothing if not resourceful. Even when manufacturers are slow to notice Linux users, the same isn't true the other way around. As more and more people run Linux, this becomes less and less of a problem. In time, hardware manufacturers may be building for Linux first and Windows second. In the meantime, check out the Linmodems.Org web site at www.linmodems.org and you should be up and running shortly.

So just how do you transform a Winmodem into a Linmodem? Well, let me give you an example.

Among the more common Winmodems out there are those based on the Conexant chipset; these are starting to be very well supported. For the latest driver, just head on over to the Linuxant (no relation to Conexant) web site at www.linuxant.com. You will be able to find precompiled packages for a number of popular Linux distributions.

Identifying the Winmodem is your first step. You can use the KDE Control Center to get a listing of your PCI hardware, where you will get a lot of detail. You can also shell out and use the lspci command for a quick list of all the PCI devices found on your system. Here's what it looks like:

```
$ lspci
00:00.0 Host bridge: VIA Technologies, Inc. VT8367 [KT266]
00:01.0 PCI bridge: VIA Technologies, Inc. VT8367 [KT266 AGP]
00:06.0 Communication controller: Conexant HSF 56k
Data/Fax/Voice/Spkp    (w/Handset) Modem (WorldW SmartDAA) (rev 01)
00:08.0 Ethernet controller: Realtek Semiconductor Co., Ltd.
RTL-8139/8139C (rev 10)
00:11.0 ISA bridge: VIA Technologies, Inc. VT8233 PCI to ISA
Bridge
00:11.1 IDE interface: VIA Technologies, Inc. Bus Master IDE
(rev 06)
00:11.2 USB Controller: VIA Technologies, Inc. USB (rev 18)
00:11.5 Multimedia audio controller: VIA Technologies, Inc.
VT8233 AC97    Audio Controller (rev 10)
01:00.0 VGA compatible controller: nVidia Corporation NV11
[GeForce2 MX DDR] (rev b2)
```

In some cases, you will find precompiled driver packages. These are the RPMs, as discussed earlier. Some are specific to your release, and others will be generic. In the case of my Conexant-based Winmodem, I downloaded the RPM package and installed it.

As per the instructions that followed the RPM install, I typed the following command:

```
/usr/sbin/hsfconfig
```

A short dialog followed, asking me for the country (Canada, in my case), after which the program compiled and installed my driver for me. It even linked the newly created device, /dev/ttySHSF0, to /dev/modem. I was ready to use my modem without a care.

Shell Out From the shell prompt, I can verify the location of my modem with this command:

```
$ ls -l /dev/modem
```

The system then responds with this information, presented as one unbroken line:

```
lr-xr-xr-x   1   root    root   8 Sep  9   11:23
/dev/modem  -> /dev/ttySHSF0
```

The Winmodem/Linmodem Roundup

Clearly, none of this whole Winmodem problem applies if you are using an *external* modem or happen to be among the lucky ones using a cable modem connection or high-speed DSL access from your local phone company. For others out there, it can be a bit more complicated. Remember, however, that *many of these modems* can be made into useful and productive members of Linux society with a visit to the right web site. I've already given you the address of the Conexant web site; here's a few more that could help:

- Conexant modems (HCF and HSF): www.linuxant.com
- Smart Link modems: www.smlink.com/download/Linux
- Lucent modems: www.physcip.uni-stuttgart.de/heby/ltmodem
- PCTel modems: http://linmodems.technion.ac.il/pctel-linux/

Devices under the Skin

It is only natural to view devices as hardware. After all, the console is a large, glowing screen in front of you and your keyboard feels real enough. When you bought a new hard drive for your computer, it sure had some heft to it. Without sounding too metaphysical, devices, from the Linux kernel's perspective, are nothing but special files in the /dev directory. The way in which you define those files also defines how the system treats devices in the real, physical world.

Major Minor

The definitions for these devices are created with a command called mknod by passing a device type, a major number, and a minor number definition. For example, I can create a copy of my null device like this:

```
mknod /dev/null2 c 1 3
```

The second parameter is the device name. You should already be in the /dev directory, or you must specify the full path. This is followed by the device type, which in this case is c, for *character* device. Another option is to create a block or *buffered* device using the b option. Each of these options is followed by the major and minor numbers.

 Note There is one exception to the major/minor rule. You can also create a *named pipe*, also known as a *FIFO*, using the p option. This file type is used by applications for interprocess communication. Essentially what happens is that one process writes to the named pipe, and another reads from it. Think of it as a file that lives mostly in system memory rather than disk: one that is emptied as it is read.

The *major* number tells the system what kind of device you are talking about. The *minor* number identifies which device of that type you are talking about. For instance, you'll find that your IDE hard drives have a major number of 3, and your SCSI disks have a major number of 8. Meanwhile, all serial ports are 5 (including the console, by the way), parallel ports are 99, and SCSI tape drives are 9. If you are curious, do an ls -l on /dev:

```
ls -l /dev | more
```

On the minor side, you'll notice an interesting pattern as well. My first IDE disk drive is called /dev/hda. Its major number is 3, and its minor number is 0. The first partition on /dev/hda (hda1) is major 3 and minor 1. The second partition is major 3 and minor 2. Same story goes for my second IDE hard drive. Called /dev/hdb, its first partition, hdb1, is major 3 with minor 64. On the second partition, the minor number is incremented to 65 and then to 66 for the third partition.

```
brw-rw----   1 root     disk       3,    0 Jan 30   2003 /dev/hda
brw-rw----   1 root     disk       3,    1 Jan 30   2003 /dev/hda1
brw-rw----   1 root     disk       3,   64 Jan 30   2003 /dev/hdb
brw-rw----   1 root     disk       3,   65 Jan 30   2003 /dev/hdb1
```

Quick Tip Sometimes, the device entries are a symbolic link pointing to another device location (as is the case on a Mandrake system). Just follow those links, and you'll see that the definitions are the same. For instance, these two lines represent hda and hda1. Notice that the major and minor numbers are the same as above:

```
brw-------   1 root root 3, 0 Dec 31   1969
/dev/ide/host0/bus0/target0/lun0/disc

brw-------   1 root root 3, 1 Dec 31   1969
/dev/ide/host0/bus0/target0/lun0/part1
```

On a number of distributions, such as Red Hat, Debian, and others, the commands necessary to regenerate these files are contained in a script called MAKEDEV, which lives in /dev. To do its work, the script uses the same mknod command I talked about earlier.

Incidentally, if you ever find yourself having deleted a device, you can use this script to recreate it. For instance, pretend that you accidentally deleted your audio devices (/dev/audio and /dev/audio1). You can recreate them as follows:

```
cd /dev
./MAKEDEV -v audio
```

The -v option is not necessary, but it does give you some information as the script executes. For instance, here is a small portion of the output from the previous command:

```
create mixer       c 14 0 root:sys 666
create sequencer   c 14 1 root:sys 666
create midi00      c 14 2 root:sys 666
create dsp         c 14 3 root:sys 666
```

What? More Devices?

I've covered a lot of ground here, but I am by no means finished. Those things we attach to our computers aren't much good if we don't put them in context with the tools we use them for. Those tools tend to require a somewhat more in-depth examination. For instance, burning CDs isn't just about creating collections of your favorite songs. People use them for backups as well, or to make collections of digital photos for sharing with the family.

The same is true of scanners. These gizmos are incredibly handy devices for the home or office. Aside from converting nondigital pictures to place on your web site, you can use your scanner as a photocopier and as a way to send faxes when the pages require your signature (you can fax from a word processor, after all).

Services and Runlevels

When you start your system, a number of messages go scrolling by on the screen. Some have to do with hardware detection, but you will also see a number of things starting (starting named, starting sendmail, and so on). Unless you have already made changes to your system, these are all the result of either default configurations or requests for services you made when you installed your system.

Now that you are fresh from your exploration of processes, it is time to take it to the next level. As you progress through this book, I suggest that you add various programs or settings to your start-up files. This chapter covers how this is done for the various Linux distributions.

Daemons and Other Not-So-Scary Things

When your system boots up, it starts a number of services. Among these can be a web server, such as Apache; an X window font server; sendmail, an email transport system; and any number of other programs, such as the xinetd daemon, your network listener.

Note Because I casually tossed out the term "xinetd" and called it a daemon, it is only fair that I explain what I mean by that. By definition, a *daemon* is a program that after being spawned (either at boot or by a command from a shell) disconnects itself from the terminal that started it and runs in the background. If you then disconnect from the terminal session that started the program or log out entirely, the program continues to run in the background.

What daemons do there, all by themselves with no one to control them, is a function of what the daemon is for. The `inetd` daemon listens for network connections, while `syslogd`—another process I will discuss in detail when I cover logs—watches, monitors, and logs information.

The inittab File

Of all the processes on your system, one of them is the master process and the parent (grandparent, great-grandparent, and so on) of every other process. Its process ID is always 1 and will always be 1. That process is called `init`, and its main job is to read its configuration file and start processes as defined there.

Which services or programs get started are decided by the *runlevel* at which your system boots. Take a look at the file called `/etc/inittab` for the runlevel in Figure 8-4. The line you are looking for is near the bottom of the following listing (`initdefault`), but on your system, it is most likely near the top of the file itself, because Figure 8-4 displays only a partial listing. I included the comment lines so you could see what the levels mean on my test Linux system.

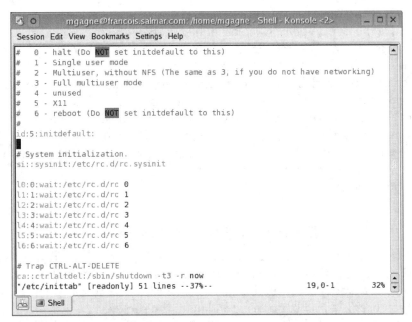

FIGURE 8-4   A sample view from the `/etc/inittab` file.

So, my system starts at runlevel 5. To find out what gets started, I do a long listing (`ls -l`) of `/etc/rc.d/rc5.d,` as in:

```
ls -l /etc/rc.d/rc5.d
```

Here is a partial listing of what I see there:

```
lrwxrwxrwx  1 root root 17 Mar  9 14:51 S10network ->
../init.d/network*
lrwxrwxrwx  1 root root 18 Mar  9 15:09 S11internet ->
../init.d/internet*
lrwxrwxrwx  1 root root 19 May 13 14:19 S11mysql-max ->
../init.d/mysql-max*
lrwxrwxrwx  1 root root 17 Mar  9 14:51 S11portmap ->
../init.d/portmap*
lrwxrwxrwx  1 root root 16 Mar  9 14:51 S12syslog ->
../init.d/syslog*
lrwxrwxrwx  1 root root 17 Mar  9 14:36 S13partmon ->
../init.d/partmon*
lrwxrwxrwx  1 root root 17 Mar  9 14:41 S14nfslock ->
../init.d/nfslock*
```

Notice the arrows pointing to other files in the `/etc/rc.d/init.d` directory. These are simply symbolic links to the actual files that start and stop the various services. If a link to the file exists, that service is started.

At some point in this book, I might tell you to add a command to your startup script. This usually refers to the `rc.local` boot script. Depending on your system and the initial configuration, you might not be able to find an `rc.local` file. A Debian system is a good example of that. If the file doesn't exist, then how do you create it and where do you put it? Another question: How do you get the system to recognize it at boot time?

Good questions.

The rc.local File and Runlevels

To get the scoop on `rc.local`, I need to give you the scoop on runlevels and a handful of scripts that run each time your system comes up. What gets executed at boot time is partly defined by symbolic links located in an `rc#.d` file. The # represents a number corresponding to the runlevel.

What is this runlevel? In your `/etc/inittab` file, you will find an entry that says something like this:

```
id:3:initdefault:
```

Note the 3 at the beginning of the line. This tells you that when the system comes up, it will, by default, switch to runlevel 3, which is full multiuser mode with a command-line login. If your system says 5, this means you are booting directly to the graphical desktop. What starts at each of these runlevels will be found in an accompanying /etc/rc#.d directory; in my case, rc3.d. Yeah, it's true. I'm still a command-line guy who starts his X desktop with the startx command (I'll talk about that later).

On a Red Hat or Mandrake system, you'll find this rc.local file hiding under /etc/init.d. Didn't I just say that it would be in the rc3.d directory? It is. More or less.

If you change directory to /etc/rc3.d, you'll see a number of script files either starting with an S or a K. Do an ls -l, and you will notice they are all symbolic links pointing back to a directory somewhere else. On a SUSE system, the rc#.d directories are under /sbin/init.d, but you will still find those S or K files and they point to /sbin/init.d. In the case of my Red Hat system, they point back to the /etc/rc.d/init.d directory:

```
lrwxrwxrwx  1 root root 11 Mar 18 22:56 S99local ->
../rc.local
```

On a Debian system, these scripts point back to /etc/init.d, which is where I would create my rc.local file. On my own system, it turns out that rc.local is executed by a call to S99local. On a Debian system, for instance, look for or create an S99local file under the appropriate runlevel directory.

My use (or Red Hat's) of S99local is to some degree convention, but you can be somewhat more arbitrary. The first part of that name, S, means start (K means kill), and 99 is simply a high enough number that it is likely the last thing your system executes on boot. The local part is just a name that means something to me. You might call it rclocal or systemlocal or iceberg. So, if I want this file started with my runlevel 3 on a Debian system, I would create a symbolic link like this:

```
ln -s /etc/init.d/rc.local /etc/rc3.d/S99local
```

Switching between Runlevels

It is possible to change runlevels on your system without rebooting. One way is to start and stop a specific initialization script. To start and stop system services, you must be running as the root user:

```
/etc/rc.d/init.d/named stop
```

This would stop the name server (covered in Chapter 9, "Network and Internet Connections,") assuming, of course, that the named script was in /etc/rc.d/init.d. However, if you want to switch to all processes that are supposed to be running at runlevel 5 and you are at runlevel 3, you can have init do this for you:

```
init 5
```

Beware of changing runlevels. You may impact other users that are running other processes. If others are using the system, make sure you warn them.

If you aren't sure what runlevel your system is currently at, try typing the runlevel command:

```
/sbin/runlevel
```

The system may respond in one of two ways. You may get an N followed by a number like this:

```
N 3
```

This indicates that the system is at level 3 and that this is the previous level as well. The other possible answer might be something like 3   5, indicating that the system was previously at runlevel 3 but that it was recently changed to runlevel 5.

The chkconfig Command

On some systems, such as Red Hat and Mandrake, you will find another way to add or delete services at boot time. Look for the command chkconfig. This command provides a simple interface for updating or reporting on system start-up scripts in the /etc/rc.d directory. With chkconfig, the process of creating and maintaining the symbolic links that define what services get started is easily taken care of.

```
chkconfig version 1.3.8 - Copyright (C) 1997-2000 Red Hat, Inc.
This may be freely redistributed under the terms of the GNU Public
License.
usage:   chkconfig --list [name]
         chkconfig --add <name>
         chkconfig --del <name>
         chkconfig [--level <levels>] <name> <on|off|reset>)
```

To find out what services get started at boot time, you can use the --list option. Adding a service name at the end of it will return information only for that service. For instance, let's see when and where the xinetd service gets started:

```
[root@testsys root]# chkconfig --list xinetd
xinetd          0:off  1:off  2:off  3:on   4:on   5:on
6:off
```

If you want to completely stop a service from starting automatically, you can use the --del option and specify the service. In this example, I am removing the advanced power management daemon (apmd) from the automatic start-up:

```
[root@testsys /root]# chkconfig --del apmd
```

Adding is the same process, but with the --add option. That said, you may also want to specify what services start based on specific runlevels. If I do a list of my apmd service after the delete, all runlevels will show as being off:

```
[root@testsys /root]# chkconfig --list apmd
apmd       0:off   1:off   2:off   3:off   4:off   5:off   6:off
```

If, for some strange reason, I did want the apmd running but only when booting in runlevel 3, I would use this command:

```
[root@testsys /root]# chkconfig --level 3 apmd on
```

To configure multiple runlevels, tack them together as one number. Using the previous example, use this variation on the command to start apmd with runlevels 3, 4, and 5:

```
[root@testsys /root]# chkconfig --level 345 apmd on
```

Runlevels the Graphical Way

Manipulating runlevels is not something you will be doing every day. Still, you may find that a nice, friendly graphical interface makes the job just that much more fun when it does come up. Several tools are available to do this job and each distribution's system administration tool (drakconf for Mandrake, for example, or YaST for SUSE) provides a means of doing this. There are also release agnostic tools, including your old friend Webmin. To get to the Webmin SysV init configuration screen on your server, use the following link (substituting *your_server* with the name of your server, of course):

```
http://your_server:10000/inittab/index.cgi
```

KDE also provides an excellent tool called KSysV (command name: `ksysv`). If the package isn't already installed, look for the package name `kdeadmin-ksysv`. Because it is not a platform-specific tool, you will see a configuration wizard pop up the first time you use it. You'll be asked to pick your Linux distribution type: Mandrake, Debian, Red Hat, and so on. The reason for this is something I mentioned earlier in this section. Start-up files haven't yet adhered to one single format or file structure layout (but they are getting there).

That's all there is to that step. The next screen is a confirmation with a Finish button. Once you click that, the main KSysV window pops up (Figure 8-5).

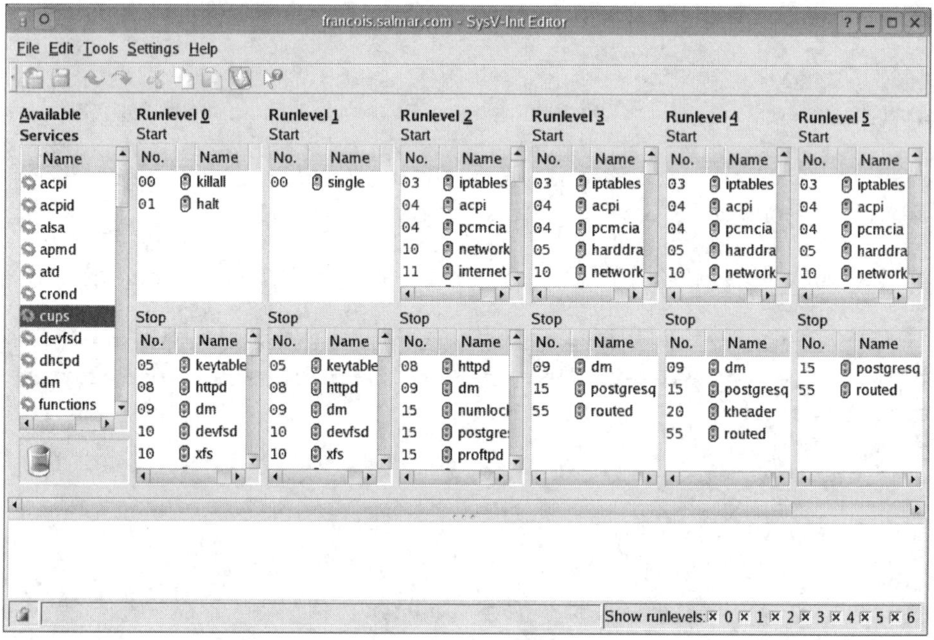

Available Services		Runlevel 0 Start		Runlevel 1 Start		Runlevel 2 Start		Runlevel 3 Start		Runlevel 4 Start		Runlevel 5 Start	
Name		**No.**	**Name**	**No.**	**Name**	**No.**	**Name**	**No.**	**Name**	**No.**	**Name**	**No.**	**Name**
acpi		00	killall	00	single	03	iptables	03	iptables	03	iptables	03	iptables
acpid		01	halt			04	acpi	04	acpi	04	acpi	04	acpi
alsa						04	pcmcia	04	pcmcia	04	pcmcia	04	pcmcia
apmd						10	network	05	harddra	05	harddra	05	harddra
atd						11	internet	10	network	10	network	10	network
crond		**Stop**		**Stop**		**Stop**		**Stop**		**Stop**		**Stop**	
cups		**No.**	**Name**	**No.**	**Name**	**No.**	**Name**	**No.**	**Name**	**No.**	**Name**	**No.**	**Name**
devfsd		05	keytable	05	keytable	08	httpd	09	dm	09	dm	15	postgresq
dhcpd		08	httpd	08	httpd	09	dm	15	postgresq	15	postgresq	55	routed
dm		09	dm	09	dm	15	numlocl	55	routed	20	kheader		
functions		10	devfsd	10	devfsd	15	postgre:			55	routed		
		10	xfs	10	xfs	15	proftpd						

Show runlevels: ☒ 0 ☒ 1 ☒ 2 ☒ 3 ☒ 4 ☒ 5 ☒ 6

FIGURE 8-5   KSysV, KDE's system runlevel editor.

Through this interface, you can easily start and stop processes (and restart them in one pass), edit their configuration files directly, or remove them from the list of processes completely. If you choose a process that does not already start in a desired runlevel, just drag it from the list on the left into the runlevel of your choice. When you are done, click the disk icon to save your changes.

Clicking directly on a service in an active runlevel brings up a box that enables you to work with the running process (Figure 8-6).

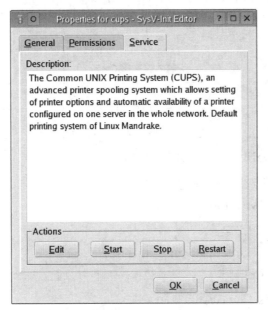

FIGURE 8-6   Getting the skinny on a service from KSysV.

From there, you can start, stop, or restart, but, perhaps more interesting for the new administrators out there, you can also get some information on just what this process does. Click the Service tab, and KSysV divulges what it knows about the specified service.

Creating Your Own Startup Scripts

As I mentioned earlier, the classic method of adding your own start processes is to put them in the rc.local script (or whatever you wind up calling it). You could just as easily create your own rc script by copying one of the existing ones and making modifications to the new version. A nice, simple one to look at is the script that starts your printer daemon, cups.

```
cd /path_to/init.d
cp cups my_service
vi my_service
```

Make sure that you put the final script in the appropriate init.d directory for your system, and you can even work with the final script in your graphical runlevel editor.

Resources

Linux Hardware Compatibility HOWTO

www.tldp.org/HOWTO/Hardware-HOWTO/index.html

Hardware Compatibility List at Red Hat

http://hardware.redhat.com

Linmodems.org (Winmodems under Linux)

www.linmodem.org

LinuxPrinting.org (Linux printer database)

www.linuxprinting.org

Linux USB Device Overview

www.qbik.ch/usb/devices/

9

Network and Internet Connections

I'm going to start this chapter with a little Networking 101. It will be fun—really. For those of you who already know everything about TCP/IP and how IP networks operate, you can skip ahead a few paragraphs.

Communication over the Internet takes place using something called the TCP/IP protocol suite. TCP/IP stands for Transmission Control Protocol/Internet Protocol, and it is the basic underlying means by which all this magic communication takes place. Everything you do on the Net, whether it is surfing your favorite sites, sending and receiving emails, chatting via some instant messaging client, or listening to an audio broadcast—all these things ride on TCP/IP's virtual back.

TCP/IP is often referred to as a *protocol suite*, a collection of protocols that speak the same language. Essentially, this comes down to the transmission and reception of IP packets. Those packets have to get from place to place, and that means they need to know how to get there. IP packets do this in exactly the same way that you get from your house to someone else's house. They have a home address from which they go to a remote address.

Each and every computer connected to the Internet has a unique address called an *IP address*, four numbers separated by dots, such as 192.168.22.55. Some systems that are always online—banks, web sites, companies, and so on—have a *static* address. Dial-up connections for home users tend to be shared: when you aren't connected, someone else may be using the same address, which is referred to as a *dynamic* IP address.

You may be wondering how a symbolic web site address such as www.marcelgagne.com translates to the dotted foursome I mentioned above, and that would be an excellent question.

Think of the real world again. We don't think of our friends as 136 Mulberry Tree Lane or 1575 Natika Court, but rather by their names. To find out where our friends live, we check the phone book or ask them. The same holds true in the digital world, but that phone book is called a *domain name server* (DNS). When I type a symbolic (human-readable) address into my web browser, it contacts a DNS assigned by my Internet Service Provider (ISP) and asks for the IP address. With that IP address, my packets almost know how to get to their destinations.

Almost?

To reach an address in the real world, you get out of your driveway and enter some road to which all other roads are connected. If you drive long enough, presumably you get to Rome (having often been told that "all roads lead to Rome"). Before you can get to Rome, you enter your default route, namely, the street in front of your house. The same principle exists in the virtual world. For your IP packages (an email to your mother, for instance) to get to its destination, it must take a particular route, called a *default route*. This is the IP address of a device that knows all the other routes. Your ISP provides that route.

That concludes Networking 101. Not particularly complicated, is it?

Before You Begin

Connecting to the Internet is one if those things you set-up once, then forget about. Many offices are likely already hooked up directly into an existing network or router, so connecting to the Internet is simply a matter of assigning a default route. This is all part of your basic system installation.

Nevertheless, you may be setting up your Internet after the fact, putting together an email server, a web server, or deploying thin clients. Understanding Linux networking is still an important skill for the systems administrator. In this chapter, I'm going to give you all the skills you need to navigate the Linux network waters.

Note The tools I will cover in this chapter are generic. In other words, you should be able to use these methods of setting up and working with network connections regardless of which distribution you are using. That said, many distributions provide their own administrative tools, designed to make the process that much friendlier. SUSE has YaST2 (command name: `yast`) and Mandrake has the Mandrake Control Center (command name: `drakconf`). Another option is Webmin, which I will cover in Chapter 11.

I'll begin by showing you how to set up a dial-up Internet connection. Before you begin, you do need to get some information from your ISP up front. The basics are:

- Your username and password
- The phone number your modem will be dialing to connect
- The IP address of the DNS (name servers)
- The IP address of your SMTP and POP3 email hosts
- The IP address of your news server (optional)

All of this information likely came with your contract when you first signed up with your ISP. Armed with this information, you are ready to begin.

Getting on the Net

As I write this, there are three very popular methods of connecting to the Internet, notwithstanding your own connection at the office. These are cable modem, DSL service from the phone company, or good old-fashioned dial-up modem. The first two are usually referred to as *high-speed* or *broadband* connections, and dial-up access is usually made fun of.

With all the press and hype about high-speed service, you would think that this is all people run. Think again. As I write this, the vast majority of people in North America are still connecting through a dial-up connection. Make no mistake; as Mark Twain might have remarked, the rumors of the demise of dial-up access are greatly exaggerated. You may be among the majority who are still using dial-up; I'll cover that in detail.

Connecting to the Net with a Modem

Most ISPs provide dial-up access through the *Point-to-Point Protocol*, or PPP. The KDE program that gets you connected to the Internet with a modem is called KPPP. On a standard KDE setup, you'll find it under Kicker's big K by choosing the Internet menu, then clicking Internet Dialer. On Mandrake, look under Networking, then Remote Access; and Red Hat has it under Extras and Internet. You can always just start the application with the command kppp & from an X window terminal session or by using your old friend, the <Alt+F2> combo—once again, just type kppp.

Quick Tip You may have noticed in the paragraph above that I added an ampersand (&) to the end of the kppp command. When you start a command from a shell prompt, it normally runs in the foreground, meaning that you can't start another process at the shell until the current one finishes. (You could, of course, open up another shell.) The ampersand tells the shell to put the process in the background so that you can run other things.

When KDE's Internet connection tool comes up for the first time (Figure 9-1), there isn't much to see, because nothing has been configured. You'll see a blank Connect To list, as well as blank login ID and password fields.

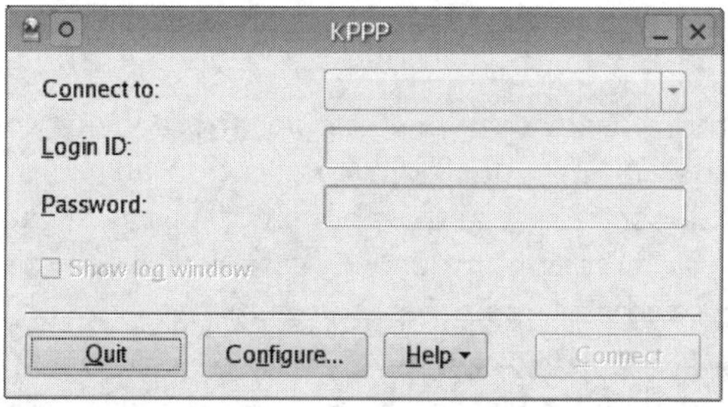

Connect to:	
Login ID:	
Password:	

☐ Show log window

Quit   Configure...   Help ▾   Connect

FIGURE 9-1   First time with KPPP.

To get started, click the Setup button. This will take you to the KPPP Configuration screen.

I realize that the Accounts tab is the first, but I want to talk about the Device tab for a moment. I covered devices back in Chapter 8, "Devices and Services," specifically the issue of modems, and it is particularly relevant here. If you click on that tab, you'll notice that the modem device is set to /dev/modem, which is a symbolic link to the actual port for the modem. That might be /dev/ttyS0, but it could be many other things as well.

If you find yourself having problems here when you dial out, it may be that the link wasn't set properly. Never fear; click on the drop-down list, and you will see a number of potential devices. After choosing a device, click on the Modem tab and choose Query Modem. If KPPP successfully sees your modem, you should see something similar to Figure 9-2.

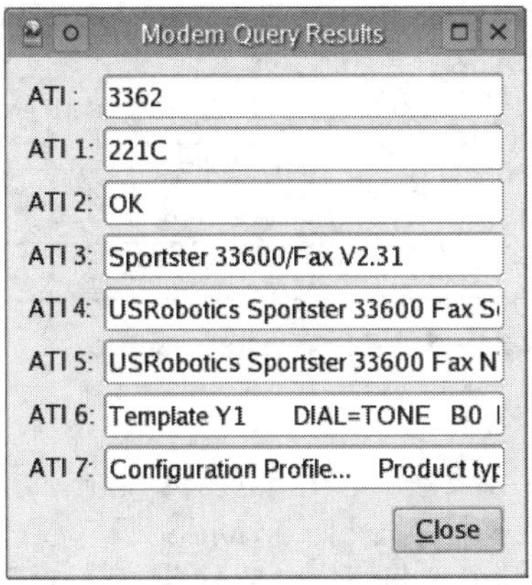

FIGURE 9-2   Modem query results.

Let's get back to the Accounts tab now. As you can probably infer from this screen, it is possible to configure and maintain several dial-up accounts from here. Most people will probably use just one, but you can also use it to set up multiple profiles of the same account. If you happen to be a road warrior or globetrotter with a notebook, you can create profiles for the various cities you visit.

From the Account setup window, click New to create a new account. Skip by the Wizard option, which tends to be for European sites, and choose the Dialog Setup instead. You'll be asked for a connection name, a phone number for your ISP, and the authentication type (Figure 9-3). This defaults to PAP authentication, which most ISPs today use. If your ISP still has you go through some kind of authentication script, known as an *expect/send dialog*, choose Script-based from the list.

FIGURE 9-3   New account setup.

Notice that you have some additional tabs on the menu. The IP tab enables you manually to enter the IP address provided by your ISP. Because most dial-up accounts use dynamic addresses, that is the default selection, and you probably don't have to change anything. The same goes for the next tab, the Gateway tab. This is usually set for you as you connect. Once again, you can override this setting by providing a static gateway address, if your ISP provides it.

The last tab is one you will probably need to worry about: the DNS tab. In all likelihood, you will want to configure an address here as indicated by your ISP. Click the Manual button. Enter the DNS address you were given into the DNS IP Address field, then click Add. If you have a second address, enter it in the same way.

Of course, you may have to do the most work in the Login Script tab, where you may have to provide your dial-up configuration with the appropriate dialog for a connection. This is also something your ISP should have provided

When you click OK, you'll find yourself back at the configuration screen. Click OK one final time, and you return to the initial KPPP window, with one difference. In the Connect to connection list, your new connection should be visible (Figure 9-4). Enter your login name and password, click Connect, and you are on your way.

FIGURE 9-4   With my account configured, I am ready to connect.

Before moving on, notice the Show Log Window check box. If you find that you are having problems connecting, checking this box will show you a login script window as the connection takes place. This can help you debug any problems you might have with the connection.

Cable Modems and High-Speed DSL

For the most part, if you installed your Linux system with the cable modem connected, it is probably already working, and you have nothing left to do. If, however, you are already up and running and you are just now getting a cable modem, you may need a few pointers. Quite frankly, with a modern Linux distribution, there isn't much to it these days.

To begin with, cable modems aren't modems in the classic sense. The so-called modem is connected to your cable TV service on one side and to an Ethernet card inside your PC on the other. High-speed access through your phone company's DSL service is similar, in that it provides you with an external, modem-like device (in many cases, it is really a router) that also connects to an Ethernet card.

The Ethernet card, which should be automatically detected by your system, gets an IP address from the cable modem via the Dynamic Host Configuration protocol (DHCP). Although this address may appear permanent, in that it rarely (if ever) changes, it is nevertheless dynamic, because your actual Ethernet card gets its address whenever it connects.

The process of getting your system configured varies a little bit from distribution to distribution, but only cosmetically. When you install your new Ethernet card for access through the cable modem, the system autodetects it on reboot. As part of that process, the system asks you whether you want to configure the card. The answer is yes, of course. Next, the system asks whether you want to supply an IP address or have it autoconfigure via DHCP. With a cable modem, as with DSL, choose autoconfiguring.

Now that I've told you how incredibly *easy* it is to do this, I'm going to mention that there are many different providers of high-speed cable and DSL access. If your system doesn't autorecognize and configure your connection, you may need to do a little research. For cable modems, the answers vary, but start by checking out the Cable Modem HOWTO at www.tldp.org for details on your particular geographic location.

If you are on a phone company DSL service, look on your distribution disks for the rp-pppoe package (PPP Over Ethernet) and install it. You can get the package from Roaring Penguin at www.roaringpenguin.com/pppoe, but you probably have it on your CDs. Make sure that you check there first. In fact, it may already be installed on your system.

Once the package is installed, open a shell (Konsole) and switch to the root user. Do this by typing su - root at the shell prompt. You'll be asked for the root password. After entering it, type:

```
adsl-setup
```

This is basically a fill-in-the-blanks session. Your phone company assigned you a username and password, along with some connection information. Using the information your company provided, answer all of the questions. The information is case-sensitive, so be careful entering it. When you have answered everything, type the following at your shell prompt:

```
adsl-start
```

That's it. You have no doubt guessed that there is also an adsl-stop command, as well as adsl-status, which, among other things, tells you your IP address. If you install the RPM package from your distribution, adsl-start runs automatically when you reboot your system, so you don't need to worry about it each time.

Getting Down to the Details

Linux is almost synonymous with the server world. When asked, I tend to champion the use of Linux on the desktop as quickly as I champion it in the server world. Nevertheless, Linux's strength and flexibility comes through in the server world. You might argue that the whole point of running Linux is to have access to the unparalleled networking capabilities inherent in the OS. That and rock-solid reliability. And excellent performance. And flexibility. And open source code that you can modify as needed. And...

Before I discuss Linux's networking capabilities, I need to cover the basics of TCP/IP networking.

Warning As you start to work your way through this chapter, you'll notice that a number of networking protocols, environments, tools, and so on will be presented. I could warn you every step of the way about the dangers of these tools, but I want to cover the concepts here. Once you have finished this chapter, please make sure that you read Chapters 22, "Remote Control", and 23, "Security," which cover secure computing and security, and take what you find there to heart.

Because I am going to cover a lot of ground, I'll give you some good markers to let you know when it makes sense to take a breather. How much information am I talking about? Well, think of this chapter as a Wagner opera.

A Light-Speed Introduction to TCP/IP, Part 1

Let's talk about basic TCP/IP configuration for a moment, shall we? Once again, I'll start with the non-GUI approach and discuss the bits and bytes of networking as it relates to TCP/IP, which we all know stands for Talk Clearly Please, Internet Politeness. Actually, that's a lie. It stands for Transmission Control Protocol/Internet Protocol, and it is the basic, underlying means by which communication is possible across the Internet.

At this point, we enter into one of the more technical and geeky sections of the book. I'm not apologizing for it. Although somewhat complicated at times, this stuff can actually be a lot of fun. As I mentioned earlier, a large part of network configuration happens either magically at install time or can be dealt with easily by using the tools provided by your particular distribution. That said, when it comes time to get into more complicated issues like DNS (which I will discuss shortly), a deeper understanding of the process will help you immensely. I'm just letting you know that now might be a good time to make a fresh cup of coffee.

Protocols and Suites

In discussions of TCP/IP, you will often hear the word "protocols." In fact, TCP/IP is often referred to as the *TCP/IP protocol suite*. In other words, it is a collection of protocols that speak the same language. Any information transmitted using the TCP/IP protocol suite is done with IP packets, the fundamental bundles of information for IP-based protocols. Eventually, everything either becomes a packet or comes from a packet.

Packets are transported across your network to the various application protocols in this suite. These transport protocols tend to be either Transmission Control Protocol (TCP) or User Datagram Protocol (UDP).

TCP is referred to as a *connection-oriented* protocol, which means that you connect to a specific application and this connection stays up until such a time as you disconnect. When you telnet into another computer, you are using TCP as your transport protocol. TCP also breaks up large chunks of information into numbered IP packets and routes them to their final destination. The packets are numbered, because they can theoretically take different paths to get to their destination, where they are reassembled according to their numbers.

On the other hand, UDP is referred to as a *connectionless* protocol. No connection has to be created, other than running the specific application daemon. UDP sends information through datagrams, which are small, packet-like chunks of data. Unlike with TCP packets, there is no numbering information and no checking to make sure that the datagrams arrive in the right order. There is no guarantee of delivery either. Any consistency checking must be done by the application. So why would anyone in his or her right mind want to use UDP as his or her transport protocol?

Note Most application protocols that use UDP can also use TCP. The reverse is also true, but somewhat fewer TCP protocols use UDP.

The answer is performance. Because UDP doesn't have to worry about numbering, disassembling, and reassembling packets, it tends to be more efficient—if you don't need to worry about getting all the data all the time. For fast, private networks, UDP is probably not a bad transport mechanism for certain less-critical applications. The Simple Network Management Protocol (SNMP) is an example of a UDP application protocol.

In this TCP/IP protocol suite, you also have a number of application protocols (some UDP, some TCP, and some both). These include the Simple Mail Transport Protocol (SMTP), Post Office Protocol (POP), and File Transfer Protocol (FTP) to name just a few. These are called *services*, and services are addressed by their respective port numbers.

Services and Ports

Your system's master process, the one that got the system going (after you pushed the On switch, that is) is called `init`. The process ID for `init` is 1. It is always 1. If you want to explore it further, you can find `init` in your process table using `ps`:

```
# ps ax | grep init
1    ?    S         6:03  init
```

One of the services that `init` starts when your system boots is `inetd`. Its job is to listen for network requests, which it references by way of Internet socket numbers or ports. For instance, when you telnet to your system by typing `telnet mysystem`, you are actually requesting that `inetd` on `mysystem` starts an `in.telnetd` process that handles communication over port 23. So far, so good. Then, `in.telnetd` starts a process that eventually asks you for your login name and password, and, miraculously, you are then logged in.

Basically, `inetd` listens to find out what other daemons should wake up to answer the port request. If you want to see what those service numbers translate to, do a more (or `less`) on `/etc/services`, a text file that lists the known TCP service ports. Here's a small sample from that file:

```
tcpmux          1/tcp           # TCP port service multiplexer
echo            7/tcp
echo            7/udp
discard         9/tcp           sink null
discard         9/udp           sink null
systat          11/tcp          users
daytime         13/tcp
daytime         13/udp
netstat         15/tcp
qotd            17/tcp          quote
msp             18/tcp          # message send protocol
msp             18/udp          # message send protocol
```

```
chargen         19/tcp          ttytst source
chargen         19/udp          ttytst source
ftp-data        20/tcp
ftp             21/tcp
fsp             21/udp          fspd
ssh             22/tcp          # SSH Remote Login Protocol
ssh             22/udp          # SSH Remote Login Protocol
telnet          23/tcp
```

Notice that I have services that use both TCP and UDP as their transport protocols. Your own /etc/services file will contain a list of the more common port numbers. The services file has a very simple format. First, the service is listed, followed by some white space, a port number, a slash, and then the transport protocol for that service. You can also leave some white space again and add descriptive comments. Your version of this file will have a couple hundred (or more) services listed. Even so, this is by no means an exhaustive list. The Resources section at the end of this chapter provides a link to a much more complete list.

From a resources perspective, it makes sense to have a single process listening rather than one for each and every service. For those of you who can remember and visualize such things, picture Lily Tomlin as the telephone operator who (eventually) patches people through to the party to whom they wished to speak. She is inetd, and the people to whom you wish to speak are the service deamons. You request extension 23, and eventually she puts you through.

When inetd starts, it reads a file called inetd.conf. You can find this one in your /etc directory, just like the services file. Here are a couple of sample lines from inetd.conf:

```
#
# These are standard services.
#
ftp     stream     tcp  nowait     root /usr/sbin/tcpd in.ftpd -l -a
telnet     stream  tcp     nowait  root     /usr/sbin/tcpd
in.telnetd
#
# Shell, login, exec, comsat and talk are BSD protocols.
#
shell     stream     tcp  nowait     root /usr/sbin/tcpd in.rshd
login     stream     tcp  nowait     root /usr/sbin/tcpd in.rlogind
#exec     stream     tcp  nowait     root /usr/sbin/tcpd in.rexecd
```

IP Addresses, Networks, and Subnets, Oh My!

Pay no attention to that man trying to scare you away. While the following terms may appear like arcane words from a strange alternate universe, they are in fact the stuff that networks are made of. All those packets have to go somewhere and getting them there is what I am going to talk about next.

When you address a snail-mail envelope, you are triggering a chain of events that has its equal in the network world: moving something from one address to another.

What Are Domains?

Anybody who has ever surfed the Net from a browser knows about domain names—the dot-coms, the dot-orgs, and the dot-whatevers. Domain names always appear in the format:

```
somecomputer.somedomain.top_level_domain
```

The idea behind all these names is to provide an easy-to-remember address to a specific computer in much the same way that your house or apartment has an address. I say easy-to-remember, because the real address is something entirely different. This is the `number.number.number.number` format of addressing and the only one that actually really matters to computers on the Internet. In fact, the whole point of a domain name server (DNS) is to translate those friendly names back into something the computers and routers of the Internet can deal with.

The `somecomputer` part of the domain is pretty much arbitrary. If I have a machine called natika, that becomes my host name. What you usually call the domain is actually the domain name itself combined with the *top-level domain* (TLD). The TLDs most North Americans are familiar with are .com, .org, .edu, .net, .gov, and .mil, but there are substantially more than just these. If you live outside the United States, your top-level domain is your country's two-letter code. For instance, .ca represents Canada and .jp represents Japan. Canadians, with their proximity to the United States, can use either the .ca TLD or three of the classic United States TLDs, .com, .org, and .net, as shown in Table 9-1.

TABLE 9-1   Traditional U.S. Top-Level Domains

Domain	Description
.org	Organizations, nonprofits, and so on
.com	Businesses
.edu	Universities and educational institutions
.mil	Military
.gov	Government
.net	Networks and service providers

The rules have relaxed quite a bit since these original domains were put in place. Anybody can get a .com, .org, or .net TLD without necessarily being a business, an organization (non-profit or otherwise), or a network services provider. Furthermore, several new TLDs were introduced just recently, in addition to the two-letter country TLDs. These new domains are presented in Table 9-2.

TABLE 9.2   New Top-Level Domains

Domain	Description
.aero	Aerospace and air transport industry
.biz	Businesses
.coop	Nonprofit cooperatives
.info	Pretty generic; no restrictions
.museum	Museums
.name	Personal and family names
.pro	Accountants, lawyers, and physicians

Believe it or not, there isn't a lot more that can be done in terms of coming up with new .com names. Pretty much anything you might want has already been registered. That is the reason that, for the first time, new TLDs were considered.

Note The job of administering all those two-letter country codes or TLDs goes to the Internet Assigned Numbers Authority (IANA). When you see an email coming in from somebody@mydomain.gr, you can use IANA's listing (www.iana.org/cctld/cctld-whois.htm) to find out just what the .gr stands for. (It is Greece, by the way.)

IP Addresses and Networks

Getting back to those IP address numbers: How are they defined?

Finding the answer to this question requires looking at public and private addressing schemes. Because both use the same format for defining IP addresses, let's start there. An IP address, say 192.168.22.56, is often referred to as consisting of four octets. In other words, four dotted 8-bit sections. All told, this gives you a 32-bit addressing scheme that can generate nearly 4.3 million separate IP addresses. While that's an awful lot of computers, it just isn't enough. This is why the IPv6 standard is replacing the old IPv4 standard. The new standard ensures that the addresses don't run out any time soon.

Note My local IP address of 192.168.22.2 can also be read as 3232241154. How is this possible? Well, follow me through these little calculations and you'll see. Take the first octet (in this case, the leftmost) and multiply it by 256 cubed. Add to that the second octet times 256 squared plus the third octet times 256 plus the fourth octet. Confused? Here it is as I fed the calculation into the command-line calculator, bc:

((192*256^3)+(168*256^2)+(22*256)+2) = 3232241154

If I type ping 3232241154, the system responds as though I had typed ping 192.168.22.2. Try it yourself. It's more work than you ever want to do, but it is fun.

Warning You must not assign IP addresses willy-nilly. Even if your network is not connected to the Internet in some way, do not use a routable address. As system administrator, it is your job to make sure that the IP addresses you assign to PCs and other devices in your office environment are unique, sane, and legitimate.

This whole issue of running out of network addresses does have a positive effect. As it turns out, the odds of your ISP being willing to provide you with IP addresses for every machine on your network are pretty slim, but as I said, that's a good thing. The standard nonprivate network addressing scheme is, by necessity, routable throughout the Internet. Your local network should not be. Making every machine visible to the world just increases the amount of work you are going to have to do to keep crackers out. Crackers might be able to see and work at breaking through your web server, but the internal network is problematic, because they have to get through your gateway or firewall before they can direct their attention to the rest of your network.

The three common network classes are Class A, Class B, and Class C. *Class A networks* cover a range of addresses starting at 1.0.0.0 and going all the way to 127.0.0.0. *Class B networks* run from 128.0.0.0 all the way through to 191.255.0.0, and *Class C networks* occupy the space from 192.0.0.0 to 223.255.255.0. There are also two other classes of networks, which I won't spend a lot of time talking about,: the multicast addresses, which run from 224.0.0.0 to 239.255.255.255.0, and the "don't touch because this is reserved" space, which runs from 240.0.0.0 through to 255.255.255.255.

If you are creating a local network in your home or company, you should use a subnet of addresses as defined by RFC1918. Although the other addresses require that they be assigned to you, the private network addresses can be used any way you see fit. This private space is defined as shown in Table 9-3.

TABLE 9-3   Private Network Addresses

Class	Address Range	Number of Hosts
Class A	10.0.0.0 to 10.255.255.255	Over 16 million hosts
Class B	172.16.0.0 to 172.31.255.255	Around 65,000 hosts
Class C	192.168.0.0 to 192.168.255.255	254 possible hosts

Note RFC stands for Request For Comments. Started in 1969, these documents were and continue to be efforts to define the Internet (originally the ARPANET), computer communications, networks in general, protocols, and so on. Some of these documents eventually became the standards for the Internet under the Internet Engineering Task Force (IETF). RFCs are a kind of blueprint for the Internet.

You'll notice that when addresses are used in this book, they follow the pattern in Table 9-3. In fact, I tend to gear my examples to the Class C network scheme, because it represents a small network of just a few computers, which is what my own office is using.

Subnets, Netmasks, and Broadcast Addresses

Even when you have a large network assigned to you, you may want to break up the network into small *subnets*. This is, in fact, what is happening when your ISP gives you an address within a Class A, B, or C network. Normally, you won't subnet a Class C network, because it's already quite small (254 possible hosts), requires minimal maintenance, and is well within the capacities of most office backbones. ISPs routinely subnet Class C networks, because they rarely assign complete Class C networks anymore (the running out of addresses thing again). Class B and Class A networks almost demand subnetting, which I will talk about shortly. Imagine some 65,000 hosts hanging off a batch of routers in your office (Class B), or even worse, over 16 million hosts (Class A).

The *netmask* is designed to isolate your network from every other network. Talking to other computers inside that network then requires a router, which is how your computer winds up talking to other computers on the Internet. Here's what constitutes being part of a subnet: Any computer you can talk to without the aid of a router is on your subnet. Specifically, if your computer's network is the same as another's and your netmask matches the netmask of that other computer, you are on the same subnet.

The following line shows the IP address 192.168.22.2 as a binary representation:

```
11000000 . 10101000 . 00010110 . 00000010
```

Each octet is represented by 8 bits and, as it turns out, 8 bits is just enough to represent the numbers 0 through 255.

Netmasks

What about the netmask? If you are dealing with an internal private network, you almost don't have to worry about it. When you give a host an IP address, there is a default netmask. The standard netmask for a Class A network is 255.0.0.0. For a Class B network, it is 255.255.0.0. Finally, for a Class C network, it is 255.255.255.0. To understand why these are the defaults, it helps to understand what a netmask does. The answer is pretty much what the name implies: A netmask masks or covers up those parts of the IP address that aren't part of your subnet. The default subnet mask for my 192.168.22.2 address is 255.255.255.0. Let's line them up as in my earlier example:

```
11000000 . 10101000 . 00010110 . 00000010
11111111 . 11111111 . 11111111 . 00000000
```

The first line is the address. The second line is the netmask. Because the 255 translates to 11111111, the 192 in my address is masked. In other words, my computer in that part of the network effectively becomes invisible. The same goes for the 168 and the 22. You can't touch those. Those numbers represent my network, and the only thing I can see are other computers in that same network. That's what the netmask does: It defines which part of your IP address is your network. So, all that's left over for you to play with are those last 256 numbers (0 through 255), right? Not quite.

If you accept this standard netmask, your networks have not been divided into subnets themselves. The Class C network, for instance, will only have 254 usable addresses. That's because the .0 address is reserved to represent the network itself (192.168.22.0) and the .255 becomes the broadcast address (192.168.22.255). Everything else is up for grabs.

Broadcast Addresses

"So, what's a broadcast address?" you ask. Well, I'll tell you. Sending information (a packet) to the broadcast address is akin to sending it to every host on the network. You are, in effect, broadcasting. For instance, I could broadcast `ping` over my network with this command:

```
ping -b 192.168.22.255
```

Some versions of the `ping` command require that you use the `-b` flag when you do a broadcast `ping`.

Participation in a network is defined by the network side of your IP address, your netmask, and your broadcast address. Any host within the same network can, by definition, talk to any other host within that network without the need for a router. A router, quite simply, is a device that enables a computer to talk to another computer not on the same network by taking care of moving information between those networks.

Subnets

If I break up a network into small networks, that's called *subnetting*. If I create subnets from my larger network, I then need a router for those subnets to talk to each other. Routers cost money. Separating your network from somebody else's just makes sense when you think of the Internet and several million other hosts, but how about in your own company? Why would you want to do such a thing?

A Class C network can consist of over 1.5 million hosts. From an office administration point of view, that's insane. A Class B network can consist of some 65,000 hosts. Not quite insane, but still crazy. On the other hand, a Class A network of 254 hosts, although more than okay for a small office, isn't much for a medium-sized office of a hundred employees or so. Toss in a few network printers, a handful of servers, and a PC on every desk, and it's amazing how quickly you can use up 254 addresses. But 65,000 hosts? That's a bit much, and there's no in-between network definition.

Pretend that you have 2,000 hosts and a couple hundred network printers that you want to configure into your corporate network. That still qualifies as an administrative nightmare. Still, let's say you could do it. Standard Ethernet rules say you can have no more than 1,024 hosts on a single network segment. That leaves you a bit short if you just try to string them all together. Even if you could, long before you get to that number, you'd discover that collisions, errors, and just plain traffic on your network would make the network unusable. Breaking up the network into something manageable and efficient is what subnetting is all about.

Before I continue with how this happens, I should talk about Classless InterDomain Routing (CIDR). That means taking all that stuff I told you about default netmasks and putting it away for a few minutes. Pretend I never told you about all of that—but only for a few minutes.

Intermezzo

To help me explain CIDR, let's continue with the 2,000-host network. You'll use the private Class B network so every host will have an address somewhere between 172.16.0.1 and 172.31.255.254. The default netmask under normal conditions would be 255.255.0.0, which in binary format looks like this:

```
11111111 . 11111111 . 00000000 . 00000000
[ network portion ] . [   host portion   ]
```

Those first two octets define your network as being 172.16.0.0. A computer at 172.16.10.1 can then see another computer at 172.16.12.17 if both computers are on the same backbone. The 172.16.10.1 computer cannot, however, talk to a computer at 172.21.10.1, because the subnet mask won't allow it. Now, if you apply a subnet of 255.255.255.0 to that large Class B network, you have essentially created a whole bunch of 254-host networks, or subnetworks, with which to work. The host portion is as a result much smaller:

```
11111111 . 11111111 . 11111111 . 00000000
[        network portion       ] . 00000000
```

Because these are now separate networks, they will need routers to transport packets from one segment to another. The problem is that you still have a minimum of 254 hosts per network, or subnetwork. On the Internet itself, this waste of addresses was a formula for disaster as IP address space quickly ran out. Is there a way to divide even a Class C network into smaller networks?

Go back to my 255.255.255.0 subnet mask. The network portion is identified by the number of bits; in this case, it's 24 bits. In the example before that, it was 16 bits. (Just count the 1s.) Finally, in a Class A network, the netmask is 8 bits. You can write the network and netmask definition like this:

```
Class A      10.0.0.0/8
Class B      172.16.0.0/16
Class C      192.168.22.0/24
```

That's eight 1s for the Class A network's netmask, 16 for the Class B, and 24 for the Class C. This is the important part here. The netmask defines the network. So what would happen if you mucked about with this nice, clean netmask? That was the whole point of CIDR.

What CIDR did was permit the use of a netmask of anything from 13 to 27 bits to define the network, thus giving up. Using the CIDR scheme, you could take a Class C network and split it into two or more networks by adding bits to the netmask. For instance, if I want to break my Class C network of 254 possible hosts into two separate networks of 128 hosts, I should use a netmask of 255.255.255.128, which using the CIDR format I can write as 192.168.22.0/25 instead. How does this work? Have a look at the following:

```
11111111 . 11111111 . 11111111 . 10000000
```

Notice the extra 1 in the preceding binary representation. Those 1s are my netmask. They define my network. That means I only have 7 bits left in which to specify IP addresses. That's because I can create only the numbers 0 through 127 with seven binary digits. Get it? I also wind up with two networks. As for any network definition, I need to reserve space for one network address and one broadcast address, leaving me with 126 hosts. My first network would be 192.168.22.0 with a broadcast address of 192.168.22.127. That extra 1 in the last octet is the break, the wall through which neither network is allowed to pass without a router. The second network would be 192.168.22.128 with a broadcast address of 192.168.22.255.

Using CIDR notation, you can create more interesting subnets yet. Sticking with the Class C example, 192.168.22.0/26 would create four class C networks of 64 hosts each. Why? Because 6 bits is enough to define only the numbers 0 through 63. And 192.168.22.0/27? That becomes eight Class C networks of 32 hosts each, because 5 bits is good enough to define only the numbers 0 through 31.

What happens if you go in the other direction? What happens when you use a /23 mask? The host part of the network now has 9 bits. That's good enough to generate numbers running anywhere from 0 to 511, meaning you could create two Class C networks of 512 hosts each. A /22 mask leaves 10 bits, which allows four networks of 1024 addresses each, because 10 bits enables you to define numbers from 0 to 1023. This process is called *supernetting*, and other than getting you all excited about the prospect, I'm going to slide back to the discussion on local network configuration and leave you with those thoughts. Check the Resources section for the RFC editor link and put CIDR into the Search field if you want the deep-down, nasty details.

Setting Up Your PC Network

Although we did cover this earlier in the chapter, setting up dial-up connection to the Internet using PPP and a modem is not the way it is generally done in an office network. I say generally because, in early 2004, as I write these words, I still work with a handful of companies who use a dial-up modem connection to access the Internet. It occasionally gets complicated, ugly, and very slow, but sometimes, because of location, a company just doesn't have a choice.

Instead, most businesses install Ethernet cards into their computers and link them through RJ45 Ethernet cabling through hardware hubs and finally to routers connected to a high-speed Internet connection.

Drivers

An Ethernet card is configured by loading the appropriate driver into the running system. While it is possible to compile these drivers into the kernel, the favored approach is through loadable modules. These are defined in /etc/ modules.conf. Here's the relevant information from my modules.conf file:

```
alias eth0 rtl8139
alias eth1 tulip
```

In this case, I have a couple of no-name (low-name) PCI cards, one running the RealTek 8139 driver, and the other running the Tulip driver.

Setting the IP Address

Again, setting the IP address depends on the system—more on that in a moment.

Before I get into the system specifics, there is actually a universal way of setting an address. In fact, this is what actually happens under the surface by the scripts that bring up interfaces at boot time. The command is called /sbin/ifconfig. To see all the interfaces on your system, type:

```
/sbin/ifconfig -a
```

You should see something like this come back to you:

```
eth0      Link encap:Ethernet  HWaddr 00:20:18:89:29:A6
          inet addr:192.168.22.100  Bcast:192.168.22.255
Mask:255.255.255.0
          UP BROADCAST RUNNING MULTICAST  MTU:1500  Metric:1
          RX packets:1318777 errors:0 dropped:0 overruns:0 frame:0
          TX packets:1238307 errors:0 dropped:0 overruns:0 carrier:0
          collisions:26510 txqueuelen:100
          Interrupt:9 Base address:0x1000
lo        Link encap:Local Loopback
```

```
inet addr:127.0.0.1  Mask:255.0.0.0
UP LOOPBACK RUNNING  MTU:3924  Metric:1
RX packets:108877 errors:0 dropped:0 overruns:0 frame:0
TX packets:108877 errors:0 dropped:0 overruns:0 carrier:0
collisions:0 txqueuelen:0
```

You may actually see more information, depending on the number of cards you already have configured. What's interesting here is that you can do everything related to starting, stopping, and reconfiguring the interface from the command line. Have another look at the first three lines for eth0:

```
eth0      Link encap:Ethernet  HWaddr 00:20:18:89:29:A6
          inet addr:192.168.22.100  Bcast:192.168.22.255
Mask:255.255.255.0
          UP BROADCAST RUNNING MULTICAST  MTU:1500  Metric:1
```

The interesting piece of information in the first line is the hardware address (HWaddr). This is also referred to as the Media Access Control (MAC) address. This is your card's hardware address and like the Little Prince's rose, it is unique in all the world. The second line is what you think of as the normal network address (IP, netmask, and so on). Finally, in the third line, you see that the card is up and running (UP). Taking that card down can be done with your friend, ifconfig:

```
/sbin/ifconfig eth0 down
```

To change the address to something else (like the answer to life, the universe, and everything), you can use the same command:

```
/sbin/ifconfig eth0 192.168.22.42 netmask 255.255.255.255 up
```

Notice that I changed the card address and brought it up with one command.

Of course, in real life, these things happen automatically when you boot your system. There is no need to manually bring up interfaces other than for testing. On a Red Hat or similar system, you'll find most of the configuration files exist in a directory called /etc/sysconfig. Your default network address is defined in the network file.

```
NETWORKING=yes
HOSTNAME=mailhost.mydomain.dom
GATEWAY=192.168.22.10
```

The details of various interfaces are sitting in the `/etc/sysconfig/`
`network-scripts` directory. On my test machine, I have four interfaces: one
for `lo` (the loopback address), another for `eth0` (my first Ethernet card), `eth1`,
and finally, a `ppp0` interface for my dial-up connection. For each interface,
there is an `ifcfg-interface` file with the details of that interface. When the
system boots and the `/etc/rc.d/init.d/network` script executes, it is this
information that the scripts read to bring up the interfaces. The following is
from the `ifcfg-eth0` file in the network-scripts directory:

```
DEVICE=eth0
IPADDR=192.168.22.10
NETMASK=255.255.255.0
NETWORK=192.168.22.0
BROADCAST=192.168.22.255
ONBOOT=yes
BOOTPROTO=none
```

On my Debian system, all the information is in the `/etc/network/`
`interfaces` file. Here is a sample configuration on my network, including a
single `loopback` interface (127.0.0.1) and one card for the internal network
interface at `eth0`:

```
# This is the loopback interface
iface lo inet loopback
# Our single ethernet card
iface eth0 inet static
address 192.168.22.3
network 192.168.22.0
netmask 255.255.255.0
broadcast 192.168.22.255
gateway 192.168.22.10
```

I can now bring up my `eth0` interface with the `ifup` command and take it
down with the `ifdown` command.

Routing

Simply having a configured network interface isn't enough. Your system needs
to know what to do with packets once they leave your Ethernet card or dial-

up modem. You do this with the `route` command. Take a look at the previous line from the Debian `network` script:

```
route add -net ${NETWORK} netmask ${NETMASK} dev eth0
```

By plugging in the appropriate numbers, you wind up with this line:

```
route add -net 192.168.22.0 netmask 255.255.255.0 dev eth0
```

By executing this command after configuring your card with `ifconfig`, you are telling the system what to do when it sees packet addresses within that 192.168.22.0 network—redirect them to the `eth0` interface. When the packets generated belong to something outside that network, you rely on a different kind of route: the *default route*. This address usually refers to a router that is connected to other routers and hosts. Eventually, one of these will hopefully know where this packet belongs. That, in a rather crude nutshell, is how the Internet works. In the following example, I configure my system to look to another host on my network as the default route for all nonlocal network traffic:

```
route add default gw 192.168.22.10
```

The simplest form of this command is `/sbin/route`.

```
$ /sbin/route
Kernel IP routing table
Destination      Gateway Genmask          Flags Metric Ref Use Iface
testsys.mydomai  *       255.255.255.255 UH    0      0   0   eth0
192.168.22.0     *       255.255.255.0   U     0      0   0   eth0
127.0.0.0        *       255.0.0.0       U     0      0   0   lo
default          netgate 0.0.0.0         UG    0      0   0   eth0
```

The previous command goes ahead and tries to resolve the numerical addresses into symbolic ones. You can speed up this process by passing the -n flag and using only a numerical display.

Using netstat

You can also use the `netstat` program to display essentially the same information as displayed by the `/sbin/route` command above by using the -r flag. The `netstat` program is important for other reasons as well. By using the program with the -a and -p flags, you can find out about every connection (or port) open on your system and which programs are using those ports.

Note Learn to use and appreciate the `netstat` program; it can be extremely useful in determining if there are people using your system who should not be there. Does every one of those connections make sense to you? Are there live connections from a host you don't recognize? These are things to think about when you explore network security later on in this book.

In the following example, I also use the -n flag, which tells `netstat` not to worry about resolving IP addresses into symbolic addresses. It also makes the program run a bit faster, because no name resolution is performed. Finally, this can be quite a long listing, so I pipe the whole thing to `more`.

```
# netstat -apn | more
Active Internet connections (servers and established)
Proto Recv-Q Send-Q Local Address      Foreign Address      State
PID/Program name
tcp         0     20 192.168.22.10:22   192.168.22.100:1014
ESTABLISHED
4003/sshd
tcp         0      0 192.168.22.10:22   192.168.22.100:1015
ESTABLISHED
6122/named
tcp         0      0 192.168.22.10:53   0.0.0.0:*
LISTEN
6122/named
tcp         0      0 127.0.0.1:53       0.0.0.0:*
LISTEN
6122/named
tcp         0      0 0.0.0.0:80         0.0.0.0:*
LISTEN
1231/httpd
tcp         0      0 0.0.0.0:443        0.0.0.0:*
LISTEN
```

The PID is the process ID of the running program that is using the connection.

Domain Name Services (DNS)

This whole discussion of IP addresses brings up one of the more frightening topics in the world of Linux administration: the ever-unpopular domain name server (DNS). The job of the DNS, quite simply, is to provide a mechanism whereby you can turn those IP numbers into a symbolic name, such as `arbitrary.domain_name.com`, and vice versa.

You don't necessarily need a DNS. In fact, running your own DNS (if you don't have to) is often more trouble than it is worth. Even on a home system where you've decided to share that one Internet connection with the other PCs in your house, you may find a DNS is completely unnecessary. Simple entries in your hosts file can define your local network.

 Warning All right, this isn't meant to scare you away from running a DNS. You may, in fact, need to run a DNS. That said, one of the most common holes in networks, not to mention one of the most common means by which networks are compromised, continues to be DNS. If you must run a DNS, stay on top of your `bind` package releases. Keep an eye on security bulletins, and upgrade your DNS software whenever necessary.

The **/etc/hosts** File

Once upon a time, a long time ago, there was no DNS. There was a simple file on every network-connected host: the `/etc/hosts` file. You still have a hosts file on your computers, but it isn't used to define every network-connected system, just yours and perhaps a handful of others that you need quick access to. The format is quite simple: an IP address followed by some white space (I like to use tabs) followed by the fully qualified domain name of the computer and then any aliases by which that host is known. Here's an example:

```
# /etc/hosts file
# IP Address      Fully qualified domain name     Aliases
127.0.0.1         localhost.localdomain           localhost
192.168.22.100    scigate.mycompany.com           scigate         devsys
192.168.22.2      nexus.mycompany.com             nexus
192.168.22.3      speedy.mycompany.com            speedy
```

The first two lines are comments. The first "real" line is the 127.0.0.1 line, which defines my `localhost` interface. The next three lines define different systems on my network. Notice that the machine called scigate.mycompany. dom has aliases of scigate and devsys. That means I can get to that machine by using either of those names.

The `/etc/hosts` file is only visible to users on the machine on which that file resides. That means you need to have a `/etc/hosts` file on every system in your network, and those files have to be up-to-date. I'm sure you can see where this is going. If you only have two or three hosts on your network, managing the appropriate files is not time-consuming. Once that list starts to grow, it is time to start thinking about running some kind of local name service.

Note   Incidentally, DNS is not the only solution to consider. Another is network information service (NIS). Where DNS is strictly a name resolution system, NIS performs a number of other lookup functions that I'll explore in a later chapter.

Your own computer's host name, by the way, is contained in a file called `/etc/HOSTNAME`. That's how the system remembers to set that information between reboots. On a Debian system, that file has the same name in lower-case letters: `/etc/hostname`.

Will the Real DNS Please Stand Up

BIND is the de facto package that runs DNS. If you see something called named running on your system, you have BIND. BIND stands for Berkeley Internet Name Domain, and despite the Berkeley in the name (that's where it all began), the home of BIND is actually the Internet Software Consortium (ISC, `www.isc.org`), where you can always find the latest and greatest BIND. Your Linux distribution vendor will also have precompiled binaries of this DNS software, but it usually follows behind what you can find at the ISC site.

Setting up your own DNS can be a fairly complicated affair (and I will cover that), but as I have already mentioned, you may not need to do so. If you are already tied in to an existing network that is connected to the Internet, the simple solution is to point to existing name servers by adding them to your `/etc/resolv.conf` file. I talked about this earlier in the chapter when I discussed a dial-up connection to the Internet. A single line (or two) pointing to your ISP's name server will serve under the circumstances. For example:

```
domain mydomain.dom
nameserver XXX.XXX.XXX.XXX          (first DNS)
nameserver YYY.YYY.YYY.YYY          (second DNS)
```

What this does is set up as a DNS client, rather than a server. The first line is your default search domain (usually your own). If you try to do a lookup (using the `host` or `nslookup` programs), you do not need to specify your domain name. For instance, if I were trying to find the address of a host called speedy on my network, I would type this command:

```
$ host speedy
speedy.mydomain.dom has address 192.168.22.3
```

As part of doing the lookup, the default domain is appended to the host name I specified.

Before I get into the nitty-gritty, you should also be aware of the /etc/nsswitch.conf file. This text file is one that I will visit in more detail later in Chapter 19, "Linux File Sharing," where I cover NFS and NIS. For now, simply be aware that the order in which certain information, such as host names, is looked up is defined in this file. The line that refers to the hosts file looks something like this:

```
hosts:        files nisplus nis dns
```

With this configuration, the local host file is searched first (`files`), followed by the NIS (`nisplus` and `nis`), and finally the DNS (`dns`). This is designed to speed up the lookup process. If you want to telnet to a host called host1.natika.dom, and that information is in your /etc/hosts file, the system looks no further. Consequently, it is possible to modify this file to force a different order.

TABLE 9-4   Service Options

Option	Option Meaning
files	Use the local files to look up information
nis (or yp)	Use NIS for this information
nisplus	Use NIS+
dns	Use DNS to find the information; only applies to hosts
[NOTFOUND=return]	If you haven't found the information, stop searching

Setting Up Your Own Name Server

Generally speaking, if you are running a single site with a simple dial-up connection to the Internet and you're not running server services, you do not need to set up a DNS. As previously mentioned, you should save yourself some trouble and let your ISP do it for you. If, however, you're running a public web server, if multiple servers and clients are sharing a connection, or if you're distributing mail through a local domain, then read on, brave hearts. It's time to set up a real DNS. But first, consider a few weasel words about BIND and DNS.

Note Unfortunately, the prevalence of BIND and a permanently available service on most servers makes it a tempting target for crackers and script kiddies. In fact, the SANS Institute (www.sans.org) routinely places DNS and BIND at the top of its list of means by which security is compromised.

Please make sure that you are running the latest version of BIND.

Quick Tip Before you dive into this whole DNS configuration thing, I'll make it easy on you. If you visit my web site (www.salmar.com/marcel) and check the Downloads section, you'll notice some generic DNS configuration files. If you want to save yourself a lot of typing and all you need is a DNS for your small PC network, look for the quick and easy package there.

Defining Your Domain

The point of this exercise is not to turn you into an ISP. If this is what you are trying to do, you are going to be doing quite a bit more reading on DNS services and you'll certainly need more information than I will give you here. Nevertheless, the following is the premise for this DNS.

You have a Linux server that provides printing, TELNET (or SSH) access, maybe web services for your Intranet, a little mail perhaps, and it also shares your outside connection with an internal network. The internal network in this example is going to be based on a private address Class C network at 192.168.22.0.

The `/etc/named.conf` File

The `/etc/named.conf` file represents the top of your DNS pyramid. The first thing to note is that anything starting with double forward slashes (`//`) or slash-star star-slash constructs (`/* stuff goes here */`) represents comments. The first version is C++ type comments, while the second is good, old-fashioned, C-style comments.

Let's start by having a look at a pretty basic `named.conf` file. This one is actually from a Red Hat system, from a base package called `caching-name-server`. While you are at it, install the `bind` and the `bind-util` packages. The Debian people will want to pick up the `bind` and the `dnsutils` packages.

The `/etc/named.conf` File

Let's start with something simple. The following information is a listing of the default configuration file for a caching-only name server. This is what `named` reads when it starts up:

```
// generated by named-bootconf.pl

options {
        directory "/var/named";
        /*
        * If there is a firewall between you and nameservers you want
        * to talk to, you might need to uncomment the query-source
        * directive below.  Previous versions of BIND always asked
        * questions using port 53, but BIND 8.1 uses an unprivileged
        * port by default.
        */
        // query-source address * port 53;
};

//
// a caching only nameserver config
//
controls {
        inet 127.0.0.1 allow { localhost; } keys { rndckey; };
};
zone "." IN {
```

```
        type hint;
        file "named.ca";
};

zone "localhost" IN {
        type master;
        file "localhost.zone";
        allow-update { none; };
};

zone "0.0.127.in-addr.arpa" IN {
        type master;
        file "named.local";
        allow-update { none; };
};

include "/etc/rndc.key";
```

The very first line is interesting, because you are looking at the name of the
utility that will enable you to convert an old-style named.boot file to a new
named.conf for BIND 8 or 9. The program listed is a perl script called named-
bootconf.pl, which you will find in /usr/sbin. Should you have that old
BIND 4 named.boot file lying around from a previous name server, here is
what you do:

```
cd /etc
named-bootconf < named.boot > named.conf
```

Going back to your named.conf file, notice also the comments in both C
and C++ formats. The format of the file is pretty much the same throughout:
some statement definition with various options inside curly brackets.

```
zone "0.0.127.in-addr.arpa" {
        type master;
        file "named.local";
};
```

The statement in this case is zone with options called type and file. Have
a look at these, starting with the ones you see in the default named.conf file.

- `options`: Refers to things that affect the name server configuration globally and is the very first statement you run across. The best example in this case is the directory option, which defines where all name server configuration files will live. While you can specify another place for your files, this is the accepted standard.
- `zone`: Define parts of your domain, specifically as they relate to networks and subnetworks inside your organization. These sections are the heart of your DNS. The most basic zone references the entire domain, because the domain and the network are essentially one and the same. Large organizations may have hundreds of zones in their domains.
- `acl`: Enables you to define IP address lists for access control of some definition.
- `logging`: Specifies what to log and where.
- `include`: Enables you to include other files in your configuration, rather than putting everything in this one file.

And yes, you guessed it, there are even more.

Zones

Ack! Don't zone out yet. You're almost there.

The first zone you'll encounter is the `named.ca` zone, which is listed as type `hint`. Essentially, this is exactly what it sounds like: If your DNS can't find the answer, it would at least like some kind of hint. That hint is a list of the top-level domain name servers in the world and their addresses. This is your cache file. Because this is a list of top-level servers and the list does change from time to time, it is in your best interest to keep this copy up-to-date. To get the latest and greatest copy, use this command:

```
dig @e-root-servers.net > newcache_file
```

You will want to be connected to the Net, of course, and you will want to use the same name as your current cache file (`named.ca`) when you have what you need. By the way, `dig` is a command-line tool used to query name servers.

 Note Your DNS is not alone. In fact, the whole point of DNS is that each server is actually part of some greater entity—a distributed database of address information that spans the world.

The next zone is your `localhost` zone. The file name is `named.local` in the example (and in the caching name server defaults). The file type is `master`, meaning that it is the primary source of information for anything having to do with this zone. For this zone, it doesn't make sense, but in another zone, you might find the type set to `slave` with a list of `masters` followed by an IP address list to get the appropriate zone information, as follows:

```
zone mydomain.dom {
type slave;
masters {t ip_addr; };
}
```

Take a look at that `named.local` file:

```
@       IN      SOA     localhost. root.localhost.  (
                                2004032701 ; Serial
                                28800      ; Refresh
                                14400      ; Retry
                                3600000    ; Expire
                                86400 )    ; Minimum
        IN      NS      localhost.
1       IN      PTR     localhost.
```

The first line has a very important keyword: SOA, which means start of authority—as in this is where it all begins. IN tells the system that this is an Internet record. They pretty much always are in DNS files. Then, `localhost.` followed by `root.localhost.` represent the fully qualified domain name (or FQDN) for this domain and the place to email the domain administrator (you). The period instead of an at sign (@) is not an error in this file, so leave it as is.

Note Notice the trailing period at the end of the domain name. This is important. A period indicates that this is the whole domain name and not relative to the domain in the zone record. The @ sign indicates the called domain. If you set up a zone for `mydomain.dom`, @ might be replaced with `mydomain.dom`. Once again, note the trailing period. This is also true for IP addresses inside zone files.

Quick Tip Notice the semicolons at the end of each option.

The next thing to look at is the serial number, which you can see is a date. The last two zeroes in that example represent 100 possible changes to the file within that day. Why the changes? Every time you modify a name server record, you must increment that serial number for the zone to be reloaded. If you make changes (add a host) and you find that your updated information is not showing up in a query, you probably haven't updated the serial number. At that point, you need to restart the named daemon.

The second number (Refresh) tells secondary name servers how long they should wait before refreshing their information by contacting the primary name server. If contact fails or the primary is offline, the next number (Retry) becomes important. How long, in seconds, do you wait before trying to contact the primary again? If the primary server cannot be contacted after repeated trials, you might have to start thinking that it is gone for good and that any cached information relating to its domain is quite possibly useless. For that, you have an Expire number.

Your Own Zone File

To get information to and from that 192.168.22.0 domain I told you about, you need to create your own zone records. You will need two files: the primary zone file and a corresponding reverse lookup file. The *primary zone file* is called in the named.conf file as follows:

```
zone "mydomain.dom" {

    type master;
        file "named.hosts";
```

It looks quite similar to the zone definition for localhost, but instead of that reverse number address (0.0.127.in-addr.arpa), you list a domain name. This is what a simple file for this zone might look like:

```
@       IN      SOA     mydomain.dom. root.mydomain.dom. (
        2004032701      ; serial, todays date + todays serial #
        28800           ; refresh, seconds
        14400           ; retry, seconds
        604800          ; expire, seconds
        86400 )         ; minimum, seconds
        0       IN      NS      ns.mydomain.dom.
        0       IN      MX      10 mail.mydomain.dom.
                                ; Primary Mail Exchanger
ns      0       IN      A       192.168.22.10
```

```
mail            0       IN      A       192.168.1.11
gateway         0       IN      A       192.168.22.99
www             0       IN      CNAME   gateway.mydomain.dom.
@                       TXT     "My Company Name, maybe."
;       Other hosts
natika          0    IN    A        192.168.22.1
nexus           0    IN    A        192.168.22.2
speedy          0    IN    A        192.168.22.3
ultraman        0    IN    A        192.168.22.4
```

Some interesting new records here include the MX record, which indicates where mail to this domain should be sent—in other words, where the machine that handles delivery of mail sent to that domain is. The 10 that you see is called the weight. A lower number implies a server whose weight is more important in the hierarchy of finding a valid mail exchange host. If one server is down, the second (or third) will be tried.

```
IN      MX      10 mail.mydomain.dom.   ; Primary Mail Exchanger
IN      MX      20 mail2.mydomain.dom.  ; Secondary Mail Server
```

The NS record specifies the location of the DNS. You can have multiple NS records. In fact, if you are connected to the Internet through your ISP, you may use them as a secondary DNS and put the address here.

The A type records simply indicate maps from the host name to the relevant IP address, and the CNAME, or canonical name, is just an alias for a previously defined A record.

Note Do not use an alias (CNAME) for your MX record.

Finally, you'll see the TXT record. This is pretty much what it looks like: a free-form text field where you can put company information, such as who this DNS belongs to, or contact information. You can also choose to have nothing there at all.

And Now the Reverse DNS Zone

The last file you are going to look at is your local reverse IP mapping. Internet hosts must be able to resolve your address not only by name, but also by doing a lookup on the IP number. The first thing you need to do is look at how this is configured in the named.conf file. Notice that the zone name is your network address (192.168.22.0) minus the trailing zero and mapped in reverse format. The `in-addr.arpa` is always suffixed in this way:

```
zone "22.168.192.in-addr.arpa" {
        type master;
        file "named.rev";
};
```

Now, here is the `named.rev` file:

```
@                   0       IN      SOA     mydomain.dom.
ns.mydomain.dom.  (
                                    200101311          ; Serial
                                    28800    ; Refresh
                                    14400     ; Retry
                                    604800   ; Expire
                                    86400)   ; Minimum TTL
                    0       IN      NS      ns.mydomain.dom.
11                  0       IN      PTR     mail.mydomain.dom.
99                  0       IN      PTR     gateway.mydomain.dom.
1                   0       IN      PTR     natika.mydomain.dom.
2                   0       IN      PTR     mgagne.mydomain.dom.
3                   0       IN      PTR     speedy.mydomain.dom.
```

Note This whole `in-addr.arpa` thing is meant to specify that the file and its addresses conform to the Arpanet addressing methodology. The truth is that all DNS files conform to the Arpanet addressing methodology. In the early days of the Internet, however, several methods of addressing were either being used or worked on. This method of naming the reverse lookup file is there for historical reasons (and perhaps a little nostalgia).

Other than the fact that you use this file for reverse address mapping, the records you find here are pretty much the same as in the previous file (`named.hosts`). The new records are PTR records. These serve more or less the same purpose as the A records in the previous file, but the information is reversed. First, you have the number (of which only the last octet is required), which is followed by the host name.

Does It Work?

Now that you have everything, it is time to shut down your named process (if it is running) and start or restart it. Next, use the dig command to see how well you did. In the previous files, you have a host on the network called speedy at 192.168.22.3. Try doing a lookup on the address to see if it finds speedy:

```
# dig -x 192.168.22.3
;; Got answer:
;; ->>HEADER<<- opcode: QUERY, status: NOERROR, id: 25921
;; flags: qr aa rd ra; QUERY: 1, ANSWER: 1, AUTHORITY: 1,
ADDITIONAL: 1
;; QUESTION SECTION:
;3.22.168.192.in-addr.arpa.        IN        PTR
;; ANSWER SECTION:
3.22.168.192.in-addr.arpa. 0       IN        PTR
speedy.mydomain.dom.
;; AUTHORITY SECTION:
22.168.192.in-addr.arpa. 0         IN        NS        ns.mydomain.dom.
;; ADDITIONAL SECTION:
ns.mydomain.dom.           0       IN        A         192.168.22.10
;; Query time: 2 msec
;; SERVER: 127.0.0.1#53(127.0.0.1)
;; WHEN: Sun Apr  1 03:50:37 2001
;; MSG SIZE  rcvd: 112
```

What's All This about Lame Servers?

If you watch your logs closely, there is a distinct possibility that you will see messages about lame servers being reported. Simply stated, a *lame server* is one that has been designated as being authoritative for the domain but that doesn't agree. Unfortunately, if you are regularly communicating with such a server and it is not yours or under your control, these errors are of little use. In fact, they can be downright annoying precisely because you can't do anything about them. To get rid of these annoying little messages, edit your /etc/named.conf file and add these lines:

```
logging  {
category lame-servers{ null; };
};
```

Who Gets to See the Information?

When you run a name server, you are usually offering services for your network, but you may also be providing information about your mail exchange server or your web site to the rest of the world. Obviously, the world needs to know how to get vital information to you. What they don't need to know is what is inside your network. Queries about your private network should not be for public consumption. Furthermore, restricting access reduces malicious use of your DNS.

You can disable queries for any zones you don't want public by adding the allow-query option to the global options paragraph at the top of your /etc/named.conf file.

```
// generated by named-bootconf.pl
options {
    directory "/etc/nsdata";
    /*
    * If there is a firewall between you and nameservers you want
    * to talk to, you might need to uncomment the query-source
    * directive below.  Previous versions of BIND always asked
    * questions using port 53, but BIND 8.1 uses an unprivileged
    * port by default.
    */
    // query-source address * port 53;
    allow-query { 192.168.22.0/24; localhost; };
};
```

From here on in, only the internal 192.168.22.0/24 network and the localhost address are allowed free reign of the DNS. To allow remote sites to query valid zones in the DNS, add an allow-query option that specifies "any" host access, as follows:

```
zone "mydomain.dom" {
        type master;
        file "mydomain.hosts";
        allow-query { any; };
};
```

If you try to do an nslookup on an address on your internal 192.168.22.0 network from a remote machine on the Internet, you'll get a message similar to this:

```
*** www.mydomain.dom can't find 192.168.22.3: Query refused
>
```

DNS Wrap-up

The previously presented information should be enough to get you going with a simple DNS setup. While it is fairly easy to set up your own domain name services, it can also be quite complex. If you need additional information, check the various man pages or the Resources section at this end of this chapter.

Time Synchronization

In the world of PC hardware, the whole notion of trying to keep time can be quite a frustrating experience. Cheap PC clocks have been known to drift wildly, leaving you asking that age-old question: What time is it really?

rdate

If you take a look at your `/etc/inetd.conf` file, you'll notice an entry like this one:

```
time    stream  tcp    nowait  root    internal
time    dgram   udp    wait    root    internal
```

Using the `rdate` command is one way of synchronizing with a trusted machine. For this to work, however, you must check that the services are active on the server machine by making sure that their entries in the `/etc/inetd.conf` file are not commented out. Then, a client can synchronize with this trusted time server by using the command:

```
rdate -s server_name
```

The `-s` flag means set. If you are logged in as root, you can use this to reset your own computer's clock with another on your network. If you are just curious, use the `-p` flag (print), which only reports the date and time, making no changes to your system.

Although this is often referred to as a brute force approach to synchronizing the time and date, it does work. If your operation doesn't require a huge amount of accuracy (down to the split second) and you just want to make sure that your systems more or less agree with each other, putting this command in a nightly `cron` job is probably sufficient.

If you'd like more information, read on.

NTP

What if you have a network of inexpensive PCs that all have wandering clocks? What if you don't have a host on this network that you can trust?

This is where NTP comes in to play. Originally maintained by professor David L. Mills, with the assistance of numerous volunteers over the years, the idea of NTP is to make it possible to synchronize the time of one Internet-connected computer with another.

You will probably find that NTP is on your Linux system distribution CD. The odds are, however, that it did not get installed by default, so you may have to do that. A word of caution: When you look for it, you may find it as xntpd rather than ntpd.

NTP is configured using the /etc/ntp.conf file.

There are also a handful of programs you should be aware of. The first is the NTP program itself, called xntpd, a daemon that runs on both the server and client sides, enabling the synchronization to take place.

When you first set things up, you may want (or be tempted) to quickly synchronize with a time server out there on the network. A common method of doing this is through the use of the ntpdate command. Say that my /etc/ntp.conf file is all set up and things are ready to roll. Now I want to quickly set up my machine to some reasonably accurate standard. I type the date command and get something like this: Thu Dec 7 15:41:14 EST 2000. This is, as it turns out, at least an hour off. I then run ntpdate:

```
ntpdate server_ip_address
```

When I run the date command again, it returns Thu Dec 7 14:46:40 EST 2000, so I guess my clock was off. Ideally, I don't want to do this again, because the ntpdate command is considered a brute force approach to setting system time, as mentioned previously. It's time to start xntpd:

```
xntpd
```

The NTP client/server now starts to run in the background and updates itself according to the defaults set up earlier.

Resources

Common IP Port Numbers (IANA web site)

www.iana.org/assignments/port-numbers

DNS HOWTO

www.linuxdoc.org/HOWTO/DNS-HOWTO.html

ISC (BIND and DNS)

www.isc.org

Linux Router Project

www.linuxrouter.org

RFC Editor

www.rfc-editor.org

Time Server Web Site

www.eecis.udel.edu/~ntp

Becoming One with the Shell

Think of this chapter as an extended Shell Out section. That means that it is time to transform you into a master of the shell.

The things I want to talk about here are basic commands you will need throughout the course of this book and your time with Linux. One of the things I hope to show you is how flexible some of these commands are. With most, you can modify the basic function with command-line switches, flags, or options, and thereby have them yield far more information than a simple execution of the command itself. A little thirst for exploration will open you up to the real potential of everyday commands.

These days, you can do almost every aspect of Linux systems administration via graphical tools, from configuring system services, creating users, setting up printers, moving files around, and so on. That said, the shell is still a powerful and *fast* alternative to doing everything graphically. You'll appreciate that lean speed at those times when you have to fix a problem over a modem or a slow Internet connection. And did I mention power? I'm fond of saying that learning to wield the shell is akin to getting a black belt in martial arts. Sure you can throw a kick, but can you break a stack of bricks doing it?

Before I wrap up this chapter, I will also cover editors. Editors aren't a luxury or an option, but an eternal necessity in the life of the system administrator. Every once in a while, you will have to edit some configuration file or other to get your work done. I'll give you some pointers for making this as simple and painless as possible.

Linux Commands: An Easy Start

When you talk about commands, it invariably means working at the shell level: the command prompt. That's the dollar sign prompt ($), and it is common to many command shells. When you are logged in as the root user, you will usually have a different prompt. That symbol (#) goes by many names. In North America, we call it the pound sign or the hash mark. My English lit friends tell me it's an octothorpe. Others call it the tic-tac-toe board. I'm going to call it the *root prompt*.

Anyway, you want to be at just such a command prompt to begin your experimentation. If you are running from a graphical environment, click the Terminal Window icon to start a terminal (or shell) session. KDE users will be starting a Konsole (command name : `konsole`). Konsole (Figure 10-1) supports tabbed shells so you can run multiple shell sessions from one Konsole window. Just click Session on the menu bar and select New Session. You can then click back and forth from one shell to the other. You can even cut and paste between sessions. This is very handy if you are working on multiple systems.

GNOME users, meanwhile, will likely start up a `gnome-terminal`. Like Konsole, it also features tabs to give you easy access to multiple sessions. To say that there are a great number of terminal emulators might be understating things. You also have the venerable `xterm`, `rxvt`, and `Eterm`, to name just a few.

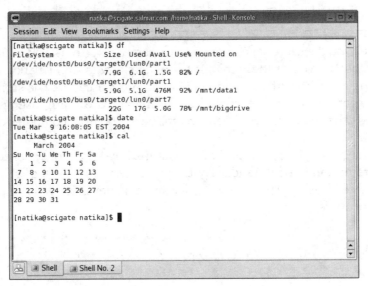

```
[natika@scigate natika]$ df
Filesystem           Size  Used Avail Use% Mounted on
/dev/ide/host0/bus0/target0/lun0/part1
                     7.9G  6.1G  1.5G  82% /
/dev/ide/host0/bus0/target1/lun0/part1
                     5.9G  5.1G  476M  92% /mnt/data1
/dev/ide/host0/bus0/target0/lun0/part7
                      22G   17G  5.0G  78% /mnt/bigdrive
[natika@scigate natika]$ date
Tue Mar  9 16:08:05 EST 2004
[natika@scigate natika]$ cal
     March 2004
Su Mo Tu We Th Fr Sa
    1  2  3  4  5  6
 7  8  9 10 11 12 13
14 15 16 17 18 19 20
21 22 23 24 25 26 27
28 29 30 31

[natika@scigate natika]$ 
```

FIGURE 10-1   Running commands from a bash shell inside Konsole.

Commands to Know and Love, Part 1 **Throughout this** chapter, I'll toss in little boxes like this one. If these commands are not already in your arsenal, then spend a few minutes playing with them and finding out what they do.

date   Date and time.

df   Show me how much free space my disks have.

who   Who is logged on to the system?

w   Similar to who but with different information.

cal   Show me a calendar

tty   Identify your workstation.

echo   Hello, ello, llo, lo, o, o, o...

        Try typing echo "Hello world."

last   Who last logged in, and are they still logged in?

Working with Files

Let me tell you the secret of computers, of operating systems, and of the whole industry that surrounds these things: *Everything is data*. Information is the be all and end all of everything we do with computers. Files are the storehouses for that information, and learning how to manipulate them, use and abuse them, and otherwise play with them will still be the point of computers 20 years from now.

The next thing I want to do is talk about the three most overlooked files on your system: standard in, standard out, and standard error. A facility in manipulating these "files" will provide you with amazing flexibility when it comes to doing your work.

Commands to Know and Love, Part 2

ls   List files.

cat   Concatenate files.

       Try cat /etc/profile

sort   Sort the contents of a file or any output.

       Try sort /etc/passwd

uniq   Return only the unique lines—you do this after sorting.

wc   Word count—returns a count of words, characters, and lines.

       Try wc /etc/passwd

cp   Copy files.

mv   Move, or rename, a file.

rm   Remove, or delete, a file.

more   Allows easy paging of large text files

less   Like the more command, but with serious attitude

File Naming Conventions

Valid filenames may contain almost any character. You do have to pay some attention to the names you come up with. Your Linux system will allow filenames up to 255 characters long. How you define filenames can save you a lot of hassle, as I will soon demonstrate.

Some valid filename examples include:

- fish
- duck
- program_2.01
- a.out
- letter.to.mom.who.I.dont.write.often.enough.as.it.is
- .bash_profile

Notice the last name in particular. It starts with a period. Normally, this type of file is invisible with a default listing. Starting a file name with a period is a way to make a file somewhat invisible. This is good to know if you don't want to burden file listings with a lot of noise. It is also the way that a cracker might hide his or her tracks should they break into your system—by creating a directory that starts with a period. To see these so-called *dot-files*, use the ls command with an -a flag (ls -a).

Listing Files with Emotion!

The ls command seems so simple, and yet it has a number of options that can give you tons of information. Change to something such as the /etc directory or somewhere similar, and try these options:

```
cd /etc
ls --color
ls -b
ls -lS
ls -lt
```

The first listing shows different types of files and directories in color. The second (-b) shows octal representations for files that might have been created with control characters. Depending on the terminal you are using, the default is to show question marks or simply blanks. If you need to access or delete the file, it helps to know what it is really called. The third and fourth options control sorting. The -lS option gives you a long listing (lots of information) sorted by file size. The last option, -lt, sorts by time, with the newest files at the top of the list and the oldest at the bottom.

A Peek at Metacharacters

Metacharacters are special characters that have particular meaning to your shell—that dollar sign or hash mark prompt where you do your work. The asterisk (*) metacharacter means "match any number of characters," and the question mark (?) means "match a single character." For example, you could list all files containing the string "ackle" by using this command:

```
$ ls *ackle*
hackle hackles      tackles
```

Similarly, you could find all of the words that start with the letter "h" like this:

```
$ ls h*
hackle hackles
```

To see all of the seven-letter words in your directory, use this command:

```
$ ls ???????
hackles       tackles
```

Each question mark represents a single letter position.

File Permissions in the Shell

Back in Chapter 6, "Using Konqueror for File Management," I showed you how to look at file permissions with Konqueror. When you use the `ls -l` command, you are doing the same thing: looking at basic Linux security at the file or directory level. Here is an example of a long `ls` listing:

```
$ ls -l
total 3
drwxr-x---   5 root     system   512  Dec 25 12:01   presents
 -r-xr--r--  1 zonthar  users    123  Dec 24 09:30   wishlist
 -rw-rw----  1 zonthar  users    637  Nov 15 09:30   griflong
```

The first entry under the total column shows a directory (I'll talk about the next nine characters in a moment). The first character is a d, which indicates a directory. Right at the end of each line, you'll find the directory or filename;

in my example, they are `presents`, `wishlist`, and `griflong`. Because the first character in the permissions field is `d`, `presents` is a directory.

Those other nine characters indicate permissions for the user or owner of the file (first group of three), the group (second group of three), and others or everyone else (last three). In the first line, user root has read (`r`), write (`w`), and execute (`x`) permissions, and the system group has only read and execute. The three dashes at the end imply that no one else has any permissions. The next two files are owned by the user called `zonthar`.

Quick Tip Remember *user, group,* and *other* (ugo). You will find them useful later when I cover changing file and directory permissions.

Not-So-Hidden Files

When you take your first look at valid filenames, remember that I mentioned that files starting with a period are hidden. As a result, creating directories or files in this way is a favorite trick of system crackers. Get used to the idea of listing your directories and files with an -a option so that you see everything that's there. Look for anything unusual.

Keep in mind, however, that a number of applications create dotted directory names in your home directory so that you are generally not burdened with seeing all of the configuration areas. That's great, except that you should know what you've got on your disk. Always balance your need for convenience with a healthy curiosity. A quick `ls -a` in your home directory will show you some files (and directories) you will become very familiar with as time goes on. Here is an example of what you will see:

```
.Xclients   .bash_history   .bash_profile   .gnupg   .kde
```

Strange Filenames That Just Won't Go Away

Every once in a while, you do a listing of your directory and some strange file appears that you just know isn't supposed to be there. Don't panic. It's not necessarily a cracker at work. You may have mistyped something, and you just need to get rid of it. The problem is that you can't.

Case in point: I accidentally created a couple of files with hard-to-deal-with names. I didn't want them there, but trying to delete them did not work. Here are the files:

```
-another_file
 onemorefile
```

Here's what happens when I tried to delete the first one:

```
[mgagne@scigate tmp]$ rm -another_file
rm: invalid option — a
Try `rm —help' for more information.
```

What about that other file?

```
[mgagne@scigate tmp]$ rm onemorefile
rm: cannot remove `onemorefile': No such file or directory
```

The problem with the first file is that the hyphen made it look like I was passing an option to the rm command. To get around this problem, I'll use the double-dash option on the rm command. Using two dashes tells the command that what follows is not an option to that command. Here I go again:

```
[mgagne@scigate tmp]$ rm -- -another_file
[mgagne@scigate tmp]$
```

Bravo! By the way, this double-dash syntax applies to many other commands that need to recognize potentially weird filenames. Now, what about the second file? It looked fine, didn't it? If you look very closely, you'll see that there is a space in front of the leading o, so simply telling rm to remove the file doesn't work either, because "onemorefile" is not the filename. It is " onemorefile" actually. So, I need to pass that space as well, and to do that I give the full name (space included) by enclosing the filename in double quotes.

```
[mgagne@scigate tmp]$ rm " onemorefile"
[mgagne@scigate tmp]$
```

More on rm, or "Oops! I didn't really mean that."

When you delete a file with Linux, it is gone. If you didn't really mean to delete (or rm) a file, it is time to find out if you have been keeping good backups. The other option is to check with the rm command before you delete a file. Rather than simply typing rm followed by the filename, try this instead:

```
rm -i file_name1 file_name2 file_name3
```

The -i option tells rm to work in interactive mode. For each of the three files in the example, rm pauses and asks if you really mean it.

```
rm : remove 'file_name1'?
```

If you like to be a bit more wordy than that, you can also try:

```
rm --interactive file_name
```

but that goes against the system administrator's first principle.

 Note System administrators believe in simplifying things. If your solution makes things more complicated, something has gone terribly wrong.

Of course, in following that principle, you could remove all of the files starting with the word file by using the asterisk.

```
rm -i file*
```

Making Your Life Easier with alias

You might find that you want to use the -i option every time you delete anything, just in case. It's a lot easier to type Y in confirmation than it is to go looking through your backups. The problem is that you are adding keystrokes, and everyone knows that system administrators are notoriously lazy people. Then there's that whole issue of the first principle. That's why we shortened "list" to simply `ls`, after all. Don't despair, though—Linux has a way. It is the `alias` command:

```
alias rm='rm -i'
```

Now, every time you execute the `rm` command, it will check with you beforehand. This behavior will be in effect only until you log out. If you want this to be the default behavior for `rm`, you should add the `alias` command to your local `.bashrc` file. If you want this to be the behavior for every user on your system, you should add your `alias` definitions to the system-wide version of this file, `/etc/bashrc`, and save yourself even more time. Depending on your distribution, there may already be `alias` definitions set up for you. The first way to find out what has been set up for you is to type the `alias` command on a blank line.

```
[root@website /root]# alias
alias cp='cp -i'
alias ls='ls --color'
alias mv='mv -i'
alias rm='rm -i'
```

Using the `cat` command, you can look in your local `.bashrc` file and discover the same information.

```
[root@website /root]# cat .bashrc
# .bashrc
# User specific aliases and functions
alias rm='rm -i'
alias cp='cp -i'
alias mv='mv -i'
# Source global definitions
if [ -f /etc/bashrc ]; then
        . /etc/bashrc
fi
```

Well, isn't this interesting? Notice the two other commands here, the `cp` (copy files) and `mv` (rename files) commands, and both have the `-i` flag as well. They too can be set to work interactively, verifying with you before you overwrite something important. Let's say that I want to make a backup copy of a file called `important_info` using the `cp` command.

```
cp important_info important_info.backup
```

Perhaps what I am actually trying to do is rename the file (rather than copy it). For this, I would use the mv command.

```
mv important_info not_so_important_info
```

The only time you would be bothered by a confirmation message is if the file already existed. In that case, you would get a message similar to:

```
mv: overwrite 'not_so_important_info'?
```

Forcing the Issue

The inevitable next question is "What do you do if you are copying, moving, or removing multiple files and you don't want to be bothered with being asked each time when you've aliased everything to be interactive?" The answer is this: Use the -f flag, which, as you might have surmised, stands for force. Once again, this is a flag that is quite common with many Linux commands—either a -f or a —force.

Imagine a hypothetical scenario in which you move a group of log files daily so that you always have the previous day's files as backup (but just for one day). If your mv command is aliased interactively, you can get around it like this:

```
mv -f *.logs /path_to/backup_directory/
```

> *Note* Yes, I know that mv looks more like *move* than *rename*. In fact, you do move directories and files using the mv command. Think of the file as a vessel for your data. When you rename a file with mv, you are moving the data into a new container for the same data, so it isn't strictly a rename—you really are moving files. Looking at it that way, it doesn't seem so strange. Sort of.

The reverse of the alias command is unalias. If you want your mv command to return to its original functionality, use this command:

```
unalias mv
```

Standard Input and Standard Output

It may sound complicated, but it isn't. Standard in (STDIN) is where the system expects to find its input. This is usually the keyboard, although it can be a program or shell script. When you change that default, you call it *redirecting* from STDIN.

Standard out (STDOUT) is where the system expects to direct its output, usually the terminal screen. Again, redirection of STDOUT is at the discretion of whatever command or script is executing at the time. The chain of events from STDIN to STDOUT looks something like this:

```
standard in  -> Linux command  ->  standard out
```

STDIN is often referred to as fd0, or file descriptor 0, while STDOUT is usually thought of as fd1. There is also standard error (STDERR), where the system reports any errors in program execution. By default, this is also the terminal. To redirect STDOUT, use the greater-than sign (>). As you might have guessed, to redirect from STDIN, you use the less-than sign (<). But what exactly does that mean? Let's try an experiment. Randomly search your brain and pick a handful of names. Got them? Good. Now type the cat command and redirect its STDOUT to a file called random_names:

```
cat > random_names
```

Your cursor will just sit there and wait for you to do something, so type those names, pressing <Enter> after each one. What's happening here is that cat is taking its input from STDIN and writing it out to your new file. You can also write the command like this:

```
cat - 1> random_names
```

The hyphen literally means standard in to the command. The 1 stands for file descriptor 1. This is good information, and you will use it later. Finished with your random names list? When you are done, press <Ctrl+D> to finish. <Ctrl+D>, by the way, stands for EOF, or end of file.

```
Marie Curie
Albert Einstein
Mark Twain
Wolfgang Amadeus Mozart
Stephen Hawking
Hedy Lamarr
^D
```

If you cat this file, the names will be written to STDOUT—in this case, your terminal window. You can also give cat several files at the same time. For instance, you could do something like this:

```
cat file1 file2 file3
```

Each file would be listed one right after the other. That output could then be redirected into another file. You could also have it print out the same file over and over (cat random_names random_names random_names). The cat command isn't fussy about these things and will deal with binary files (programs) just as quickly. Beware of using cat to print out the contents of a program to your terminal screen. At worst, your terminal session will lock up or reward you with a lot of beeping and weird characters.

 Quick Tip If you get caught printing the contents of a program to your terminal screen and all of the characters appear as junk, try typing echo and then pressing <Ctrl+V> and <Ctrl+O>. If you can still type, you can also try typing stty sane and then pressing <Ctrl+J>. Some systems also provide a command called reset, which returns your terminal session to some kind of sane look.

Redirecting STDIN works pretty much the same way, except that you use the less-than sign instead. Using the sort command, try working with the file of random names. Many commands that work with files can take their input directly from that file. Unless told otherwise, cat and sort will think that the word following the command is a filename. That's why you did the STDIN redirection thing. Yes, that's right: STDIN is just another file.

```
sort random_names
```

The result, of course, is that you get all your names printed out in alphabetical order. You could have also specified that sort take its input from a redirected STDIN. It looks a bit strange, but this is perfectly valid.

```
[mgagne@scigate tmp]$ sort < random_names
Albert Einstein
Hedy Lamarr
Marie Curie
Mark Twain
Stephen Hawking
Wolfgang Amadeus Mozart
```

One more variation involves defining your STDIN (as you did previously) and specifying a different STDOUT all on the same line. In this example, I am redirecting from my file and redirecting that output to a new file:

```
sort < random_names > sorted_names
```

Pipes and Piping

Sometimes the thing that makes the most sense is to feed the output from one command directly into another command without having to resort to files in between at every step of the way. This is called *piping*. The symbolism is not that subtle: Imagine pieces of pipe connecting one command with another. Not until you run out of pipe does the command's output emerge. The pipe symbol is the broken vertical bar on your keyboard, usually located just below or (depending on the keyboard) just above the <Enter> key and sharing space with the backslash key. Here's how it works:

```
cat random_names | sort | wc -w > num_names
```

In this example, the output from the cat command is piped into sort, whose output is then piped into the wc command (that's "word count"). The -w flag tells wc to count the number of words in random_names. So far, so good.

That cat at the beginning is actually redundant, but I wanted to stack up a few commands to give you an idea of the power of piping. Ordinarily, I would write that command as:

```
sort random_names | wc -w > num_names
```

The cat is extraneous, because sort incorporates its function. Using pipes is a great timesaver, because you don't always need to have output at every step of the way.

tee: A Very Special Pipe

Suppose that you want to send the output of a command to another command, but you also want to see the results at some point. Using the previous word count example, if you want a sorted list of names, but you also want the word count, you might have to use two different commands: one to generate the sorted list and another to count the number of words. Wouldn't it be nice if you could direct part of the output one way and have the rest continue in another direction? For this, use the `tee` command:

```
sort random_names | tee sorted_list | wc -w > num_names
```

The output from sort is now sitting in a file called `sorted_list`, while the rest of the output continues on to wc for a word count.

STDERR

What about STDERR? Many commands treat the error output differently than STDOUT. If you are running the command at your terminal and that's all you want, there is no problem. Sometimes, though, the output is quite wordy and you need to capture it and look at it later. Unfortunately, using the STDOUT redirect (the greater-than sign) is only going to be so useful. Error messages that might be generated, such as warning messages from a compilation, will go to the terminal as before. One way to deal with this is to start by redirecting STDERR to STDOUT, and then redirecting that to a file. Here's the line I use:

```
command_name 2>&1 > logfile.out
```

Remember that file descriptor 2 is STDERR and that file descriptor 1 is STDOUT. That's what that 2>&1 construct is all about. You are redirecting fd2 to fd1 and then redirecting that output to the file of your choice. Using that program compilation example, you might wind up with something like this:

```
make -f Makefile.linux 2>&1 > compilation.output
```

Quick Tip You could eliminate the final greater-than sign from the preceding example. When you use the 2>&1 construct, the system assumes that what follows is a filename.

The Road to Nowhere

If the command happens to be verbose by nature and doesn't have a quiet switch, you can redirect that STDOUT and STDERR noise to what longtime Linux users like to call the *bit bucket*, a special file called /dev/null—literally, a road to nowhere. Anything fed to the bit bucket takes up no space and is never seen or heard from again. When I was in school, we would tell people to shut up by saying, "Dev null it, will you?" As you can see, we were easily amused.

To redirect output to the bit bucket, use the STDOUT redirection:

```
command -option > /dev/null
```

If, for some strange reason, you want to sort the output of the random_names files and you do not want to see the output, you can redirect the whole thing to /dev/null in this way:

```
sort random_names > /dev/null
```

Using the program compilation example where you had separate STDOUT and STDERR streams, you can combine the output to the bit bucket.

```
make -F makefile.linux 2>&1 /dev/null
```

That's actually a crazy example, because you do want to see what goes on, but redirecting both STDOUT and STDERR to /dev/null is quite common when dealing with automated processes running in the background.

Linux Commands: Working with Directories

There is another batch of commands suited to working with directory files. Remember, directories are just another type of file.

Commands to Know and Love, Part 3

pwd	Print working directory.
cd	Change to a new directory.
mkdir	Make or create a new directory.
mv	Move directories, or like files, rename them.
rmdir	Remove or delete directories.

One way to create a complicated directory structure is to use the mkdir command to create each and every directory.

```
mkdir /dir1
mkdir /dir1/sub_dir
mkdir /dir1/sub_dir/yetanotherdir
```

To save yourself a few keystrokes, you could use the -p flag instead. This tells mkdir to create any parent directories that might not already exist. If you happen to like a lot of verbiage from your system, you could also add the —verbose flag for good measure.

```
mkdir -p /dir/sub_dir/yetanotherdir
```

To rename or move a directory, the format is the same as you used with a file or group of files. Use the mv command:

```
mv path_to_dir new_path_to_dir
```

Removing a directory can be just a bit more challenging. The command rmdir seems simple enough. In fact, removing this directory was no problem:

```
$ rmdir trivia_dir
```

Removing this one, however, gave me an error:

```
$ rmdir junk_dir
rmdir: junk_dir: Directory not empty
```

You can use rmdir to remove an empty directory only. You need the -p option (as in *parents*) to remove a directory structure. For instance, you could remove a couple of levels like this:

```
rmdir -p junk_dir/level1/level2/level3
```

All of the directories from junk_dir on down will be removed, but only if they are empty of files. A better approach is to use the rm command with the -r, or recursive, option. Unless you are deleting only a couple of files or directories, you will want to use the -f option as well.

```
$ rm -rf junk_dir
```

Warning Beware the `rm -rf *` command. Better yet, *never use it*. If you must delete an entire directory structure, change directory to the one above it and explicitly remove the directory. This is also the first and best reason to do as much of your work as possible as a normal user and not root. Because root is all-powerful, it is quite capable of completely destroying your system. Imagine that you are in the top-level directory (*/*) instead of `/home/myname/junkdir` when you initiate that recursive delete. It is far too easy to make this kind of mistake. *Beware!*

There's No Place Like $HOME

Yeah, I know. It's a pretty cheesy pun, but I like it.

Because you've just had a chance to play with a few directory commands, I'd like to take a moment and talk about a very special directory. Every user on your system has a home directory. That directory can be referenced with the `$HOME` environment variable. To get back to your home directory at any time, simply type `cd $HOME` and no matter where you were, there you are. Actually, you only need type `cd` and press <Enter> to get home. The `$HOME` is implied.

The `$HOME` shortcut is great for shell scripts or anytime you want to save yourself some keystrokes. For instance, say you want to copy the file `remote.file` to your home directory and you are sitting in `/usr/some_remote/dir`. You could use either of the next two commands:

```
cp remote.file /home/my_username
cp remote.file $HOME
```

The second command saves you keystrokes, and the more time you spend doing system administration, the more you will love shortcuts like this. To save the maximum keystrokes, you can also use the tilde (~), a special character synonym for `$HOME`, as in:

```
cp remote.file ~
```

More on File Permissions

What you can and can't do with a file, as defined by your user or group name, is pretty much wrapped up in four little letters. Look at the following listing (using `ls -l`) for an example. The permissions are at the beginning of each line.

```
-rw-r--r--    1 mgagne mgagne       937 May 17 13:22 conf_details
-rwxr-xr-x    1 root   root    45916220 Apr  4 12:25 gimp
-rw-r--r--    1 root   root         826 Feb 12 09:43 mail_test
-rw-r--r--    1 mgagne mgagne     44595 May 17 13:22 sk_open.jpg
```

Each of these letters in turn can be referenced by a number. They are `r`, `w`, `x`, and `s`. Their numerical representations are 4, 2, 1, and "it depends." To understand all of that, you need to do a little binary math.

Reading from right to left, think of `x` as being in position 0. The `w`, then, is in position 1 and the `r` is in position 2. Here's the way it works:

2 to the power of 0 equals 1	(`x` is 1)
2 to the power of 1 equals 2	(`w` is 2)
2 to the power of 2 equals 4	(`r` is 4)

To specify multiple permissions, you can just add the numbers together. If you want to specify both read and execute permissions, simply add 4 and 1 and you get 5. For all permissions (`rwx`), use 7.

File permissions are referenced in groups of three `rwx` sections. The `r` stands for read, the `w` means write, and the `x` denotes that the file is executable.

Although these permissions are arranged in three groups of three `rwx` combinations, their meaning is the same in all cases. The difference has to do with who they represent rather than the permissions themselves. The first of these three represents the user, the second trio stands for the group permissions, and the third represents everybody that doesn't fit into either of the first two categories.

The commands you will use for changing these basic permissions are `chmod`, `chown`, and `chgrp`.

Commands to Know and Love, Part 4

`chmod`	Change the mode of a file, in other words its permissions.
`chown`	Change the owner of the file or directory.
`chgrp`	Change the group of the file or directory.

User and Group Ownership

Suppose you have a file called `mail_test` and you want to change its ownership from the root user to natika. You first have to log in as root, because only root can change root's ownership of a file. This is very simple:

```
chown natika mail_test
```

You can also use the `-R` option to change ownership recursively. Try it with a directory called `test_directory`. Once again, it belongs to root, and you want every file in that directory and below to be owned by natika.

```
chown -R natika test_directory
```

The format for changing group ownership is just as easy. Let's change the group ownership of `test_directory` (previously owned by root) so that it and all its files and subdirectories belong to group accounts:

```
chgrp -R accounts test_directory
```

You can even combine the two formats. In this example, the ownership of the entire `finance_data` directory changes to natika as the owner and accounts as the group:

```
chown -R natika.accounts finance_data
```

 Quick Tip You can use the `-R` flag to recursively change everything in a subdirectory with `chgrp` and `chmod` as well.

So now files and directories are owned by some user and some group. This brings us to the next question.

Who Can Do What?

From time to time, you will need to modify file permissions. One reason has to do with security. The most common reason, however, is to make a shell script file executable. For this, you use the `chmod` command:

```
chmod mode filename
```

For instance, if you have a script file called `list_users`, you make it executable with:

```
chmod +x list_users
```

That command will allow execute permissions for all users. If you want to make the file executable for the owner and group only, you specify it on the command line like this:

```
chmod u+x,g+x list_users
```

The u means user (the owner of the file, really), and g stands for group. The reason you use u for the owner instead of o is that the o is being used for other, meaning everyone else. The

```
chmod +x list_users
```

command can then be expressed as

```
chmod u+x,g+x,o+x list_users
```

Unfortunately, this starts to get a bit cumbersome. Now let's look at a much more complicated set of permissions. Imagine that you want your `list_users` script to have read, write, and execute permissions for the owner, read and execute for the group, and read-only for anybody else. The long way is to do this is as follows:

```
chmod u=rwx,g=rx,o=r list_users
```

Notice the equal sign (=) construct rather than the plus sign (+). That's because the plus sign adds permissions, and in this case you want them to be absolute. If the original permissions of the file allowed write access for other, the plus sign construct would not have removed the execute permission. Using the minus sign (–) removes permissions. If you want to take away execute permission entirely from a file, you can do something like this:

```
chmod -x list_users
```

One way to simplify the `chmod` command is to remember that r is 4, w is 2, and x is 1, and add up the numbers in each of the three positions. rwx is then 4+2+1, or 7. You can translate r-x to 4+1, and x is simply 1. That monster from the second to last example can then be rewritten like this:

```
chmod 751 list_users
```

Who Was that Masked User?

Every time you create a file, you are submitted to a default set of permissions. Go ahead. Create a blank file using the `touch` command and call it `fish`.

```
[mgagne@testsys tmp]$ touch fish
```

Now have a look at its permissions by doing an `ls -l`.

```
[mgagne@testsys tmp]$ ls -l
total 0
-rw-rw-r--    1 mgagne    mgagne          0 Nov  5 11:57 fish
```

Without doing anything whatsoever, your file has read and write permissions for both the user and group, and read permission for everybody else. This happens because you have a default file creation mask of 002. You can discover this using the `umask` command.

```
[mgagne@testsys tmp]$ umask
002
```

The 2 is subtracted from the possible set of permissions, `rwx` (or 7). 7–0 remains 7, while 7–2 is 5. But wait—5 stands for `r-x`, or read and execute. How is it that the file only shows a read bit set? That's because newly-created files are not set executable. At best, they provide read and write permissions for everyone. Another way to display this information is by using the `-S` flag. Instead of the numeric output, you'll get a symbolic mask displayed.

```
[mgagne@testsys tmp]$ umask -S
u=rwx,g=rwx,o=rx
```

If you have an application that requires you to provide a default set of permissions for all of the files you create, change `umask` to reflect that inside your scripts. As an example, pretend that your program or script created text files that you wanted everyone to be able to read (444). Because the execute bit won't be a factor anyway, if you mask out the write bit using a 2 all around, then everybody will have read permission. Set your `umask` to 222, create another file (use `duck` this time), and then do an `ls -l` to check things out.

```
[mgagne@testsys tmp]$ umask 222
[mgagne@testsys tmp]$ touch duck
[mgagne@testsys tmp]$ ls -l
total 0
-r--r--r--    1 mgagne    mgagne          0 Nov  5 12:58 duck
```

The setuid Bit

Aside from those three permission bits (read, write, and execute), there is one other very important one: the s bit, sometimes referred to as the setuid or setgid bit, depending on its position.

The reasoning behind this particular bit is as follows. Sometimes you want a program to act as though you are logged in as a different user. For example, you may want a certain program to run as the root user. This would be a program that you want a nonadministrative user to run, but (for whatever reason) this program needs to read or write files that are exclusively root's. The sendmail program is a perfect example of that. The program needs to access privileged functions to do its work, but you want regular (nonroot) users to be able to send mail as well.

The setuid bit is a variation on the execute bit. To make the hypothetical program, ftl_travel, executable by anyone but with root's privileges, you change its permissions as follows:

```
chmod u+s ftl_travel
```

The next step, as you might guess, is to combine full permissions and the setuid bit. Start by thinking of the setuid and setgid bits as another triplet of permissions. Just as you could reference r, w, and x as 4, 2, and 1, so can you reference setuid as 4, setgid as 2, and other, which you don't worry about.

So, using a nice, complicated example, let's make that command so that it has read, write, and execute permissions for the owner, read and execute permissions for the group, and no permissions for anyone else. To those with execute permission, though, you want to have it setuid. You could also represent that command either symbolically or in a numerical way.

```
chmod u=rwxs,g=rx,o= ftl_travel
chmod 4750 ftl_travel
```

The 4 in the front position represents the `setuid` bit. If you want to make the program `setgid` instead, you can change that to 2. And, yes, if you want the executable to maintain both the owner's permissions and that of the group, you can simply add 4 and 2 to get 6. The resulting set of permissions is as follows:

```
chmod 6750 ftl_travel
```

Changing the `setuid` bit (or `setgid`) is not strictly a case of providing administrative access to nonroot users. This can be anything. You might have a database package that operates under only one user ID, or you may want all users to access a program as though they were part of a specific group. You will have to decide.

Note You cannot use the `setuid` or `setgid` bit for shell scripts (although there are perl hooks to do this). This won't work for security reasons. If you need to have a script execute with a set of permissions other than its own, you will have to write a little C program that wraps around your script, and then allow the program rather than the script to have `setuid` (or `setgid`) permissions.

The lesson here is that making something setuid immediately raises security issues. Know why you are taking this approach and consider the risks.

File Attributes

Unfortunately, the first time most people run across file attributes is usually after their system has been cracked. What happens is that you try to update a package that you know has been modified and the system does not let you. So you try to delete the file and that still doesn't work. You check your user ID, and you are logged in as root, and still you cannot get rid of the file or update it with a clean version. What is going on? Isn't root supposed to be all-powerful?

You have probably just run across a file with the immutable attribute set, which means that under no circumstances can you move, rename, delete, or write to the file.

For the most part, users never wander into this territory and it tends to be a largely ignored aspect of the Linux ext2fs file system. The first command to look at here is lsattr, which (you guessed it) lists the attributes of any given file. Normally, your stock system has none of these permission-like bits set, so using the lsattr command shows something like this:

```
[mgagne@testsys mgagne]$ lsattr LSAdocs
-------- LSAdocs/LSA01- Introduction
```

The dashes all represent position markers for a number of attributes that can be set or changed using the chattr command.

```
chattr +attribute file_name
```

You can also use a minus sign (–) to remove attributes or the equal sign (=) to set a number of attributes at the same time. Some of the attributes must be set by the superuser alone. These are a and i. The i attribute is the one that makes a file immutable, and it's the most interesting one to me. Now, why would you want to bother yourself with any of this? Think back to how I introduced this section and my immutable file. You can do the same thing to protect yourself. Take those system files that you absolutely do not want anybody modifying in a remote session and add this attribute.

The other root-only attribute is a. Setting this bit means that files are append-only. In other words, you cannot simply overwrite the files. This might be good for log files that you don't want someone suddenly clearing out. Here's an example of this append attribute in action:

```
[mgagne@testsys mgagne]$ chattr +a test.txt
chattr: Operation not permitted while setting flags on test.txt
[mgagne@testsys mgagne]$ su - root
Password:
[root@testsys /root]# touch test.txt
[root@testsys /root]# chattr +a test.txt
[root@testsys /root]# /usr/games/fortune -l > test.txt
bash: test.txt: Operation not permitted
[root@testsys /root]# /usr/games/fortune -l >> test.txt
```

When I first tried to set the attribute, I was working as a regular user and you can see where that got me. I tried again, but this time switched to the root user first. I used the touch command to create a blank file, and then set the append attribute. The first time through, I simply redirected the output of the fortune program (using the greater-than sign) but was refused, even though

I was running as root. Only when I started appending my output to the file was I allowed to do so.

The other permissions you can set in this way are:

- Attribute A: Don't update the access time information on files. For frequently accessed files that don't change a great deal, this attribute can provide performance improvements. The catch, of course, is that you can't track access time on the files.
- Attribute c: When this file is not being accessed, the system automatically compresses it. Any time the file is accessed, it is uncompressed. This may or may not be valid on your system, because it was not yet fully implemented as of this writing.
- Attribute d: Files marked in this way will not be backed up by the dump command. (For more on the dump command, see Chapter 13, "Backup and Restore.")
- Attribute s: Think of this as the paranoia bit. If you set this on a file, it will be completely zeroed out when you delete it. In other words, someone scanning your disk at the bit level will see no trace that it ever existed.
- Attribute S: All files tagged with this bit are automatically synchronized to the disk whenever any changes are made.
- Attribute u: This is another bit that was not yet implemented at the time of this writing. The idea is that you can undelete a file flagged in this way, even after you have deleted it.

Finding Anything

One of the most useful commands in your arsenal is the find command. This powerhouse doesn't get anywhere near the credit it deserves. Generally speaking, find is used to list files and redirect (or pipe) that output to do some simple reporting or backups. There it ends. If anything, this should only be the beginning. As versatile as find is, you should take some time to get to know it. Let me give you a whirlwind tour of this awesome command. Let's start with the basics:

```
find starting_dir [options]
```

One of those options is -print, which only makes sense if you want to see any kind of output from this command. You could easily get a listing of every file on the system by starting at the top and recursively listing the disk with the command:

```
find / -print
```

Although that might be interesting and you might want to redirect that to a file for future reference, it is only so useful. It makes more sense to search for something. For instance, look for all of the JPEG-type image files sitting on your disk. Because you know that these images end in a .jpg extension, you can use that to search.

```
find / -name "*.jpg" -print
```

Depending on the power of your system, this can take a while and you are likely to get a lot of Permission Denied messages (particularly as you traverse a directory called /proc). If you are running this as a user other than root, you will likely get a substantial number of Permission Denied messages. At this point, the usefulness of find should start to become apparent, because a lot of images stashed away in various parts of the disk can certainly add up as far as disk space is concerned. Try it with an .avi or .mpg extension to look for video clips, which can be very large.

If what you are trying to do is locate old files or particularly large files, then try the following example. Look for anything that has not been modified (this is the -mtime parameter) or accessed (the -atime parameter) in the last 12 months. The -o flag is the "or" in this equation.

```
# find /data1/Marcel -size +1024 \
\( -mtime +365 -o -atime +365 \) -ls
```

A few techniques introduced here are worth noting. The backslashes in front of the round brackets are escape characters, which are there to make sure the shell does not interpret them in ways you do not want it to—in this case, the open and close parentheses on the second line. The first line also has a backslash at the end. This is to indicate a line break, as the whole command does not fit neatly on one line of this page. Were you to type it exactly as shown without any backslashes, it would not work; however, the backslashes in the second line are essential. The preceding command also searches for files that are greater than 500KB in size. That is what the -size +1024 means, because 1024 refers to 512-byte blocks. The -ls at the end of the command tells the system to do a long listing of any files it finds that fit my search criteria.

Earlier in this chapter, you learned about setuid and setgid files. Keeping an eye on where these files are and determining if they belong there are important aspects of maintaining security on your system. Here's a command that will examine the permissions on your files (the –perm option) and report back on what it finds.

```
find / -type f \( -perm -4000 -o -perm -2000 \) -ls
```

You may want to redirect this output to a file that you can later peruse and decide on what course of action to take. Now, take a look at another find example to help you uncover what types of files you are looking at. Your Linux system has another command called file that can deliver useful information on files and what they are, whether they are executables, text files, or movie clips. Here's a sample of some of the files in my home directory as reported by file.

```
$   file $HOME/*
code.layout:      ASCII text
cron.txt:         data
dainbox:          International language text
dainbox.gz:       gzip compressed data, deflated, original
                  filename, last modified: Sat Oct 7 13:21:14
                  2000, os: Unix
definition.htm:   HTML document text
gatekeeper.1:     troff or preprocessor input text
gatekeeper.man:   English text
gatekeeper.pl:    perl commands text
hilarious.mpg:    MPEG video stream data
```

The next step is to modify the find command by adding a -exec clause so that I can get the file command's output on what find locates.

```
# find /data1/Marcel -size +1024  \
\( -mtime +365 -o -atime +365 \) -ls -exec file {} \;
```

The open and close braces that follow -exec file mean that the list of files generated should be passed to whatever command follows the -exec option (in other words, the command you will be executing). The backslash followed by a semicolon at the end is required for the command to be valid. As you can see, find is extremely powerful. Learning to harness that power can make your administrative life much easier. You'll encounter find again at various times in this book.

Using grep

What does `grep` mean? Global regular expression parser—but that definition of the acronym is just one of many. Don't be surprised if you hear it called the "gobble research exercise program" instead. Basically, the purpose of `grep` is to make it easy for you to find strings in text files. This is its basic format:

```
grep pattern file(s)
```

As an example, say you want to find out if you have a user named natika in your `/etc/passwd` file. The trouble is that you have 500 lines in the file.

```
[root@testsys /root]# grep natika /etc/passwd
natika:x:504:504:Natika the Cat:/home/natika:/bin/bash
```

Sometimes you just want to know if a particular chunk of text exists in a file, but you don't know which file specifically. Using the `-l` option with `grep` enables you to list filenames only, rather than lines (default behavior of `grep`). In the next example, I am going to look for Natika's name in my email folders. Because I don't know whether Natika is capitalized in the mail folders, I'll introduce another useful flag to `grep`: the `-i` flag. It tells the command to ignore case.

```
[root@testsys Mail]# grep -i -l natika *
Baroque music
Linux Stuff
Personal stuff
Silliness
sent-mail
```

As you can see, the lines with the word (or name) "Natika" are not displayed—only the files. Here's another great use for `grep`. Every once in a while, you will want to scan for a process. The reason might be to locate a misbehaving terminal or to find out what a specific login is doing. Because `grep` can filter out patterns in your files or your output, it is a useful tool. Rather than trying to scan through 400 lines on your screen for one command, let `grep` narrow down the search for you. When `grep` finds the target text, it displays that line on your screen.

```
[root@testsys /root]# ps ax | grep httpd
1029 ?        S        0:00 httpd
1037 ?        S        0:00 httpd
1038 ?        S        0:00 httpd
```

```
  1039 ?          S        0:00 httpd
  1040 ?          S        0:00 httpd
  1041 ?          S        0:00 httpd
  1042 ?          S        0:00 httpd
  1043 ?          S        0:00 httpd
  1044 ?          S        0:00 httpd
 30978 ?          S        0:00 httpd
  1385 pts/2      S        0:00 grep httpd
```

Here, the `ps ax` command lists the processes, and then the | pipes the output to the `grep` command. Notice the last line that shows the `grep` command itself in the process list. You'll use that line as the launch point to one last example with `grep`. If you want to scan for strings other than the one specified, use the `-v` option. Using this option, it's a breeze to list all of the processes currently running on the system but ignore any that have a reference to root.

```
ps ax | grep -v root
```

And speaking of processes…

Processes

You are going to hear a lot about *processes*, process status, monitoring processes, or killing processes. Reducing the whole discussion to its simplest form, all you have to remember is that any command you run is a process. Processes are also sometimes referred to as jobs.

Question : So what constitutes a process?

Answer : Everything.

The session program that executes your typed commands (the shell) is a process. The tools I am using to write this chapter are creating several processes. Every terminal session you have opened, every link to the Internet, every game you have running—all of these programs generate one or more processes on your system. In fact, there can be hundreds, even thousands, of processes running on your system at any given time. To see your own processes, try the following command:

```
[root@testsys /root]# ps
  PID TTY          TIME CMD
12293 pts/5     00:00:00 login
12316 pts/5     00:00:00 su
12317 pts/5     00:00:00 bash
12340 pts/5     00:00:00 ps
```

For a bit more detail, try using the u option. This shows all processes owned by you that currently have a controlling terminal. Even if you are running as root, you will not see system processes in this view. If you add the a option to that, you'll see all of the processes running on that terminal—in this case, revealing the subshell that did the su to root.

```
[root@testsys /root]# ps au
USER    PID    %CPU %MEM  VSZ  RSS  TTY     STAT START TIME COMMAND
root    12293  0.0  0.4   2312 1196 pts/5 S      21:23 0:00 login —
mgagne
mgagne  12294  0.0  0.3   1732 976  pts/5 S      21:23 0:00 -bash
root    12316  0.0  0.3   2156 952  pts/5 S      21:23 0:00 su - root
root    12317  0.0  0.3   1736 980  pts/5 S      21:23 0:00 -bash
root    12342  0.0  0.2   2400 768  pts/5 R      21:24 0:00 ps au
```

The most common thing someone will do is add an x option as well. This shows you all processes, controlled by your terminal or not, as well as those of other users. Administrators will also want to know about the l option, which stands for long. It is particularly useful, because it shows the parent process of every process, because every process has another process that launched, or spawned, it. This is the parent process of the process ID. In sysadmin short form, this is the PPID of the PID. When your system starts up, the first process is called init. It is the master process and the superparent of every process that will come until such a time as the system is rebooted. Try this incarnation of the ps command for an interesting view of your system:

```
[root@testsys /root]# ps alxww | more
```

F	UID	PID	PPID	PRI	NI	VSZ	RSS	WCHAN	STAT	TTY	TIME	COMMAND
100	0	1	0	0	0	1120	120	134005	S	?	0:07	init [3]
040	0	2	1	0	0	0	0	12d42b	SW	?	0:00	[kflushd]
040	0	3	1	0	0	0	0	12d4a0	SW	?	0:03	[kupdate]
040	0	4	1	0	0	0	0	123282	SW	?	0:00	[kpiod]
040	0	5	1	0	0	0	0	126896	SW	?	0:03	[kswapd]
140	1	336	1	0	0	1212	0	134005	SW	?	0:00	[portmap]
040	0	350	1	0	0	0	0	1ad198	SW	?	0:00	[lockd]
040	0	351	350	0	0	0	0	1aa906	SW	?	0:00	[rpciod]

Again, this is a partial listing. You noticed, of course, that I threw a couple of new flags in there. The double w, or ww, displays each process' command-line options. A single w truncates the options at a half a line.

The columns you see there tell you a little bit more about each process. The F field indicates the process flag. A 040 in that position indicates a process that forked, but didn't exec, whereas a 140 means the same, but that superuser privileges were used to start the process. The UID field represents the user ID, while PID and PPID are the process and parent process ID that I covered earlier. PRI and NI (priority and nice number) will feature later when I discuss performance issues. In fact, there are quite a number of information flags for the ps command. Every system administrator should take some time to read the man page. More importantly, play with the command and the various flags. You will be enlightened.

Forests and Trees

With all of the information displayed through ps, you can be forgiven if your head is starting to hurt a bit. It is a little like trying to see the forest but being overwhelmed by the sheer number of trees. And yet, all of these processes are linked in some way. Luckily, your stock Linux distribution contains tools to make this easier. One of them is called pstree. Here's a sample of what you get by simply typing the command and pressing <Enter>:

```
init-+-aio/0
     |-atd
     |-bonobo-activati
     |-crond
     |-cupsd
     |-devfsd
     |-events/0
     |-gconfd-2
     |-httpd2-+-advxsplitlogfil
     |         `-5*[httpd2]
     |-ifplugd
     |-kalarmd
     |-kblockd/0
     |-kdeinit-+-artsd
     |         |-karm
     |         |-12*[kdeinit]
     |         |-kdeinit---bash
     |         |-kdeinit-+-aspell
     |         |         `-2*[gs]
     |         |-kdeinit---bash---pstree
     |         `-soffice.bin
     |
```

```
|-12*[kdeinit]
|-kdeinit---perl
|-kdesud
|-kicker
|-klogd
|-knotes
|-kontact
|-kopete
|-lockd
|-login---bash---startx---xinit-+-X
```

This is only a partial listing, but notice that everything on the system stems from one super, ancestral process called `init`. Somewhere under there, I have a login that spawns a shell. From that shell, I start an X window session from which spawns a WindowMaker application. Even so, there are GNOME and KDE applications in there as well.

If you want a similar output, but in somewhat more detail, you can go back to your old friend, the `ps` command. Try the `f` flag, which in this case stands for forest (as in forest view). The following output is the result of my running `ps axf`. Once again, this is a partial listing, but unlike the `pstree` listing, you also get process IDs, running states, and so on.

```
$ ps axf

 1894 tty6     S   0:00 /sbin/mingetty tty6
 2513 ?        S   0:00 /sbin/ifplugd -w -b -i eth1
 3099 ?        S   0:00 login -- mgagne
 3169 tty1     S   0:00  \_ -bash
 3228 tty1     S   0:00  \_ /bin/sh /usr/X11R6/bin/startx
 3241 tty1     S   0:00  \_ xinit /home/mgagne/.xinitrc -- -
deferglyp
 3242 ?        S  65:16  \_ /etc/X11/X :0 -deferglyphs 16
 3247 tty1     S   0:00  \_ /bin/sh /usr/bin/startkde
 3256 tty1     S   0:13  \_ magicdev
 3304 tty1     S   0:00  \_ kwrapper ksmserver
 3270 tty1     S   0:00 /usr/lib/gconfd-2 13
 3273 ?        S   0:01 kdeinit: Running...
 3278 ?        S   0:01  \_ kdeinit: klauncher
 3300 ?
```

In the Linux world, you can find a number of programs devoted to deciphering those numbers, thereby making it possible to find out what processes are doing and how much time and resources they are using to do it. This in turn makes it possible to manage the resultant information.

Interrupting, Suspending, and Restarting Processes

Every once in a while, I start a process that I think is going to take a few seconds. It will be something like parsing a large log file, scanning for some text, extracting something else, sorting the output, and finally sending the whole thing to a file. All very ad hoc in terms of reporting. The trouble is this: two and a half minutes go by, and I start to get a little impatient. Had I thought that the process would take a while, I might have started it in the background.

When you start a process by typing a command name and pressing <Enter>, you normally start that process in the foreground. In other words, your terminal is still controlling the process and the cursor sits there at the end of the line until the process completes. At that point, it returns to the command or shell prompt. For most (not all) processes, you can run things in the background, thus immediately freeing up your command line for the next task. You do this by adding an ampersand (&) to the end of the command before you press <Enter>.

```
[root@testsys /root]# sh long_process &
```

Unfortunately, I've already confessed to you that I wasn't thinking that far ahead and now I am sitting here, looking at a flashing cursor, wondering if I did something wrong and just how long this thing will take. Now, I don't want to end the process, but I wouldn't mind being able to temporarily pause it so I can have a look at its output and decide whether or not I want to continue. As it turns out, I can do precisely that with a running process by pressing <Ctrl+Z>.

```
[root@testsys /root]# sh long_process
Ctrl-Z
[1]+  Stopped                 sh long_process
```

The process is now suspended. In fact, if you do a ps ax and you look for long_process, you'll see this:

```
5328 ?          RN    2267:04 ./setiathome -nice 19
 5617 tty1       R     3294:01 wmaker
32118 tty1       S        0:00 sh /usr/X11R6/bin/startx
11091 ?          S        0:00 kdeinit: Running...
11127 tty1       S        0:00 rxvt -bg black -fg white -fn fixed
```

```
11128 pts/0    S      0:00 bash
11139 pts/0    S      0:00 ssh -l www website
11177 ?        S      0:00 smbd -D
11178 ?        S      0:00 smbd -D
11219 pts/2    T      0:01 sh long_process
```

Quick Tip Want to see what jobs you have suspended? Try the jobs **command.**

I added a few additional processes in the above command snapshot. That's because I wanted to show you the state of the processes. That S you see in the third column of most of these processes means that they are sleeping. At any given moment or snapshot of your system, almost every single process will be sleeping and a small handful will show up with an R to indicate that they are currently running or runnable, sometimes referred to as *being in the run queue*. The T you see beside the suspended process means that it is traced, or suspended.

Two other states you might see processes in are D and Z. The D means that your process is in an uninterruptible sleep, and it is likely to stay that way—usually not a good sign. The Z refers to a process that has gone zombie. It may as well be dead and will be just as soon as someone gets that message across.

Getting back to the suspended process, you have a few choices. You can just restart it from where it left off by typing fg at the shell prompt; in other words, you can continue the process in the foreground. The second option is to type bg, which tells the system (you guessed it) to run the suspended process in the background. If you do that, the process restarts with an ampersand at the end of the command just as it did earlier.

```
[root@testsys /root]# bg
[1]+ sh long_process &
```

Your other option is to terminate the process, or kill it.

Killing Processes

You can usually interrupt a foreground process by pressing <Ctrl+C>, but that does not work with background processes. The command used to terminate a process is called `kill`, which as it turns out is an unfortunate name for a command that does more than just terminate processes. By design, `kill` sends a signal to a job or jobs. That signal is sent as an option (after a hyphen) to a process ID, as in:

```
kill -signal_no PID
```

For instance, you can send the SIGHUP signal to process 7612 like this:

```
kill -1 7612
```

Signals are messages. They are usually referenced numerically, as with the ever popular `kill -9` signal, but there are a number of others. The ones you are most likely to use are 1, 9, and 15. These signals can also be referenced symbolically with these names.

Signal 1 is SIGHUP. This is normally used with system processes such as `inetd` and other daemons. With these types of processes, a SIGHUP tells the process to hang up, reread its configuration files, and restart. Most applications will just ignore this signal.

Signal 9 is SIGKILL, an unconditional termination of the process. Some admins I know call this "killing with extreme prejudice." The process is not asked to stop, close its files, and terminate gracefully. It is simply killed. This should be your last resort approach to killing a process, and it works 99 percent of the time. Only a small handful of conditions will ever ignore the `-9` signal.

Signal 15, the default, is SIGTERM, a call for normal program termination. The system is asking the program to wrap it up and stop doing whatever it was doing.

Remember when you suspended a process earlier? That was another signal. Try this to get a feel for how this works. If you are running in an X display, start a digital `xclock` with a seconds display updated every second:

```
xclock -digital -update 1 &
```

You should see the second digits counting away. Now, find its process ID with:

```
ps ax | grep xclock
```

Pretend the process ID is 12136. Let's kill that process with a SIGSTOP:

```
kill -SIGSTOP 12136
```

The digits stopped incrementing, right? Restart the clock.

```
kill -SIGCONT 12136
```

As you can see, `kill` is probably a bad name for a command that can suspend a process and then bring it back to life. For a complete list of signals and what they do, look in the man pages with this command:

```
man 7 signal
```

If you want to kill a process by specifying the symbolic signal, you use the signal name minus the `SIG` prefix. For instance, to send the `-1` signal to `inetd`, you could do this instead:

```
kill -HUP `cat /var/run/inetd.pid`
```

Note that those are backward quotes around the previous command string.

Working With Editors

Now on to the wonderful world of editors. I'm talking here about computerized line editors, as opposed to the kind that want to know whether your book will be delivered in time for the original deadline.

There will be times when you need to work with an editor, whether to edit a configuration file, to write a script, or to do some quick edits on the company web site. In the Linux world, there are many alternatives.

Meet Kate

Your KDE desktop comes with a very nice and very powerful editor called Kate (command name : `kate`). With colorful language-sensitive syntax highlighting (bash, C, C++, perl, HTML, and others), tabs, project development control, multifile search and replace, and a built-in Konsole, this is one great editor. To see Kate in action, look at Figure 10-2. You can start Kate on its own or specify a filename to start with.

```
kate /etc/rc.d/rc.local
```

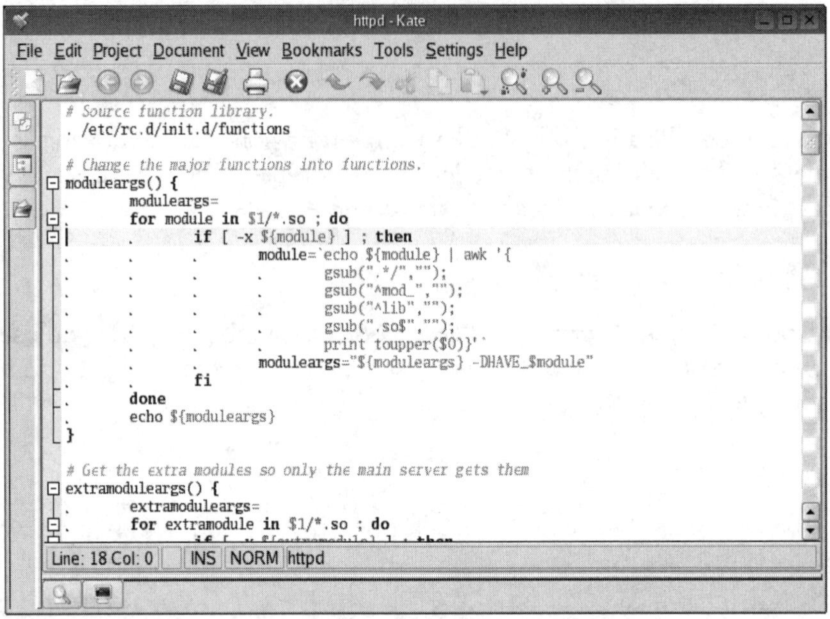

FIGURE 10-2   The Kate editor: easy, powerful, and elegant.

Look down the left side of the program window and you'll see three tabs. Pausing your mouse cursor over each one will bring up a tool tip identifying its function. The topmost tab, the Files tab, provides quick access to currently and recently worked on files. Another nice way to keep certain files handy is to bookmark them. You can do this from Bookmarks on the menu bar. The next tab is the Projects tab. The idea behind this is to provide a mechanism for organizing files and folders (for quick access) that constitute the various parts of a project. Finally, the Selector tab is just a file navigator from which you can select which file to open. Once one is open, you can also define (from a small icon menu at the top of the window) the type of view you prefer. The default is a friendly icon view. You might prefer, as I do, the detailed view, which provides such additional information as file size and modification date and time.

Now, let's move to the bottom of the Kate editor window and look at the tabs there. There's a magnifying glass and a terminal. Pause your mouse pointer over the magnifier and the tool tip will indicate Find in Files. A pause over the terminal icon identifies it as Terminal.

Click the magnifying glass and a detailed search wizard appears. You can specify the pattern of text you are looking for (perhaps all instances of the word "print"), the directory you want to search in (including subdirectories), and the types of files. When you have entered all of the information in your search criteria, click the Search button to begin. A list of files appears below the search fields. To close the search, click the magnifier icon a second time.

Next is the terminal tab. Click this and a terminal window opens with the shell active in the current working directory (Figure 10-3). I find this feature particularly handy when I am working on one system, then want to transfer the edited files to another, remote system, such as when I'm editing web pages. As with the search feature, clicking the tab a second time closes the terminal window.

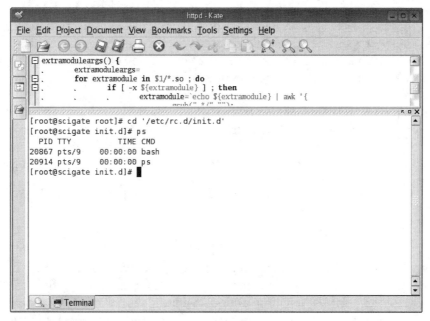

FIGURE 10-3   Kate with an open terminal session.

For years, I've been a fan of vim, the next editor I will discuss, but lately I've taken quite a liking to the KDE programmer's editor and its elegant and powerful interface. Still, there are times when you won't have access to Kate and times when a slow, remote connection makes a graphical editor too painful to consider. It's at those times that you'll be thankful for a simple shell window and vim to help you get your work done.

I Am vi, the Great and Powerful

You can almost hear a fearsome voice echoing eerily around the walls of your office or home. If there is one editor that strikes fear in the hearts of newbies everywhere, it is certainly vi (or vim), the visual editor. vim, by the way, stands for vi improved, and it is the version of vi that you will find in your Linux system. Anyhow, pay no attention to that fearsome voice behind the program. Once you get to know it, vi is not so frightening. To start vi, enter the command name on its own or start it by specifying a file name:

```
vi /tmp/test_file
```

To start entering information, type i to go into insert mode. Type several lines, then press <Esc> when you are done editing. Moving around with vi is easy. Depending on the terminal emulator you are using, you can usually simply use your cursor keys. In the absence of cursor key control, the up, down, and sideways motions are all implemented with single keystrokes. To move left, press the letter "h." To move right, type "l." The letter "k" is up, and "j" is down. (A little further on, I've included a quick cheat sheet.)

When you work with vi, the <Esc> key is your friend. If you don't know where you are or what mode you are in (insert, replace, append), press the <Esc> key. You'll go back to normal vi command mode. Your second best friend is u or U, which stands for undo. The uppercase undo will undo every change to the current line and the lowercase undo will undo the last change only.

:q, :w, :wq, and ZZ

All done editing? When it comes time to save your work, press <Esc> to get out of whatever mode you are in, and type ZZ. Another way to exit is to type :wq (write and quit). At any time during an editing session, you can type :w to save your current work. Finally, if you really don't want to save anything you have done, type :q!. The exclamation point essentially says that you won't take no for an answer. Had you modified the file and simply typed :q, vi would warn you that you were trying to exit from a modified file without having saved your changes.

vi keystrokes and their functions

These commands enable you to move around:

k	Line, or cursor, up.
j	Line, or cursor, down.
l	Single character, or cursor, right.
h	Single character, or cursor, left.
w	Move one word right.
b	Move one word left.
^	Move cursor to the first character in a line.
0	Move cursor to the very beginning of a line.
$	Move cursor to end of a line.
G	Jump to the end of a file.
gg	Jump to the beginning of a file.

You can also type a number followed by gg and jump to that line.

These commands enable you start inserting text in various ways:

i	Start inserting text before the current character.
I	Start inserting text at the beginning of the line.
a	Start inserting text after the current character.
A	Start inserting text after the last character in the line.
o	Open a blank line below the current position.
O	Open a blank line above the current position.

These commands let you delete or change characters, lines, and so on:

x	Delete a single character.
3x	Delete three characters.
dd	Delete a whole line.
20dd	Delete 20 lines.
dw	Delete a word.
cw	Change an entire word; press <Esc> to finish.
5cw	Change five words; press <Esc> to finish.
r	Replace a single character.
R	Start replacing text; press <Esc> to stop.

Quick Tip Need help while in vi? Make sure you aren't in insert or replace mode, and then type :help.

I urge you to not let vi frighten you. Get to know it. The likelihood that you will ever log on to a modern Linux or UNIX system that doesn't have some form of vi installed is virtually nonexistent. That said, if you need more information than I've given you here, consider the vi tutor. This little tool is distributed as part of the vim documentation. It is essentially a text file that tells you what to do and how to do it as you read it. To start the tutor, type vimtutor.

When the tutorial starts, you should see a picture like the one in Figure 10-4. The entire tutorial takes between 25 and 30 minutes for most people to complete.

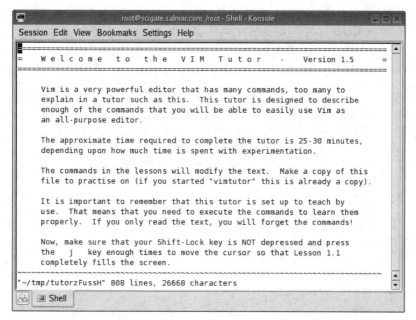

FIGURE 10-4   Learning `vi` or `vim` from the `vimtutor`.

Recovering a vim Session

From time to time, you may find yourself trying to edit a file but someone else, maybe you, is already editing it. That session may be open or something may have happened to terminate it accidentally. As a result, you get a nice, long-winded message along the lines of "swap file found" and a whole lot of information on what you can do about it. Here's a shortened version of that message:

```
E325: ATTENTION
Found a swap file by the name "textfiles/.listing1.swp"
          owned by: mgagne    dated: Sun Dec 28 14:43:20 2003
          file name: ~mgagne/textfiles/listing1
```

To locate these files, you can use the famous `find` command and look for anything with a .swp extension. A better way is to have `vi` report on these for you. You can check for the existence of swap files by using the -r option, which will provide you with a little more information than the simple find.

```
Swap files found:
   In current directory:
1.     .linux_companies.swp
            owned by: mgagne    dated: Mon Sep 15 14:38:55 2003
            file name: ~mgagne/textfiles/linux_companies
            modified: YES
            user name: mgagne    host name: francois
          process ID: 2266
2.     .sas.swp
            owned by: mgagne    dated: Mon Sep  8 09:49:02 2003
            file name: ~mgagne/textfiles/sas
            modified: no
            user name: mgagne    host name: ultraman
          process ID: 6340
   In directory ~/tmp:
      -- none --
   In directory /var/tmp:
      -- none --
   In directory /tmp:
      -- none --
```

Power vi: Start-up Options

Next time you need a reason to use vi over one of the other editors, consider some of these quick tricks for getting to what you want as quickly as possible.

This will take you right to line 100 in the file called (in this case) ftl_program.c:

```
vi +100 ftl_program.c
```

This can be a great little timesaver when you are compiling programs and something goes wrong, as in the following example:

```
gcc  -O2 -Wall  -c -o ftl_program.o ftl_program.c
ftl_program.c:100: parse error before `<'
make: *** [ftl_program.o] Error 1
```

Another useful start flag is the same one you use to search for text inside a file: the forward slash (/). In the next example, I want to get back to the same place I was working on in my file. To mark my place, I had written my name on a blank line. This `vi` starter gets me right to where I was working:

```
vi +/Marcel ftl_program.c
```

Note the plus sign before the slash.

Here's a last little teaser before you run off to the man pages or a bookstore for the latest and greatest 500-page `vi` reference guide. By design, `vi` is a text editor and basic text is our medium. As demonstrated earlier, you can press <Ctrl+V> to insert control characters into your text, but you can also edit binary files. Here's a crazy example. There's a great little game that you probably installed when you set up your system. It's called XBill, a wonderful piece of strangeness where you must stop a renegade program known only as Bill from spreading a most insidious computer virus, which is cleverly disguised as an operating system.

Okay, I know that I can get the source and modify the program without going into the scenario I am about to describe, but trust me, there may be times when you have a binary file of some kind with no source and all you need is a simple modification. You don't want to entertain this lightly. Changing things in this mode could leave you with a nonfunctional program or worse, but you are still going to do it. Just remember to make a backup. In my case, I made a copy of the XBill program in my home directory. If you pause in the middle of a game, you get the message in Figure 10-5.

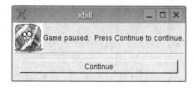

FIGURE 10-5   The original XBill pause message.

For reasons I won't go into at this time, I didn't like the fact that it said "Continue." I would rather it said "Ah go on." Because I only have the source, I start `vi` with the `-b` option which lets me edit a binary file. To make life just a bit easier, I am going to combine that with another helpful little command line option:

```
vi -b +/"Press Continue" xbill
```

This puts me right on the line I want. There I change "Continue" to "Ah go on." I also need to find and change the word "Continue" on its own. Figure 10-6 displays the message I receive when I press Pause during a game now.

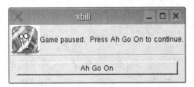

FIGURE 10-6 My new xbill pause message in action.

Note Notice that I used exactly the same number of letters for my change. Because this is a binary, the amount of space I had to work with to make my change was defined at compile time. Breaking this rule may get you the dreaded Segmentation fault (core dumped) message. Using less space is *probably* okay if you fill with spaces.

Still More Editors: Emacs, Pico, and NEdit

As I mentioned in my introduction to editors, there are many editors available to the Linux user. Many of these are either installed as part of your distribution or included on the distribution CD.

One of my old favorites is another non-graphical editor that makes a nice alternative for people who, having gotten up close and personal with vim, would prefer something else. It's called Pico (command name : pico), which stands for Pine Composer. Pico is the full-screen editor distributed with PINE, a great text-based email client distributed by the University of Washington.

Then, there's the venerable Emacs. When talking about Emacs, it becomes almost difficult to classify it as strictly an editor. The brainchild of Richard M. Stallman, founder of the Free Software Foundation, GNU Emacs is more than just a nice, powerful, if somewhat complex, editor. It's a mail reader, news-reader, web browser, program development environment, LISP interpreter, and more. To do Emacs justice, you would have to write an entire book. For some, this is too much editor, yet many professional programmers tend to think differently and consider Emacs indispensable. Either way, you owe it to yourself to try this incredibly powerful and customizable tool.

Finally, I'd also like to mention NEdit (command name: `nedit`), another editor I've taken quite a liking to. This is another multipurpose, graphical programmer's editor. I like the fact that NEdit manages to pack its many powerful features into a small, lightweight, and easy to use package.

Resources

GNU Emacs

www.gnu.org/software/emacs

NEdit

www.nedit.org

PINE Information Center (the home of Pico)

www.washington.edu/pine

vim Homepage

www.vim.org

XBill

www.xbill.org

11

Web-based Administration

As we go through this book together, I'm going to cover a number of graphical and command line tools. Each is suited to a particular job, although in some cases, such as KDE's Control Center, a single tool covers a lot of ground.

Command-line tools are wonderfully universal. All it takes to access them and work with them is a text-based terminal via the secure shell (ssh) or, if absolutely unavoidable, telnet. If a secure shell client isn't available at the PC in question, there is almost assuredly a web browser and with a web browser, you've got a friendly face to a powerful system administration tool. It's called Webmin, and it's the brainchild of Jamie Cameron of Australia.

Introducing Webmin

Webmin is exactly what the name implies: a web-based system administration tool. Although this book concerns itself with Linux, Webmin's strength comes partly from its multiplatform support. Once you are familiar with Webmin on any Linux distribution, you'll find it just as easy on Solaris, AIX, HPUX, or any number of other UNIX and UNIX-like operating systems. With a consistent, cross-platform look and feel, Webmin makes it easy to administer your systems from anywhere in the world, as long as you have a browser and a network connection, of course.

Webmin is also flexible enough to let you securely offload some of that administrative work on others. Want to hand off printer administration to someone else? Webmin makes it easy, and I'll show you how a little later. It's also an easy program to work with in that the browser-based interface is something everyone is familiar with. Over the years, I have turned Webmin over to other users who aren't very Linux savvy but who can deal with those system functions that I've provided them on a custom-tailored menu.

Because most modern Linux distributions include Webmin, you will very likely find it on your CDs. This package requires only that you have perl loaded on your system, which is standard in most Linux installations. Webmin comes with its own mini web server, so Apache isn't even necessary. You can get the latest and greatest Webmin from the official Webmin site at www.webmin.com. It is available in tarred and gzipped bundles or in a single RPM package. For most, this will be the easiest way to install Webmin.

If you choose to use the tar bundle, extract it into a temporary directory and run the "./setup.sh" script. This installation procedure does ask a few questions, but for the most part, you can pretty much just accept the choices as they are presented. The final question you'll be asked is whether you want Webmin to automatically start at boot time, and that is certainly a good idea.

Running Webmin

Webmin's mini web server runs its own little web server on port 10000. To connect to Webmin, point your browser to the server at port 10000:

```
http://your_server:10000/
```

This is probably fine for administering local systems, but remote administration and on untrusted networks, you'll probably want to use the encrypted
Webmin connection. For the SSL-enabled version, try this instead:

```
https://your_server:10000/
```

On the first connection to the SSL-enabled Webmin, you'll be presented
with a security certificate and told that the system is unable to verify the identity of the server. If you are running this on your own server, you can safely
accept it.

When you connect, you'll be asked for a username and password. On most
package-based Webmin installations, that usually means the root user and
password. Enter the information into the form, click Login, and you should be
looking at the main Webmin screen (Figure 11-1).

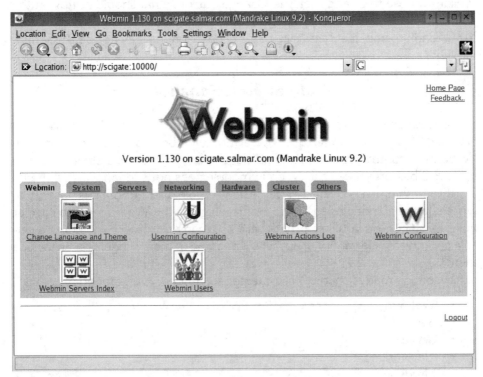

FIGURE 11-1   The friendly and simple face of Webmin.

Webmin's many functions are presented in a handful of tabbed categories. Each of the tabbed categories may include additional submenus or represent a specific service. I'll get to some of those in a second, but first I will show you one thing in particular. That's the theming section, where you can change Webmin's default style. It may seem like a strange place to start, but depending on how Webmin was installed on your system, you may be looking at something altogether different than what I am showing you here.

Click on Webmin Configuration, then choose Webmin Themes. You can also get to that module directly by using the URL

```
http://your_server:10000/webmin/edit_themes.cgi
```

and substituting your own server's name for *your_server*. The various themes are listed in a drop-down box to the right of the Current Theme label. In that list, you'll find the tabbed style listed as "Old Webmin theme" or something similar. Choose that, and click the Change button. That should put us on the same page. If you're happy digging or you absolutely have to have the MSC.Linux theme, just be aware that my descriptions may not be the same.

Modular Functionality

Administration tools provided in Webmin are referred to as *modules* or *Webmin modules*. You should know that there may well be modules included with Webmin to control processes and packages that may not be installed on your system. Their presence as a Webmin module does not suddenly install them.

If something isn't covered in the basic Webmin distribution, it is possible to write additional modules to suit tasks. If you go to the Webmin home page at www.webmin.com, you'll see that there are many third-party modules available covering a wide variety of applications. Some of these modules even include themes.

Webmin's many functions are categorized under seven tabbed headings:

- Webmin
- System
- Servers
- Networking
- Hardware
- Cluster
- Others

The Webmin tab is obviously concerned with things related to Webmin, such as creating additional Webmin users (covered in the next section), checking logs of Webmin events, and various Webmin configuration options.

Without listing everything that's useful in Webmin (and there is a lot), let me give you a quick tab-by-tab overview of some of the things related to the content of this book:

- **System:** Backup system, CD backup, Disks and Network File systems, LDAP Users and Groups, Running Processes, Schedule Cron Jobs, Software Packages, System Logs, Users and Groups
- **Servers:** Apache Webserver, BIND DNS Server, DHCP Server, Jabber IM Server, OpenLDAP Server, Postfix Configuration, Samba Windows File Sharing
- **Networking:** Extended Internet Services, Linux Firewall, NFS Exports, Network Configuration, Network Utilities, Shorewall Firewall
- **Hardware:** CD Burner, Partitions on Local Disks, Printer Administration, System Time
- **Others:** Command shell, SSH Login, System and Server Status, VNC Client

Explore. Get a feel for the interface. I'll revisit Webmin as an alternative to some of the servers I'll be showing you later in the book. Before leaving Webmin for now, take a look at a couple of powerful features that you will almost assuredly want to use.

Creating Webmin Users

Way back at the beginning of this chapter, I mentioned that you could unload some of your administration work to another user. Suppose you want someone to take care of the printers. From the master Webmin tab, select Webmin Users, or head straight to this URL:

```
http://your_system:10000/acl/index.cgi
```

When the page comes up, you'll see the root or admin user listed with all of the various modules assigned to it. Click on the link that says Create a New Webmin User. The username referred to on the next page does not have to be an existing username. You may choose anything you like. If you do choose an existing Linux username, you may then assign a specific Webmin password or select UNIX Authentication to keep the same password.

Below that, you can select an alternate language or a theme specifically for that user. In some cases, you may want to limit that user to access from their workstation only. Specify an IP address or a range if that is the case. The last item on this page is the list of modules you want to allow this new user to administer. To select a particular function, click the check box associated with that module (Figure 11-2). Yes, there are a lot of them!

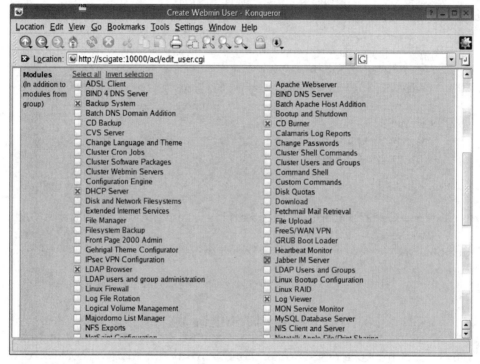

FIGURE 11-2   Creating a Webmin user and allocating module access.

 Quick Tip Be aware as you do this that certain functions (such as allowing password changes) can give the Webmin user the tools necessary to remove all of these constraints.

When you are happy with all of your choices, click Save and you can start forgetting about administering those printers.

Upgrading Webmin

It's actually very easy to keep up to date with the latest version of Webmin, and it doesn't require a reinstall at every turn. Here's what you do. .

Log in to Webmin as you normally would with your admin username and password. From the Webmin tab, click on Webmin Configration. When the next page loads, select Upgrade Webmin. If you would rather type than click, you can just jump to the upgrade module on your server like this:

```
http://your_server:10000/webmin/edit_upgrade.cgi
```

You'll see several options on the page, including upgrading from a local file, server, or another remote machine where you know the packages exist. The default, and probably best choice, is to download from www.webmin.com itself. Make sure that the Check GnuPG Signature on Package radio button is checked on before clicking Upgrade Webmin.

In between major updates to Webmin, individual modules may be updated. Scroll a little further down the page, and you'll see a couple of interesting options. One is to update the modules. The other, more interesting one (Figure 11-3) is to set an update schedule so that Webmin will go out on a regular basis, check for updates, and install them as necessary.

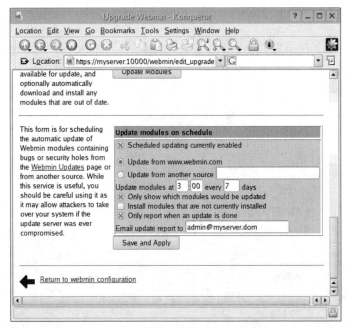

FIGURE 11-3   Configuring Webmin for scheduled upgrades.

Moving On

With the remaining administration chapters in this book, I'm going to continue showing you both graphical and command-line ways to achieve various tasks, but I'll mention Webmin as well. Just look to the end of the chapter, and I'll point you to the right place.

Resources

Webmin Home Page

www.webmin.com

chapter
12
Users and Groups

Linux is a multiuser operating system, meaning that one or more users can work on it at the same time. Each user is referenced by a user name. Each user name has a user ID or UID associated with it and one or more groups. Like user names, group names are also represented by a numeric identifier, this time called a group ID or GID. A user's UID is as unique as a group's GID.

When it comes to your files and directories, security on a Linux system is defined by means of permissions, which directly relate to the user ID. Users are either administrative users or regular users. The chief administrative user is called root. A user's ID is used to decide which commands can be executed and which files can be read from or written to.

Each user ID also has a password associated with it. That password can and should be changed on a regular basis.

When Not to Use the root User

The short answer here is that you should never use the root user unless you absolutely have to. The danger lies in the fact that the root user is virtually omnipotent on the system. A mistake can have serious implications that can wipe out your entire system. Unless you absolutely have to, it is best to work as a nonadmin user. There are other reasons as well.

The first is security. Because the root user has access to everything, it makes sense that only those that really need to have access are given the root password. The fewer people that have access to root, the better. Let me give you a few good reasons for jealously guarding root access:

- It makes maintaining security easier.
- It decreases the risk of dangerous code.
- Errors usually do not have global implications.

Yes, it is still possible for a nonroot user to do great damage to a system, but the risk is much, much smaller.

Managing Users

Never manually edit the password file. I'm not saying you can't, simply that you probably shouldn't. You'll notice I told you that even before telling you about the password file which, by the way, is /etc/passwd. On systems running with shadow passwords, there is one other file to worry about: /etc/shadow.

My reason for introducing this section with a warning is simple. I have seen far too many instances of people getting locked out of their system because of a botched modification to the password file. Suddenly, there is no user access and no root access.

 Quick Tip You should know that the vipw command lets you edit the password file and that vigr is its groups file counterpart, but I would still recommend against using these. The reason for those commands isn't to prevent dangerous typos, but to allow for proper locking of the file when updating.

Your Linux system has all of the tools you need to add and maintain users without having to resort to manually editing your password file. That said, take a look at this file:

```
root:x:0:0:root:/root:/bin/bash
bin:x:1:1:bin:/bin:
daemon:x:2:2:daemon:/sbin:
adm:x:3:4:adm:/var/adm:
lp:x:4:7:lp:/var/spool/lpd:
sync:x:5:0:sync:/sbin:/bin/sync
shutdown:x:6:0:shutdown:/sbin:/sbin/shutdown
halt:x:7:0:halt:/sbin:/sbin/halt
mail:x:8:12:mail:/var/spool/mail:
news:x:9:13:news:/var/spool/news:
```

The format of this file is actually pretty simple. Each field in the password file is delimited by a colon. First comes the username, then the password field (more on that shortly), followed by a numeric user ID, a group ID, some kind of a comment, a home directory, and a default shell or login program.

The first thing to remember is that all of this information is case-sensitive. This does make a difference, particularly when you are trying to log into the system. When you choose a username, make sure that it is no more than eight characters long. These characters can be letters or numbers and can be mixed in any way.

Note The eight-character limit is one of those truths in transition. On modern releases, you can create a username that is more than eight characters. The question then becomes one of whether an application that references the username will truncate it to eight characters or use the entire field.

I'll discuss the password field in more detail later on. For now, let's move immediately to the user ID (UID) and group ID (GID) fields. The UID is a unique numerical identification. It is used in setting and modifying security information on files and directories. The same goes for the GID, except that this number does not need to be unique. That's because it is useful to be able to set permissions based on an effective group. For instance, say you have an accounting application and you want all of the users in the accounting department to have access to it. GIDs make it easy to offer those permissions.

Notice the root user. Its UID and GID are both 0. GID 0 is also shared by the users sync, shutdown, and halt because they all share root's group permissions.

Next is the comment field. This is pretty much what it sounds like. You can enter comments relating to the identity or purpose of a user on your system. Normally, this means entering the user's full name so that he or she can be identified with commands such as `finger`. For instance, take a look at the `/etc/passwd` entry for natika, one of the users on my system.

```
natika:x:504:504:Natika the Cat:/home/natika:/bin/bash
```

Her command field contains the phrase "Natika the Cat," which is appropriate because she just happens to be my cat. If I type who to find out who is logged into the system, I get the following:

```
# who
natika    pts/1    Dec  7 14:30
```

That only tells me so much. If I then use the `finger` command, I get a lot more information, including natika's plans.

```
# finger natika
Login: natika                         Name: Natika the Cat
Directory: /home/natika               Shell: /bin/bash
On since Sun Dec  7 14:30 (EST) on pts/1 from localhost.localdomain
    5 minutes 7 seconds idle
No mail.
Plan:
To get my own Natika-only Web site and rule the cat world.
```

Note By the way, the plan that you see listed is normally blank. This is a holdover from the early days of UNIX. The idea was literally to identify what your plans were or what you were working on. Nobody really does that anymore. Most people use their `.plan` file, if they use it at all, for silly comments like natika's.

Let's get back to the password file. The next field is the home directory. When a user logs in to the system, they are placed here (in an electronic, virtual sort of way). This directory contains personal login and user-specific information. For instance, X window client files would be here as would the personal login script, the `.bash_profile`.

Finally, there is the shell itself. You can change your default login shell if you want, but the only valid shells are listed in another system file called /etc/shells. Here are the contents of /etc/shells on my system:

```
/bin/bash
/bin/sh
/bin/ash
/bin/bsh
/bin/bash2
/bin/tcsh
/bin/csh
```

It's time for me to let you off the hook and finally talk about the password field itself. You may have noticed that in my example, the only thing in the password field was a single letter, x. That's because I am using the *shadow password file* (/etc/shadow) for a higher level of security. Traditionally, the password entry was visible in the /etc/passwd file. Sadly, that makes it sound like finding out someone's password was as simple as looking at the entry in the password file, and that is not true.

First, take a fresh look at the password file from earlier. For simplicity's sake, I'll stick with the root password.

```
root:x:0:0:root:/root:/bin/bash
```

The password entry is a rather cryptic x. Here is the root entry from a classic password file:

```
root:2IsjW45pb4L56:0:0:root:/root:/bin/bash
```

As you can see, it is far from easy to guess that 2IsjW45pb4L56 might translate into the word "calculus." The problem is that the encryption algorithm used for creating passwords is well-known and it is possible through brute force methods and lots of CPU cycles to crack passwords in the password file, specifically if I have been foolish enough to use a word out of the dictionary. In fact, there are a variety of popular tools available for cracking passwords with names, such as crack and "John The Ripper," and all are available for free download. I'll cover rules for choosing good passwords later in this chapter.

The shadow password file makes it harder for users to use a password-cracking utility, because, unlike the /etc/passwd file, which is readable by all users, the shadow password file is readable only by root.(The cracker would need privileged access, at which point you have bigger problems on your hands.) The format of the file is a little different as well and includes somewhat more flexibility in how users can be configured. Have a look at the shadow password file's layout:

```
root:$1$J.tGxREA$nHqbRUyid9.hf4I6UtRBs0:11242:0:99999:7:-1:-
1:134540356
```

As in the regular password file, the fields are delimited by colons. There are nine fields in total. Starting with the user name, the shadow password file stores the password itself and then gets into a series of numbers that deal with password expiration.

The first of these (Field 3) is the number of days (starting from January 1, 1970) since the last password change, the minimum number of days before a user is allowed to change their password, and the number of days before the password must be changed. The warnings come next. Field 6 is the number of days before a user starts getting warned about changing his or her password. Field 7 represents the grace period. Here's another way of looking at this: How many days are you willing to allow a user to use the system after the user's password has expired before you disable that user's account? This brings us to Field 8, which is a representation (in days since January 1, 1970) that the account has been disabled. Finally, there is Field 9, which is reserved. Just don't worry about it.

If an entry contains -1 (as in Fields 7 and 8 in my example), it essentially means never, as in the user never gets warnings and the account is never disabled.

Before I get into how to add, modify, or remove users (delete just sounds so final), I should talk about the /etc/group file. Every user belongs to at least one group. If you use the quick and dirty method of adding a user that I'll cover next, you wind up with a GID that is equivalent to the UID.

The importance of groups is simple. There are times when you want a specific group of people to share access and rights to one or more files or applications. Rather than having to create access rights for each and every user, you can say that the accounting application is available to all the accounting folk. (Imagine that!)

I should tell you that I am not quite as worried about someone editing the group file manually. The potential for damage is not as great as with the /etc/passwd file. Take a look at the format of a sample group file:

```
root:x:0:root
bin:x:1:root,bin,daemon
daemon:x:2:root,bin,daemon
sys:x:3:root,bin,adm
adm:x:4:root,adm,daemon
users:x:100:marcel,natika,sally
```

Colons separate the fields, as they did with the passwd and shadow files. The first field is the group name. This is followed by a password field and then the unique group ID. Finally, you see a comma-delimited list of user names that are members of this group. For instance, if you have a group called "finance" and you want users albert, isaac, and marie to be part of that group, use this entry:

```
finance:x:540:albert,isaac,marie
```

Managing Groups

Dealing with group management is somewhat simpler than dealing with users (at least in the OS world), so let's tackle that first. There is another reason. Strange as it might sound, in some ways there is logic to the idea that groups precede users. Although it is true that a group without users isn't much of a group, people usually define a group before adding users to it. So it is in this world of bits and bytes.

Adding Groups

Adding a group is a simple procedure. The command is groupadd followed by a group name.

```
[root@testsys /root]# groupadd finance
```

You can also specify a group ID by using the -g flag. By default, the system assigns the next nonadmin group ID in line. Allowing this default is probably the best idea unless you are trying to clone group information from another system.

Modifying Groups

Generally speaking, the reason for modifying groups involves a name change. Realistically, changing the group ID causes you headaches, because it means changing the GID on every file to which this group originally had access. It is possible, however, that you might want to change the finance group, for example, to read accounts instead. Here's the command:

```
[root@testsys /root]# groupmod -n accounts finance
```

The -n flag, by the way, is used to refer to the new **group**.

Removing Groups

Group removal is something that too often gets forgotten in the world of managing accounts, whether they are group or user accounts. People leave a company and names change. Be vigilant. If the account or group is no longer needed, get rid of it.

To remove a group, use the groupdel command:

```
[root@testsys /root]# groupdel xpilots
```

Adding Users

The simplest possible way to add a user is to use the adduser command or useradd. If you do an ls -l, you'll notice that adduser is just a symbolic link to useradd. In its most basic incarnation, the format is:

```
useradd  username
```

The system assigns the next available UID and equivalent GID, creates a basic home directory under /home, and assigns a default shell. What defines those defaults is a file called /etc/default/useradd. Although you need to be root to look at it or modify it, here's an example:

```
# useradd defaults file
GROUP=100
HOME=/home
INACTIVE=-1
EXPIRE=
SHELL=/bin/bash
SKEL=/etc/skel
```

As you can see, the default directory prefix for a user's home directory is /home. The default shell is /bin/bash, and what shows up in the user's new home directory is a copy of what is found in /etc/skel. That's a skeleton directory. Using it as a model, useradd decides what to create for the new user.

Several other flags enable you to further customize the account creation process. The more complex form of the useradd command is summed up in this way:

```
usage: useradd [-u uid [-o]] [-g group] [-G group,...]
               [-d home] [-s shell] [-c comment] [-m [-k template]]
               [-f inactive] [-e expire ] [-p passwd] [-n] [-r] name
```

Should you decide that the default user ID is not for you, you can specify it with the -u flag. Although I am going to tell you about it, I'd like you to forget about the -o flag. It enables you to override the system's requirement that all UIDs be unique. If you decide (and you shouldn't) to use an existing UID when you create a user, make sure you also add the -o flag.

Next is the -g flag, which enables you to define the group. You might have noticed that there is a -G option as well. This is an optional, comma-separated list of other groups to which the user belongs. For example, a user might belong to the staff group as well as the finance group.

Note that when you create a user with a default group, that name becomes the GID field in /etc/passwd. On the other hand, the optional group list specified by -G adds that username to the /etc/group file. For instance, I added a group called geeks on my system. With three of the users I created, I used a -G geeks option to specify that they were also part of the geeks group. This is what the geeks group entry looks like in /etc/group:

```
geeks:x:511:mgagne,natika,guitux
```

About Home Directories

Every account you create has a home directory by default. In addition, several files are copied into it, namely those found in the SKEL directory (usually /etc/skel). This is a good thing to remember, because this is where you add files or configuration information that you want to appear in every new user's directory or profile.

Should you want to use another account as the model, or skeleton, for the creation of a new account, use the -k flag. Note that you also need to add the -m flag in this case. Let's say that you want to create a user called aeinstein, but you want him to have the same files and configurations that exist in natika's home directory. This is what you should do:

```
[root@testsys /root]# useradd -m -k /home/natika aeinstein
```

If you look in Mr. Einstein's home directory now, his files are the same as in natika's, but the permissions and ownerships are his.

Group Participation

The -g option is your opportunity to define which group a user belongs to. By default, if you specify nothing, a group is created to match the user's UID. For an environment where users access a database application to which they all have permission and must modify the information, allowing for some kind of group identification is crucial. If you need to specify an additional group or groups, use the -G option.

```
useradd -g staff -G finance,research aeinstein
```

Here, Mr. Einstein's account is created with an initial group of staff. He is also added to the groups finance and (of course) research.

Email-Only Accounts

If you are creating an account that needs to access email only and never needs to log into a shell session, the solution is to simply not give the account a shell. You do this by assigning a shell of /bin/false when creating the account.

```
useradd -g popusers -s /bin/false aeinstein
```

The command I just suggested as the user's shell, /bin/false, is one of those wonderful little commands that is a stroke of brilliance. Rather than using my own words here, allow me to quote the man page on false.

```
FALSE(1)                    FSF                    FALSE(1)
NAME
        false - do nothing, unsuccessfully
```

Yet More User-Creation Controls

Users are the *raison d'être* of a multiuser system. Consequently, the world of user-creation defaults offers another interesting file called /etc/login.defs, which controls other, more interesting things. Here's a small sample from that file:

```
PASS_MAX_DAYS   99999
PASS_MIN_DAYS   0
PASS_MIN_LEN    5
PASS_WARN_AGE   7
#
```

```
# Min/max values for automatic uid selection in useradd
#
UID_MIN                 500
UID_MAX                 60000
#
# Min/max values for automatic gid selection in groupadd
#
GID_MIN                 500
GID_MAX                 60000
```

This is quite interesting. You can set a system-wide default wherein users must change their passwords every 30 days or however often your office security policy demands. The default is 99,999 days, which translates to roughly 274 years. You can pretty much call that never. The file is well-documented, so have a look at it.

Modifying a User Account

The first example I gave you for adding a user was the simple useradd username, which is fine, except that it gives you very little control over account creation unless you go ahead and pass the appropriate information at that time. Let's pretend that you are feeling lazy or you are in a hurry—a classic sysadmin trap—and, as a result, you do not set up any additional information, such as the user's full name. How do you make changes?

With the usermod command, that's how.

```
usage: usermod [-u uid [-o]] [-g group] [-G group,...]
               [-d home [-m]] [-s shell] [-c comment] [-l new_name]
               [-f inactive] [-e expire ] [-p passwd] [-L|-U] name
```

In some ways, usermod looks quite similar to the useradd command. To change a user's default shell from /bin/bash to /bin/ash, use this command:

```
usermod -s /bin/ash natika
```

If all you want to do is change the name field, the so-called comment field, there is another command that you can use: chfn, which actually means change finger information, as in the finger command. Here's how it works:

```
[root@testsys /root]# chfn -f "Tux the Penguin" guitux
Changing finger information for guitux.
Finger information changed.
```

Deleting a User Account

Allow me a moment to say something blitheringly obvious, even if it does sound like I am repeating myself. If a user leaves, you should remove that user's login account, or username if you prefer. (You should also, as part of your regular schedule, run a check on dormant accounts, but I'll get to that shortly.) Removing a user is easy. That's why you should be careful. The command that does the job is called userdel, and it has one optional flag: -r.

```
userdel [-r] user_name
```

The -r flag, which is optional, tells userdel to not only remove the user, but also the user's entire home directory. If you omit the flag, you have to manually clean up the directory yourself. Making this decision is where you should be exceptionally careful. Have you checked the user's home directory to make sure it doesn't contain information you might need later? Take a moment and have a look around as root. A good practice might be to do a backup of that account (and maybe two) and file it semi-permanently, until such a time as you are absolutely sure there is nothing useful in that account.

The bottom line, as always, is to use your good judgment.

Note If the user has received any mail, even from the system, a mailbox with his or her username may be in the /var/spool/mail directory. You should remember that, as well, when removing the user. You might also consider changing the ownership of the user's files to something such as root so that only the administrator account has access.

Checking the Password File

As if you didn't already have enough things to do, let me give you yet another job. On a regular basis, you should run a report to identify accounts or logins that have gone dormant. (This is a nice way of saying accounts for people who are gone and who are not coming back anytime soon.)

As you might recall, the finger command will display the information relating to the last time an account was used. Try typing this command to list each user ID and to check the last login time:

```
finger `sort /etc/passwd | cut -f1 -d":"` | grep -i log | more
```

Note that the single quotes just before the `sort` command and just before the pipe symbol are actually *back quotes* or *back ticks*. The back quote is usually found with the tilde (~) just under the <Esc> key on a keyboard.

The output of this command looks something like:

```
Login: aeinstein                    Name: A. Einstein
Never logged in.
Login: guitux                       Name: Tux the Penguin
Last login Mon Jan  8 14:54 (EST) on tty2
Login: halt                         Name: halt
Never logged in.
Login: lp                           Name: lp
Never logged in.
Login: mail                         Name: mail
Never logged in.
Login: mgagne                       Name: Marcel Gagne
Last login Wed Mar  7 17:29 (EST) on 1 from website
Login: named                        Name: Named
Never logged in.
Login: natika                       Name: Natika the Cat
```

Warning You must use your good judgment, which is an absolute requirement for system administration, on this one. Some of these accounts—`sync` and `lp`, for instance—are system accounts. It only makes sense that no one will have ever logged in through them. On the other hand, Mr. Einstein (at the top of the list) has never logged in either, and his is certainly not an admin login. It could be that this is a new account (and it is) or that you created an account for a user and it was never used. In the latter case, you should probably get rid of that account.

I used that example to give you a feel for your command-line prowess. I should tell you, however, that there is a cleaner way to do this. Your Linux system comes with a handy little command called lastlog that does just this sort of thing.

```
[root@scigate /root]# lastlog | more
Username    Port   From           Latest
root        tty1                  Wed Mar  7 17:18:40 -0500 2001
bin                               **Never logged in**
daemon                            **Never logged in**
adm                               **Never logged in**
lp                                **Never logged in**
sync                              **Never logged in**
shutdown                          **Never logged in**
mgagne      1      scigate        Wed Mar  7 17:29:55 -0500 2001
postgres                          **Never logged in**
www                               **Never logged in**
natika      8      localhost.locald Thu Dec  7 14:30:15 -0500 2000
guitux      tty2                  Mon Jan  8 14:54:55 -0500 2001
```

Note You can't edit or modify this file, but the lastlog command information comes from the file /var/log/lastlog.

Here is another thing you should do: Every once in a while, run the command pwck. By default, it walks through your /etc/passwd and /etc/shadow files and does some basic integrity checks, such as making sure that the right number of fields is present and that each name is uniquely identified.

```
# pwck
```

For the group file, the companion command is grpck.

```
# grpck
```

KUser

As with the command-line tools, adding users under KDE requires that you do so as root. When you launch the KDE User Manager (command name kuser), you are asked for the root password. When the program starts, a window appears (Figure 12-1) with two tabs, one for Users and the other for Groups.

To add an additional user, click User on the menu bar, and select Add. (You can also click the Add User icon below the menu bar.) A new window appears asking you to enter the name of the new user. This username should be in lower case with a minimum of five and a maximum of eight characters.

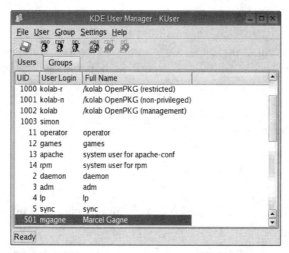

FIGURE 12-1   KUser, the KDE user and group manager.

When you press <Enter>, the User Properties dialog opens (Figure 12-2).
You don't really need to add anything new here, but there are fields provided
to further identify the person for whom you are creating the login. For instance,
you can choose to enter his or her full name, office location, or home address.

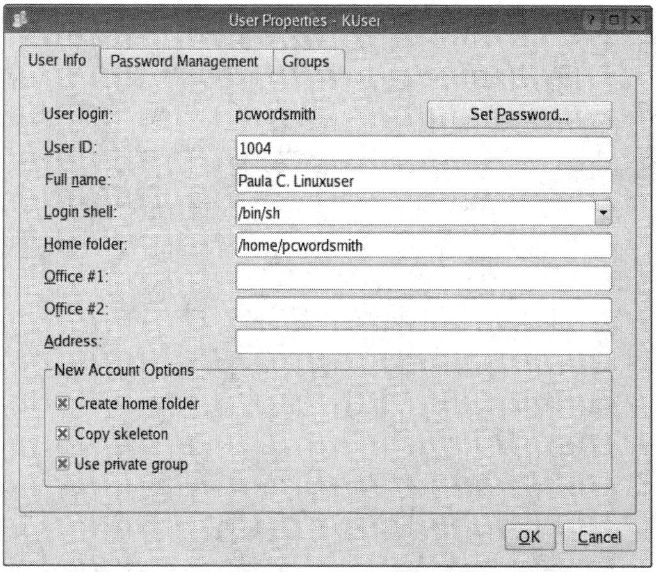

FIGURE 12-2   Changing user properties with KUser.

The most important item on this window is the Set Password button. Click that, and you are asked to enter a password (Figure 12-3). In fact, you are asked to enter it twice, once for verification. Note that when you do enter the password, you don't actually see it, but rather stars echo your keystrokes. When you are done, click OK.

FIGURE 12-3   *Password changes must be verified.*

This takes you back to the User Properties screen, where you can simply click OK to finish. Before you do that, however, take a look at some of the other settings you can apply to a user. Click on the Password Management tab, and you'll see a number of settings associated with password aging (Figure 12-4). For added security, you may wish to have passwords expire regularly. It is also possible that you want to provide a temporary employee with a username and password, but that you want that account to automatically expire after a few days.

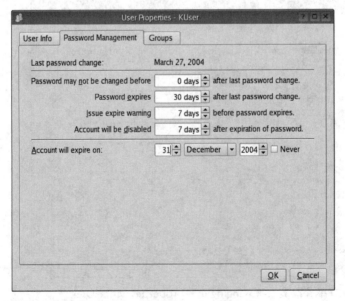

FIGURE 12-4   *Setting password aging.*

Finally, you have the Groups tab. Here, you can specify the primary group associated with a particular user as well as any additional groups they might belong to—perhaps marketing needs to have access to sales' files, for example. When it's all done, click OK to close the New User dialog and return to the main KUser screen. To save your changes, click File on the menu bar and select Save. Alternatively, you can click the diskette icon just below the menu bar.

Adding groups is even easier. Click Group on the menu bar and select Add, or just click the appropriate icon. A small dialog box appears with an auto-matically selected group number. Add your new group name, and click OK (Figure 12-5).

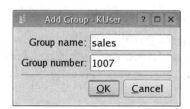

FIGURE 12-5   Adding a group is very easy.

Finally, to change an existing user or group, simply double-click on that user or group in the KUser list.

Other User Adminstration Tools

In this chapter, we looked at user and group administration both from the com-mand line and through KDE's KUser tool. Aside from these methods, many other distributions offer some friendly methods of getting the same job done. Mandrake, for instance, has userdrake, part of the Mandrake control center suite of tools (drakconf). SUSE has its famous YaST2 do-it-all administration tool. You get the idea.

For a more universal option and for those times when you aren't sitting at a Linux desktop, there's always Webmin, that wonder of browser-based admin-istration. To get to the Users and Groups screen, look under the System tab or head straight for this URL (on your own server, of course):

```
http://your_server:10000/useradmin/index.cgi
```

What Next?

For those of you administering your own systems at home or in a small office, I'll leave it there. For others who have to administer their company's system and its however many users, it's time to educate those users. Set a time and date and enforce good passwords as of that date. At first they'll hate you for it, but that's part of your job as IS—to be hated. As we move increasingly (and hopefully) to open and networked systems, we must become increasingly conscious of security on our systems. Passwords are the first level of protection and, properly implemented, still one of the best.

I Logged In from Where?

Have a look at what happens when I log into a machine. Everything looks normal. I have a login name, and a request for my password. I enter the password and voila, I am in. But hold on—read that little one-line message that appears after I enter the password:

```
login: mgagne
Password:
Last login: Thu Jan  8 16:00:39 from energize
```

What the heck is energize? Energize is the host name of the computer from which I last logged in apparently, except I don't have a system called energize. Furthermore, I don't know anyone with that system, and I always log in from the same place. The only explanation is that somebody from a system called energize logged into the server with my login name and password.

This is just a hypothetical situation, but it does illustrate one other habit that you should consider training your users to adopt. If they are logging in from the same PC day in and day out, that message should never change. If they do not recognize the host name in the last login message, they should make it a policy to alert you.

Another command you may want to run from time to time is `last`. Pipe the output of this command to `more` (or `less`), and you get a list of all the recent logins to your system, including system boots.

```
# last | more
mgagne   vc/1                  Fri Mar 12 21:18 - 09:46 (6+12:28)
reboot   system boot 2.6.3-4mdk Fri Mar 12 21:18         (10+19:22)
francois vc/2                  Fri Mar 12 19:32 - 20:14   (00:41)
root     vc/2                  Fri Mar 12 19:32 - 19:32   (00:00)
```

Finally, check the `lastlog` command. This isn't the same thing as `last` in that it only shows the last login associated with each particular user name, including a number of system user names that will never (and should never) log in. Here's a small sample from one of my test systems:

```
rpcuser                              **Never logged in**
sshd                                 **Never logged in**
ftp                                  **Never logged in**
postgres                             **Never logged in**
mgagne             vc/1              Wed Mar 24 14:59:55 -0500 2004
francois           vc/2              Fri Mar 12 19:32:58 -0500 2004
inewton                              **Never logged in**
natika             pts/3   wsltsp1   Thu Mar 11 20:44:57 -0500 2004
```

Security isn't just the domain of the system administrator. After all, you've got plenty on your plate. Any help is appreciated. You need to get the users involved. Let them know that system security is their business as well as yours.

13

Backup and Restore

You can get almost anyone you ask to agree that backups are a good idea. You can also pretty much guarantee that many people don't back up as often as they should. While I won't name names, I've known a number of people over the years who, despite touting the benefits of regular backups, treat their important data as shown on the next page.

- Backups are done "occasionally" or "very occasionally."
- Backups are not verified. ("They must be okay, right?")
- Backups are not labeled. ("What did I back up and when?")
- A backup is put on a single floppy diskette that is used over and over.
- A backup is put on a single tape that is used over and over.
- Backups are saved to another directory on the same disk.

The single disk entry in that list is a true story. The user in question had only a single floppy disk for all of his important documents, because he was worried about the hard disk crashing! (Yes, the floppy diskette eventually failed, and all of the data was lost.) Because there is no point in boring you with a list that goes on and on, I'll stop for now. Suffice it to say that when the system crashes and data has to be recovered, it's always important data.

So, what's the best way to protect that important data? In one word: backups.

Backup Everything? And to What?

Do you really need to back up everything? There's absolutely no doubt that this is the best-case scenario. If you find yourself missing a file, any file, you can get back to it. On the other hand, there's an awful lot of stuff on that disk that never changes. Installing a default Linux system from scratch takes very little time and that includes most programs. Almost all of the important system configuration files are to be found under the /etc directory, and you can compress that directory to a single, relatively small file. Add all of your users' data, and that backup can be a monstrous beast requiring several tapes, CDs, DVDs, or whatever media you happen to choose.

Floppy diskettes, that backup medium of old, are still around (but a lot less floppy), perhaps because we still have lots of disks floating around. The amount you can store on them is severely limited. These days, you can put the equivalent of a hundred or more disks on a USB key that you can put in your pocket along with your keys. Rewritable CD-ROMs are another alternative, raising the bar to 700 megabytes of storage. DVDs increase that capacity even further. Given that CD and DVD writers are also extremely inexpensive now, they look particularly attractive as backup media.

Large corporate systems can have several gigabytes of data or more, however, and even a DVD writer reaches its limits quickly under those circumstances. Ideally, every system should have some kind of large storage capacity backup, such as a tape drive. That's right. Whatever you may have heard, tape is alive and well. Network backups are possible (and many large-scale backup systems are built this way), but they add a layer of complexity, and tape sometimes still features in that picture. I will discuss some of these systems later in the chapter.

Basic Tools in Every Linux System

Your Linux distribution contains an incredible collection of tools for a variety of applications. The same is true for keeping your data safe. Without buying or downloading anything else, you can start getting into a healthy habit of regular backups.

The most popular commands out of the box are cpio and tar. Other command-line tools such as dd, dump, and afio are also available, although afio might not be included in all distributions. For simplicity and universality, tar and cpio are quite useful and powerful, and they are still tools I use on a regular basis on systems with large-capacity tape drives. These days, however, I am increasingly doing regular synchronization backups using rsync and CD-ROM backups. I'll discuss these options in a bit, but I'd like to start by telling you a little bit about those simple, always there, command-line tools, cpio and tar.

Using cpio

The main advantage of cpio over tar is that it does a somewhat better job of packing data on your backup medium, and it handles errors better as well, particularly when dealing with tape. There is one other advantage: When using tar, you tend to work in terms of short lists of directories or files. With cpio, you can largely customize the files that wind up in an archive. For instance, you can work from a list of files and pipe that list directly to cpio:

```
cpio -ov > /dev/st0 < /tmp/list_of_files
```

The -o option writes out an archive directed to /dev/st0 (the SCSI tape drive) and takes the list from a file called list_of_files. You can then go back and check the backup by reading the tape and checking the table of contents. This is done with the -t option:

```
cpio -ivt < /dev/st0
```

To extract a file from that archive, you need to know how it was stored (the path to the archive). The command is fairly simple. Say you want to restore a file called lost_file; use the command:

```
cpio -iv lost_file < /dev/st0
```

Working with tar

The next candidate for included backup tools is my old friend, `tar`. I confess that I probably use `tar` more than any other command. It's partly out of habit, because I have been tarring files for a number of years, and it's also partly because single-file archives are always delivered tarred and in some way compressed (as in `cool_new_software.tar.gz`).

Linux's `tar` isn't your plain old `tar`; it's GNU `tar`. This means it has some advantages over the regular `tar`, which makes it that much more interesting. For instance, with GNU `tar` it's possible to do compression on the fly—both standard `compress` compression and `gzip` compression. You can also specify multivolume backups. Here's an example:

```
tar -cvf /dev/fd0 /mydata
```

In this example, I am backing up the directory `/mydata` to a floppy. Yes, I know what I said about floppy disks, but every once in a while, nothing beats the convenience of using them. Unfortunately, as I mentioned earlier on, there's only so much space. What if your floppy is really too small for that amount of data, but you still want to use diskettes? No problem, assuming you don't need a huge number of floppies. Use the `-M` flag. When `tar` gets to the end of the first disk, it prompts you for the next volume in your multivolume backup.

```
tar -cvMf /dev/fd0 /mydata
```

You can't use compression on multivolumes—sorry—so to compress data, use the `-z` flag. For instance, if I want to archive `/mydata` and `gzip` it to my SCSI tape drive on the fly, I use this command:

```
tar -czvf /dev/st0 /etc
```

For a good, old-fashioned `zcat`-type of compression, as with the command `compress`, use a capital `Z` flag instead of the lowercase `z`. Another compression type is `bzip2`. In addition, you can have `tar` do `bzip2` compression on the fly. On most systems, you specify this with the `-j` option.

Quick Tip The `-p` option may well be the most important `tar` option of them all. This tells `tar` to preserve permissions and ownership information when doing restores. If you are using `tar` to back up system files, you definitely want to do this.

Backing Up Windows Workstations

Linux works nicely with a number of other computer systems, including Windows. With a few simple commands, Linux will happily safeguard data in those systems as well.

You probably have Samba installed already. If you don't, never fear. Chapter 18 is devoted to it entirely. For now, here's a quick Samba example. Pretend that you have a Windows PC called speedy on your network. The user has shared the C: drive with the name SPEEDY_C. I can mount that share on a Linux system running Samba like this:

```
smbmount //speedy/speedy_c /mnt/linux_mount_point
```

Then, I simply back it up to my tape drive like this:

```
cd /mnt/linux_mount_point
tar -cvf /dev/st0 .
```

I'm jumping ahead a little bit, but I just wanted to show you that it is possible to use Linux tools to do Windows backups. More on this later.

Everything works. So, what's wrong with that? Well, for one thing, straight tar isn't the greatest when it comes to error recovery. Although errors don't generally occur, this is a concern. I've seen systems backed up with tar for years with few problems or none at all, so while I urge caution, it's not all bad. You could use cpio, which has better error handling for read errors, but neither tar nor cpio is particularly quick if you want to restore something.

Plus, older versions of these commands, which still exist on some platforms, don't back up all files. Here's another minus: To find a file, you may have to travel the entire length of the tape searching for it. There is no index at the beginning, and if you don't remember the exact pathname, just finding the file can take quite some time.

The real plus with cpio and tar is this: Every Linux/UNIX under the sun (including Sun OS) has cpio and tar. This assures cross-compatibility, an important consideration.

Selecting a Backup Medium

On the question of medium, here's how I see things. Floppy diskettes are extremely convenient for storing small collections of files, but their capacity is very limited. CD-RW is reliable and access is reasonably quick, but the capacity (although much larger than a floppy diskette) is still limited. A 2GB Jaz drive is quite hot, but 2GB is pretty much it at the moment, and spare cartridges can be pricey. It's good for infrequent backups and data that doesn't change much, but there are limits. You could use a spare hard disk, but multiple archives of your data are a bit difficult with that scenario. It's very fast, though. Then there's tape.

Tapes themselves are relatively inexpensive. At this writing, I can buy a 12GB DDS tape for about $10. The number one advantage to tape, however, is capacity. There is no other medium, short of maybe another hard disk, that provides the backup capacity of today's tape drives, and certainly not at a comparable cost. It is now possible to get Linux-compatible tape drives that can back up an astounding 50GB on a single tape.

Large capacity makes for another great advantage: unattended backups. You can pop in a tape before you head out for the night, rather than sitting around watching files list to the screen. With a little ingenuity, you can verify a backup, capture a list of what has been backed up, and have the result mailed to you in the morning. For instance, take a look at the following hastily constructed script that (I am quite sure) could be a lot prettier.

```
#!/bin/bash
#
# 4mm.dataonly  -  This Short Backup Script backs up only my data
# Marcel Gagne
#
mkdir /usr/local/.Admin
# Set up some file pointers for short backup
sb_log=/usr/local/.Admin/dataonly.log
sb_errlog=/usr/local/.Admin/dataonly.err
# Do we capture the file list, or send it to dev null?
# file_log=/usr/local/.Admin/backup.log
file_log=/dev/null
admin_dir=/usr/local/.Admin
# Do a little cleanup.
mv $sb_log $sb_log.old
mv $sb_errlog $sb_errlog.old
# Prepare report headers
#
echo "=================================================" > $sb_errlog
echo "What follows is a report of errors encountered" >> $sb_errlog
echo "during the backup or its subsequent verify." >> $sb_errlog
echo "=================================================" >> $sb_errlog
```

```
echo "Data Only Nightly Backup. <'date'>" >> $sb_log
echo "======================================================" >>
$sb_log
#Get on with actual backup
#
echo "** Moving to data directory..." >> $sb_log
cd /root
echo "***Nightly Backup Starting : `date`..."  >> $sb_log
echo "Backup errors ..." >>$sb_errlog
tar -cvf /dev/st0 . 2>>$sb_errlog
# Verify Backup
# start by rewinding the tape
mt -f /dev/st0 rewind
echo "****Verifying the Backup : `date` *** " >> $sb_log
echo "Restore and verify errors . . ." >>$sb_errlog
tar -vtf /dev/st0 2>>$sb_errlog
echo "*****Nightly Backup Completed : `date`..." >> $sb_log
# Report on this, will you?
cat $sb_errlog >> $sb_log
mail -s "Dataonly backup status report" root < $sb_log
```

When I come in the next morning, my backup has completed and I have an email message telling me when it started and how long it took. If the tape generated messages to STDERR (standard error), I'll see it in that message.

Another thing I toss in there is an option to list the files on backup and restore. Warning: This can chew up a lot of disk space, which is why my file_log has the option of going to either a file or to /dev/null. Because my 4mm DAT can back up 4GB to 8GB, I can have this happen every night with a cron job (see Appendix B, "Scripting and Automation") and not worry about it. All I have to do is remember to put the tape in. Here's a cron entry for a backup that runs at 11:00 PM every night, Monday to Friday:

```
0 23 * * 1-5 /usr/local/.Admin/4mm.dataonly
```

K3b for a Friendlier Burn

One of the friendliest tools for creating and copying audio and data CDs is called *K3b*. You may have K3b available on your system, but if it isn't, simply visit www.k3b.org. Both the source code (it is GPL-ed, after all) and precompiled binaries are available. The program name (should you wish to run it from the shell or via the <Alt+F2> launcher) is k3b.

When you fire up K3b for the first time, you may get a little warning message alerting you to this fact and advising that you should consider running K3bSetup2 (program name `k3bsetup`). Click Yes here to start the setup program automatically. Because, as you might expect, `k3bsetup` requires root permission, you will be asked for the password before continuing.

The K3b setup program (Figure 13-1) is essentially an assistant that lets you assign a CD burning group, identify your hardware (specifically CD/DVD readers and writers), and locate the various programs it will need to do its job (`cdrdao`, `cdrecord`, and so on). Quite frankly, you probably won't have to do anything here. However, if your CD writer isn't automatically selected, you can click the Add button and insert a path to the device. The programs are listed in the bottom half of the K3bSetup dialog under the Found Programs tab. If some programs aren't automatically located, odds are that the search path isn't properly identified. In that case, click the Search Path tab and add the new program directory. When you are happy with your settings, click OK.

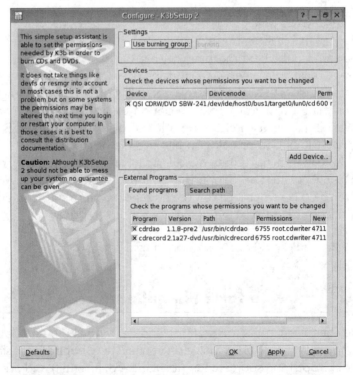

FIGURE 13-1   The K3b initial setup screen.

Getting Familiar with K3b

K3b's interface is friendly and very easy to use. It is broken up into three main windows, with two top frames and one larger frame at the bottom. The top-left frame is your file navigator, showing your directories in the familiar Konqueror-like tree format. Just click the plus sign to open a directory or the minus sign to collapse it. The top-right frame displays the contents of whatever folder you have selected on the left side. You can resize each of these windows to suit you. Just click on the separator (or line) between each, and drag it up or down or left to right.

Creating a CD of any kind in K3b is done with *projects*, and that is where the bottom window comes into play. For starters, that window displays a few quick access projects. They are New Audio CD Project, New Data CD Project, New Data DVD Project, and Copy CD. These are just the most common options. Click File on the menu bar, and select New Project to see a number of other choices (Figure 13-2).

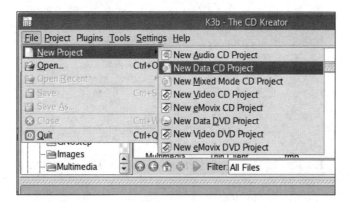

FIGURE 13-2   Selecting a data project for backup.

Because this chapter is about backing up data, I'll let you explore ripping and burning song collections on your own.

In the following example, I'm going to work with CD-RWs, or rewriteable CDs, because you can use them over and over again. Before you reuse your CD-RW, be sure to blank it first. Pop the disc into your CD rewriter, click Tools on the menu bar. Then, under the CD submenu, select Erase CD-RW.

A window appears (Figure 13-3), showing you some options for blanking the CD-RW. From there, you can select which CD writer you wish to use (if you have more than one), the speed at which you want to perform the operation, and whether you want a fast blank or a complete erase. When you are happy with your choice, click the Start button in top-right corner of the window. Just below all of this is an Output window, which displays the progress of blanking. After your successful completion message, click Close to banish the window.

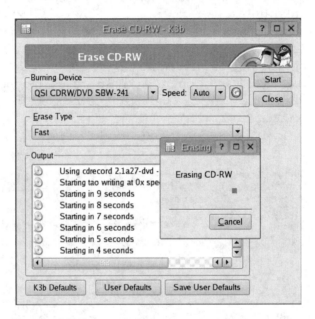

FIGURE 13-3   Prior to the backup, blank the CD-RW.

Now you are ready to back up your data. Start a new data project. A tab with a sequentially-generated name appears in the bottom window, which is now divided in two (Figure 13-4). The left side includes a small icon representing a CD with the current project name next to it. The right side houses a blank list with headings for file Name, Type, Size, Local path, and Link.

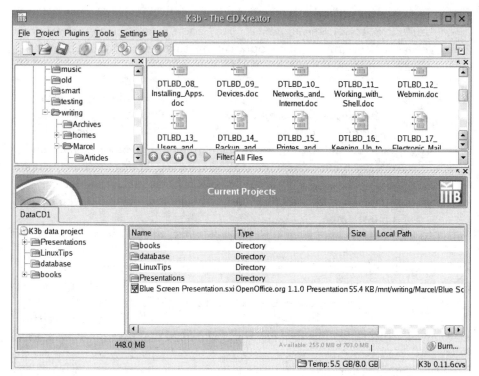

FIGURE 13-4   Adding files and directories to our data project prior to backing up.

To fill this project, simply drag directory or files into the project window in the bottom-left half of K3b. As you add each directory, K3b calculates the amount of space all of this takes. Consequently, it may take a few seconds for a large directory to appear as K3b works on these calculations. A colored bar stretches along the bottom, indicating the amount of space you still have left to create your data CD.

After you add everything you want, click the Burn button in the bottom-right of the K3b window. You can also right-click the current project tab and select Burn there. A new Write window appears, with five tabs labeled Writing, Settings, Volume Desc, Filesystem, and Advanced.

I won't cover everything on every tab here, but I will tell you about a few of the more important settings, starting with the Writing tab. If your device is capable of high-speed burning, you may want to change the setting for Speed.

The default is Auto, but depending on what your CD writer tells K3b, that may be very slow. Your unit might be able to handle much better performance. You might also check the Burnfree option's box to avoid buffer underruns.

> *Quick Tip* A rather odd-sounding option is Simulate, located on the Writing tab. After all, why go through the process and not do anything? The idea is to see whether a disc can be written properly at the current speed. Everything happens as it would, except that the laser is turned off. This is also where the Writing on the Fly option comes into play. If your system performance is such that you can burn a disc without writing out an image first, make sure you check this option on.

The Volume Desc tab allows you to set some label information for your CD, such as the name, who created it, and which system it was intended for. You don't actually need to enter anything here. It is information only.

Look under the Filesystem tab and you'll find a couple of important settings related to data backups. The first has to do with whether you will ever be looking at this CD using a Windows system. If so, make sure you check on the Generate Joliet extensions box. Under Permissions, check on Preserve File Permissions if this CD is a backup of your data. Should you ever need to recover from this CD, you'll want to have the proper ownership and permissions of files and directories maintained.

Over at the Advanced tab, you'll find a number of miscellaneous options related to how data is written on your CD. For most users, these can be left alone, but you should take a moment to consider the implications of each setting. There is one *particularly important* setting here. Make sure that you check on the box for Allow Leading Period. Linux uses leading dots on a filename to identify it as a hidden file or directory. Dotfiles are often configuration files as well, defining your personal settings for a particular application. In a backup, you will definitely want to preserve these files.

Ready to Burn that Backup?

When you're done and ready to go, click on the Burn button located in the top-right corner of this dialog box. A new progress window appears with status information on the current CD creation (Figure 13-5).

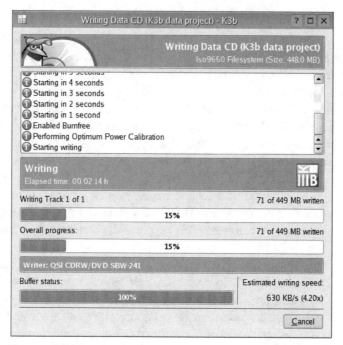

FIGURE 13-5 During a backup, K3b reports on the status of the burn.

That's it. With your data safely backed up, you can sleep soundly at night.

Keeping Your Data in rsync

Another fascinating approach is to back up from one machine to the other. As crazy as it may sound on the surface, many people I know who do regular backups are doing theirs to a disk on another machine. Machine A backs to Machine B, which backs to C, which backs to A. In the absence of another machine, others still are backing up to a second disk on the same machine or sometimes, a USB- or FireWire-connected external drive.

Given that adding an extra hard drive to a system is extremely inexpensive these days and high-capacity tape drives can still cost substantially more, it isn't that unusual to find this kind of solution being used.

"Data, Meet rsync."

The ideal solution in any of these scenarios is to do one big backup; simply make sure that the backup is always up to date. In other words, back up only what has changed. The result is a perfect mirror: one directory and its accompanying subdirectories are mirrored either locally or on a remote system. One of the best tools available to achieve this mirroring is a program called rsync.

With rsync, you can synchronize files and directories on one system with that of another. Because only those files that have been modified are transferred, the process can be very quick. You can do this with single files, whole directories, and subdirectories while maintaining file ownership and permissions, links, symbolic links, and so on. rsync has its own transport, but you can use OpenSSH to secure the transfer (something I'll cover later). You can even mirror with anonymous rsync if you wish, but I am getting ahead of myself.

You can find rsync at http://rsync.samba.org, and it is freely distributed under the GPL. That said, you may not have to go hunting for rsync. Your Linux distribution may already come with this handy piece of software, so check your distribution CDs first. If you go for the source instead, you'll find that building the package is simply a matter of the classic extract and build five-step (as described in Chapter 7, "Installing New Applications").

This magic synchronization of files and directories is done using a client and server setup. At least one machine must play the role of server; although nothing stops you from running an rsync daemon on every one of your machines, however, the client machine must also have the rsync program installed. The server gets its information about who can access what from a configuration file called rsyncd.conf. You'll find that it probably lives in the /etc directory. The following listing is from an rsync server I just set up:

```
hosts allow = 192.168.22.0/24
use chroot = no
max connections = 4
log file = /var/log/rsyncd.log
gid = nogroup
uid = nobody

[website]
    path = /mnt/data1/website
    read only = no
    comment = All our websites
```

```
[mailman]
    path = /mnt/extradrive/mailman
    read only = no
    comment = Mailman lists and archives

[marcel]
    path = /mnt/backups/marcel
    read only = no
    comment = Backup area for Marcel
```

This configuration file needs a little explaining, but it is all very simple once you get the hang of it. For starters, if you've used Samba at all, you might have noticed that the format of the file is quite similar. Given that the author of rsync, Andrew Tridgell, is also one of the authors of Samba, that won't seem so strange. Backup areas are identified by a name in square brackets (website, mailman, and so on). The chief bits of information there are the path to the disk area and some kind of comment.

In each of these sections, I also specified read only = no, but I could just as easily have added that to the top section (the one without a name in square brackets). That's the global section. Anything put up there applies to all other sections, but can be overridden later. Pay particular attention to the gid and uid sections—namely, the group and user ID while the file transfer takes place. The default is nobody, but you need to make sure that this is the case on your system. One of my servers has no *nobody* group, but has a *nogroup* group instead.

The hosts allow section identifies my local subnet as being the only set of addresses from which transfers can take place. The log file line identifies a file to log information from the daemon. You can also specify a maximum number of connections, specific users who are allowed to transfer files (auth users), and a whole lot more. Run man rsyncd.conf for the full details. When your configuration is set, you can launch the rsync daemon, which interestingly enough is exactly the same program as the rsync command itself. You can run rsync from xinetd or inetd or as a daemon. To run it as a daemon, do the following:

```
rsync --daemon
```

That's it. Now it's time to put this setup to use. You might want to test out your rsync connection by issuing the command:

```
rsync remote_host::
```

Note the double colon at the end of the server's name. The result should be something like this, assuming a server called sciserv:

```
$ rsync sciserv::
website      All our websites
mailman      Mailman lists and archives
marcel       Backup area for Marcel
```

Now, pretend that I am on the server where my mailman files live (mailman is a mailing-list manager). Using the following command, I can launch rsync to back up this entire area. Because this is the first time, I see something like this:

```
$ rsync -av /home/mailman sciserv::mailman/
building file list ...
```

Depending on the size of the directory you are copying, the "building file list…" process might take a few minutes. Before we look at the results, I should tell you something about the flags used with the command. The -v for verbose is kind of a giveaway, but the simple -a hides some amount of complexity in that it is the same as using the -rlptgoD flags. In order, this means that rsync should do a recursive copy; copy symbolic links; preserve permissions, modification times, and group and owner information; and, with the final D, copy special files (device and block). When you press <Enter>, files go scrolling by, after which you see something like this:

```
mailman/tests/test_message.py
mailman/tests/test_runners.py
mailman/tests/test_safedict.py
mailman/tests/test_security_mgr.py
mailman/tests/testall.py
wrote 85515773 bytes read 149192 bytes 482619.52 bytes/sec
total size is 84949774 speedup is 0.99
```

I included the tail end of my mailman directory transfer, but at the end, you'll notice that rsync provides a synopsis of the data transferred and the rate at which it was sent. When I run rsync again a little later with only a few things changed in my mailing lists, the process is much faster, because the program transfers only those files that are changed. Consequently, I get these results:

```
wrote 580445 bytes read 6326 bytes 31717.35 bytes/sec
total size is 84950558 speedup is 144.78
```

If you want this whole process to happen magically, you can set up a cron job to run whenever you like, and your data would always be up-to-date. Just remove the -v flag from the command to keep the output quieter.

One other thing that rsync should be able to do in order to be completely useful is delete files. If you are mirroring files and directories from one system to another, it stands to reason that you want that mirror to represent exactly what is on the original. If files have been deleted, you want them deleted on the backup server as well. This is where the --delete parameter comes into play. Assume that I routinely backed up a directory called system_info and that I deleted a configuration file called sys001.conf.

```
$ rsync -av --delete /home/marcel/system_info sciserv::marcel/
building file list ... done
deleting system_info/sys001.conf
system_info/
wrote 504 bytes read 40 bytes 43.52 bytes/sec
total size is 55084 speedup is 101.26
```

The above command ensures that any files that were deleted in my directory are deleted on the remote server as well.

Before wrapping up with rsync, you should consider secure data synchronization. It is possible to use ssh as the transfer agent for rsync. You simply use the -e ssh parameter.

```
rsync -av -e ssh /home/marcel/
  Mail sciserv:/mnt/backups/
  marcel/
```

The remote system (sciserv) asks for a username and password, something that may not be necessary when creating public shares. The sharp-eyed will notice that the above command has only one colon between the backup server and the path. The path is also interesting, because in every example before, I used the symbolic name for the backup area; but in this case, the full path is specified. That's because when using ssh, rsync (by default) writes into the home directory of the authenticating account, which may well be different from the share defined in /etc/rsyncd.conf.

Quick Tip When backing up to tape or CD, administrators historically used what it called a *grandfather system*. You keep a backup for each day of the week, rotating the first tape when you get to the end. You also keep a weekly backup, rotated every four or five weeks, and several monthly backups as well. With an `rsync` backup, it's harder to track this, but not impossible. Simply create multiple backups locations labeled for each day of the week. That way, you can always go back seven days for a particular file.

No Remote Necessary

Here's a final tip: You can take advantage of the mirroring capabilities of `rsync` without having to specify a host. In all of these examples, I made the assumption that we are backing up to another host. That doesn't have to be the case. Picture a large USB drive connected to the main system. That type of drive makes an inexpensive backup solution, but it isn't necessarily connected to a different host. Here's how you would handle this case.

As part of the setup, you still create a `rsync` configuration file defining the backup areas. Say that this drive is mounted at `/mnt/bigusbdrive`. Furthermore, you break up this file system so that there is a backup area for each day of the week defined in your `rsyncd.conf` file. Here's the command for the Monday backup:

```
rsync -av directory_name /mnt/bigusbdrive/monday
```

As you can see, the command is virtually identical to the earlier examples, except that it is not specifying a host (followed by a double colon) on the command line.

Backing Up with dump

The `dump` command is half of a duo, the other part being the `restore` command. The idea behind `dump` is to take a complete backup of a file system as opposed to a single directory or a list of directories. The first backup you do with `dump` is called a *full backup*. From there, you can speed up the backup process by doing incremental backups. In other words, you can back up only what has been modified since the last full backup. You do this by instituting levels. A *level 1* backup only saves those files that have changed since the last level 0 backup. A *level 2* backup only saves files that have changed since the last level 1 backup. (Are you seeing a pattern developing?) There are nine possible levels of incremental backups. The following is the essence of a full backup that I have just run on my system. The zero indicates a *level 0*, or full backup. The u flag tells dump to update /etc/dumpdates after it successfully completes. Immediately after the f flag, I specify the device to which the backup should occur. Finally, just before the pipe symbol, I specify the file system:

```
# dump -0uf - /dev/hdb1 | cat > /dev/st0
    DUMP: Date of this level 0 dump: Wed Apr 16 16:43:54 2003
    DUMP: Date of last level 0 dump: the epoch
    DUMP: Dumping /dev/hdb1 (/mnt/data1) to standard output
    DUMP: Label: none
    DUMP: mapping (Pass I) [regular files]
    DUMP: mapping (Pass II) [directories]
    DUMP: estimated 1590653 tape blocks.
    DUMP: Volume 1 started at: Wed Apr 16 16:44:03 2003
    DUMP: dumping (Pass III) [directories]
    DUMP: dumping (Pass IV) [regular files]
    DUMP: 6.25% done, finished in 1:15
    DUMP: 13.09% done, finished in 1:06
    DUMP: 19.90% done, finished in 1:00
    DUMP: 26.99% done, finished in 0:54
```

Notice anything strange? Instead of specifying my tape drive directly (after the f flag), I used a hyphen to redirect to standard out, and then I piped the whole thing to cat and redirected that to the tape drive. If that sounds convoluted, consider this: The dump command wants to know the density of the tape in bits per inch (the d flag) and the number of feet in the tape (the s flag) so that it can figure out how many tapes it will need. As it turns out, the only thing I know for sure is that my tape drive can back up 30GB uncompressed and that I only have 15GB of data. Doing it this way overrides the need to supply the tape size information.

Quick Tip The dump and restore commands work with ext2 and ext3 file systems only.

Now, here is a `dump` of the same file system one day later, using a level 1 backup:

```
# dump -1uf - /dev/hdb1 | cat > /dev/st0
   DUMP: Date of this level 1 dump: Thu Apr 17 17:16:35 2003
   DUMP: Date of last level 0 dump: Wed Apr 16 16:43:54 2003
   DUMP: Dumping /dev/hdb1 (/mnt/data1) to standard output
   DUMP: Label: none
   DUMP: mapping (Pass I) [regular files]
   DUMP: mapping (Pass II) [directories]
   DUMP: estimated 29280 tape blocks.
   DUMP: Volume 1 started at: Thu Apr 17 17:16:49 2003
   DUMP: dumping (Pass III) [directories]
   DUMP: dumping (Pass IV) [regular files]
   DUMP: 94.33% done, finished in 0:00
   DUMP: Volume 1 completed at: Thu Apr 17 17:22:06 2003
   DUMP: Volume 1 took 0:05:17
   DUMP: Volume 1 transfer rate: 91 KB/s
   DUMP: DUMP: 29072 tape blocks
   DUMP: finished in 317 seconds, throughput 91 KBytes/sec
   DUMP: level 1 dump on Thu Apr 17 17:16:35 2003
   DUMP: DUMP: Date of this level 1 dump: Thu Apr 17 17:16:35 2003
   DUMP: DUMP: Date this dump completed:  Thu Apr 17 17:22:06 2003
   DUMP: DUMP: Average transfer rate: 91 KB/s
   DUMP: DUMP IS DONE
```

As you can see, the whole thing took just over five minutes and backed up only what had changed since the day before. My `/etc/dumpdates` file looks like this now:

```
/dev/hdb1 0 Wed Apr 16 16:43:54 2003
/dev/hdb1 1 Thu Apr 17 17:16:35 2003
```

You can see that Wednesday's backup was a level 0 (second column), and the following day's backup was a level 1.

Restoring with—You Guessed It—restore

When it comes time to `restore` from a `dump` tape, you must recreate the file system with the `mke2fs` command (mke2fs /dev/hdb1), change directory to that file system (/mnt/data1 in this case), and then restore your data to it.

```
# restore -rf /dev/st0
```

This will overwrite everything, and you must start with your level 0 backup. You can also do an interactive restore by specifying the -i flag. You will find yourself at a restore> prompt where you can enter an interactive session and specify individual directories or files.

I'll admit that the dump and restore system is not the prettiest of systems, but it works well and comes with every major Linux distribution.

Other Backup Solutions

All of the solutions I've mentioned are great for single-server implementations, but in a more complex environment, you may need something somewhat more tuned to large enterprises. In this arena, we are generally talking about network backup solutions. The core software runs on a main server with a large-capacity tape drive or a tape jukebox. Client software is installed on the various servers and PCs in the organization, and data is streamed across the network.

For a sophisticated and powerful backup solution that just happens to be free, check out AMANDA, the Advanced Maryland Automatic Network Disk Archiver, from the University of Maryland at College Park (www.amanda.org). AMANDA, a non-GUI tool, can back up a large number of clients to a single location on a high-capacity tape drive. You can also back up Windows clients using Samba and use standard Linux backup tools to store the data. Furthermore, AMANDA is free software.

You can also find many commercial products. One of my personal favorites is Arkeia (www.arkeia.com), a powerful and very cool backup program that looks like something from the future. This program can handle up to 200 clients simultaneously—Linux, UNIX, Windows, and more—while writing on as many as 32 tape drives. If you'd like to take this great program out for a test drive, Arkeia offers a little something called Arkeia Light, a free version of the same product, but with support for only one Linux server, one tape drive, and two clients (either Linux or Windows) in either a personal or commercial environment.

Another package worth your consideration is BRU Pro from the Tolis Group. BRU Pro is also capable of backing up several machines to multiple tape drives simultaneously. Bru Pro runs on a Linux server, but there are clients for many different platforms (UNIX of various flavors, Mac OS X, Windows, and more). Check it out at www.bru.com.

Last but not least is our old friend Webmin. Look under the System tab and you'll find Backup System. This is a front end to the tar command (with or without compression) that allows for scheduled backups as well. You can get to it directly from your own browser at:

```
http://your_system:10000/backup/
```

Final Words

Do your backups.
Label your backups.
Verify your backups.
If possible, store backups off site.
Do backups regularly.
Remember that no piece of data is ever as important as the day you need to recover it.

Resources

AMANDA
www.amanda.org

Arkeia
www.arkeia.com

BRU
www.bru.com

K3b
http://k3b.kde.org

Printers and Printing

Printing seems like one of those constants of the computer world that should be so simple as to require next to no thought. Of course, you need to print things. Paper output is a part of doing business. Why, then, does printing continue to confound? Over the years, I have seen and read many different estimates regarding system administrators and printers. In particular, I'm interested in the question of how much time the average administrator devotes to this simple thing. One figure, which had a fairly strong argument backing it up, put printer administration at around 25% of a system administrator's time. Granted, this information goes back a few years, but I haven't seen much since then to convince me that this figure has changed. In fact, with many manufacturers cutting costs and pushing cheaper (both in quality and price) printers to market, things aren't getting any better.

This chapter examines how printing works and what processes are involved at the system level. I want you to walk away with an understanding, not of graphical printer admin tools, but of printing's dirty underbelly. On the subject of tools, I'll also explore some of the alternative tools that are available to make the whole printing experience just that much easier to deal with. The beauty of working with Linux is that you don't have to do things the way they are defined right out of the box. Many other options exist. Armed with the nuts and bolts of printers and printing, you should be able to print just about any type of document to just about any type of printer.

Selecting Printers for Linux

Beware.

Before you buy any printer to run with your Linux system, make sure you ask your dealer if it will work with Linux. I don't mean to frighten you into thinking that this is an impossible task, by the way. In fact, the "Does it work with Linux?" question is becoming less and less of a problem, but you can still save yourself an awful lot of headaches by asking first. Another way to protect yourself is to check out the hardware compatibility list (see Chapter 8, "Devices and Services") for Linux systems. This is a great idea for any kind of hardware add-on. For printers, though, you have an additional option that goes one step further.

Even seasoned Linux users like myself occasionally get stuck or caught with a printer that doesn't work. Some time ago, I bought an HP710C printer, and I just assumed (what do they tell us about assuming) that anything from HP would just work with Linux. After all, they make that great OS, HP-UX. As it turns out, being wrong is extremely easy. This particular printer used something called Printing Performance Architecture (PPA), a closed protocol whose secrets were only available to the Windows platform.

Looking around the Net, I found that a guy named Tim Norman and a group of devoted developers had put an early driver together. Unfortunately, at the time, you could print in black and white only, but Tim and his team were working on a color driver. So, I printed in black and white until a color driver finally became available. Had I known about Grant Taylor's printer compatibility list at LinuxPrinting.org (`www.linuxprinting.org`), I wouldn't have had to wait, because I wouldn't have bought the printer in the first place.

One of the most useful things at LinuxPrinting.org is a search engine that lets you select a particular manufacturer and get a report on all of its printers, what level of support the company offers, and what kind of tweaking you might need to do to make the printers work. This is especially good if you already have a particular printer and you want to know what filter or drivers are out there for your Linux system. (I'll delve into filters momentarily.)

If you are feeling less than adventurous or you haven't already spent money on a printer, you can use the safer reporting option. Simply ask to see which color inkjet printers (or laser printers, or whatever type you are looking for) work perfectly. The resulting report lists printers by manufacturer with appropriate links to detailed descriptions of individual models.

The safest approach of all is to get a PostScript printer. These, unfortunately, tend to be the more costly choice. I'll talk more about PostScript later.

Getting Information on LPD

The classic LPD print system is covered in many places, including my own first book. If you wish to follow this approach, the chapter that covers this is even available online in PDF format (`www.marcelgagne.com/LSAbook/lsach13.pdf`). That sample chapter also covers some great tools for working with Postscript files, creating custom print filters, and more. Although I highly recommend that you check it out, I also highly recommend that you consider using CUPS as your print system. So, without further ado, let's move on to printers and printing.

CUPS

This might seem like a silly thing to mention, particularly if your printer was automatically detected, configured, and tested at boot time. Nevertheless, there are things that you might want to do with your printer, and I should probably cover some of these now. Furthermore, *printing is one of the most important functions a personal computer can perform*. It's good to get it right. On that note, I'm going to spend a little bit of time talking about printers and printing. Trust me, it's going to be lots of fun.

Printing under Linux works on the basis of *print queues*. At its simplest, this means that whenever you send something to the printer, it is queued in a directory where it awaits its turn at the printer. This de-queuing is known as *spooling*. Consequently, the process that sends the print jobs from the queue to the printer is called the *spooler*. That spooler can be one of a small handful of programs, all of which are transparent to you when you print from applications. Here's a quick roundup of the more popular spoolers.

CUPS, the Common UNIX Printing System, is designed to be a platform-independent printing system that works across a great number of UNIX flavors, including Linux. CUPS uses the Internet Printing Protocol (IPP), a next-generation printing system designed to allow the printing of any job to any printer, anywhere. At this point, CUPS certainly looks like the spooler of the future. Most modern Linux distributions include CUPS, and KDE uses it transparently.

The second most likely spooler you will run into is *LPD*, the classic UNIX spooler. LPD has been around for a long, long time and continues to be distributed with pretty much every Linux out there.

Whether it is CUPS or LPD, KDE handles printing beautifully. Adding, configuring, or removing a printer is done through the KDE Control Center. After activating the Control Center, click on Peripherals (in the left side category window) and select Printers.

I'll start with adding a printer. Because adding hardware, like adding software, is an administrative function, click the Administrator button at the bottom of the Printing Manager window first. A window pops up, asking you for the root password (Figure 14-1).

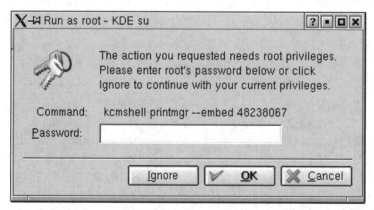

FIGURE 14-1   Accessing the printer configuration requires the root password.

After entering the password, you are looking at the same interface, but things are a little different. For starters, the window to the right is now surrounded by a *red border*. Furthermore, some of the icons have gone from being grayed out to being active. If the toolbar and icons are not visible, right-click in the printer list window (at the top of the Printers configuration window). A pop-up menu appears (Figure 14-2), from which you should select View Toolbar or View Menu Toolbar. Both have the same menu options but are presented somewhat differently.

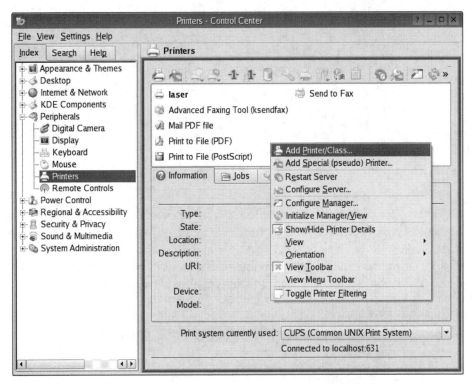

FIGURE 14-2   Toolbar menu options in the KDE printer configuration manager.

One of those is the Add Printer/Class icon. Clicking that icon brings up the KDE Add Printer wizard. Click Next through the welcome screen (Figure 14-3), and you can select the type of printer, whether it is connected directly to your PC with a parallel or USB cable or via the network in some way. Network-connected printers could be good old LPD printers, Microsoft Windows-connected and -shared printers (SMB), CUPS, HP JetDirect, IPP, or others. Click on the one you are looking to connect, and click Next.

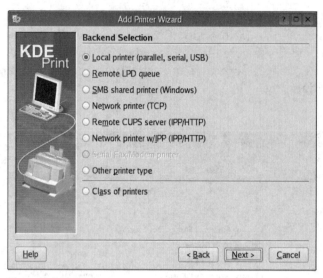

FIGURE 14-3   The KDE Add Printer wizard.

When you click Next after selecting your connection, you face different choices, based on whether the printer is local or on the network. For a local printer, your choices are parallel port, serial port, or some kind of USB connection. After you click Next again, the wizard loads its printer database. Select your vendor and model from the list (Figure 14-4), and click Next.

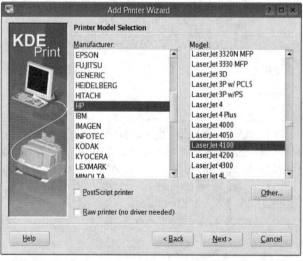

FIGURE 14-4   Selecting a printer vendor and model.

Depending on the printer, there may be more than one suitable driver. Consequently, you may be asked to choose between one or more additional drivers on the next screen. Usually, the default choice is the best. Click Next, which brings you to the Printer Test screen. The information regarding your new printer is displayed, and you have the option of sending a test page to the printer. I *strongly recommend* that you print a test page before moving on.

At this point, you can also click the Settings button and personalize certain defaults; for instance, the default page size (U.S. letter, A4, and so on), margins, print quality, or, in the case of a color inkjet like mine, how ink cartridges are accessed and used. If everything looks as you expect it to on your test page, click Next one more time. Now you see the banner selection screen. Simply put, would you like a banner page before or after your print job has completed? Unless you are in an office with many people trying to keep their jobs straight, you probably don't want to waste the paper. Luckily, the default is no banners of any kind.

Click Next to see the Printer Quota Settings (Figure 14-5). You might be asking what the heck a printer quota is and why you should care. Once again, if this is your home printer, you can just click Next, and completely ignore this. In some office environments, it may be practical or necessary to limit the number of jobs any single user can print to a printer in a given time period—per hour, per day, per week, or even per minute. The size of job can be based on the number of pages or the amount of data sent.

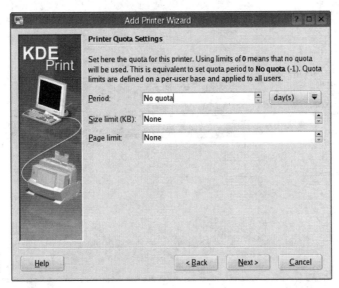

FIGURE 14-5   You can add restrictions on printer use.

Click Next, and it is time for the User access settings where you can decide who can and can't use your printer. You can either specify a list of *denied users* where everyone can use your printer except those listed or a list of *allowed users* where only those listed can use the printer. It is at times like this that Linux reminds you it is a *multiuser* system.

After making all of these decisions, you come to the General Information, or summary screen. Enter a name for this printer (a one-word name is best), followed by a location and a description. In reality, the only thing you need to enter is a name for the printer. Click Next, and you have a final opportunity to review the choices you've made. At this point or at any point before now, you can still click Back and make different choices. If you are happy, click Finish, and you are done. Congratulations; you've added and configured a printer.

Now, have a closer look at the Printing Manager (Figure 14-6). Take a moment to move your mouse slowly over the various icons at the top and take note of the tool tips. You can do a lot in terms of printer modification and administration here. If you are looking to share your Linux printer with Windows workstations in the office or home, you can even export the driver for use. Notice the tabs as well: Information, Jobs, Properties, and Instances.

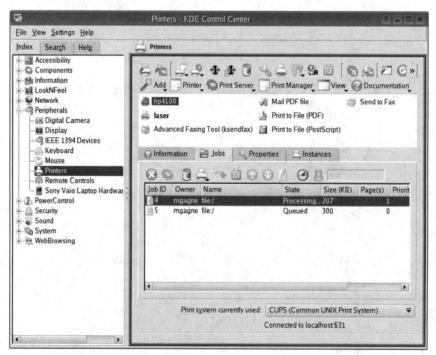

FIGURE 14-6 The KDE Control Center Printing Manager provides all of the information you need.

Information is just that, basic information about your printer, such as its name, location, and so on. Under the Jobs tab, you can see all the jobs currently waiting in your print queue.

Let me tell you about a great way to work with printers, monitor print jobs, and so on. For quick access to your printing subsystem, right-click on the application launcher (the big K), select Panel Menu>Add>Special Button, and click on Print System. A *new icon* appears in your Kicker panel. Click on that icon, and all of your printers appear in a pop-up list (along with quick access to other print system tools). Click on the appropriate printer icon, and a window opens with a list of jobs waiting to be printed (Figure 14-7).

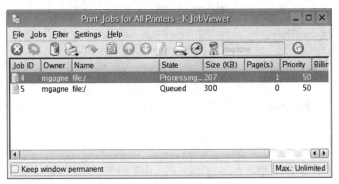

FIGURE 14-7   Checking on queued print jobs.

 Quick Tip   You can also call this program as `kjobviewer`.

From the jobs list, you can delete jobs, change the order in which they print, or redirect them to another printer if yours is particularly busy. Using the Properties tab, you can change some of the characteristics that you assigned to your printer when you configured it, such as quotas, banner pages, and so on—just make sure you are in Administrator mode.

That brings us to the *Instances*. Each printer you create has at least one instance, the default instance. The idea behind this is that you can create multiple instances of the same printer. Say you have a color printer and that you often switch between a high-quality color mode (for photographs) to a lower-quality draft mode when you want to conserve that expensive colored ink. Just add another instance of the same printer but with different characteristics.

Now that you have added a printer, configured it, and given yourself supreme power over all print functions, it is time to print something. Luckily, this is the easiest part of all. Whenever you print from any KDE application (Kmail, Konqueror, and so on), you are presented with a common printer dialog (Figure 14-8).

FIGURE 14-8   The common KDE Print dialog.

From that window, you can select the printer of your choice or click Properties and change the number of copies, the paper size, and a number of other settings associated with that particular printer and that particular job. If you want to see those details up front, click on the Expand button for a somewhat more *panoramic* view. Finally, you can even start from here to add yet another printer. Notice that little icon to the left of the Properties button, the one that looks a bit like a magic wand? Clicking this fires up the Add Printer wizard.

Yes, we've come back around to where we started.

Kprinter

Part of the KDE print system includes a tool that doesn't get anywhere near enough attention. That tool is kprinter, a universal KDE printing front end that you can call from anywhere by using your <Alt+F2> shortcut. Have a look at Figure 14-9 for an idea of what it looks like.

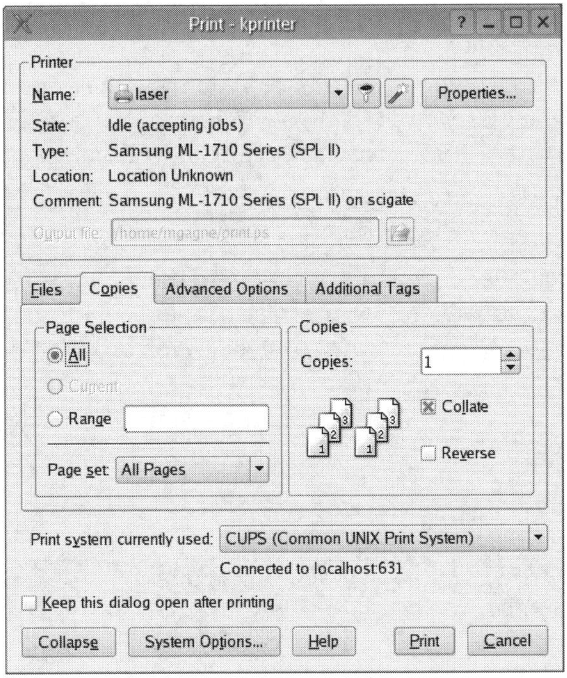

FIGURE 14-9   Sending jobs to the printer with kprinter.

What I like about kprinter is that you can manually add a list of files that you would like to have printed by navigating your directories (see the Files tab). Then, you can modify your job by selecting number of copies from the Copies tab and so on.

You can also substitute `kprinter` for such simple commands as `lpr` in scripts where you would like to have a nice graphical popup for the user. Being able to use the command in this way just provides an added layer of flexibility to the print system.

```
kprinter /path_to/some_file
some_command | kprinter
```

Other Printer Administration Tools

The KDE printer admin tools are nice in that they provide a consistent look and feel for dealing with anything from adding a printer to printing to checking up on print jobs. As with so many things in the Linux world, there is more than one way to do things.

One of those ways is your old friend, Webmin. The printer administration module is under the Hardware tab. If you prefer, you can also jump to it directly. From the location bar on your browser, type the following path to your server:

```
http://your_server:10000/lpadmin/index.cgi
```

Another, often overlooked tool, is built in to the CUPS software. CUPS has its own web-based administrative interface running on port 631, and it requires no additional software to install. Just use your Web browser by pointing to this URL on your server:

```
http://your_server:631
```

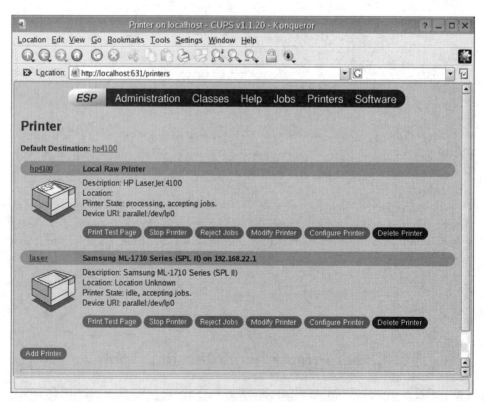

FIGURE 14-10   The built-in CUPS web administration tool.

Resources

CUPS

www.cups.org

Linux Printing HOWTO

www.linuxdoc.org/HOWTO/Printing-HOWTO/index.html

Linux Printing Usage HOWTO

www.linuxdoc.org/HOWTO/Printing-Usage-HOWTO.html

LinuxPrinting.org

www.linuxprinting.org

chapter
15

Electronic Mail

Getting email flowing in an organization involves the following components. On the server end, the basic components are a mail transport agent (MTA) and a local delivery agent (LDA). The client side consists primarily of a mail user agent (MUA), which usually, but not always, lives on the user's PC. Later in this book, I'll cover two of the most popular email packages for the Linux desktop: Kmail and Evolution. For the remainder of this chapter, I'm going to concentrate on what you need to do to implement electronic mail on the server side.

Postfix

Many of the popular Linux distributions today include Postfix (written by Wietse Venema) as their choice for default mail transport agent. In my first book, I covered sendmail instead of Postfix, but I've come to really appreciate the benefits of Postfix as a sendmail replacement. The advantages of Postfix include enhanced security, relatively simple configuration, and excellent performance.

Note Postfix's increased security comes partly from its modular design. Each process handles some portion of the mail delivery cycle and none of these processes run setuid root. As has been observed, Postfix doesn't even trust itself.

The next step is to configure Postfix.

Setting Up Postfix

In most Linux installations, the configuration files for Postfix are located in the /etc/postfix directory. This is also where you will find access control files, user alias definitions, and so on. Every Postfix installation I've seen also provides a number of sample configuration files for a huge number of parameters to help you fine-tune your own installation. These sample files, such as sample-smtp.cf, are heavily documented. I recommend that, at some point, you have a look through them to see what else might be of benefit to you. For the time being, I'm going to cover the most important and basic parameters in the main configuration file that is called, oddly enough, main.cf.

Using your favorite editor, open main.cf and look for the following lines:

```
myhostname = gateway.mycompany.dom
mydomain = mycompany.dom
```

As you can see, the first variables of interest here have to do with defining your own fully-qualified domain name (FQDN). You may or may not have to set these. On my own mail server, these two parameters remain commented out. That's because if your system is properly configured with a domain name server (DNS), you don't actually need to enter this information. $myhostname is derived from your server's FQDN which, in my example, is gateway.mycompany.dom. The $mydomain variable is further identified by stripping off the server part of the FQDN and leaving the domain behind, for example `mycompany.dom`.

The next variable of interest is closely tied to the last two:

```
mydestination = $myhostname, localhost.$mydomain, mycompany.dom,
mysecondcompany.dom, mythirdcompany.dom, someotherdomain.dom
```

Notice that the line above can wrap on multiple lines, but for readability, you could rewrite it using multiple lines. As long as you included a comma between each entry but the last, feel free to get creative. Here is the same line reformatted:

```
mydestination =
        $myhostname,
        localhost.$mydomain,
        mycompany.dom,
        mysecondcompany.dom,
        mythirdcompany.dom,
        someotherdomain.dom
```

The `$mydestination` variable is a list of all the domains and systems for which your server will accept mail. These are your local domains (not necessarily the same as a *localhost*). On my server, I process mail and receive mail for a dozen or so different domains. In the above example, I could receive mail for user@localhost, user@mysecondcompany.dom, user@someotherdomain.dom, and so on.

Some companies do not route the mail directly from their servers. In some cases, usually when your own network uses a single, shared connection, your ISP may not allow you to directly send your own mail. Some go so far as to block port 25 (SMTP) as a means of protecting against spam. In these situations, you may have to specify an external relay host, usually your ISP's mail server. Use the command:

```
relayhost = myisp.mailserver.dom
```

Quick Tip I mentioned that some settings were already properly defaulted on my system, such as the hostname. Aside from the variables I've given you above, Postfix often works right out of the box with the default settings. What are those settings? You can find out by typing `postconf`.

Stopping and Restarting Postfix

After making configuration changes, you need to let the `postfix` program know about them. Luckily, it isn't necessary to shut down the `postfix` system to do this. You simply can tell `postfix` to reload its configuration by using the command:

```
postfix reload
```

If, at this point, you happen to be watching the output of your `/var/log/maillog` file, you should see something like this:

```
Apr 17 20:54:51 gateway postfix/master[24819]: reload configuration
```

Of course, if need be, you can shut down postfix entirely and then restart it with these two commands:

```
postfix stop
postfix start
```

Setting Up Users and Aliases

You can add users to your Linux system as I discussed in Chapter 12, "Users and Groups." Use the graphical interface (KUser), or go straight to the command line with the `adduser` command. Remember that you must be logged in as the root user to do this.

```
adduser user_name
```

You then assign a password with the `passwd` command.

```
passwd user_name
```

One of the things you will likely want to do is create an alias for your office (or perhaps several aliases). This is a fairly simple process. Aliases are also useful if you want to add something like `sales@mycompany.dom` that you want redirected to two salespeople. Another useful alias, `office@mycompany.dom`, sends mail to everybody. Here's how it's done.

The file you need to edit is called `aliases`. The location of the aliases database is defined in `main.cf` like this:

```
alias_database = hash:/etc/postfix/aliases
```

Using your favorite editor, open the file. The format of the aliases file is simple:

```
alias_name:     real_name1,real_name2,real_name3, . . .
```

The `alias_name` part is the name for which you are creating the alias. In the preceding example, this is sales or office. After the colon, press Tab (or just insert spaces) and type your list of user names separated by commas. White space at the beginning of a line implies the continuation of an alias. Here's an example using office:

```
office: john,myrtle,bonnie,gilbert,elvis,tux
```

The six email addresses listed after `office:` will receive copies of any mail addressed to `office@mycompany.dom`. Now, save your work and run the command:

```
newaliases
```

A Quick Conversation About hash

A database format is, of course, what we are talking about here. When I showed you how to add aliases and rebuild the database, I also mentioned the line in `main.cf` where the aliases database is defined:

```
alias_database = hash:/etc/postfix/aliases
```

As we go along here, I'm going to mention a few other databases. The `hash:` prefix that you see before the path to the database defines the format. In the case of the `aliases` file, there is also an `aliases.db`, which the `newaliases` command creates. Another way to create this database would be with the postmap command:

```
postmap hash:/etc/postfix/aliases
```

This literally means make a hash database called `aliases.db` from the `aliases` text file. If you do this, you don't need to run `newaliases` or restart `postfix`. The same technique can be applied to some of the other hash databases I will be covering shortly.

Setting Up the POP3 or IMAP Server

Most email clients use either POP3 or IMAP for reading email. The POP3 and IMAP servers listen for mail pickup requests from users. Both protocols are usually part of the imap package. To check if you have imap installed, use this version of the rpm command:

```
rpm -q imap
```

If the system responds with imap-2002d or something of the sort, the package is already loaded. If not, mount your distribution CD-ROM and install imap. You may also need to activate those services in the /etc/xinetd.d directory. You'll find paragraphs there for IMAP and POP3. The key is to make sure the services aren't disabled. Here's what my pop-3 file looks like:

```
service pop-3
{
        socket_type             = stream
        protocol                = tcp
        wait                    = no
        user                    = root
        server                  = /usr/sbin/ipop3d
        disable                 = no
}
```

As long as disable is set to no, the service is active. You will now need to refresh the xinetd process for this change to take effect. Find the process ID for xinetd, and send a SIGHUP to it. Careful with that -1! Remember that forgetting the hyphen in this case could down the whole system because init, the master process, has a PID of 1.

```
kill -1 `cat /var/run/xinetd.pid`
```

Not-So-Stupid Postfix Tricks

Once your organization becomes relatively complex, you will find yourself wanting to do things with email that may not seem immediately important. The first and most important thing is, of course, that the mail flows and that you can send and receive. I'm willing to bet that the first enhancement that comes to mind for people is spam control, or unsolicited commercial email

(UCE). But that, as they say, is just the beginning. On that note, I'm going to save the best for last—or is it the worst?

Let's get to the good stuff, shall we?

The Multiple Domain, Similar Address Dilemma

Imagine for a moment that you have decided to register several domains, all of which reside on the same machine. After all, your Linux system is more than capable of handling the load and you don't want to bother starting from scratch for what might be low-traffic domains anyway. What you do want, though, is a standard method of getting information-only mail to your virtual companies. You might even want that mail to go to different places. Here's what you want in a nutshell:

```
info@mycompany.dom
info@myseconddomain.dom
info@myinfosite.dom
```

Now, you can only have one info login on your system. If info is not a user on your system, you could add an info alias to direct info mail to a real user, rather than creating the pseudo-user. For instance, if mary was to get info's mail, you would have an `aliases` entry like this:

```
info:   mary@somedomain.dom
```

The problem comes when you want all of these different info addresses to go to different people. You can't have two `alias` entries for info. The way to get around this is to use the `virtusertable` feature. Look for this line in your `main.cf` configuration file:

```
virtual_maps = hash:/etc/postfix/virtusertable
```

This will give you the path to the virtual user table and the means to set up these different domains with equivalent users. The format of the file is simple:

```
username@somedomain.dom      realuser@someotherdomain.dom
```

In the case of my info example, my `virtusertable` would look like this:

```
info@mycompany.dom           mary@localdomain.dom
info@myseconddomain.dom      tom@remotedomain.dcom
info@myinfosite.dom          natika@bigschool.edu
```

Finally, you need to get Postfix to start using the new database. From the `/etc/postfix` directory or wherever you have decided to configure the table, run this command:

```
postmap hash:/etc/postfix/virtusertable
```

The Multidrop Domain

Here's another scenario. Pretend that mail bound for `myinfosite.org` was all to go to one user because there is only one user at `myinfosite.org`. You don't want to lose important mail if people send to that address, but use Webmaster when you have only info set up as an alias. Generally, mail that is improperly addressed is probably not mail you want, but if you want to play it safe, how do you make sure that all mail gets through no matter whom it is addressed to within that domain?

Strangely enough, the answer is the same as in the previous section—namely, your old friend `virtusertable`. Here's an entry that directs all mail for `myinfosite.dom` to andy@mycompany.dom:

```
@myinfosite.dom       andy@mycompany.dom
```

Once again, recreate your `virtusertable` database, and you are on your way.

```
postmap hash:/etc/postfix/virtusertable
```

Stop the Spam!

Here's a great tip for getting rid of some of the spam that keeps pounding your mail server. In case you've been away for a while, *spam* is a euphemism for unwanted email. The sheer bulk of spam directed at your server can slow things down to a crawl. When you run your own server, you aren't completely powerless. Start by adding the following to your `main.cf` configuration file:

```
smtpd_helo_required = yes
disable_vrfy_command = yes
```

The first of these two settings, smtpd_helo_required, specifies that any incoming server must identify itself with the HELO command. Failure to do so means that the email is dropped. While it shouldn't be a problem, you should consider that it is possible that emails from friends whose clients don't properly identify themselves might also get dropped. The second variable, disable_vrfy_command, refuses VRFY queries, which a potential cracker might use to locate valid user names on your system.

Of course, spammers use a large number of annoying techniques to get past your system, including sending out email to thousands of people on your server and just hoping that some of the email addresses are valid. Because they are already relaying through a site other than their own anyway, they don't care if some of it bounces. It doesn't affect them. The problem is that it affects you. Many spammers also don't provide proper hostnames, return addresses, and sometimes the header information is completely invented. To reduce some of the traffic that falls into these categories, the following additions to main.cf might also be in order:

```
smtpd_recipient_restrictions =
            reject_invalid_hostname,
            reject_non_fqdn_sender,
            reject_non_fqdn_recipient,
            reject_unknown_sender_domain,
            reject_unknown_recipient_domain,
            reject_unauth_destination,
            reject_unauth_pipelining
            permit_mynetworks,
        reject_non_fqdn_hostname
```

Another trick is to block access to email from particularly annoying domains. Here's an example: some time ago, I dealt with an incident of bulk emails being sent through a relay. The format of the spam was hundreds of email addresses to the same domain, mostly to users that did not exist on that system anyhow. Presumably, the spammers were looking to hit at least some legitimate email addresses.

The solution is to block all access from a particular domain in the access database. You'll recognize this somewhat from our discussion of hash maps. The location of this file is defined by this variable:

```
smtpd_sender_restrictions = hash:/etc/postfix/access
```

Start by editing your `access` file, and add the name of the domain you want to reject with the word "REJECT" separated by white space.

```
spammer.dom          REJECT
anotherspammer.dom   REJECT
```

To activate the new `access` database, use the `postmap` command.

```
postmap hash:/etc/mail/access
```

Track Those Emails

Sometimes, it may be necessary to track the email messages that make their way across your system. What are those reasons? You may have noticed an increase in email abuse, either internal or external, where forwarding a copy of each message to an administrator would be desirable. By using the `always_bcc` parameter, a blind carbon copy of each message will be delivered to an administrative user of your choice. Since that person will be getting a lot of messages, it makes sense to create a temporary user account. Tracking and logging messages in this way can be quite a daunting task.

Here's how you do it. Edit your main.cf file and add the following line:

```
always_bcc=adminuser@yourdomain.dom
```

The adminuser is the one you created to receive a copy of all this email. Reload postfix and that username will start receiving a copy of every email that goes across the system. To activate the feature, reload postfix.

```
postfix reload
```

Postfix via Webmin

Webmin provides extensive configuration options for Postfix, and you should certainly familiarize yourself with it. Webmin provides multiple modules to administer everything, including dealing with messages in the current mail queue, client and server restrictions, logging, and a whole lot more. You'll find Postfix configuration under Servers in Webmin, or you can just jump to it by entering the URL in your browser's location bar like this:

```
http://your_server:10000/postfix/index.cgi
```

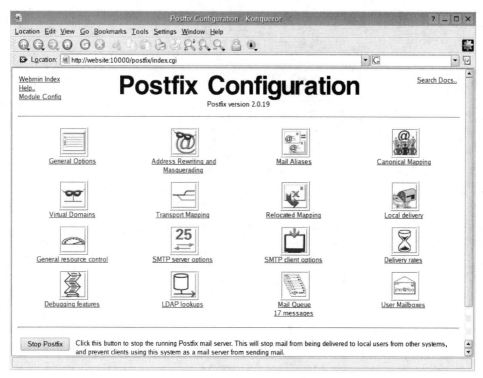

FIGURE 15-1   Webmin makes Postfix configuration easier.

Resources

Postfix

www.postfix.org

16

LDAP

Part of the data we take for granted at home is our email. Closely related to that very topic are those ever-growing lists of people with whom we communicate. Sure, you could carry your own list of contacts, but what about the corporate address book and its wealth of information? How can you get to that?

Introducing LDAP

One way to do this is with LDAP. *LDAP* is an acronym for *Lightweight Directory Access Protocol*. I like to think of it as directory assistance for your network, although it can be a great deal more. LDAP can provide you with basic directory information such as name, address, phone numbers, and email addresses, but its database can also serve as a central user database for logins and passwords as well.

A directory is a collection of entries, as you might expect in any database. Each entry is made up of attributes—more importantly, globally unique distinguished names, and I do mean globally. Each attribute also has types with associated values. For instance, an email address is defined as `mail`, and a person's full name is referred to as `cn` for common name. All of this data is organized inside of a hierarchical structure. The database represents an *organization*. Inside that organization are *organizational units*. Inside organizational units are *people*. A person is described by *attributes* of different *types* and *values*. Trust me. This will all make sense when you see it in action.

While it may seem frighteningly obvious, to do something with LDAP, you need to get the LDAP software. You can download the latest version directly from www.openldap.org.

In all likelihood, you already have a copy of OpenLDAP on any recent distribution CD. The big advantage of building LDAP from source is that you will be working with the latest and greatest. Note that a default `openldap` package installed with your distribution may have everything you need to access an LDAP server, but not the server itself. That package is usually called `openldap-servers`, and in Debian, it is called `slapd`. If you decide to go with a source bundle, which is identified by its release date, you can build it with these basic steps:

```
tar -xzvf openldap-stable-20040614.tgz
cd openldap-2.2.13
./configure
make depend
make
make install
```

When installing from the `openldap-servers` RPM, I received this message:

```
Generating self-signed certificate...
cd To generate a self-signed certificate, you can use the utility
/usr/share/openldap/gencert.sh...
```

By default, the source distribution installs in /usr/local. If you are going
to run a server, then the configuration aspects aren't too scary for the server
anyhow, because everything you need to worry about is in one file:
slapd.conf. That install path is important, because it will affect the location
of the file. On my Mandrake test system, the RPM package puts it in
/etc/openldap. On another system, on which I built OpenLDAP from
scratch, the file is in /usr/local/etc/openldap. Have a look at that file. To
simplify things, I'm going to accept all of the defaults at the beginning of the file
and concentrate on the database definition.

```
database         bdb
suffix           "dc=your_domain, dc=dom"
rootdn           "cn=Manager, dc=your_domain, dc=dom"
# Cleartext passwords, especially for the rootdn, should
# be avoided.  See slappasswd(8) and slapd.conf(5) for details.
# Use of strong authentication encouraged.
rootpw               itsasecret
# rootpw               {crypt}ijFYNcSNctBYg
# The database directory MUST exist prior to running slapd AND
# should only be accessible by the slapd/tools. Mode 700 recommended.
directory        /var/lib/ldap
# Indices to maintain
#index  objectClass                              eq
index   objectClass,uid,uidNumber,gidNumber      eq
index   cn,mail,surname,givenname                eq,subinitial
# samba searches on sid
#index  sambaSID                                 eq
```

I've already done a little editing here, and I'll go over a few of these changes.
For starters, you should change the suffix information to reflect your domain
name. As you can see, the domain is broken up into its constituent parts. Think
of rootdn as the root user for administering LDAP, consequently the name
can be something other than root. Following that hierarchical format, that person exists within an organization.

Next, take a look at the directory parameter. That directory can exist anywhere you want, but it does have to exist before you start adding information.
I've chosen to use the default directory as created by the RPM install. Finally,
I'm going to jump back a couple of lines and look at that password note. That
little warning above about plain text passwords is important. In the simplest

form, I could just enter my password of itsasecret. To generate an encrypted password, use this little perl script:

```
perl -e 'print("userPassword: {CRYPT}".crypt("secret","salt")."
");'
```

The `"secret"` is your password, and the `"salt"` is a two-character key designed to provide a pseudo-random seed so that the crypt routine can generate a password. By doing this, you can generate an encrypted password rather than using the plain text version.

```
perl -e 'print("userPassword: {CRYPT}".crypt("itsasecret","MG")."
");'
userPassword: {CRYPT}I5ToCN7ZovZmQ
```

Since the core of an LDAP server (or at least, what makes it useful) is a database, we need just a little more information in our slapd.conf file. Specifically, we need to include some database schema definitions. These are already defined for you and LDAP installations included with major Linux distributions will have some of these defined as below:

```
include          /usr/local/etc/openldap/schema/core.schema
include          /usr/local/etc/openldap/schema/cosine.schema
include          /usr/local/etc/openldap/schema/misc.schema
include          /usr/local/etc/openldap/schema/inetorgperson.schema
```

Before you start adding include statements, check your own slapd.conf file, particularly if you are using the one supplied with your distribution CDs. Your distribution may include more than the four above, but the ones above are pretty much the minimum. So far, so good. It's time to start up the LDAP server. Obviously, this is going to vary depending on where you or your distribution decided to install the software. The daemon that does all the work is called `slapd`, and that is pretty much all you need to know to start it.
```
/usr/sbin/slapd
```
In all likelihood, you'll find yourself back at the root prompt without any additional information. So how are you supposed to know if anything worked? Well, you can try this little command:

```
ldapsearch -x -b '' -s base "(objectclass=*)" namingContexts
```

The -b flag specifies the search base. Here we're using the default. If all has gone well up to this point, you should get something that looks like the following:

```
# extended LDIF
#
# LDAPv3
# base <> with scope base
# filter: (objectclass=*)
# requesting: namingContexts
#

# search result
search: 2
result: 0 Success

# numResponses: 1
```

Specifically, you are looking for the line that says namingContexts which is, after all, what we asked for. Does it look like what we defined in slapd.conf? It should.

Good. Now we need to enter some real information into the database. I'll cover some nice graphical tools to do this shortly, but before we start adding a lot of data, we need to seed the database at a fairly basic level. You do this by creating an LDIF file (LDAP data interchange format). Warning: This gets a little wordy, but I will explain. Each stanza represents an entry into the data hierarchy. Each subsequent stanza builds on the one above it. Look at the description: attribute, and you'll see what each represents.

```
dn: dc=salmar,dc=com
objectClass: top
objectClass: dcObject
objectClass: organization
dc: salmar
o: salmar
description: Salmar Domain

dn: cn=Manager,dc=salmar,dc=com
objectclass: organizationalRole
cn: Manager
```

```
dn: ou=people,dc=salmar,dc=com
ou: people
objectClass: top
objectClass: organizationalUnit
description: Salmar Address Book

dn: cn=Marcel Gagne,ou=staff,o=salmar
cn: Marcel Gagne
sn: Gagne
objectclass: top
objectclass: person
objectClass: organizationalPerson
objectClass: inetOrgPerson
mail: mggagne@salmar.com
telephoneNumber: 555-0918
givenname: Marcel
```

 Note In the above example, make sure you change my domain (salmar.com) to yours. Furthermore, make sure that your lines have no leading or trailing spaces. This can make the data import fail.

Creating this definition file doesn't give you a database. To get this information, you need to use the `ldapadd` command. Pretend that I saved this file as `staff.ldif`. The command is as follows:

```
ldapadd -f staff.ldif -xv -D "cn=Manager,dc=salmar,dc=com" -w secret
```

The `-w` lets you pass your simple authentication password. A `-W` tells the command to prompt you for the password. You could, if you wanted to, add as much information to this LDIF file as you needed. You could also add more later. The stanzas describing the root, domain, and administrator do not need to be added each time. What's done is done. Because my database looked a little lonely with only one name, I decided to add another, historic figure.

```
dn: cn=Isaac Newton,ou=staff,dc=salmar,dc=com
cn: Isaac Newton
sn: Newton
objectclass: top
objectclass: person
```

```
objectClass: organizationalPerson
objectClass: inetOrgPerson
mail: inewton@salmar.com
telephoneNumber: 555-0930
givenname: Isaac
```

Take note of those attributes. They are part of this globally-defined, unique list of names that I talked about at the beginning and contained in those schema files. How an `inetOrgPerson` can be defined is described in RFC 2798. Look there for details.

It might help at this point to pause and look over what we've done. Start by taking a look at that LDIF file we created for adding our initial data (including Mr. Newton's information). If you look at the "dn=" line in each paragraph, you should see a pattern there. What you have is a hierarchical directory (Figure 16-1). The domain definition is first under the root (dc=salmar,dc=com), followed by an administrator entry (cn=Manager) followed by an organization unit (people) and finally, entries for each person.

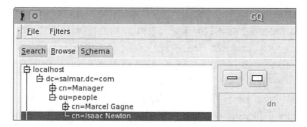

FIGURE 16-1   LDAP is a hierarchical directory.

Okay, we are pretty much done. The big question, of course, is "What do we get for our troubles?" Oh, and "Did it work?" In searching for an answer to these questions, start with Netscape. Because Konqueror is LDAP-enabled, it will do what we want here. Using your own domain (of course), do a lookup by entering a URL such as:

```
ldap://server_name/cn=some name,ou=org_unit,dc=your_domain,dc=dom
```

Figure 16-2 shows the results I get when I use my own LDAP configuration.

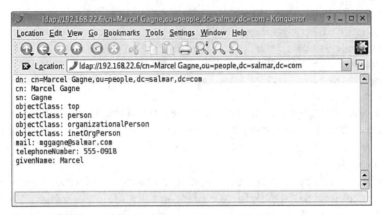

FIGURE 16-2   Using Konqueror to do an LDAP lookup.

KAddressBook

Wonderful! The information we so laboriously entered is now visible in the browser. That's nice, but it's not quite an address book either. For that, we can use KAddressBook, the KDE address book (command name :kaddressbook). You can start it on its own or select it from the side bar in Kontact. If you are using Kmail on it's own, you can also click Tools on the menu bar and select Address Book. (Kontact and Kmail are covered later in the book in Chapter 24, "Email Clients.")

Once the address book is up, click Settings on the menu bar and select Configure KAddressBook. A configuration window will appear. Select LDAP lookup from the sidebar. In the window that appears, there will likely be no LDAP servers defined. Click the Add Host button at the bottom to add your new server. A small window will appear asking for the server information (Figure 16-3). All you need to add here is the host and the Base DN (in my example, dc=salmar,dc=com).

When your server appears in the list, click the check box beside it to activate it for searching. Click OK to close the configuration window and you are back to the address book. Click Tools on the menu bar and select Lookup Addresses in the LDAP Directory (you can also click the magnifying glass icon in the icon bar). When the search window appears, put in the name (or partial name) of the person you want to search for in the search field and click the search button. The results appear in the window below (Figure 16-4).

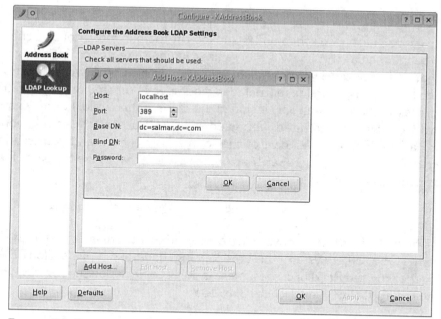

FIGURE 16-3   Adding an LDAP search host in the KDE address book

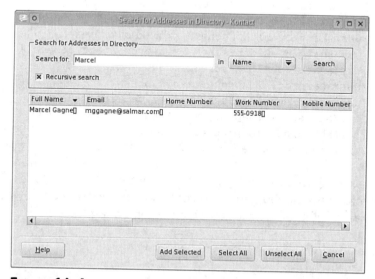

FIGURE 16-4   An LDAP search using the KDE address book

LDAP in Depth

Let's get back to those schema files and look at them in more detail. Schema files define the data and how it is organized in your directories, including the format of attributes, syntax and so on. The Red Hat package installation, which I used in my initial tests, included a number of schema files by default, whereas the source install only included the `core.schema` file. For my example to work as demonstrated, you need to include at least three additional schema files. These are all part of the source distribution, and you will find them in `/usr/local/etc/openldap/schema`. Here's what the top part of my `slapd.conf` file looks like:

```
include          /usr/local/etc/openldap/schema/core.schema
```

That's it. There are, however, several other schemas available in the schema. On another system, this time running Mandrake 10, I installed LDAP using the provided RPM packages. Here is the list of included schema from the default `slapd.conf` file in `/etc/openldap`:

```
include /usr/share/openldap/schema/core.schema
include /usr/share/openldap/schema/cosine.schema
include /usr/share/openldap/schema/corba.schema
include /usr/share/openldap/schema/inetorgperson.schema
include /usr/share/openldap/schema/java.schema
include /usr/share/openldap/schema/krb5-kdc.schema
include /usr/share/openldap/schema/kerberosobject.schema
include /usr/share/openldap/schema/misc.schema
include /usr/share/openldap/schema/nis.schema
include /usr/share/openldap/schema/openldap.schema
include /usr/share/openldap/schema/autofs.schema
include /usr/share/openldap/schema/samba.schema
include /usr/share/openldap/schema/kolab.schema
```

Let's get back to LDIF information and entering data by using LDIF files. If you had to enter all 500 names currently in your address book, you would have to create 500 LDIF entries that looked something like this:

```
dn: cn=Galileo Galilei,ou=staff,o=salmar
cn: Galileo Galilei
sn: Galilei
objectclass: top
objectclass: person
```

```
objectClass: organizationalPerson
objectClass: inetOrgPerson
mail: ggalilei@salmar.com
telephoneNumber: 555-8708
givenname: Galileo
```

Let's look at some alternatives, shall we? There are some great graphical tools out there which I will talk about shortly, but for starters, it's likely that you have this address book somewhere on your Windows email client. Perhaps you or your office is running Outlook with a large collection of email addresses. You could export that address book to a CSV file (a comma-delimited ASCII file) and, from that file, create a single LDIF file to import. The missing step, of course, is how you easily convert that CSV file to an LDIF file.

I put together this little perl script to tackle that very issue. (There is more on scripting in Appendix B, "Automation and Scripting.") You can use Kate or vi to create this (both were covered in Chapter 10, "Becoming One With The Shell").

```perl
#!/usr/bin/perl
# importcsv.pl : Create LDIF file from CSV addressbook
# Marcel Gagné

open (LDIF_FILE,"+>/tmp/loadfile.ldif");
##  This is our temporary LDIF file.

$csv_file = @ARGV[0];
open (CSVFILE,"$csv_file");
##  Open the CSV file.

while ($line = <CSVFILE>)
  {
    chomp $line;
      ($full_name, $email, $street, $city, $poscode)
         = split (",", $line, 5);
##  I only really care about the first two attributes for this
example
    ($first_name, $last_name) = split (" ", $full_name, 2);


    printf LDIF_File ("%s,"dn:
cn=$full_name,ou=people,dc=domain,dc=dom");
```

```
    printf LDIF_FILE ("%s","cn: $full_name");
    printf LDIF_FILE ("%s","sn: $last_name");
    printf LDIF_FILE ("%s","objectclass: top");
    printf LDIF_FILE ("%s","objectclass: person");
    printf LDIF_FILE ("%s","objectclass: organizationalPerson");
    printf LDIF_FILE ("%s","objectclass: inetOrgPerson");
    printf LDIF_FILE ("%s","mail: $email");
    printf LDIF_FILE ("%s","givenname: $first_name");
}

close CSVFILE;
exit (0);
```

Make sure you substitute your own domain in the script. Save the file as importcsv.pl, then make the script executable and run it.

```
chmod +x importcsv.pl
./importcsv.pl myfile.csv
```

The script takes one argument, and that is the pathname of your CSV file. You could modify this to take a second argument that would then be the LDIF file's pathname, but I chose to use a default name in /tmp (namely /tmp/loadfile.ldif).

That's great. You can now import all of that data with the following command:

```
ldapadd -c -f loadfile.ldif -xv -D "cn=Manager,dc=salmar,dc=com" -W
```

The -W flag tells the ldapadd command to ask for the password at the command line, but the really interesting flag is the -c option. Because of the sheer number of LDAP entries this perl script might be generating, we don't want the LDAP command to choke every time it encounters an error. The -c tells the command to continue regardless of any errors it might encounter.

GQ, A Graphical LDAP Tool

Suddenly, we have an LDAP database populated with all of the data from the corporate address books (or, for the more popular among you, personal address books). This is a great approach for that initial load, but what do you do when you want to casually add data to this directory? This constant creation of LDIF files can get a little tedious. If you check your Linux distribution CD, you might just find a little Gtk-based package called GQ, a rather innocuous name for a wonderful tool that provides an LDAP directory browser, schema browser, and import/export utility. Best of all, it lets you add, delete, or modify single entries in your LDAP directory using a nice, friendly graphical interface (Figure 16-5).

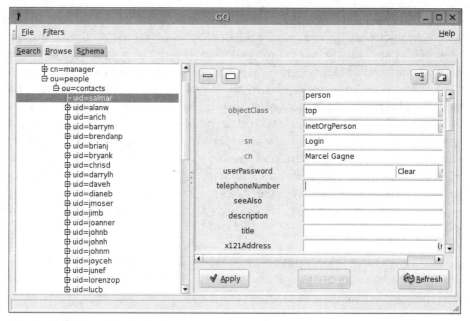

FIGURE 16-5   GQ is a graphical LDAP browser/editor.

You can also pick up the latest version of GQ from Bert Vermeulen and Peter Stamfest at Biot.com (`http://biot.com/gq`). As per my description, building GQ requires that you have Gtk installed (version 1.2 or better). Beyond that, the install process follows the standard extract and build five-step.

```
tar -xzvf gq-1.0beta1.tar.gz
cd gq-1.0beta1
./configure
make
su -c "make install"
```

Sure, I know that you all know this stuff, but nothing satisfies me like seeing a program get built from scratch on your own system. Am I right? I digress.

Start the program by simply typing the command name at a shell prompt:

```
gq &
```

If you have an LDAP server configured and running on that host, gq automagically takes note of it and offers it as a default. Notice that the program window has three tabs: Search, Browse, and Schema. From the Search tab, you can enter all or part of a name in your LDAP directory and find it. There are three fields here. The first is your name search field, the second is your LDAP server, and the third lets you specify where in your directory the search takes place, such as dc=salmar,dc=com in my sample organization. If you leave the name field blank, gq will return all the names in your LDAP directory.

From the Browse tab, you can add or modify an entry. To modify an existing name, click down through the directory tree until you find the entry you want. Click on that entry, and a box opens on the right side from which you can modify or update any information. You can also right-click in the left list and specify Delete (to remove an entry) or New to create a brand new entry.

I'm going to wrap up this discussion in a moment, but I do want to show you one last thing. Click on File, and choose Preferences (pressing <Ctrl+P> works as well), and you'll see a number of configuration options which you can explore for yourself. I do want to point out the Server tab, however, which lets you add other servers to administer (or query). Click on Server, then New and fill in the appropriate information.

Other Graphical LDAP Clients

One of the first places you might want to look for an alternative is Webmin. You'll find LDAP Users and Groups under Webmin's System tab. To get to it directly on your server, use this quick link:

```
https://your_server:10000/ldap-useradmin/index.cgi
```

Another tool well worth your while is called Luma (available at http://luma.sourceforge.net). This is a great-looking QT Python application and as such, doesn't require you to compile anything. You do, however, need the PyQT and python-ldap packages to use it.

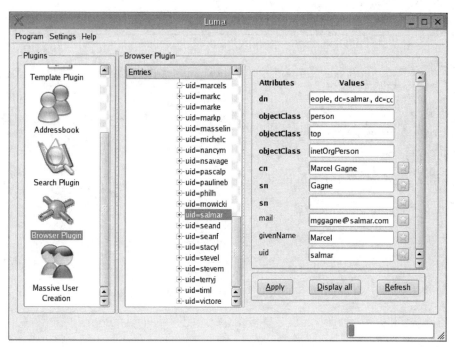

FIGURE 16-6   Using Luma to administer an LDAP server.

Going Further

In this chapter, I've given you the basics for setting up an LDAP server. Still, this is a very complex topic covering an extremely flexible piece of network infra-structure that can burrow into almost every part of your system, including user authentication. When you start dealing with this aspect of directory services, a well thought-out configuration is essential.

Getting that deep is beyond the scope of this book; there are large and heavy tomes covering that single topic alone. To create a basic directory server and address book, you shouldn't have any problems with the information given here. To go further, I highly recommend that you take some time at the OpenLDAP web site. The `www.openldap.org/faq/data/cache/73.html` page is a good place to start.

Resources

GQ

http://biot.com/gq

Luma

http://luma.sourceforge.net

OpenLDAP

www.openldap.org

17

Web Services

The corporate web site is a mainstay of the modern business. The costs of hosting a domain have dropped, and most businesses provide, at the very least, the equivalent of a full-page or multipage ad for the world to see. It's just part of the cost of doing business, and for many small companies, it is a cost they can easily afford. So why would you want to run your own web server?

Web sites can be far more complex than a one-page ad, however, and having control over your own server (as opposed to remote hosting) can offer you some interesting possibilities beyond just advertising. These include interactive pages or local programs that can provide information in your own databases. Even if you choose to continue hosting off-site, you may still want to run your own web server. Another exciting possibility is the creation of a groupware server or web-based email system. Imagine being able to access your email from any PC with a browser and from anywhere in the world. Web servers aren't just about serving up static pages anymore. They are part of your corporate information structure.

The Apache Web Server

Linux distributions come with the world's most popular and most flexible web server: the Apache server. Like other open source projects, the Apache server can be built from scratch and customized at will. It also provides extensive module support, allowing you to plug in additional functionality, such as database support modules or SSL encryption.

The name Apache is actually a homonym for the original description of the server in its early development. Originally, it was based on the NCSA httpd web server. Developers kept patching and enhancing the code. When asked what their project was, legend has it that the developers called it a "patchy" web server. I suppose they could have said a patchwork server, but Apache caught on, and the rest, as they say, is history.

You can always pick up the latest code for the Apache server from the Apache web site, but it is almost guaranteed to already be in your Linux distribution, providing you with a precompiled, easy-to-install version that will invariably include a number of the more popular modules, such as database and PHP support. If you want to or would prefer to build your Apache server from scratch, I'll show you how in a moment.

Building Apache from Source

The first thing to do is get the latest source from the Apache Software Foundation web site (www.apache.org).

From there, download the source and save it to a temporary directory. For this example, I'll work with release 2.0. The first thing I did was extract the source into my directory, as follows:

```
tar -xzvf httpd-2.0.49.tar.gz
cd httpd-2.0.49
./configure --with-apxs2 --enable-modules=most --enable-mods-
shared=all --enable-ssl
```

This configures Apache for installation into the default directory structure of /usr/local/apache. In the case of a Red Hat installation (along with some others), the default directory is /home/httpd. If you want a different installation directory, use the --prefix option:

```
./configure --prefix=/home/httpd (other options follow)
```

The configure script has a number of additional flags or options that you can set. You might want to run ./configure --help before you start your installation. For now, I'll keep it simple and use the defaults as in my first example. When the configure script has finished creating its Makefiles, type make followed by make install to complete the installation.

```
make
make install
```

A number of defaults are assumed if you choose the standard configuration. For instance, your document root is assumed to be /usr/local/apache2/htdocs, and your cgi-bin directory is assumed to be /usr/local/apache2/cgi-bin which, for the most part, should be just fine.

Once your server is installed, you need to start it with the apachectl command.

```
/usr/local/apache2/bin/apachectl start
```

You stop the server by using the stop option instead of start—but I bet you figured that out. To test your installation, fire up your favorite browser—Netscape, Lynx, or Konqueror—and point it to your new server. Assuming that you just did your installation on a server called your_server, use this URL:

```
http://your_server
```

You should get a page that looks very much like Figure 17-1.

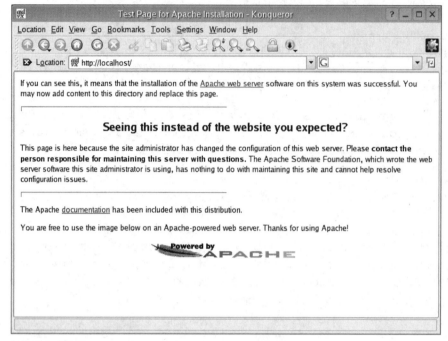

FIGURE 17-1   The face of a fresh Apache installation.

At this point, you could actually start putting web pages (HTML documents) into your server's document root. Using my build from source example, that would be the `/usr/local/apache2/htdocs` directory.

If you look at your running processes, the server itself will generally show up as `httpd`. If your web server was installed as part of a Debian apt-get or basic installation, there is a good possibility that the executable is actually called apache rather than `httpd`. You can verify this by listing the apache package files with this command:

```
dpkg -L apache | more
```

A Brief Visit to PHP Land

Before I delve into the configuration option, I'd like you to consider building PHP (or installing it from your CD packages). At the time of this writing, the latest release was php-4.3.6, which is what I use in the example below. Once again, this is something you can work with by using the packages provided by your distribution. Still, building the package from source does provide you with the latest and greatest in terms of both features and security. While this is mostly another example of the extract and build process I described in Chapter 7, "Installing New Applications," there are a few configuration flags associated with the Apache server you just created.

```
tar -xzvf php-4.3.6.tar.gz
cd php-4.3.6
./configure --with-apxs2=/usr/local/apache2/bin/apxs --with-mysql
--with-pgsql
make
make install
```

The two most popular open source databases are arguably PostgreSQL and MySQL. The above configure statement builds PHP with support for both. Once the `make` has been completed, you may want to change a parameter or two in the `php.ini` configuration file. On most pre-packaged installs, the file will be in `/etc`. Assuming you built from source, the default will be `/usr/local/etc`.

Now, to get your Apache server to work with PHP pages, you need to add this directive into your `httpd.conf` file:

```
AddType application/x-httpd-php .php .phtml
```

Finally, we want pages called `index.php` to automatically load when we visit a directory on our web server in much the same way that pages called `index.html` are automatically loaded. Look for this line in your `httpd.conf`:

```
DirectoryIndex index.html index.html.var
```

If it doesn't already exist because you built from source, add `index.php` so that the line looks like this:

```
DirectoryIndex index.html index.html.var index.php
```

Basic Apache Configuration

Most of the configuration information is in one file: the `httpd.conf` file. If you built from scratch, you'll find the configuration files in `/usr/local/apache2/conf`.

On my preinstalled Debian Apache server, the `httpd.conf` file lives in the `/etc/apache` directory and, on my Red Hat system, it is in `/etc/httpd/conf`. It's a good idea to look around in this directory, because some systems break up the `httpd.conf` file as is the case with my Mandrake 10 system, where most of the settings I will be mentioning are in `commonhttpd.conf`.

Because I gave you a number of possible directories, you might be wondering where you should be looking if you did not install from source. One way to find out exactly where this file is on your system (other than running the `find` command) is to ask the Apache executable itself by calling it with the `-V` flag. This will show you the compile time settings of a number of parameters, including paths to configuration files. For the sake of this example, I am going to assume that the Apache executable is in your PATH.

```
httpd -V
```

On my Debian system, I type `apache -V` instead. Look for a line that says SERVER_CONFIG_FILE. It indicates the full path to the configuration file.

Before we continue, I should tell you that any change to the web server requires a restart of the server. With any current Apache installation, this is done using the `apachectl` program (as demonstrated previously).

Common Changes

The `httpd.conf` file is generally a well-documented file, and it pays to get familiar with the settings if you are going to get fancy with your server. The first thing I want to look at is the server name. Your host may be known by different names on the same network. A common example is the classic `www.mydomain.dom` format. Your server may respond initially as `myserver.mydomain.dom`, but you may want to force the www form. Note that this has to be a valid host name for your server. Change the `ServerName` setting.

```
ServerName www.mydomain.dom
```

Other parameters you may want to change are the user ID and group ID your server runs as. These are the `User` and `Group` configuration parameters. The root user still starts the server, but the Apache binary switches to this user for its operation. Some sites have a user called www to run web services. Others use a user called nobody. Mine uses one called apache. You may use

whatever nonroot user your server is configured for. This is defined in the
`httpd.conf` file where you find these lines:

```
User apache
Group apache
```

Every once in a while, something goes wrong with a document, and the
server generates an error message with a note to contact the administrator of
the site. The server maintains this information in the `ServerAdmin` parameter.
The administrator may well be at some address other than that of the server.
Find and modify the line that looks like this:

```
ServerAdmin webmaster@somedomain.dom
```

You may want to make other changes, and there is certainly a lot that you
can do with those changes. As luck would have it, Apache comes with its own
HTML documentation. After the default installation completes, you should
see a link to the documentation on the test page.

Now that you have an Apache server running with PHP, let's do something
practical that has nothing to do with running a web site. How does free web-
based email for your company sound?

SquirrelMail

How many of you have a separate hotmail or Yahoo email account for those
times when you are on the road and can't get to your email? That's just nuts,
and there's no reason not to have access to your own email if you are running
your own server. That's where SquirrelMail comes into play.

Billed as "Webmail for Nuts," this is an email package you need to check out.
SquirrelMail is written in PHP with full IMAP support. It is themeable, is customizable, includes an address book, supports MIME, and more. Best of all, it
is distributed free of charge under the GPL. You can get Squirrelmail at
`www.squirrelmail.org`.

Before I get into how to install SquirrelMail, you need to make sure that
IMAP is installed and running on your system. The IMAP service is part of the
same package that handles POP3. (I covered this in Chapter 15, "Electronic
Mail," when I discussed setting up a Postfix email server.) In any modern Linux

distribution that uses `xinetd` for your network services, edit your `/etc/xinetd.conf.d/imap` file. It should look something like this:

```
service imap
{
        socket_type                 = stream
        wait                        = no
        user                        = root
        server                      = /usr/sbin/imapd
        log_on_success              += DURATION USERID
        log_on_failure              += USERID
        disable                     = no
}
```

Make sure that `disable` is set to `no`. For the changes to take effect, restart `inetd` (or `xinetd`) with:

```
kill -HUP `cat /var/run/xinetd.pid`
```

Remember, those are back quotes in the command.

Pretty much everything related to the installation of SquirrelMail happens in the same directory. Once you have downloaded your source, change directory to your Apache server's document root. Because I compiled my Apache server myself, that would be in `/usr/local/apache2/htdocs`. On many default package installations, document root is at `/var/www/html`. From document root, extract the SquirrelMail distribution and do a little name changing.

```
cd /usr/local/apache2/htdocs
tar -xzvf squirrelmail-1.4.2.tar.gz
mv squirrelmail-1.4.2 squirrelmail
cd squirrelmail
```

As you have probably figured out, there won't be any `make` or `make install` here. In fact, when I use my browser to access my mail, I'm going to do something simple, like `http://myserver/squirrelmail`. The real reason for this is that I don't want to have to remember version numbers every time I try to get to my mail, hence the rename. The big gotcha you may run into here has to do with the data directory; it has to be writable by the web server software. That means you need to change some ownerships. You'll need to know what username and group ID your web server runs as. You can find this out by looking for these lines in your `httpd.conf` file:

```
User apache
Group apache
```

Depending on your default installation, this may be nobody or apache as well. Armed with this information, execute the following command from the SquirrelMail install directory (in my example, I will use the apache username and group):

```
chown -R apache data
chgrp -R apache data
```

You could also save yourself a couple of keystrokes by typing it all on one line, like this:

```
chown -R apache.apache data
```

But you already knew that, didn't you? Okay, we are almost there. A little configuration magic and we are ready to go. Still in the SquirrelMail installation directory, look for an executable file called configure and execute it in this way:

```
./configure
```

This will bring up a menu much like the following:

```
SquirrelMail Configuration : Read: config_default.php (1.4.0)
---------------------------------------------------------------
Main Menu --
1.   Organization Preferences
2.   Server Settings
3.   Folder Defaults
4.   General Options
5.   Themes
6.   Address Books (LDAP)
7.   Message of the Day (MOTD)
8.   Plugins
9.   Database

D.   Set pre-defined settings for specific IMAP servers
```

```
C.   Turn color on
S    Save data
Q    Quit

Command >>
```

Walk through the various menu items and configure them for your site. Of particular importance are Options 1 through 4. Take special note of the Server settings menu item; this is where you'll need to enter your domain name and mail server information. Make sure that you also take a look at Option D, which asks for the type of IMAP server you are running. (Many default package installations are still using the uw IMAP server.) When you are done, save your work and point your browser to your SquirrelMail installation.

```
http://your_server/squirrelmail/
```

If all has gone according to plan, you should see something that looks like Figure 17-2.

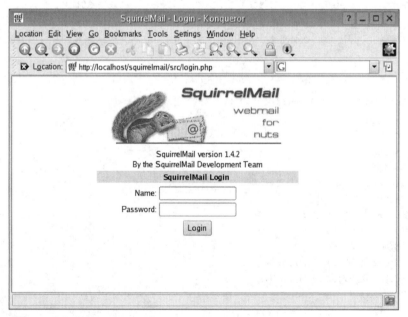

FIGURE 17-2   Logging in to SquirrelMail.

Plugins, Plugins, and More Plugins

SquirrelMail supports plugins, and developers and supporters of the packages have been as busy as, well, squirrels gathering up nuts for the winter. Look for the plugins link on the SquirrelMail web site menu, and you'll see just what I mean. Several very useful plugins are included with SquirrelMail, and you may want to activate them. For instance, there's a feature to import an email address into your address book (abook_take), an appointment calendar (calendar), a spell checker (squirrelspell), and more.

To activate a plugin, go back into your SquirrelMail directory on your web server and run `./configure` again. Now, choose Option 8 for plugins. On the next menu, you should see a list under Available Plugins. Select the one you want by typing its number and pressing <Enter>. When you are done, save your work and exit. Now log back into SquirrelMail, and the plugin you asked for will have been activated.

I started this by mentioning that there are plugins you will probably want from the SquirrelMail web site, plugins that aren't included with the basic package. For instance, one I kind of like is a weather plugin that shows me the temperature, pressure, and so forth, just below my folder list, on the left side. Let's say that you want to install this plugin. Start by downloading it from the SquirrelMail web site. Then, `cd` to wherever you have SquirrelMail installed. You'll find a directory called `plugins`. Once there, extract the plugin you just downloaded (note that being in Canada, I downloaded the Canadian weather plugin).

```
cd /usr/local/apache2/htdocs/squirrelmail/plugins
tar -tzvf /path_to/can_weather_2.2.2.tar.gz
```

When you extract any plugin, make sure that you look at the accompanying README. Sometimes you need to modify something, and sometimes you just need to activate your plugin. To activate my plugin, I run `./configure` once again,

See my weather report in SquirrelMail's left folder list (Figure 17-3)? Look around. Experiment. You'll find that there are many options to give SquirrelMail that personal or corporate touch.

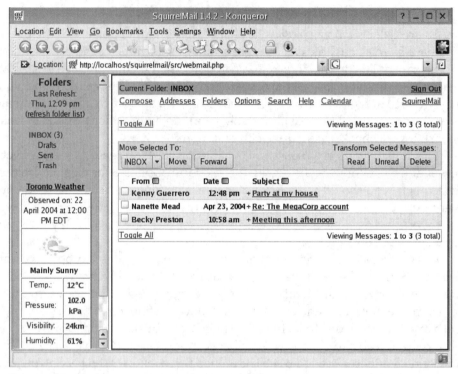

FIGURE 17-3   SquirrelMail with the weather plugin activated.

Congratulations; your email is now always as near as the nearest browser.

Before I introduce you to another powerful use for an internal web server (and I promise you, you will like this), I'm going to take a little side trip and tell you about an open source database called PostgreSQL.

An Introduction to PostgreSQL

PostgreSQL is an advanced multiuser relational database management system (RDBMS) distributed freely along with its source code. Originally written in 1985 and worked on by many developers worldwide, PostgreSQL is fast, is powerful, supports most (if not all) SQL standards, and (best of all) is free. You probably don't even have to go looking for PostgreSQL, because it is packaged as part of most major Linux distributions. In fact, on some systems, PostgreSQL is part of the default installation.

Still, if you want to work with the latest and greatest version of the software, it makes sense to download the source and build it yourself. Even if you do have PostgreSQL preinstalled, there are some basics that you will need to configure, so let's go through the process together. To get things started with PostgreSQL in this environment, it is usually just a question of typing `service postgresql start`.

Of course, the latest version is available by visiting the PostgreSQL web site (`www.postgresql.org`) or by visiting one of the mirrors (the main site can get busy, so it provides a list of alternate sites). Should you decide to go the source route, download the latest bundle, extract it to a temporary location, change directory to the source directory, and build PostgreSQL using these steps:

```
tar -xzvf postgresql-7.4.2.tar.gz
cd postgresql-7.4.2
./configure
make
make install
```

The distribution directory (`postgresql-7.4.2`, in this case) has a nice `INSTALL` file that you'll want to take a moment to read, because there are some options related to the configure script that you may find useful. For instance, by default, PostgreSQL installs in the `/usr/local/pgsql` directory, and you may want to use another location.

When the compile is done, PostgreSQL has to know how to find its libraries. You can always modify your environment variable to include `/usr/local/pgsql/lib` in the `LD_LIBRARY_PATH`, but it's probably easier to add the path to the `/etc/ld.so.conf` file. This is a text file that tells the system where to search for libraries. Because it is straight text, just add the path to your libraries and run this command as root:

```
ldconfig
```

If you decided to install a PostgreSQL binary from your CD, a `postgres` user will likely already have been created as part of the installation. Otherwise, create a `postgres` user with its home directory being the PostgreSQL install directory. Then, assign a password to the user and log in as `postgres`. If you built your database along with me, you will be in the `/usr/local/pgsql` directory. The next step is to create a data directory.

```
mkdir data
```

To initialize the database for the first time, use:

```
$ bin/initdb -D /usr/local/pgsql/data
```

That is, of course, the data directory that you just finished creating. You will see a number of messages going by as PostgreSQL reports on what it is doing. Some default permissions are set. In addition, a default database is created along with PostgreSQL's own database (pg_database) for user and other database information. Several views are then created, after which you should get a message like this:

```
Success. You can now start the database server using:
/usr/bin/postmaster -i -D /var/lib/pgsql
    or
/usr/bin/pg_ctl -i -D /var/lib/pgsql start
```

Either option will work, but the second is a better choice, because it launches the process in the background for you. You will also want to add this to your start-up files (rc.local) for system boot.

> *Quick Tip* I've been going through a source install here, but it is important that you make sure that the "postmaster" is running with the -i flag to allow for TCP and web connections to the database. That is true even if you are using an RPM or deb installation and running from /etc/init.d/postgresql.

Next, you need to create some default PostgreSQL users, add Root, and add the user named nobody. Start by logging in as your postgres user and execute the following commands to add users root and nobody to your PostgreSQL system:

```
bin/createuser root
```

When you are prompted for root's UID, accept the default. When asked whether or not user root is allowed to create databases, answer y. When asked whether root is allowed to create users, I answered n. Now, do the same thing for user nobody. The only difference is that I answer n to the question of whether user nobody is allowed to create databases as well. Depending on the version of PostgreSQL that you are using, the question of whether or not a user is allowed to create other users may be worded this way:

```
Is user "whoever" a superuser?
```

The answer is still n. Finally, with the creation of user nobody, you are asked whether createuser should create a database for nobody. Answer y, and you are finished creating users.

Raising The Bar: eGroupWare

Now that you have a database installed and running, it's time to turn your attention to groupware solutions.

What sets groupware apart is the scope of the web-based intelligence it provides and the collaborative possibilities it opens. Groupware suites may include centralized electronic mail, calendars, address books, discussion forums, call tracking, and any number of other applications. One web-based groupware suite that I think is well worth checking into is eGroupWare.

eGroupWare is a GPL suite with an open source API so that applications can easily be created and added to the system. Among the applications included are email, calendaring, an infolog for tracking customer calls and setting up to-do lists, a trouble ticket system, forums, personal and corporate addressbooks, knowledge base, Wiki documentation system, and more. There's also a site manager feature so individual users can create and deploy their own web sites. eGroupWare does all this while sporting a slick-looking and very business ready face (Figure 17-4).

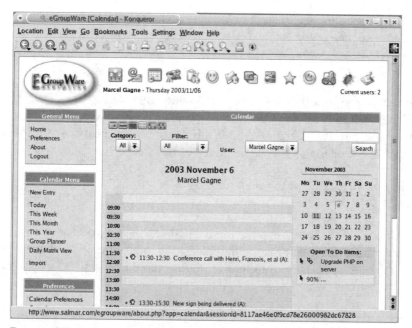

FIGURE 17-4   eGroupWare's calendar view.

eGroupWare supports the two most popular open source database formats, namely MySQL and PostgreSQL. In the following example, I will show you how to run it with PostgreSQL, but the setup is just as easy, and only slightly different, with MySQL. To get in on the eGroupWare action, start by downloading the package from `www.eGroupWare.org`. Tarballs and binary packages are both available.

To install from the tarred and gzipped bundle, extract the package into your web server's document root. In my built-from-source Apache installation, that is `/usr/local/apache2/htdocs`. Once again, a default RPM-based install (such as Red Hat) often has it at `/var/www/html`.

```
cd /var/www/html
tar -xzvf eGroupWare-relnum.tar.gz
```

This creates a directory called `egroupware`. Now, assuming that your Apache server runs as user and group apache, change the permissions on the directory tree in this way:

```
chown -R apache.apache egroupware
```

With a PostgreSQL installation, your next step is to create a PostgreSQL user to access the database. Do this by switching to your postgres user:

```
su - postgres
createuser egroupware
    Shall the new user be allowed to create databases? (y/n) y
    Shall the new user be allowed to create more new users? (y/n) n
    CREATE USER
```

When asked whether this user is allowed to create other databases, say yes. When asked whether this user can create other users, make that one a no. You are almost there. All that's left to do is create a database for eGroupWare. Still logged in as the postgres user, type the following:

```
    createdb -U egroupware egroupware_db
    CREATE DATABASE
```

You could, if you don't like the idea of just calling it egroupware, use pretty much any name you want for the database, or modify the name slightly as I did above. After this, you are done with the command line work. Time to fire up your browser and finalize eGroupWare's settings. Open up Mozilla, Konqueror, or any Javascript-enabled browser, and point to your web server like this:

```
http://yourwerbserver/egroupware/setup
```

On this screen, you enter the relevant information for your setup to create your header configuration file (`header.inc.php`). If you changed your DB user from egroupware to something else, make sure you identify it here. The same holds for the database name. You should also assign a header password and an administration password. The header password lets you modify or recreate the configuration file you are building now.

When you are finished, you are taken to the setup/header login screen. Because you have already created the header file, chances are you do not wish to do it all over again. Your concern now is the actual eGroupWare setup.

Once you have logged in using the admin password, the setup checks to see if your database has been properly created and the appropriate user ID defined in the header creation step. If everything has gone well up to this point, you'll be at Step 1 of the local configuration. Click Install to create the application tables and install the eGroupWare suite of applications. The system will chug along for a couple of minutes while it does its thing.

When everything has been completed, check the browser's screen to make sure that no error messages have been reported and click the Recheck My Installation button. If all has gone well, you can go to Step 2 and create your admin account (the option also exists to create three demo accounts, but you do not have to do this). Step 3 lets you define the default language, and Step 4 is for individual application management. From this dialogue, you can specify whether you want all of the applications (this is the default) or just some of them. When you log out from here, your installation will be completed.

It's time to start doing things with eGroupWare. Start by logging in with your admin account. This most likely means pointing your browser to `http://your.server.dom/egroupware`. Along the top of the screen, you'll see a number of icons representing the various groupware services. To the left, menus appear based on the functions of the current application, although a smaller menu with Home, Preferences, About, and Logout is always there. That look and feel can be modified to suit your personal tastes by clicking Preferences.

If you are the administrator, you can make changes for the entire organization. You can even force some defaults so that users cannot change them, a useful feature for the corporate administrator. User accounts can be created with predefined applications delivered to their specific login based on groups. For instance, the support group may need access to the trouble ticket system (Figure 17-5). Using this group-based approach provides you with a consistent set of tools for your users. Create your groups first, decide which applications they will need access to, and create your users based on those groups.

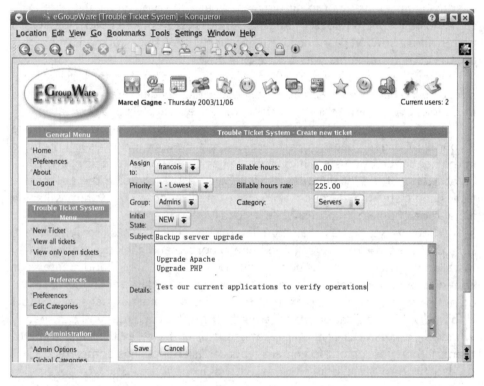

FIGURE 17-5   Entering a trouble ticket with eGroupWare.

In terms of the future and ongoing support, you'll find that eGroupWare has a very active community of users and developers. There are several mailing lists and an IRC channel, should you find yourself needing answers to your questions.

Moving On

As you can see, running an Apache web server isn't strictly restricted to serving up web sites. With SquirrelMail or eGroupWare, your entire organization is connected, and collaboration is only a step away.

Using a web browser for either straight electronic mail or the full groupware suite means that you don't have to install client software on each and every PC. Furthermore, it also means that your personal information is no longer tied to a particular workstation.

Resources

Apache Web Server
httpd://httpd.apache.org

eGroupware
www.egroupware.org

PostgreSQL
www.postgresql.org

SquirrelMail
www.squirrelmail.org

chapter
18
Samba

Samba was originally developed by Andrew Trigdell in the land down under. Using the server message block (SMB) protocol, Samba makes it possible to share resources between a surprisingly wide variety of operating systems. SMB, like many networking protocols, continues to evolve as developers do what developers do. Consequently, the current version (or incarnation, if you prefer) of the SMB protocol is actually called CIFS, for common Internet file system.

In case you are wondering where NetBIOS fits into this picture, that's what SMB evolved from, although NetBIOS isn't a protocol so much as an application programming interface (API) designed to provide the building blocks for creating LAN software.

Samba can provide file-sharing services between Microsoft Windows, OS/2, VMS, AIX, HPUX, Linux, and many others. Although most people tend to think of Samba as the means by which you replace Windows servers of various flavors with Linux machines, Samba is much more flexible than that. For instance, the lone Windows PC in my office has Client for Microsoft Networks loaded so that it can share files in the Network Neighborhood.

Let's say that this PC, which is called speedy, has a share called natika_c, which is actually the entire C: drive. From my Linux workstation, I can mount that drive using this command all on one line:

```
# mount -t smbfs -o username=natika,password=secret
//speedy/natika_c /mnt/natika
```

If I had a Samba share defined on my Linux server, I could mount it from another Linux server as though I was mounting a Windows share. I've got a small notebook called wiltravl running Linux. On a somewhat larger server called testsys, I've got Samba running. It has a share defined called winstuff. You might recall that with NFS, I specified the file system type with the -t flag, passed the appropriate options, and told it about the directory I was mounting to use this command all on one line:

```
# mount -t smbfs -o username=marcel,password=itsasecret //testsys/
winstuff
```

If I use the df command, I see the file system mounted as one of my local drives.

```
[root@wiltravl /root]# df
Filesystem            1k-blocks      Used Available Use% Mounted on
/dev/hda1              1517920    1405640     35172  98% /
/dev/hda5              2514172    1737840    648620  73% /data1
//testsys/winstuff     6109952    4611072   1498880  75%
/mnt/winstuff
```

Pretty cool stuff. With Samba, you can also make printers available to the Windows machines on the network. By the way, nothing stops you from being able to use Samba-exported printers from Linux either. If you want, you can even use Samba as your file-sharing system across your network, thereby replacing NFS.

Now that I have told you about some of the great things you can do with Samba, I suppose I should tell you how you go about doing them.

Getting and Building Samba

Just about every Linux distribution CD-ROM comes with a version of Samba, which you can install using rpm or dpkg, depending on your distribution. Debian users can, of course, use apt-get to pull in the latest distribution from the Debian site. But if you really want the latest and greatest, you need to get yourself to the Samba web site (www.samba.org). From there, you'll be asked to choose a local mirror from where you can download the Samba source code.

Go to the Download section. The Samba team makes it easy to decide what you need. The latest source is always called samba-latest.tar.gz. If you prefer, you can also find recent binaries for a variety of platforms, but they won't necessarily be as up to date as the source files. To build and install Samba from source, unpack the tarball into a temporary directory:

```
tar -xzvf samba-latest.tar.gz
```

This creates a directory suffixed with the current release number of the Samba source. When I wrote this next section, the Samba code was sitting at version 3.0.1.

```
cd samba-3.0.1
more README
cd source
./configure
make
make install
```

By default, Samba installs in the /usr/local/samba directory. If you prefer to have it install in another directory, you can use the --prefix=/path/to_dir flag when you do the ./configure step. After the installation has completed (assuming that you accepted the defaults), you need to create a Samba configuration file, which will live in /usr/local/samba/lib. The easiest way to do this is to copy the sample file provided along with the source into the appropriate directory:

```
cd /tmp_install_dir/samba-3.0.1/examples
cp smb.conf.default /usr/local/samba/lib/smb.conf
```

If you are working from a preinstalled Samba, particularly if you are running on an RPM-based system, you should look for a default `smb.conf` file in the `/etc` directory.

Using your favorite editor, open the `smb.conf` file and change these two parameters: `workgroup` and `server string`. For the `workgroup` parameter, I called mine ACCOUNTING with a server name of Testsys Samba Server. Next, find the `security` = variable, and set it to `user`. You should also set your password creation backend (`passdb` =) to `tdbsam`. Don't worry, it will all make sense shortly.

```
security = user
passdb backend = tdbsam
```

Now, let's start the Samba daemons.

```
/usr/local/samba/bin/smbd -D
/usr/local/samba/bin/nmbd -D
```

You'll want to add this to your startup scripts in `rc.local`. Say that your server is called myserver. To test Samba and see if you have done everything right, type the command:

```
/usr/local/samba/bin/smbclient -L myserver
```

If everything worked smoothly, you should see something like this appear on your screen:

```
Anonymous login successful
Domain=[ACCOUNTING] OS=[Unix] Server=[Samba 3.0.2a]

Sharename        Type        Comment
---------        ----        -------
homes            Disk        Home Directories
print$           Disk
pdf-generator    Printer     PDF Generator (only valid users)
IPC$             IPC         IPC Service (Testsys Samba Server 3.0.2a)
ADMIN$           IPC         IPC Service (Testsys Samba Server 3.0.2a)
hp4100           Printer     HP LaserJet 4100
laser            Printer     Samsung ML-1710 Series
```

Notice anything interesting when you did that? Without doing anything other than starting Samba with a valid configuration file, your printers are available as resources on the network. It is not necessary to define each printer individually. Samba takes for granted that they are shared resources—you are running a server, after all.

You can also use your Windows workstations to test all of this. Keep in mind that you need to have Client for Microsoft Networks installed on the PC in question. If you are doing this on an existing network of Windows PCs, this is very likely the case. Double-click the Network Neighborhood icon, and then double-click Entire Network. You should see the workgroup you just specified in your list. If you don't see it right away, don't despair. Windows can take a while to notice that a new workgroup or server has been added to the Network Neighborhood. If you are in a hurry, reboot the Windows PC.

Adding Samba Users

To do anything other than view public information on the server, you must be able to authenticate with the server. For that, you need to add some user accounts. The command for maintaining Windows users under Samba is pdbedit. To list the users currently in the database, use the -L flag, like this:

```
/usr/local/samba/bin/pdbedit -L
```

 Quick Tip For those of you who may have used Samba in the past, the smbpasswd command is still there, but you should switch, because smbpasswd will go away in time.

To get a more detailed listing of the users on the system, add a v to the command line as shown:

```
/usr/local/samba/bin/pdbedit -Lv
```

Note that passwords cannot be listed, only changed. When listing user information, you can also specify a single user on the command line.

```
/usr/local/samba/bin/pdbedit -Lv ggalilei
```

To add a new user, you must first create a Linux user name (Chapter 12, "Users and Groups") or use an existing user name. Then, do the following:

```
/usr/local/samba/bin/pdbedit -a -u username -f "Full Name"
```

The -a flag tells pdbedit to add a new user. The -u specifies the user name, while the -f flag indicates the user's full name. This is free form and must be inside double quotes if there are spaces; for example, when you use a first *and* last name. Pretend we have an employee named Isaac Newton with a Linux user name of inewton. The new command would be:

```
/usr/local/samba/bin/pdbedit -a -u inewton -f "Isaac Newton"
```

When you finish all of this, the system asks you for a password. For security reasons, you won't see the password as you type it. After you press <Enter>, you are asked to confirm the password by typing it again. Assuming everything went well, the system replies with something that looks like this:

```
Unix username:        inewton
NT username:
Account Flags:        [U            ]
User SID:             S-1-5-21-1077647134-3928151642-242114519-2004
Primary Group SID:    S-1-5-21-1077647134-3928151642-242114519-
2005
Full Name:
Home Directory:       \\francois\inewton
HomeDir Drive:
Logon Script:
Profile Path:         \\francois\inewton\profile
Domain:               FRANCOIS
Account desc:
Workstations:
Munged dial:
Logon time:           0
Logoff time:          Mon, 18 Jan 2038 22:14:07 GMT
Kickoff time:         Mon, 18 Jan 2038 22:14:07 GMT
Password last set:    Tue, 23 Mar 2004 18:11:54 GMT
Password can change:  Tue, 23 Mar 2004 18:11:54 GMT
Password must change: Mon, 18 Jan 2038 22:14:07 GMT
```

That's all there is to it. The next part of this operation takes place on the PC itself. Obviously, this will vary depending on the version of Windows you are working with. For instance, with XP, right-click on My Computer, and select Properties. The System Properties dialog appears with a number of tabs. Click the Computer Name tab. There's a space where you can enter some kind of description for the computer and below that a button labeled Change. Click it, and you'll be able to enter the computer name and the workgroup that you will be a part of, such as ACCOUNTING. After making the changes, reboot so that they take effect.

Configuring the Server

The order in which I've taken you through this process may seem a bit strange, but there is some method to my apparent madness. Samba is a complex beast with more parameters and configuration tweaks than I can possibly cover here. In fact, entire books have been devoted to Samba. Still, I can present you with the information you need to set up a server and start doing useful things. Because configuring a server exactly the way you want it will probably be a work in progress, you'll find that taking this process in stages reduces the chance of things simply not working. You have a working server, and you've decided on a means of password authentication. Now, let's get to the meat.

The notion of using a server like this is to provide what Samba calls *shares*: exported directories that can be mounted by Windows or Linux systems as drives. In Windows, these drives are associated with a drive letter, such as M:. There are also a number of configuration sections. Both shares and configuration sections are identified by a header in square brackets. Some of the ones you'll see as you look at your smb.conf file are as follows:

- [global]: These are parameters that affect the whole server and, as a result, everything that comes after it. You already encountered this when you set up encrypted passwords, a server name, and a workgroup. You've already seen two very important variables from this section:

  ```
  security = user
  passdb backend = tdbsam
  ```

- [homes]: This section defines home directories for users connecting to the system. By using a specific configuration macro in this section (and there are many), the Samba server automatically attaches the client to a share based on the user name. To set up a home section in this way, use the following example:

```
[homes]
    comment = Home Directories
    browseable = no
    path = /home/%u
    writable = yes
```

The %u macro substitutes the user's name as they authenticate with the Samba server. This assumes that you use /home as your top-level directory for people's home directories (as discussed in Chapter 12). In a system where home directories start from /disk2/users, the path changes accordingly.

- [printers]: The printers section is magic. With Samba, you can define individual printers as shares, or you can have Samba automatically make any printers you have defined in your /etc/printcap file available without any additional work. I'll cover this more when I talk about printing.

Go ahead and start using Samba's file sharing. Rather than testing this from a Windows PC at this time, try it from the command line. You do not have to be on a different machine to do this. Assume that you are still working with the user guitux.

```
smbclient //myserver/guitux -U guitux
```

The -U option specifies your Samba user login. Next, the system prompts for that user's password, which is the Samba password you created earlier.

```
Password: ********
Domain=[ACCOUNTING] OS=[Unix] Server=[Samba 3.0.2a]
smb: \>
```

At the prompt, you should be able to type dir and see the files in guitux's home directory. While you are there, type help at the smb prompt and have a look around.

The PC Side

The simplest setup involves setting up your Windows workstations to be part of the workgroup you have defined. Since so many people are still running earlier versions of Windows, I'll start there. On pre-XP machines, click the Start button and select Settings, then Control Panel. Double-click the Network icon. When the dialog box comes up, the Configuration tab is visible.

Look for the list defined by the phrase, "The following network components are installed." Before you can do any kind of Samba networking, you need to have Client for Microsoft Networks installed. The same is true for File and Printer Sharing for Microsoft Networks. If these are missing, get your Windows CD (the files may actually be on your disk if the system was preinstalled) and perform the following steps.

For Client for Microsoft Networks, click Add, choose Client, and then click the Add button again. You'll get a list of clients on the right and their manufacturers on the left. Click Microsoft in the left window. You should now see Client for Microsoft Networks at the top of that list. Click OK, and you should find yourself back at the network components list.

To install File and Printer Sharing for Microsoft Networks, you do the same sort of thing, except you specify Service instead of Client. When you get to the list of manufacturers, you should see it there. Click OK.

Now, click the Identification tab, and enter your PC's name and the workgroup name in the fields provided.

On a Windows XP system, the Windows sharing is usually already installed. You can check by going into your Network Connections (under the Control Panel) and right-clicking on the network interface to display Properties. You should see "File and Printer Sharing for Microsoft Networks" installed. To set your PC up with a workgroup, open the control panel and double-click on the System icon. A window labeled "System Properties" will appear. Click on the Computer Name tab. There, you can change the computer's descriptive name. The Computer Description text box is just a comment field that would appear if you were to query the client in Network Neighborhood (choose View>Details) or with `smbclient -L`. To give your computer a network name and join a workgroup, click the Change button you see there (Figure 18-1).

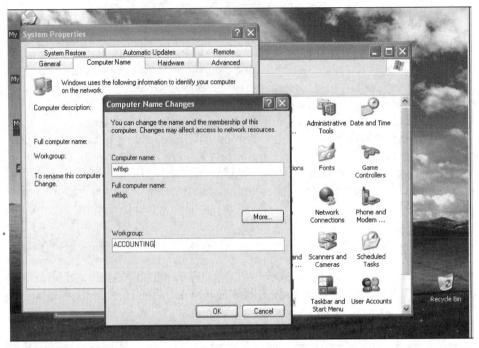

FIGURE 18-1　Specifying a workgroup in Windows networking.

Printing with Samba

As I mentioned earlier, the basics of printer definition and sharing are in a paragraph called, strangely enough, `[printers]`. Mine looks like this:

```
[printers]
        comment = My System Printers
        path = /var/spool/samba
        print ok = Yes
        guest ok = Yes
        browseable = No
```

The permissions here are pretty wide open. Anybody can browse these printers on the network and anybody can print to them. The `path` variable is the temporary spool directory where print files are kept while they are printed. In the case of printers, `browseable` is set to `No` here, because this isn't a share. All `/etc/printcap` printers automagically appear in the browse list.

You might recall that when I checked on the newly created server by executing `smbclient -L new_server`, it automatically listed all of the printers that were available. The normal method of creating a new printer in Windows is to click the Start button and then select Settings>Printers. Next, double-click the Add Printer icon, and select a network-connected printer. When you click Browse, you get the Network Neighborhood list of servers that you can navigate to find the printer you want.

From the Linux side, you can also create print queues that print to remote Samba printers. I'll talk about that, but if you are in a hurry, you can do something even simpler and quicker. If all you want to do is momentarily use a printer on the network and it is managed by a Samba server, try this trick.

Pretend that you are on a notebook called wltravl with no printers configured and that you want to be able to do a quick text print to a printer on a server called testsys. The printer is called laser. From the command line, type:

```
smbclient //testsys/laser
```

Assuming that you still have your printer settings so that guest printing or public access is allowed, press <Enter> at the password prompt and you should see this:

```
Password:
Domain=[ACCOUNTING] OS=[Unix] Server=[Samba 3.0.2a]
smb: \>
```

At the prompt, type `print` followed by the name of the file you want to print.

```
print /etc/profile
```

When you are done, all you have to do is type `quit` at the `smb: \>` prompt. The really cool thing about this is that you can do that with Windows printers on the network as well: If a PC has a printer that you need and that printer is shared on the network, you can do the very same thing. Do you want to see what a PC has available to share? Use `smbclient` with the `-L` option to list the information.

Printing from the Windows Client

To set up a printer in Windows, click the Start button and select Settings> Printers. Double-click the Add Printer icon. You should now see the Add Printer

Wizard. Click Next, choose Network Printer by clicking the radio button, and then click Browse.

You may need to click the plus sign (+) beside the appropriate host. Click the appropriate printer, and then click OK. The wizard then asks you for the printer type and manufacturer. At this point (because I don't know what printers you own), the rest is up to you.

Accessing the Network Neighborhood

So far, I've been talking from the perspective of providing file sharing to Windows users, but what about the other way around? As we work to deploy Linux desktops, we may encounter environments where a Windows server is still providing shared folders and printers. Even if the server is running Samba, those shared folders need to be accessible to both Windows and Linux desktops.

How easy is it to take advantage of the Network Neighborhood from a Linux desktop? Well, given that Samba on Linux does a great job of providing the same file and printer sharing that Windows servers used to, and sometimes still, provide, it should not be surprising that Samba client software tends to come as part of the standard installation on most modern Linux distributions. What that means is that you can connect to a Windows share on the network using the smbclient program. For example, the command smbclient -L sedna produces a report of shares that looks something like this:

```
Domain=[ACCOUNTING] OS=[Windows 5.1] Server=[Windows 2000 LAN
Manager]

        Sharename       Type        Comment
        ---------       ----        -------
        SEDNA_C         Disk
        IPC$            IPC         Remote IPC
        Reports         Disk
        Policies        Disk
```

Assuming that you have the permissions to view the Reports folder, you can connect to it like this:

```
smbclient //sedna/reports -U winuser
```

In this example, I am connecting to a Windows XP box from my Linux work-station as user winuser. The system then asks me for a password, after which I arrive at a Samba prompt like this one:

```
Domain=[ACCOUNTING] OS=[Windows 5.1] Server=[Windows 2000 LAN
Manager]
smb: \>
```

From there, type `help`, and `smbclient` offers up a list of all the things you can do while connected via the commands at your disposal. A number of them are obvious: `dir`, `copy`, and so on. While this is all good, it's not pretty in the graphical sense, and you can't use this while working in your graphical file man-agers or inside OpenOffice.org's applications.

Let's look at how you would access this machine using Konqueror. Open up Konqueror either as file manager or browser, and in the Location field, type:

```
smb:/
```

Samba servers or Windows machines advertising network shares first appear in the browser window under their workgroup name (ACCOUNTING, SALESGRP, or what have you). In Figure 18-2, you'll see a Konqueror session with a two panel view (click Window on the menu bar and select Split View>Left/Right). The basic network browser view with three active work-groups is in the left panel. In the right panel, I've clicked on the ACCOUNTING workgroup to show the computers that make up part of that group.

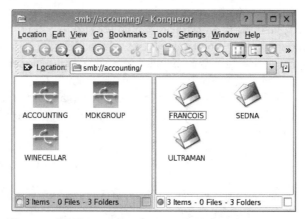

FIGURE 18-2   Browsing workgroups with Konqueror.

To read, write, or otherwise make use of the files shared on those computers, double-click on the computer's corresponding folder—the folder for François' computer, for instance. All of the available shared directories (or folders) are then visible (Figure 18-3).

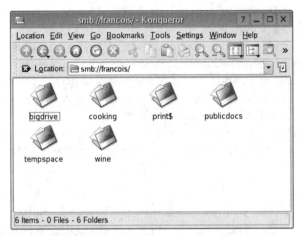

FIGURE 18-3   *Once connected, browsing is basic file manager navigation.*

From here, it's all classic drag and drop, graphical file manager browsing. By clicking (or double-clicking, depending on your configuration), you can go inside the cooking folder, for example, locate the appropriate document, and open it with OpenOffice.org Writer (right-click on the file and select Open With). Just like that, you're editing a document on a shared Windows resource.

Ideally, you don't want to go through this whole navigation process each and every time. To bring a given network share a few clicks closer, simply bookmark the appropriate shared folder.

Over on the GNOME side of things, you have Nautilus. You will find the process very similar to what you just did with Konqueror. Start Nautilus, and type the following in the Location bar:

```
smb:///
```

Nautilus then displays the active workgroups on the network (Figure 18-4).

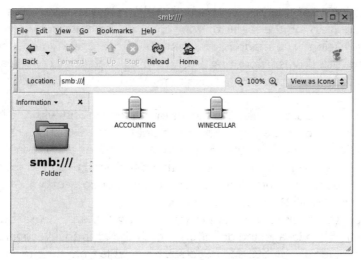

FIGURE 18-4   Nautilus in SMB browse mode.

From there, you can double-click on one of the workgroups to select a computer. Then, from the list of computers, double-click on your choice to browse the individual resources offered (Figure 18-5). Be aware that while you move around from computer to computer like this, you may occasionally be asked for a username and password for that computer or even the specific folder.

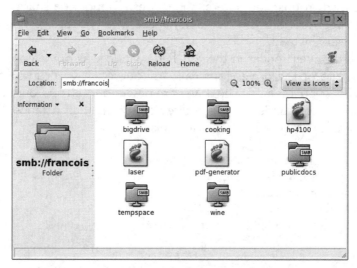

FIGURE 18-5   Windows and Samba shares are easily accessed.

As with the Konqueror example before this, you can save yourself a little time by bookmarking the folder of your choice. The only problem with both of the suggestions I've made is that neither of them lets you permanently mount network drives. Mounting a drive for all users isn't complicated, but it's not quite the point-and-click ease that Windows users on your network have access to.

For a more robust and flexible means of working in and with the Network Neighborhood, you simply must take a look at Smb4K, a super-classy SMB browser tool that is also flexible and powerful. Furthermore, it enables you to preview shares, mount shares locally without the need to run as root, reconnect automatically on startup, and more. To get your copy of Smb4K, head on over to `http://smb4k.berlios.de/index.php`.

At the time of this writing, Smb4K was sitting at 0.4.0 release, but I found it a very capable package and definitely worth the time to investigate. Binary packages for Debian, SUSE, and Fedora are available from the site as is the full source. Building Smb4K from source is a simple case of the classic extract and build five-step (Chapter 7, "Installing New Applications").

When you have installed the package, run the program by calling `smb4k`. As soon as you start Smb4K, it scans the network looking for active shares. You can fine-tune the functionality, including such options as whether you want shares to be automatically reconnected by clicking on Settings in the menu bar and selecting Configure Smb4K. The graphical interface is intuitive and easy to navigate, and the package is very easy to use.

The display is divided into two sections. On the left side, the navigation panel lists workgroups, computers, and shares. To mount a share, right-click on it and select Mount. If you would rather see what you are getting into first, choose Preview instead.

Mounted drives appear in the top-right window as drive icons. Double-clicking on one of the drive icons calls Konqueror. If you run `df` from the command line, you'll see that the drives are now mounted for your use in your own home directory under an `smb4k` directory prefix. For instance, the listing for the example in Figure 18-6 looks like this:

```
Filesystem        Size  Used Avail Use% Mounted on
//SEDNA/Reports   4.0G  3.0G  1.1G  75%
/home/marcel/smb4k/SEDNA/Reports
//FRANCOIS/wine   13G   8.8G  3.3G  73%
/home/marcel/smb4k/FRANCOIS/wine
```

FIGURE 18-6   Smb4K is an excellent and powerful SMB browser.

Now, any of my applications—KDE, GNOME, shell-based, or anything for that matter—can access the shares.

The GUI Way to Administer Samba

Now that I have gone ahead and made you do all this the command-line way, let me show you the GUI way as provided by the Samba team. When you installed Samba, you also installed a web client called SWAT. Aside from providing an easy-to-use, point-and-click means of setting up shares, printers, and configuring various functions of the server, SWAT also offers complete online help for any of the configuration parameters you might run into. Figure 18-7 shows SWAT in action.

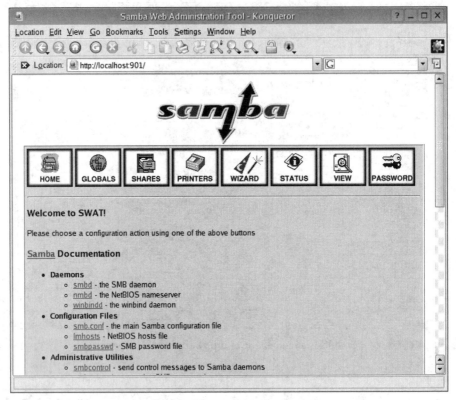

FIGURE 18-7   SWAT: Samba's own web administration tool.

To use SWAT, you may need to set up the service in your `inetd.conf` file. The following entry comes from an RPM-based installation of Samba:

```
service swat
{
        port    = 901
        socket_type    = stream
        wait    = no
        only_from = 127.0.0.1
        user    = root
        server  = /usr/sbin/swat
        log_on_failure  += USERID
        disable = no
}
```

The path to the SWAT executable depends on how you installed Samba. If you did a default source build (as I did earlier), you'll find it in `/usr/local/samba/bin`, and that is the path that you specify in the `/etc/xinetd.d/swat` file. When you've made that change, remember to reset the `xinetd` master process.

```
kill -HUP `cat /var/run/xinetd.pid`
```

Note that those are back quotes in the command. The URL to get to SWAT is `http://my_server:901/`, where `my_server` is your server's IP address.

Webmin also provides an interface for administering Samba. That module can be found under the Servers tab. Assuming your server was called your_server, you could use this quick link to get to the page:

```
http://your_server:10000/samba/index.cgi
```

Backing Up Windows Workstations

I touched briefly on backing up Windows workstations in Chapter 13, "Backup and Restore." You can avoid backing up your Windows workstations (to some degree) by having your users store all their data on a Samba server. Just make sure that each user has a network share on which to do and store all their work. If you follow this approach, by backing up the server, you back up all the workstations as well.

If data is stored on the PC, you have to do things a little differently. To back up PC client shares using a Linux system running Samba, the easiest solution is to use `smbtar`. To use `smbtar`, you must first set up shares on your Windows PCs. To do this, bring up Windows Explorer (right-click the Start button and choose Explore).

Locate the directory you want to set up a share for, and right-click that folder. You can click the drive icon itself and share the entire disk. I suggest backing up only your data files. When your Windows system needs a restore, it usually needs a clean Windows and registry installation as well.

Anyhow, right-click the folder and choose Sharing, which brings up the Properties dialog box. In this example, assume that the shared folder under my C: drive is called MYDATA. Click the Shared As radio button, and give it a share name. The default is the directory name itself, but you may want to give it a more intuitive name—it's up to you. Click OK.

Back on your Linux machine, you can now use `smbtar` to back up this directory. The format is:

```
smbtar -v -s server_name -x share_name -t tarfile
```

For `server_name`, enter the PC's network name. For `share_name`, enter the name used in the previous example. In my scenario, I would enter `MYDATA.tar_file` as the output device, which could be a filename. (Danger! Don't use up all of your disk space!) In the case of a SCSI tape drive, it might be `/dev/st0`.

```
smbtar -v -s MARYPC -x MYDATA -t /dev/st0
```

You should now see a list of files scrolling to the console screen. Other options to `smbtar` include:

```
Usage: smbtar [<options>] [<include/exclude files>]
Function: backup/restore a Windows PC directories to a local tape file
Options:            (Description)              (Default)
    -r              Restore from tape file to PC Save from PC to tapefile
    -i              Incremental mode           Full backup mode
    -a              Reset archive bit mode     Don't reset archive bit
    -v              Verbose mode: echo command Don't echo anything
    -s <server>     Specify PC Server
    -p <password>   Specify PC Password
    -x <share>      Specify PC Share           backup
    -X              Exclude mode               Include
    -N <newer>      File for date comparison
    -b <blocksize>  Specify tape's blocksize
    -d <dir>        Specify a directory in share \
    -l <log>        Specify a Samba Log Level   2
    -u <user>       Specify User Name           root
    -t <tape>       Specify Tape device         tar.out
```

If you specified an access type dependent on a password, you need to specify the username (`-u` option) and password (`-p` option) to access the PC.

Resources

Samba

www.samba.org

Smb4K

http://smb4k.berlios.de/index.php

chapter
19

Linux File Sharing (NFS)

When it comes to file sharing, you've got a number of options. For instance, you can choose from NFS, Samba, CODA, AFS, and others. When all that fails, there's always sneakernet. That last one doesn't require an awful lot of explanation: If you've got sneakers, you're connected. Throw that file onto a diskette or a tape or burn a CD, then walk it over to the remote system.

From a historical perspective, NFS is the granddaddy (or grandmamma, I can't be sure) of network file-sharing technologies. It was developed by Sun Microsystems and has been around since the '80s. Its great strength is that it is on just about every Linux and UNIX distribution.

Network shared directories are used for more than just extra space (although that is a good reason to use them). They also provide the means to have large programs or applications inhabit one linked system, thus saving the hassle of installing the same thing over and over again on every workstation. Shared directories are routinely used for email. Rather than having each user's mail distributed to each and every workstation, the mail lives in a central location, a one-stop place for backups. Speaking of backups, why not have each user's home directory remotely mounted so that his or her personal information is backed up when the server is backed up? This saves you the aggravation of worrying about each person's "important" data going missing.

Like just about everything in the world of Linux, NFS is still evolving, and different incarnations exist on different releases. Nevertheless, NFS has been around a long time, and while it has problems (which I will discuss later), it is a good, stable file-sharing mechanism that is worth looking at. On most Linux machines out there, the Linux implementation of NFS is now at version 3 with a few version 4 implementations starting to appear in distributions.

How Does NFS Work?

NFS is a client/server system that enables a local directory on the server to be made available to other client computers. These can be other Linux machines, UNIX workstations, or any other machine that can mount NFS directories. To do this, the server runs a number of processes that handle such things as permissions, authentication, maintenance of established connections, and so on. NFS uses remote procedure calls (RPC) as its mechanism for communicating information.

Starting the NFS server is usually done at boot time if you have those services set to come up at boot time. On a Debian server, most of these daemons are brought up by the `nfs-server` script.

```
/etc/init.d/nfs-server start
```

On a Red Hat or Mandrake system, you may find that you need to start both the `nfs` and the `nfslock` scripts.

```
/etc/rc.d/init.d/nfs start
/etc/rc.d/init.d/nfslock start
```

Tip On some systems, Redhat and Mandrake for instance, there is a command called "`service`" that can be used for this.

```
Service nfs start
```

There is actually one other program that needs to be up and running. When a directory is "exported" by the server, another program, `mountd`, tells the client which directories are available on the server. The `showmount` command can be used to query `mountd` regarding exported directories. Here's an example.

```
# showmount -e scigate
Export list for scigate:
/opt/ltsp                   192.168.22.0/255.255.255.0
/mnt/cdrom                  192.168.22.0/255.255.255.0
/var/opt/ltsp/swapfiles     192.168.22.0/255.255.255.0
```

Using the `rpcinfo` program, you can determine which RPC services are running on a server machine. The format of the command is simple. When I query a system called testsys, here's what I get:

```
# rpcinfo -p testsys
   program vers proto    port
    100000   2   tcp     111   portmapper
    100000   2   udp     111   portmapper
    100011   1   udp     764   rquotad
    100011   2   udp     764   rquotad
    100005   1   udp     772   mountd
    100005   1   tcp     774   mountd
    100005   2   udp     777   mountd
    100005   2   tcp     779   mountd
    100003   2   udp    2049   nfs
```

The -p flag tells the `rpcinfo` program to ask the portmapper on a remote system to report on what services it offers. This means, of course, that I need to be running the `portmap` daemon. If I shut down the `portmap` daemon, the results are less than stellar. Before I show you the results, let's shut down the portmapper. On a Red Hat or Mandrake system, you use the command:

```
/etc/rc.d/init.d/portmap stop
```

On a Debian or Storm Linux system, try this instead:

```
/etc/init.d/portmap stop
```

Here's the result of an `rpcinfo` probe of the same system (testsys):

```
rpcinfo: can't contact portmapper: RPC: Remote system error -
Connection refused
```

Now that you know how to check on what is available and whether or not NFS services are running, take a look at each of the daemons to learn what they do:

- `rpc.statd`: This daemon is started by the `nfslock` script along with `rpc.lockd`. Together they handle file locking and lock recovery, in the event of an NFS server crash, upon reboot. Depending on the system, you may not see `rpc.lockd` in your process status. Instead, you might simply see `lockd`.
- `rpc.quotad`: On a machine where quota support has been set up, `rpc.quotad` handles this, making sure that any limits that were set up are imposed on the exported directory.
- `rpc.nfsd`: The real workhorse of the whole NFS group of programs, this is the program that actually handles all the NFS user requests.
- `rpc.mountd`: When the client initiates a request to mount an exported directory, this is the program that looks to see whether the request meets with the permissions defined in the `/etc/exports` file.

Making a Remote File System Available

For a server to make a directory or file system available to one or more clients, you must add an entry to the `/etc/exports` file. Entries in this file, which you can manually edit with your favorite editor, have this format:

```
/name_of_dir client_name(permissions)
```

The name part is pretty simple. That's the full path to the directory you want to share on your network. The client name is the host name of the client machine. This can just as easily be an IP address. Furthermore, you can use a wildcard to make every host within a domain available. For instance, say your domain is myowndomain.dom and you want all machines in that domain to be able to access /mnt/data on the machine acting as your NFS server. You create an entry that looks like this:

```
/mnt/data1    *.myowndomain.dom(permissions)
```

You can also use an asterisk to make every single host on every network privy to your NFS services, but this would be a very bad idea. Still, sharing that drive is pretty simple so far. Which leads us to the permissions aspect of things.

Permissions are a bit more complex. Options for the permissions (or security) section are secure, ro, rw, sync, no_wdelay, nohide, and no_subtree_check. Other groups of permissions exist that are related to the way individual users get treated. I like to think of these as the "squashing permissions." They are root_squash, no_root_squash, all_squash, anonuid, and anongid.

- secure: This option specifies that an NFS mount request must be from an Internet port number below 1024. This option is on by default. If you don't want this behavior, specify insecure.
- ro/rw: The ro permission option allows for read-only access. This is the default. It allows the client to see the files, but doesn't let the client change anything. To allow read and write access, specify rw instead.
- sync: This option is what you might call a mixed blessing. It makes sure that a commit of data follows every write operation. This is great in the event of a server crash, but the cost is a slight performance hit. The default is async, which means that the system just writes and doesn't worry about whether the operation is completed before it moves on.
- no_wdelay: This is a cousin to the sync option. If you decide that your data is relatively safe but you still want the commit option, you can elect to set this option, which lets the system do multiple commits simultaneously. The default, wdelay, delays the next write until the first is committed.
- no_hide: Say you have two directories exported in the same tree. If one of those directories is below the first, you would normally mount both on the client. If you only mounted the parent directory, you would see the second directory, but it would have no data beneath it. It is hidden. If you want to have the entire subtree visible as well, use this option. Use it with care, however, because clients have been known to have problems with this, specifically as it relates to assigning duplicate inodes. The default option is hide.

- `no_subtree_check`: If the directory you are exporting is actually a subdirectory of a file system, the directories above it may have something to say about permissions. Because you have access to the files and directories that are exported only, you must check to ensure security throughout the chain. The default is to allow `subtree_check`, which may have minor security implications. If this is a concern, remember to specify `no_subtree_check`.

I call the next few squashing permissions, because there seems to be so much talk about squashing in the list. Generally, they have to do with how the server deals with the problem of user IDs (UIDs) and group IDs (GIDs) while assigning permissions.

The thing to remember here is that NFS in a default installation deals with permissions by assuming that UIDs and GIDs are the same on both the server and the client. This isn't such a big deal if you are the one setting up all the machines *and* you define the rules *and* you can make sure that all machines have identical `/etc/passwd` files, but unfortunately this isn't always the case. The real problem starts when the user natika on the server has UID 505, but natika on the client has UID 501.

One way to deal with this is to run NIS. (I'll explain how to set up an NIS server later in this chapter.) Another way is to use some of the following squashing permissions options to change the default behavior of NFS when a mount request is honored.

- `no_root_squash`: When a user tries to gain access to a remote NFS directory, the UID and GID are treated as though they are the same on the client and server. This is not true of the root UID by default. NFS maps root's UID (0) to the anonymous user, or nobody, for security reasons. If you are the administrator of NFS domain and you are root on all machines, this might not be a problem and you may want root to have equal rights to the exported directories. To make sure this happens, use `no_root_squash`. You can also specify the default, `root_squash`, if you like to see all of these things spelled out.
- `all_squash`: As you might expect, this option means that all UIDs should be treated like root, mapping them to the anonymous user. The default is `no_all_squash`.
- `anonuid/anongid`: This option enables you to specify the UID and GID of the anonymous user to which a `root_squash` or an `all_squash` will map permissions.

Have a look at the following example:

```
# /etc/exports file
# These are just comments
#
/mnt/data1    natika(rw,no_root_squash)
/usr/local    speedy(rw)
/mnt/acctng   *.mycompany.dom(rw)
```

Obviously, the first three lines, those starting with the # symbol, are just comments. The /mnt/data1 line makes that directory available to the client called natika. It also allows root to be treated as root on this directory. The second line gives the client called speedy read-write access, but it maps root's UID to the anonymous user. Finally, the third line enables any computer in the mycompany.dom domain to mount the /mnt/acctng directory with read-write access.

Once your directories are ready to export, you can restart NFS or reboot to reread the /etc/exports file, but this is Linux. You don't reboot or restart if you don't need to. This is why you use the command exportfs. I'll show you some of the more common formats for the command. In all cases, you can add the -v flag to up the command's level of verbosity. This first variation exports all the entries in /etc/exports.

```
exportfs -a
```

Be careful with this one, because it is a Boolean command. If you execute it again, it unexports all the entries in /etc/exports.

Probably the safest option you'll usually want to use is this:

```
exportfs -r
```

It reexports all the entries in /etc/exports. If it finds that something has been deleted from the /etc/exports file, it unexports it. Now, using a command called showmount, you can look to see what your server has exported.

```
[root@testsys /root]# showmount -exports
Export list for testsys.mycompany.dom:
/mnt/data1 192.168.22.10
```

As you can see, I have one directory exported for use by a client at 192.168.22.10. You can also export directories on the fly by using a -o option to the exportfs command. This enables you to manually export a directory without updating the /etc/exports file without re-editing it. For instance, if I want to export a directory called /etc for use by a client called speedy, I can use this version of exportfs:

```
[root@scigate /root]# exportfs -o rw,no_root_squash speedy:/etc
[root@scigate /root]# showmount --exports
Export list for testsys.mycompany.dom:
/etc       speedy.mycompany.dom
/mnt/data1 192.168.22.10
```

Mounting an NFS Partition

When you mount a directory through NFS, you can use a fairly simple version of the mount command similar to what you would use for a local file system. Using the previous /mnt/data1 example, you might do this:

```
mount -t nfs testsys:/mnt/data1 /mnt/local_data1
```

For starters, the -t flag, which specifies the type of file system, is sort of optional in that the mount command is usually able to deal with many different mount types without being explicitly told what it is mounting. Next, /mnt/local_data1 is a previously created directory on my client system. The name is entirely up to you. As you can see, the format is not at all complicated for most common requirements. There are, however, other options on the mount command that you may want to consider. The most compelling reason for other than default options is the issue of hard versus soft mounting.

By default, NFS mounts are *hard mounts*. This means that if the server goes down, your client just keeps right on trying to contact the server. If the server was to go down, you would know this is happening when you issued a df command on the client with an NFS-mounted directory. The command lists your other file systems, but it just hangs as it waits for the server to respond. You can solve this with a *soft mount*, which lets the kernel stop waiting after a while. For instance, let's use the previous command, but as a soft mount:

```
mount -f nfs -o soft,timeo=120 testsys:/mnt/data1 /mnt/local_data1
```

Yes, it's true. I added something extra there, the `timeo=` option. For starters, you can see that mount options are added to the command line with the `-o` flag. The `timeo` option specifies the number of seconds I want the system to wait before it times out on the mount. You can also specify a `retrans=n` where n is the number of retries you want the mount to attempt before giving up.

Now that I've told you all about soft mounts, I'm going to let you know that for the most part, you don't want to do this. When people are in the middle of editing a file or updating information, you don't want the client system to just drop them without them having had a chance to finish. The connection may come back 122 seconds later. Who knows?

That said, let me tell you about two other mount options. You can also issue the `mount` command with a `bg` option, which puts the `mount` command in the background. That way, if the system you need mounted is unavailable, `mount` can keep trying without hanging at the command line. The last option is `intr`, which enables you to interrupt the `mount` command should it be taking too long. Because the process of mounting a file system is a kernel function, you don't normally have the option of interrupting it, but on systems where the server's presence may be unreliable on the network, these hard and soft mount options may be worthy of consideration.

Quick Tip   Other NFS mount flags you'll want to know about are `rsize` and `wsize`. Try adding these to your `mount` command, as they can definitely improve read and write performance. The default `rsize` and `wsize` is 1024. You might want to use `rsize=8192` and `wsize=8192` instead.

Specifying Mounts with /etc/fstab

When your system boots, several file systems are automatically mounted. The most obvious is the root directory (`/`), but there are others, such as `/boot`, `/usr/local`, or `/home`, depending on your system configuration. Furthermore, you may, like me, have a separate data drive that always needs to be available. Mounting it each and every single time isn't practical.

The following listing from a `/etc/fstab` file is essentially the same as the one you saw in that chapter. The very last line is one I added after the fact. In this case, it mounts a remote file system on an NFS host called testsys.

```
/dev/hda1        /               ext2      defaults            1 1
/dev/cdrom       /mnt/cdrom      iso9660   noauto,owner,ro     0 0
/dev/fd0         /mnt/floppy     auto      noauto,owner        0 0
none             /proc           proc      defaults            0 0
none             /dev/pts        devpts    gid=5,mode=620      0 0
/dev/hda5        swap            swap      defaults            0 0
/dev/hdb1        /mnt/data1      ext2      defaults            0 0
testsys:/home    /mnt/tshome     nfs       rw,bg               0 0
```

If you look back to the last section, you'll notice that the mount happens in the background (`bg`) and that the default permissions are read and write (`rw`). The local directory is called `/mnt/tshome`.

By the way, the `fstab` isn't just for booting. It can simplify mounting and unmounting, because all of the defaults and requirements that you have for a specific mount are already there. Rather than typing the name of the device, the file system type, the various options, and the mount point, once you have an entry in `fstab` you can just type `mount /whatever`. (The "whatever" is, of course, replaced with, well, whatever.)

Simplifying Network Mounts with Linux autofs

If you start using NFS in a big way, you may find that this whole business of mounting and unmounting file systems gets to be a bit tedious. You could just put the various mounts in your `/etc/fstab` and have them come up automatically, but that has its problems as well. What if that system is not always available? It may also be that you need this file system only from time to time. If that is the case, you don't want to have it permanently mounted. Then, when somebody does need it, do you really want him or her to disturb you?

The Linux `autofs` can make your life a lot easier. The idea is that you define file systems for mounting in a map file. This map describes the file system types, where they are, and which permissions may be required to mount them. The beauty is that you don't have to manually mount these file systems or even have them mounted. As soon as a user requests something in the map path, that file system is automatically mounted.

To use this tool, you need to have the `autofs` package loaded on your system. It is probably already on your distribution CD. Alternatively, you can go to the `ftp.kernel.org` site and look in the `/pub/linux/daemons/autofs` directory for the latest and greatest.

Setup is easy. Start by setting up your `/etc/auto.master` file. You define a top-level directory where your automatic mounts occur. This points back to another file (your map), which takes care of individually defining these mounts and their file system types. Here's my `auto.master` file:

```
/automnt     /etc/auto.automnt
```

You can have many such definitions. For instance, you might have mount points defined under `/misc`, `/home`, or the perennial `/mnt`. The convention is to use a `/etc/auto.map` file where map is the same name as the mount point. You can use pretty much any name you like, however, and it will still work. Now, let's have a look at the map I have defined:

```
# automount locations
# This is an automounter map and it has the following format
# key [ -mount-options-separated-by-comma ] location
# nfs servers
testsysdata     -fstype=nfs,rsize=8192,wsize=8192     testsys:/data1
testsysroot     -fstype=nfs,rsize=8192,wsize=8192     testsys:/
# samba servers
testsysdos      -fstype=smb,username=mgagne,password=secret
://testsys/dosdir
winsoft         -fstype=smb                           ://nexus/win95
# Windows PCs
natika_c        -fstype=smb,username=natika,password=secret
://speedy/natika_c
```

Notice that I have listed Samba file systems and a Windows PC as well. The Linux `autofs` can handle many different systems—it's not just for NFS. Before you can start using things, you need to start (or restart) the `autofs` process. On my test system running Red Hat, I start it from a script like this:

```
/etc/rc.d/init.d/autofs start
```

On a Debian system, the script is likely in `/etc/init.d` instead, but it uses the same keyword to start the automounter.

Note The program that actually does the work is called `automount`, so if you look for the program in a `ps ax`, you'll see that program name instead of `autofs`.

To access information on any of these systems, I need only to change directory or reference a file there. The `autofs` system does the rest for me.

Network Information Service

Like NFS, NIS is a child of Sun Microsystems, and also like NFS, it goes back to the '80s. At that time, it was called Yellow Pages, but because Yellow Pages happens to be a registered trademark, the name was changed to avoid legal troubles. Nevertheless, an echo of those Yellow Pages days is still with you when you deal with NIS. As you will soon discover in this section, the letters "yp" show up in configuration files and commands alike.

When I talked about NFS, I mentioned that NFS assumes that user and group information on the server are equivalent to user and group information on the client. The problem with this scenario is that it requires an administrator to create and maintain identical `/etc/passwd` and `/etc/group` files on each and every computer. That's not always practical, or for that matter, desirable. One way to get around this problem is NIS.

NIS (and more recently, NIS+) does far more than allow these files to be consistent across a network. Other files can be maintained as well. You can use the `ypcat -x` command to get a list of the databases already known or managed by your system. You need to have the portmapper running, so make sure it is running and then try this on your system:

```
[root@scigate /root]# ypcat -x
Use "ethers"    for map "ethers.byname"
Use "aliases"   for map "mail.aliases"
Use "services"  for map "services.byname"
Use "protocols" for map "protocols.bynumber"
Use "hosts"     for map "hosts.byname"
Use "networks"  for map "networks.byaddr"
Use "group"     for map "group.byname"
Use "passwd"    for map "passwd.byname"
```

Now you have an idea of just what kind of information you can use NIS to distribute. Of particular interest to the topic of permissions on NFS are the group and password databases. Remember that NFS expects that a user on one machine has the same UID on another. Short of always updating each and every server to reflect user and group name changes, NIS is the answer.

The first thing you need to get NIS rolling is an NIS domain name that bears no resemblance whatsoever to your Internet domain name (although it could be the same if you so choose). Let's create an NIS domain name called `mydomain.nis`. On my Red Hat system, this is done by setting the `NIS_DOMAIN` variable in `/etc/sysconfig/network`.

```
NIS_DOMAIN=mydomain.nis
```

On a Debian system, the `domainname` is pulled from `/etc/defaultdomain`. In that case, add a single line with the domain name and nothing else.

There's more to do, but before you can get there, you need to start the ypserver process (it is actually called `ypbind`). If you are running Red Hat, try:

```
/etc/rc.d/init.d/ypserv start
```

Debian users should try:

```
/etc/init.d/nis start
```

Configuring the NIS Master Server

With NIS, you can set up backup servers as well—hence the master specification in that title. For now, you concentrate on the primary master. You've defined the domain name, so now you can move on to defining the databases that will be shared. You do this by modifying a file called `/var/yp/Makefile`. (It's starting to look an awful lot like you are compiling a program, isn't it?) Open the file into your favorite editor and you'll see something like this:

```
GROUP      = $(YPPWDDIR)/group
PASSWD     = $(YPPWDDIR)/passwd
SHADOW     = $(YPPWDDIR)/shadow
GSHADOW    = $(YPPWDDIR)/gshadow
ADJUNCT    = $(YPPWDDIR)/passwd.adjunct
#ALIASES   = $(YPSRCDIR)/aliases  # aliases could be in /etc or
/etc/mail
ALIASES    = /etc/aliases
```

```
ETHERS      = $(YPSRCDIR)/ethers      # ethernet addresses (for
rarpd)
BOOTPARAMS  = $(YPSRCDIR)/bootparams # for booting Sun boxes
(bootparamd)
HOSTS       = $(YPSRCDIR)/hosts
NETWORKS    = $(YPSRCDIR)/networks
PRINTCAP    = $(YPSRCDIR)/printcap
PROTOCOLS   = $(YPSRCDIR)/protocols
PUBLICKEYS  = $(YPSRCDIR)/publickey
```

The list is fairly long and it is possible to add others. Comment out what you don't need or want. What actually gets built is decided a little later in the file. Notice the YPPWDDIR variable. It is set earlier in the file and by default is /etc, where most of these files live. Pay attention, because this isn't always true. For instance, later incarnations of sendmail put the aliases file in /etc/mail instead of /etc. Once you have the databases you want defined, look for this:

```
NOPUSH=true
```

Because you are setting up a single master NIS server in this example, set this to true. If you had secondary or "slave" servers, you would set this to false. Notice as well these two settings:

```
MINUID=500
MINGID=500
```

This is the default UID and GID information being served. As you might guess, there are security reasons for this. You don't want to advertise administrative IDs across your network. If you want to change this, do it here. If you are setting this up on a Debian system, you may find that these are already set to 100 instead of the Red Hat default of 500.

Alright. Two more very important settings before you get ready to wrap up your server configuration. Look for these two in the file:

```
MERGE_PASSWD=true
MERGE_GROUP=true
```

In all likelihood, you are using a shadow password file, and if you are not, go back and implement shadow passwords now. NIS merges the information from your /etc/shadow file into its shared copy of /etc/passwd. This is normally set to true, but you can override it. The MERGE_GROUP setting defaults to false on some systems (my Debian test system is one), so you might wind up changing the setting of this one. Look for a /etc/gshadow file. If your system is using it, set this one to true as well.

Now you are almost ready to build the new databases. The last thing you do is confirm what you want (or don't want) built. This is where you really decide what gets out of the NIS door. Look for this text in the Makefile:

```
# If you don't want some of these maps built, feel free to comment
# them out from this list.
all:  passwd group hosts rpc services netid protocols netgrp mail
\
        # shadow publickey # networks ethers bootparams printcap \
        # amd.home auto.master auto.home passwd.adjunct
```

Once again, the settings as they exist are probably what you want, but you can set things like automount files (auto.master and so on) that you'll remember from the previous sections.

Ready? No, you don't type make.

The command that initializes all these databases is called ypinit.

```
[root@testsys /root]# /usr/lib/yp/ypinit -m
The local host's domain name hasn't been set.  Please set it.
```

If you get this message, it is because the domain name is in your boot time scripts. Next time the system comes up, you won't have to worry about this, because it will already be set. Because you don't want to reboot right now, manually set the domain name with this command:

```
domainname mydomain.nis
```

Run the ypinit command again.

```
[root@scigate /root]# /usr/lib/yp/ypinit -m
At this point, we have to construct a list of the hosts which will
run NIS
servers.  testsys.mydomain.nis is in the list of NIS server hosts.
Please continue to add the names for the other hosts, one per
line.  When you are done with the list, type a <control D>.
        next host to add:  testsys.domain.nis
        next host to add:
```

Unless you want to set up secondary servers at this point, just press <Ctrl+D> and you are done. If you want to add servers, it's easy to do so after the fact. These get added into a file called /var/yp/ypservers. If you change to this directory, you'll see that this is a simple text file. When you are finished here, the ypinit process does a make for you and creates the databases. You should see output like the following:

```
The current list of NIS servers looks like this:
testsys.mydomain.nis
Is this correct?  [y/n: y]
We need some  minutes to build the databases...
Building /var/yp/mydomain.nis/ypservers...
Running /var/yp/Makefile...
gmake[1]: Entering directory '/var/yp/mydomain.nis'
Updating passwd.byname...
Updating passwd.byuid...
Updating group.byname...
Updating group.bygid...
Updating hosts.byname...
Updating hosts.byaddr...
Updating rpc.byname...
Updating rpc.bynumber...
Updating services.byname...
Updating netid.byname...
Updating protocols.bynumber...
Updating protocols.byname...
Updating mail.aliases...
gmake[1]: Leaving directory '/var/yp/mydomain.nis'
```

It is possible that when you run this the first time, it won't work quite so cleanly. The most likely scenario for a failure here is that you have told the Makefile to create databases that don't exist on your system. Pay attention to the messages, and edit the Makefile accordingly. Then simply rerun ypinit. At this point, you can also just type make (if you really, really want to).

Configuring the NIS Client

Although it is wonderful that you've done such a great job of setting up the NIS server, it isn't much good without clients. Well, clients are fairly simple, so feel free to set up lots of them.

Start by opening the file /etc/yp.conf in your favorite editor. There are three possible ways of setting up the client to look for NIS servers.

```
domain NISDOMAIN server HOSTNAME
#        Use server HOSTNAME for the domain NISDOMAIN.
```

If you choose this method, specify the NISDOMAIN and the HOSTNAME to which you would like the client to connect. You can have more than one entry of this type. Using my example of domain.nis, my yp.conf entry would look like this:

```
domain domain.nis server testsys.mydomain.dom
```

You can also set up your client to listen for NIS servers through a broadcast. The only catch here is that the servers must be on the same subnet. You cannot listen for NIS servers outside your network.

```
domain NISDOMAIN broadcast
#        Use  broadcast  on  the local net for domain NISDOMAIN
```

Once again, you replace NISDOMAIN with the NIS domain name. The advantage of this method is that you only need to configure one entry and you are done. The final option is perhaps the easiest of the bunch in terms of flexibility.

```
ypserver HOSTNAME
#        Use server HOSTNAME for the  local  domain.
```

Type the host name of the NIS server, and that is all. Make sure, however, that the HOSTNAME is listed in /etc/hosts. For my test, I used the final example with this entry:

```
ypserver testsys
```

The /etc/nsswitch.conf File

There is one last file to edit before you are finished: /etc/nsswitch.conf. Although there is more here than in yp.conf, the format is equally simple.

Basically, it is a list of file names and service options associated with it. Here's a sample from my file:

```
passwd:      files nisplus nis
shadow:      files nisplus nis
group:       files nisplus nis

#hosts:      db files nisplus nis dns
hosts:       files nisplus nis dns
```

The service options are `files`, `nis` (or `yp`—both are the same), `nisplus`, `dns`, and `[NOTFOUND=return]`, as shown in the following table.

TABLE 19-1   Service Options

Option	Option Meaning
files	Use the local files to look up information.
nis (or yp)	Use NIS for this information.
nisplus	Use NIS+.
dns	Use DNS to find the information (only applies to hosts).
[NOTFOUND=return]	If you haven't found the information, stop searching.

Of course, each file has several options listed and that can only mean that the order is somehow important. This is the search order for information retrieval. You almost always want to search your local host first, so `files` is usually the first option. It is only when you don't find the information locally that you want to look elsewhere, but even that can be changed.

Let's test things, shall we? As with the server, you need to have the NIS domain name set. You still want the information hard-coded in the appropriate configuration files, but a quick way to set it (if you haven't already) is with the `domainname` command.

```
domainname domain.nis
```

Great! Now, you need to start `yppasswdd` (to allow for password changes on the NIS server) and the NIS listener, `ypbind`. With Debian, this is the `/etc/init.d/nis` start script. With Red Hat, you'll need to start `/etc/rc.d/init.d/yppasswdd` and `/etc/rc.d/init.d/ypbind` as well.

To see the contents of the NIS server's password file, try this command:

```
ypcat passwd
```

To get the host information, use this:

```
ypcat hosts
```

Notice that you are simply specifying the name of the file served by NIS services.

Resources

Linux NFS FAQ

http://nfs.sourceforge.net

Thin Clients: The Server

For many companies and individuals looking for alternatives to their desktop operating system, Linux is the natural choice and offers many relatively painless ways to make that switch. Unfortunately, modern Linux distributions running KDE and GNOME can demand a great deal of resources, and in some cases, companies looking to make a switch have been holding on to fairly modest PC hardware. Luckily, Linux enables you to set up workstations with minimal Linux installations that offload most of the work to a powerful, central server.

This is the thin-client approach. Just how thin this client can be is a matter of which approach you choose. In fact, it can all be done without even reinstalling the client PCs.

How Thin Clients Work

Linux thin clients typically are PCs booting from an Ethernet card with a chip that asks for an address from the server, or they are PCs with a specially prepared boot diskette that performs the same network boot function. Thin-client PCs don't even need a hard drive to provide a user with all of the functions they need. Companies may also choose to use a dedicated thin-client PC built for that purpose.

After boot, the unit—whether a PC or dedicated thin-client unit—requests an IP address, netmask, and default route from the thin-client server via DHCP (Dynamic Host Configuration Protocol). As part of the network settings package that gets sent back, the thin client is told which kernel to load and where to find it. The kernel is then downloaded via TFTP (Trivial File Transfer Protocol).

The kernel loads, and the thin-client workstation boots. As with any Linux system boot, in this scenario the kernel takes control and configures all attached hardware. A file system image is then loaded into memory and becomes a temporary root file system. Additional modules are loaded and some further network configuration takes place to prepare the system. After a few seconds, a new root file system is mounted via NFS (you'll see a "pivot_root" message as this happens). At this point, the thin client is *live,* and it begins the final states of boot. The /tmp, /proc, and other file systems are created and mounted. Swap space is activated. Soon after, the graphical display starts. The workstation queries the server for a graphical login.

Although a rather simplified explanation of the process, this is essentially it. A user can now log in at the thin-client workstation and start using Linux. All this magic takes place courtesy of the Linux Terminal Server Project (LTSP). To *make* this magic happen, however, there are a few prerequisites that we need to visit on the server side. Via NFS, thin-client servers use shared drive space across the local network. (See Chapter 19, "Linux File System (NFS)," for more on NFS.) Even before we get to that stage, the PC or thin client needs to get an IP address from the network. To do that, it uses DHCP (Dynamic Host Configuration Protocol).

DHCP

Most people who use the Internet regularly probably use DHCP on a daily basis—even if they don't know it.

In a classic office network that does not use DHCP, each PC needs to be configured with a static IP address and all of the appropriate network settings: name servers, default routes, and so on. Once configured, the device reads its own local network settings when it boots and *never forgets it*. A DHCP-connected device, on the other hand, asks a central DHCP server for all that information each time it boots and *leases* an IP address from the server. From the perspective of the user, the PC automatically configures itself. That's what happens at home when you dial in to your ISP and are assigned an address.

Setting Up DHCP

For starters, you need to install the DHCP package on your system. Be aware that many distributions break up the DHCP package into a dhcp-server and a dhcp-client, though the names can vary. Debian's DHCP server package is called just dhcp, for example.

The server gets its information from the /etc/dhcpd.conf configuration file. Take a look at this very basic configuration file that I created on my test server, being sure to note the semicolons at the end of each entry:

```
#
# My DHCP configuration file
#

ddns-update-style               none;

default-lease-time              21600;
max-lease-time                  21600;

option subnet-mask              255.255.255.0;
option broadcast-address        192.168.22.255;
option routers                  192.168.22.10;
option domain-name-servers      192.168.22.10, 192.168.22.11;
option domain-name              "mydomain.dom";
option root-path                "192.168.22.6:/opt/ltsp/i386";
filename                        "/lts/vmlinuz-2.4.24-ltsp-1";

subnet 192.168.22.0 netmask 255.255.255.0 {
    range dynamic-bootp 192.168.22.70 192.168.22.90;
}
```

When I start a thin client or even a regular PC with this configuration file in place, the unit is assigned an IP address between 192.168.22.70 and 192.168.22.90—that's the meaning behind the `range dynamic-bootp` parameter near the bottom. Take a look at the rest of these settings in turn, starting from the top:

- `ddns-update-style`: DHCP version 3, which many of you will be using, requires this entry, regardless of whether you are using dynamic DNS updates on your system. This is a setting in transition with `interim` being the only functional setting. For now, you can set it to `none` as in my configuration example.
- `default-lease-time`: Each host (MAC address) that obtains an address from the server *leases* that address for a specific time, measured in seconds. If the machine reboots inside of that time, it can be assured of getting the same IP address.
- `max-lease-time`: When connecting, the client can actually request a specific lease time, also measured in seconds. You might choose to make both default and maximum lease times to be the same or you might allow a client to request a longer lease. This is your choice.
- `option subnet-mask`: This is the subnet mask assigned to clients.
- `option broadcast-address`: Next, we have the broadcast address. Unless you are subnetting, this is pretty basic.
- `option routers`: This is essentially your default route to the Internet.
- `option domain-name-servers`: You are free to list one to three name servers on this line. Separate each one with a comma.
- `option domain-name`: Another self-explanatory parameter, this is the domain name for your network.
- `option root-path`: As the name implies, this is the path to the server where the thin client will find the new root directory and all of the associated files to run. It may seem obvious, but take note of the fact that the LTSP server does not have to be the same machine as the default route or the name server.
- `filename`: This is the filename of the kernel that the thin-client workstation will download once it connects. The kernel is downloaded via TFTP, which I'll cover shortly.

All that brings us back around to the paragraph that started it all.

```
subnet 192.168.22.0 netmask 255.255.255.0 {
    range dynamic-bootp 192.168.22.70 192.168.22.90;
    range dynamic-bootp 192.168.22.120 192.168.22.150;
}
```

Here, we are essentially defining a dynamic network and specifying the addresses available for DHCP clients just logging on. Before moving on, I should tell you that the range I've defined above is a little different than the one I showed you just a couple of paragraphs back. In this example, there are actually two ranges of IP addresses up for grabs, and you could include more, depending on how you, as the systems administrator, decided to partition out IPs.

One of the reasons I've separated this out is that everything above the subnet paragraph is considered global. There can be many different subnet paragraphs (as in a Class A or B private network). That said, some of the globals start with the word "option". All of these options you see can be applied to the subnet you defined (a different default DNS address perhaps). Unless you include a different parameter, the global parameters apply.

The Webmin Approach

Configuring DHCP from the command line is actually fairly easy. Should you prefer a more graphical approach, Webmin provides a module with everything you need to configure and maintain your DHCP server. You can find DHCP configuration under Servers in Webmin, or you can just jump to it by entering the URL in your browser's location bar:

```
http://your_server:10000/dhcpd/
```

Assigning Fixed DHCP Addresses

As a longtime systems administrator, I always have had a love/hate relationship with DHCP. These feelings come from trying to work on a site where every PC in the entire organization is assigned an IP dynamically. When troubleshooting problems on the network, I also had the additional burden of trying to figure out which workstation belonged to a particular IP address.

Luckily, DHCP does allow for host-specific IP addresses. To me, if a workstation is always sitting in a fixed location—on someone's desk, for example—then a fixed IP is more than desirable. Configuring fixed DHCP addresses does require an additional step, but it's not that complicated. Have a look at the following additional paragraph in my DHCP configuration file:

```
host thinclient1 {
    hardware ethernet      00:50:41:01:82:35;
    fixed-address          192.168.22.51;
    filename               "/lts/vmlinuz-2.4.24-ltsp-1";
}
```

Quick Tip Because this requires more work than assigning a range of addresses, why would you want to do this? Well, for one, this is more secure, because any host authenticating through your DHCP server is going to assign addresses only to those cards it knows about. For another, you know which workstation has which address, so support is easier, because you always know which unit you are talking about.

The `host` parameter represents the host name (thinclient1, in this case) for this client and should have an equivalent either configured on your name server or in your `/etc/hosts` file. Next, the `hardware ethernet` address is the unique hardware address (or MAC address) that I've mentioned in the past. You can get this information in a variety of ways. Dedicated thin-client units probably have it stamped on their backs. Ethernet cards have small labels identifying their MAC addresses. You can also see the MAC address by using the `ifconfig` command. The `hardware ethernet` address is the `HWaddr` information that you see on the second line below.

```
$ /sbin/ifconfig eth0
eth0      Link encap:Ethernet  HWaddr 00:04:5A:5A:A8:2B
          inet addr:192.168.22.100  Bcast:192.168.22.255
Mask:255.255.255.0
```

Let's get back to the `dhcpd.conf` file segment we were looking at and continue with the `fixed-address` parameter. This is, quite simply, the IP address that you want to assign to that client. Finally, the last line (the `filename` parameter) is the TFTP download path to the kernel that the thin client loads when it boots from the network. And that, my friends, is the perfect segue to a discussion of TFTP.

A Trivial Primer On TFTP

Once connected with a proper IP address in hand, your thin client will download a Linux kernel from the server using a protocol called TFTP (Trivial File Transfer Protocol). The package that contains this server may be called `tftp-server`, which is the name the Red Hat and Mandrake systems I have used here, or `tftp`, as on my Debian system.

There's not much to getting TFTP running and no real configuration file to speak of. Just make sure the protocol is active. Look in your `/etc/xinetd.d` directory, and make sure that `disable` is set to `no` in the `tftp` file.

```
service tftp
{
        disable = no
        socket_type             = dgram
        protocol                = udp
        wait                    = yes
        user                    = root
        server                  = /usr/sbin/in.tftpd
        server_args             = -s /var/lib/tftpboot
        per_source              = 11
        cps                     = 100 2
        flags                   = IPv4
}
```

It's all very nice and easy (trivial?), but beware of one possible gotcha with the kernel installation. By default, the LTSP kernel, which I will cover shortly, is placed in `/tftpboot/lts`, whereas some TFTP installations may use a different directory for the TFTP files. For instance, my Mandrake test machine uses `/var/lib/tftpboot` as the TFTP transfer directory. This will make it impossible for the workstations booting up to download.

You have two choices. The first is to move the `lts` directory (installed under `/tftpboot` into your system's official TFTP download directory. Use the line:

```
mv /tftpboot/lts /var/lib/tftpboot/
```

The second way is to modify the `/etc/xinetd.d/tftp` paragraph to reflect the location of the LTSP kernel files.

The line you need to change is the `server_args` line, substituting `/var/lib/tftpboot` with `/tftpboot`. Once the change has been made, restart the `xinetd` daemon. Which of these two options you choose depends somewhat on whether TFTP is used for anything else on your system. If you are setting it up for LTSP only, it's just as easy to change the `xinetd` configuration file. Furthermore, it will make it easier to change things when newer kernels become available. The downside is that you have to move any other TFTP files into the new directory. If, instead, you choose to modify the location of the kernel files, then you have to move new kernel files into place each time you upgrade the packages. My personal choice is usually to change the `xinetd` configuration file.

LTSP 4.0 Installation Procedures

We now have all of the pieces we need to install the heart of a Linux thin-client installation. That heart is the Linux Terminal Server Project packages available at www.ltsp.org. To install the LTSP 4.0 packages, you need to switch to the root user first.

```
su - root
```

Running as the root user, use this command to begin the LTSP server installation:

```
wget -q -O - http://www.ltsp.org/ltsp_installer | sh
```

After you press <Enter>, you will see a menu much like this one:

```
LTSP Installer - v0.06
Welcome to the LTSP Installer.

This program will retrieve the LTSP packages and install them
for you.

Please select where you want to retrieve the packages from:

  1)  http://www.ltsp.org
  2)  Local disk (current directory)
  q)  Quit installation

Make a selection: 1
```

Because you are going to be installing from the web site, selecting Option 1 probably makes sense. This also ensures that you will be running from the latest version. After a few seconds (or minutes), the install script finishes downloading and the following menu will appear:

```
LTSP Installer - v0.06
Select which group of packages you want to install:

  1)  ltsp      Linux Terminal Server Project - Version 4

Make a selection (Q=Quit):
```

Given that we have only one option here, the choice is simple. Type 1, and press <Enter>.

```
LTSP Installer - v0.06

This group contains more than 1 component, which component
do you want to install:

  1)   ltsp_core
          Core packages of LTSP

  2)   ltsp_debug_tools
          Debugging tools for LTSP

  3)   ltsp_x_core
          XFree86 packages

  4)   ltsp_x_addtl_fonts
          Additional fonts

  5)   ltsp_x336
          Older XFree86 version 3.3.6 Xservers

  6)   ltsp_rdesktop
          Rdesktop setup as a Screen Script

Make a selection (Q=Quit, A=All):
```

Unless you have good reason to do otherwise, select A for All and press <Enter>.

```
      Are you sure you want to install ALL components?
```

The answer is Y for Yes. After you press <Enter> one more time, you are asked for the LTSP installation directory. The default is /opt/ltsp, but you can select any part of the system where you have sufficient space. I'll continue the installation information using the default directory structure. Should you choose otherwise, take this into consideration as you read on.

One by one, each of the component packages is downloaded and installed. How long this takes depends largely on the speed of your Internet connection.

And Then... The Kernel

This download step provides you with most of the pieces you need, but it does leave out one very important one: the kernel. Your best bet is to select the latest kernel from the LTSP Sourceforge download page. As I write this, the latest package is `ltsp_kernel-3.0.13-0.i386.rpm`. The package is a simple RPM install, but Debian and TGZ format packages are available as well. On my current, RPM-based test system, I installed the kernel like this:

```
# rpm -Uvh ltsp_kernel-3.0.13-0.i386.rpm
Preparing...
######################################### [100%]
   1:ltsp_kernel
######################################### [100%]
```

That pretty much covers all of the pieces necessary for a working LTSP installation. By this point, you should have a working NFS, DHCP, and TFTP server running on what will be your LTSP server. On to the next step.

Configuring LTSP 4

Once everything is installed, it's time to configure your system. There is no part of the LTSP configuration that cannot be done manually, but the people working on the Linux Terminal Server Project have tried to simplify that process as well by providing the `ltspcfg` configuration utility. This is separate from the main LTSP distribution, and you must install it separately. Download the package from the LTSP web site, then install it using:

```
rpm -Uvh ltspcfg-0.5-0.i386.rpm
```

After the installation completes, run the utility by opening a root shell and typing `ltspcfg`.

```
# ltspcfg

ltspcfg - Version 0.5

Checking Runlevel....: 5
Checking Ethernet Interfaces
Checking Dhcpd....
Checking Tftpd....
Checking Portmapper...
```

```
Checking nfs....
Checking xdmcp..........Found: xdm, gdm, [kdm]
Checking /etc/hosts.
Checking /etc/hosts.allow.
Checking /etc/exports.
Checking lts.conf.

Press <enter> to continue..
```

When you press <Enter>, a ncurses-based administration interface appears
(Figure 20-1). In order to run thin clients using LTSP, several services need to
be running: DHCP, TFTP, NFS (which includes the portmapper), and a login
manager (most likely KDM). Look at the top part of the `ltspcfg` window to
check whether the services are installed, enabled, and running.

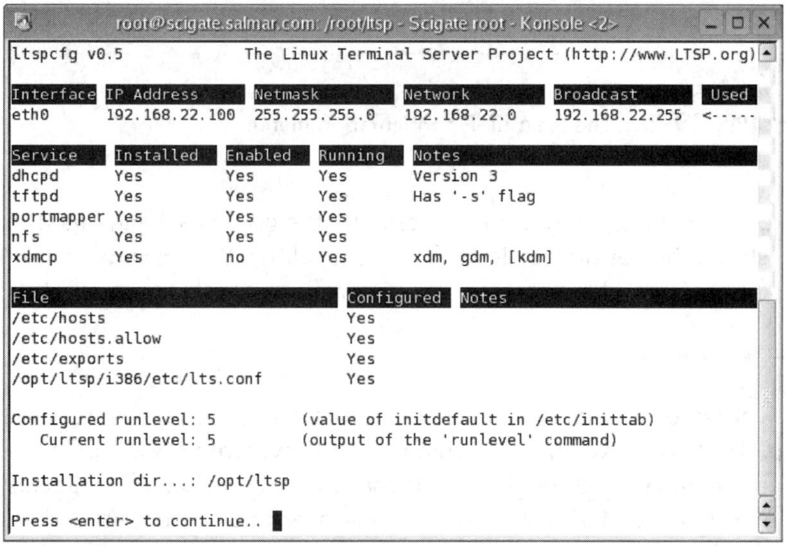

FIGURE 20-1   Checking the status of your LTSP configuration.

If there are things that still need to be installed (your TFTP server, for
instance), simply quit the configuration utility, make your changes and run it
again until you are ready to proceed. When everything is ready, choose C from
the main `ltspcfg` menu to manually configure various services. When you
press <Enter>, you'll see the various options laid out as in Figure 20-2.

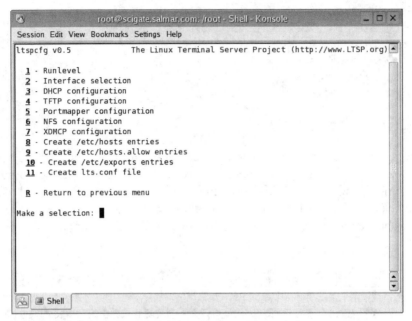

```
ltspcfg v0.5              The Linux Terminal Server Project (http://www.LTSP.org)

   1 - Runlevel
   2 - Interface selection
   3 - DHCP configuration
   4 - TFTP configuration
   5 - Portmapper configuration
   6 - NFS configuration
   7 - XDMCP configuration
   8 - Create /etc/hosts entries
   9 - Create /etc/hosts.allow entries
  10 - Create /etc/exports entries
  11 - Create lts.conf file

   R - Return to previous menu

Make a selection: █
```

FIGURE 20-2   The main LTSP configuration menu.

Take a look at item number 1. To serve up the graphical login manager, your system should be running at level 5. This modifies the `initdefault` line in your `/etc/inittab` file to 5 (should you prefer to do this manually).

```
id:5:initdefault:
```

So what does this really do? Well, if you aren't booting up into a graphical desktop, the 5 above will be a 3, which tells the system to boot up in text-only mode. To see where that happens and what that has to do with runlevels, scroll down in your `/etc/inittab` file and look near the bottom. You should see something like this:

```
# Run xdm in runlevel 5
# xdm is now a seperate service
x:5:respawn:/etc/X11/prefdm -nodaemon
```

The second item on the configuration menu is Interface Selection. If your system has more than one network interface card, you need to identify which of those interfaces the thin-client workstations will be connected to. My test system had three interfaces configured (Figure 20-3). On systems with both inside and outside interfaces, you'll most likely want to configure the private subnet interface.

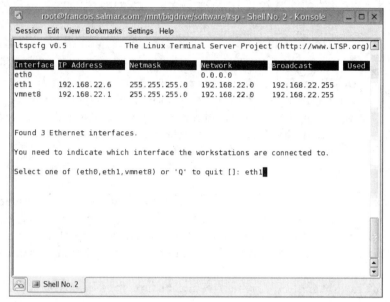

FIGURE 20-3   Which interface will your thin clients connect to?

You may be interested where this information is used. Much of LTSP's internal configurations are handled in an lts.conf file, which is created at this time under the /etc directory. If you look at the file at this point, you'll notice that it is still pretty light, containing only two important parameters:

```
# Configuration variables for LTSP
#
LTSP_DIR=/opt/ltsp
LTSP_ETH_INTERFACE=eth1
```

Note I'm making a point of mentioning this now, because there are two lts.conf files. The first, /etc/lts.conf, is used by the ltspcfg tool to keep information about the server while you configure the system. The second is /opt/ltsp/i386/etc/ltsp.conf, which is the one used by the thin clients. It contains parameters and settings that the thin clients need to operate.

Once this is written, we move on to Step 3, which creates a sample DHCP configuration file. If you used my examples earlier in this chapter, you can leave this part alone. Otherwise, go ahead and let the `ltspcfg` tool install a default `/etc/dhcpd.conf` file for you. Be aware that it is only a basic, sample file and that you will have to tweak it for your own network.

Warning Making any changes to your NFS exports file or your DHCP configuration file (`/etc/dhcpd.conf`) does require that you restart those services. I have more than once found myself wondering why a new workstation wasn't coming online, only to remember that I had not reset the dhcpd daemon. It sounds obvious, but it is also surprisingly easy to forget.

Option 4 on the menu enables TFTP, if it hasn't already been activated, as shown in the status screen (Figure 20-1). Similarly, Option 5 activates the `portmap` daemon (which we covered earlier when discussing NFS). And speaking of NFS, Option 6 turns on the NFS daemons if they haven't already been activated.

We are now at Option 7, which means it's time for a discussion of XDMCP.

XDMCP

When your Linux system comes up, you are either looking at a graphical login screen, or a simple text login prompt. The graphical login, or login manager, can also be used by remote thin-client units or PCs. XDMCP (X Display Manager Control Protocol) is the protocol that allows thin clients to login via the graphical login manager (`kdm`). Option 7 asks whether you want to start the protocol. The answer here is yes.

Note There are other login managers. GDM is popular with GNOME users and the classic XDM is still in use. Since we are concentrating on KDE, I'll cover KDM.

Immediately thereafter, you are asked another very interesting question: Do you want the graphical login manager running on the console as well? In my own office, I tend to keep the console terminal more or less permanently logged out. Consequently, a graphical login on the console isn't necessary (even though graphical logins are provided to the thin clients). The decision here is yours.

The magic that happens in the background takes place in two files, `kdmrc` and `Xaccess`. To get a graphical login screen presented to a querying host, you need to uncomment the following lines in the `/etc/X11/xdm/Xaccess` file:

```
*                              #any host can get a login window
*       CHOOSER BROADCAST   #any indirect host can get a chooser
```

Next, the configuration utility makes changes to the `kdmrc` file. On one of my systems, it is located in `/etc/kde/kdm`. On the other, it is in `/usr/share/kde/kdm`. Look for the following lines and make sure that the `Enable` parameter in the `[Xdmcp]` section is set to `true`.

```
[Xdmcp]
# Whether KDM should listen to XDMCP requests.
Enable=true
```

When you restart the window manager, you should then be able to get a remote graphical login. One way to reset the environment is to take the system down to runlevel 3 and then back to runlevel 5; this works for most systems.

```
init 3
init 5
```

If you are anxious to test this out right now, you can. All you need is a Linux client. For this example, I'll assume that you are already running in a graphical desktop. I'm going to have you type a command, but before you do, I should probably tell you what is going to happen. Your graphical KDE session is running on virtual terminal number seven. You can test this by pressing <Ctrl+Alt+F1>. You should drop out of your graphical session and back to a text screen. To get to the second, nongraphical desktop, press <Ctrl+Alt+F2> and so on, right up to virtual terminal number six. When you press <Ctrl+Alt+F7> (as in *virtual terminal number seven*), you'll be back to the graphical screen. The following command will start another graphical screen, but on virtual terminal eight! Assuming that your thin-client server is called your_tcserver, you would type:

```
X -query your_tcserver :1
```

Your X workstation queries your thin-client server for a login. The :1 at the end of the command specifies the second graphical display on your PC (the first is :0). If all has gone well up to this point, you should find yourself with a nice, graphical login screen. To switch back to your regular session, just press<Ctrl+Alt+F7>. To go back to the new session, press <Ctrl+Alt+F8>.

Back to Our Configuration

For each thin-client workstation you define, there should be an entry in your DNS tables or in your /etc/hosts file. If you are planning on providing entries on your name server zone files, you can skip this step. The same is true for a small handful of entries in your /etc/hosts file. Manually creating a handful of entries is easy, but Option 8 can create the hosts file entries for you. If you choose to let ltspcfg create entries for your /etc/hosts file, be aware that the entries will be generated as ws001 through ws254 (with IP addresses for your subnet) and a domain extension will be set to ltsp. You will probably want to do a global substitution in the file to change ltsp to your own domain name.

The next item on the menu, Option 9, has to do with system security. One way to provide or deny access is through the /etc/hosts.allow and /etc/hosts.deny files. Because some of these services, which may be controlled by the TCP wrapper, are needed by all thin-client workstations, it makes sense to put them in the /etc/hosts.allow file. These additions will be in a paragraph preceded by an ##LTSP-begin## comment line and closed with the ##LTSP-end## comment line.

```
bootpd:      0.0.0.0
in.tftpd:    192.168.22.
portmap:     192.168.22.
```

By the way, take note that the private Class C network used in this example may not be the same as in your office. Option 10 brings us back to NFS by defining those file systems that need to be exported for the thin-client workstations. By default, the entry created looks like this:

```
/opt/ltsp
192.168.22.0/255.255.255.0(ro,no_root_squash,sync)
/var/opt/ltsp/swapfiles
192.168.22.0/255.255.255.0(rw,no_root_squash,async)
```

Warning The paths mentioned are probably fine. The first entry should not be a problem at all. I do want you to think about the second, however. If you are using NFS swap (most likely), the amount of space you allow per workstation may impact on where you store this information. Imagine 50 thin-client workstations logging in, each with 64 megabytes of swap space. That starts to add up. Make sure that the file system you choose here has the capacity to handle the load.

This brings us to the last option in the menu, and that means that it's time to talk about the lts.conf file.

The lts.conf File

When you choose to execute Option 11 and write the lts.conf file, you may get a message telling you that the file is already there. That's because by this point, you have probably effected enough changes to your system's configuration that the lts.conf file has been written. There's no harm in rewriting it, so go ahead. The file, by the way, lives in /opt/ltsp/i386/ltsp/etc, assuming you chose the recommended default installation. Aside from a few comments at the beginning of the file, this is the basic information you can expect to see:

```
[Default]
        SERVER               = 192.168.22.6
        XSERVER              = auto
        X_MOUSE_PROTOCOL     = "PS/2"
        X_MOUSE_DEVICE       = "/dev/psaux"
        X_MOUSE_RESOLUTION   = 400
        X_MOUSE_BUTTONS      = 3
        USE_XFS              = N
        SCREEN_01            = startx
```

Let's look at the various parameters and what each means. The SERVER variable is the IP address of the machine on which your LTSP server will run. Nothing complicated here.

Pretty much every other variable that follows has to do with the graphical displays on the thin-client PCs or units. XSERVER generally is set to auto, but this is something you could hard code for individual workstations. The settings could be `nv`, `vesa`, `ati`, or any of the X servers supported by XFree86 version 4. We'll look at selecting parameters for individual thin clients in more detail when we discuss workstations in the next chapter. The next four variables (all prefixed with `X_MOUSE_`) are all pretty self-explanatory and relate to configuring the mouse. Meanwhile, the `USE_XFS` variable specifies whether the workstation will handle its own fonts or pull the information from the server's own font server.

The most interesting parameter here is `SCREEN_01`. The default is `startx`, which specifies that the workstation should boot up in a graphical X display, but there are a number of interesting possibilities. The other options are:

- `telnet`: When the workstation boots up in this mode, it waits for you to press <Enter>, then starts a TELNET session to the host. Obviously, your TELNET server must be running for this. (Many offices use SSH by default.)
- `shell`: This starts a local command shell, meaning local to the workstation, not to the server. From here, you could `telnet` or `ssh` to your server, or start a graphical login by typing `startx`. This mode is generally used for testing. It's also a great way to see the virtual Linux machine that gets created as part of the LTSP boot process.
- `rdesktop`: Setting `SCREEN_01` to this fires up rdesktop, a Linux-based Windows Terminal Server client, which means it uses RDP (remote desktop protocol) to communicate with and run remote Windows sessions from your Linux thin client.

How Many SCREENs?

Of course, the fact that this last variable is labeled `SCREEN_01` leads up to the obvious question: What about `SCREEN_02`? Or `SCREEN_03`?

Earlier on in this chapter, I told you about running your main X session on virtual terminal session 7, while the second X session (started with an `X -query`) ran on virtual terminal 8. You can do something similar with thin-client workstations by modifying the `lts.conf` file to include more than one `SCREEN` definition. Here's the example from my own server:

```
SCREEN_01              = startx
SCREEN_02              = telnet
SCREEN_03              = shell
```

The first virtual terminal (accessible by pressing <Ctrl+Alt+F1>) runs the graphical login served up via XDMCP. The second virtual terminal

(<Ctrl+Alt+F2>) runs a TELNET session with a prompt saying "Screen:2 – Press <Enter> to establish a connection to the server…" Finally, the third screen (<Ctrl+Alt+F3>) sits at a shell prompt.

In a default LTSP installation, all these screen definitions can be found in the /opt/ltsp/i386/etc/screen.d directory. Each is a shell script and easy to read and understand. You could, if you so wish, create your own screen definitions to better suit your own environment.

These types of screen modifications can be done globally or on a client-by-client basis. In the next chapter, you're going to look at just what sorts of things you can do with workstations. I'm also going to show you how you can run a not quite so thin, Linux thin client from a Windows desktop.

But first, what if you need extra help?

Help Me!

As complex as this whole operation sounds, it's not that difficult. That said, I've gone through this process many times now and I still miss things, usually something as silly as a typo. Thin-client computing does bring some interesting challenges into the picture, however, especially when dealing with devices connected to the thin clients themselves. Add to that the fact that a thin-client device can be anything from a vintage PC with any number of different network or video cards or any of several different types of hardware, and it's possible to run into the odd snag.

I'm going to talk about thin clients in a moment, but for now, I want to tell you about a great resource, the #ltsp IRC channel on irc.freenode.net. Many people who frequent this channel are either developers on the project or just plain enthusiastic users. If you run into problems, this is always a great place to ask questions.

Resources

Linux Terminal Server Project

www.ltsp.org

chapter
21

Thin Clients: The Clients

When I think of thin clients, I also think in terms of degree. Degree of thinness, that is. The ideal situation in deploying Linux desktops is to save money by making use of existing hardware. Your PCs may be a bit old to run the latest and greatest operating system, or the hard disk inside may not have a great deal of space. No matter; they are likely perfect for thin clients. If you felt so inclined, you could even get rid of the hard drive inside those PCs.

There is some amount of up-front work to be done to deploy thin clients, but it's also a great way to put Linux on the desktop while keeping your commitment low. After all, there's no installing to be done on the PCs. Turning a PC into a thin client is as simple as creating the appropriate boot diskette.

Converting PCs to Thin Clients

To turn an old PC into a Linux thin client, be sure that PC has an Ethernet card. In the previous chapter, I covered the various steps involved in getting such a PC on line, all of which started with a PC booting and requesting an IP address from the thin-client server. If the PCs don't already have Ethernet cards, this is a good time to consider your alternatives. Ethernet cards can be purchased with EPROM (Erasable Programmable Read Only Memory) slots so they can automatically boot from a network. The EPROMs can then be burned with Etherboot code so that they can perform an automatic boot from the network.

It isn't necessary to replace your Ethernet cards. Etherboot code, which also includes a driver for a specific Ethernet card, can also be copied to diskettes. You can then, in turn, boot from those diskettes. The tools to create these diskettes are available at the Etherboot web site at www.etherboot.org. You have two choices here. One is to download the source code for the Etherboot code, complete with all the included Ethernet card drivers. Then, simply extract and build. When you are finished, you will have a boot diskette ROM code for all of the supported Ethernet drivers. There is an easier way, however, particularly if you have only one or two different kinds of network card.

Visit the ROM-o-matic web site http://rom-o-matic.net, and you can download the appropriate boot diskette for your particular network card. Given that the Etherboot ROM code is extremely compact, downloading takes only seconds.

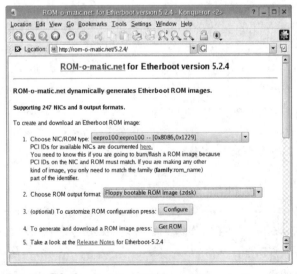

FIGURE 21-1   Let the ROM-o-matic web site create your boot diskettes for you.

From the Rom-O-Matic web page, select the Etherboot release level and click the appropriate link. The latest release is usually best, and at this writing latest means release 5.2.4. The link takes you to an easy-to-use form (Figure 21-1), from which you can select your network card type, the ROM output format (diskette, EPROM, and so on), and any local configuration options. Click Get ROM to download your Etherboot ROM to disk. You can then transfer the downloaded file to a blank diskette with this command:

```
cat eb-5.2.4-eepro100.zdsk > /dev/fd0
```

That's it. The ROM boot diskette is done. Pop it into the workstation PC and reboot. When the system comes up off the card, it will pause for a few seconds by default, giving you the opportunity for a local or network boot; network is the default. After the PC obtains its IP address from your DHCP server, the workstation should boot normally to a graphical XDMCP login.

Once a workstation is booting from the network, you're about 95% of the way there. Depending on the PC, the graphic hardware, and the fact that every PC is going to be different, you may want to do a little tweaking for individual units. Before I give you some tweaking advice, however, I want to take a moment to discuss dedicated thin clients.

Alternative Thin-Client Hardware

The advantage to using old PC hardware is obvious. There's no need to invest in yet more new hardware. One boot diskette later, your old PCs are new Linux thin clients. What could be more attractive?

Well, how about a workstation with a tiny footprint? Sitting next to me is a Jammin 125 thin-client workstation (Figure 21-2) that I purchased from Diskless Workstations (www.disklessworkstations.com). It is a mere two inches thick, and roughly six inches by seven inches on the side— slightly bigger than a thick paperback. Aside from taking up very little room on my desk, it is cool and consequently has no fan. That makes it quiet. As another bonus, it uses up very little power.

I mention this one because I happen to own one, but many other manufacturers also make dedicated thin-client units. Combined with a flat panel monitor, the result is a cool, quiet, low-power work environment that lets you take back some of that precious desktop real estate.

FIGURE 21-2 Jammin 125: a dedicated thin-client unit.

Advanced Thin-Client Configuration

This section is, to a large degree, a return to the `lts.conf` file. Looking back at the original `lts.conf` file from the last chapter, you might have noticed that everything we defined was global. One paragraph represented each and every workstation.

```
[Default]
        SERVER              = 192.168.22.6
        XSERVER             = auto
        X_MOUSE_PROTOCOL    = "PS/2"
        X_MOUSE_DEVICE      = "/dev/psaux"
        X_MOUSE_RESOLUTION  = 400
        X_MOUSE_BUTTONS     = 3
        USE_XFS             = N
        SCREEN_01           = startx
```

Because every PC is not the same, this might not work out quite as well. For instance, the mouse is defined as being a common PS/2 mouse. Suppose one of our thin-client workstations, the one called ws022, had an old Microsoft serial mouse. I could create a paragraph in the `lts.conf` file like this:

```
[ws022]
        X_MOUSE_PROTOCOL    = "Microsoft"
        X_MOUSE_DEVICE      = "/dev/ttyS0"
```

Note Section names can be host names (as the above ws022), but they can also be IP addresses or MAC addresses.

You can also combine a collection of settings that aren't specifically associated with an individual workstation by using the LIKE variable. Here's how it works: say I have two different types of mice, my PS/2 and Microsoft serial mice. I can define paragraphs strictly for each mouse configuration.

```
[msmice]
        X_MOUSE_PROTOCOL    = "Microsoft"
        X_MOUSE_DEVICE      = "/dev/ttyS0"
        X_MOUSE_BUTTONS     = 3
        X_MOUSE_BAUD        = 1200

[ps2mice]
        X_MOUSE_PROTOCOL    = "PS/2"
        X_MOUSE_DEVICE      = "/dev/psaux"
```

Then, when configuring workstations, we could use the LIKE variable name to assign a few presets to individual workstations. For example, look at these entries for ws009 and ws010:

```
[ws009]
        LIKE                = msmice
        USE_NFS_SWAP        = Y
        SWAPFILE_SIZE       = 64m

[ws010]
        LIKE                = ps2mice
        XSERVER             = vesa
        USE_NFS_SWAP        = Y
        SWAPFILE_SIZE       = 128m
```

Both of these introduce a new setting, that of NFS_SWAP. If you specify this, a swap file of the size indicated will be created on the server. The format for its filename is worstation_name.swap in a directory called swapfiles appended to NFS_SWAPDIR—for example, the swap file for workstation ws067 is `ws067.swap`. You can set the variables `NFS_SWAPDIR` and `SWAP_SERVER` in the `lts.conf` file.

```
SWAP_SERVER          = 192.168.22.20
NFS_SWAPDIR          = /mnt/bigdrive
```

I mention this, because 50 or 100 workstations all using 64 or 128 megabytes of swap space is something you need to consider when laying out where things live on your system. You certainly don't want to run out of disk space. Mind you, when the space is created (when the thin client logs in for the first time), the swap space won't continue to grow. What you allocate is what gets used.

Another very interesting configuration possibility is to add a serial or parallel printer to a workstation.

```
[ws035]
    LIKE                 = ps2mice
    SCREEN_01            = startx
    PRINTER_0_DEVICE     = /dev/lp0
    PRINTER_0_TYPE       = P
    PRINTER_0_PORT       = 9100
```

In the above example, a `PRINTER_0_TYPE` of `P` indicates a parallel printer. An `S` would indicate a serial printer. That would mean a `PRINTER_0_DEVICE` of something like `/dev/ttyS1`. The `PRINTER_0_PORT` is the network port under which the printer will be made available to the Linux print system. The printer can then be created as a system printer by configuring it as a Network Printer (TCP) as described in Chapter 14, "Printers and Printing." Printing through the thin clients use lp_server, which emulates an HP JetDirect print server. Consequently, the default network port is 9100.

Quick Tip   As you might have guessed, the `0` in `PRINTER_0_DEVICE` and the other settings, indicates the first defined printer on a thin client. There can be up to three defined printers numbered `0`, `1`, and `2`.

I could spend a long time going over all the possibilities, but I hope this is enough to give you an idea of what can be done with a thin client and how that basic configuration can be modified. For a more complete list of settings, visit my support pages for this book at `www.marcelgagne.com/MTLBD`, and look for the Thin Clients link. Alternatively, you can pay a visit to the `www.ltsp.org` site.

Linux Thin Clients, via Windows

What if you could provide all the Windows users in your office with thin-client Linux desktops? Sometimes easy access to a Linux desktop is complicated by a need to continue running legacy Windows applications. In this section, I'm going to show you a way to get the best of both worlds, while still running Windows. It isn't as fast or as good as running Linux on its own, but with the help of a package called Cygwin, it may be just what you need to bridge the gap.

Enter Cygwin

Cygwin is a collection of GNU tools ported to Windows which is done through the use of a Cygwin runtime library. Using Cygwin, a developer can use Cygwin's runtime (or the Win32 API), the gcc compiler, and accompanying debugging tools to port Unix and Linux software to Windows.

The reason for Cygwin goes beyond simply porting Linux and UNIX code to Windows. Standard bash scripts can be used on your Windows systems, thereby extending the functionality of those machines, particularly those that act as servers. Suddenly, you can have access to all those commands that you desperately miss every time you find yourself working on a Windows machine. Finally—and this is where thin clients come into play—Cygwin also provides you with the ability to run X, thereby making it possible to run graphical Linux applications on your Windows desktop. To get to that point, you are going to need to install Cygwin first. This involves a visit to the Cygwin web site at www.cygwin.com.

The install process is relatively simple. On the Cygwin web site, you'll see a link that says Install Cygwin Now. This is a link to a single, small executable called setup.exe. When you execute this file on your Windows system, it launches the Cygwin installer.

Installing Cygwin is mostly a question of clicking Next a few times, but there are a few things to consider. For instance, three install options are available. You can install directly from the Internet, download the files, or install from an existing set of files. For the latest and greatest, especially if you don't already have a copy of the files, choose to install via the Internet route. You'll then be asked for a root directory (the default is C:\Cygwin) and whether you wish to install for just one user or everyone on the system. Choose all users, and select UNIX as the default text file type. Because these are all the defaults, you can just click Next.

Choose a local temporary directory where the install will download files (I always create a tmp folder, even when working in Windows), then click Next again. After you select your Internet connection (direct, proxy, and so on), and you are presented with a mirror site selection screen. Choose a mirror, and seconds later, you see a list of package groups. Alongside each of these install sets is a plus sign. You may just want to click those to make sure that the packages you want actually do get installed (clicking the word "Update" changes it to Install, Uninstall, or Reinstall). From the perspective of running thin clients, you are going to be particularly interested in making sure that the XFree86 packages are installed. If you have tons of disk space, you could just change the default beside All (at the top of the list) to Install and then just not worry about it.

At this point, the download really begins. Because this can take a while, it is usually a good time to get another coffee.

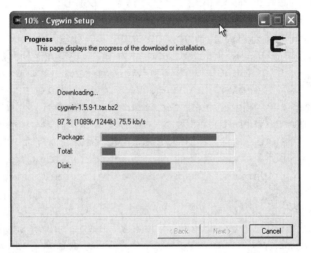

FIGURE 21-3   Installing Cygwin on a Windows XP box.

At the end of the install, the setup program creates an icon on the desktop (by default) and asks you if you want one in the Start Menu as well. Double-click on that Cygwin icon and you start up a bash shell, complete with access to a whole lot of classic Linux commands. Try df to check on your mounted partitions, or list files with ls. In addition, you can do a whole lot of the other things covered in Chapter 10, "Becoming One with the Shell." One of the real bonuses is the inclusion of the secure shell and associated tools. Using OpenSSH, you have a fully functional ssh terminal client at your disposal for secure communications and remote administration to your Linux system.

Once you've discovered the power of working with Linux, Cygwin can be a real charge in that it brings some of that functionality to Windows. Speaking of which, let's talk about graphical access to Linux. With Cygwin, access to X is done through the Xwin.exe program. Passing various flags to Xwin.exe lets you define screen size and other parameters. Look in the /usr/X11R6/bin directory for two handy files: startxwin.sh and startxwin.bat. The difference, as the extensions might indicate, is the manner in which they are run. One is a shell script meant to be run from a bash shell, and the other is a DOS/Windows batch file. Running the startxwin.sh script starts a simple graphical X terminal (xterm). From there, you can connect to your Linux system using ssh with X forwarding and run any X application:

```
ssh -X -l marcel my_system
```

You now can type any graphical Linux command and have it running under Windows. For instance, typing kcontrol while logged in from a Windows XP system, brings up the familiar KDE control panel (Figure 21-4).

FIGURE 21-4   Running Linux graphical applications from Windows.

Possibly the coolest thing to do is to use `Xwin` with the `-query` flag:

```
Xwin.exe -query your_system
```

If your system has been configured with LTSP, you will be rewarded with a graphical login from which your can run a full-blown Linux thin-client session on your Windows system. It's not quite as good as running an actual Linux thin-client session, but it comes close.

Performance Tips

Thin clients tend to be pretty efficient and fast. On older, more modest hardware, it can be amazing to see just how fast a modern desktop can run. Still, there are ways to make your thin-client experience even faster.

The first tip is to make sure your server can handle the load. Remember that every client will be running from that one machine. Combining a fast processor with lots of memory is a great place to start, but disks are also worth considering. Most of the bottlenecks in such data-intensive applications as databases have to do with disk performance. The faster, the better.

The network itself is an important part of the whole thin-client design. Most people today won't be running 10 megabit Ethernet, but these networks still exist. If possible, consider upgrading to 100 megabit cards. Consider also purchasing 100 megabit switches instead of hubs. The price difference is minimal, but it can make a huge difference in performance.

Network performance invariably brings me to screensavers. Screensavers are very cool. All of those flying things, colorful slide shows, fractals, and various things chasing other things make for great, passive entertainment. The problem is that in a thin-client network, all of that graphic network traffic can grind your network to a virtual halt. Things don't actually stop; they just feel that way. Turn the screensaver off, or set it to none so that the screen blanks out instead of firing up a trip through hyperspace.

Resources

Cygwin
www.cygwin.com
Diskless Workstations
www.disklessworkstations.com

Etherboot Project

www.etherboot.org

Linux Terminal Server Project

www.ltsp.org

Moving to the Linux Business Desktop support pages

www.marcelgagne.com/MTLBD

ROM-o-matic

http://rom-o-matic.net

22

Remote Control

Virtual Network Computing (VNC)

To system administrators in large companies with many Windows workstations, the headaches are all too familiar—simple operator error calls that require a great deal of work and time to walk users through the right steps to a solution. Wouldn't it be great if you could take control of users' desktops and do it for them while they watch and learn?

I am talking about a remote administration tool that works not only with Windows, Solaris, and DEC Alphas running OSF1, but also with that old favorite of the desktop publishing world, the Macintosh.

This great tool is Virtual Network Computing (VNC) from AT&T Laboratories in Cambridge, England. The VNC package enables you to view other computer desktops from your own desktop. For instance, I could be running an X server on a Linux machine from a Windows 95 or NT box, or doing the reverse. I can do it from my internal network or across the Internet.

Now, I know commercial packages out there can do this, but not necessarily from your Linux desktop. They also cost more than VNC. That's right: VNC is distributed free of charge. VNC may well be part of your Linux distribution already, so look on the CDs before you go hunting for it on the Internet. There are two great sites for VNC. The first is the original home of VNC, RealVNC, at `www.realvnc.com/faq.html`. The second is `www.tightvnc.org`, which is the home of TightVNC. TightVNC is a performance and featured-enhanced version of VNC and the one often included with distributions.

Let's start with the heart of VNC: the server.

```
vncserver
```

This is actually a perl script that runs the Xvnc server. Use it to run Xvnc. You may have to change the first line of the script to reflect the location of your perl binary.

You start a `vncserver` by logging on to the Linux (or UNIX) system you want to administer remotely. To start the command, type:

```
vncserver hostname:session_number
```

With VNC, you can run multiple sessions and connect to different servers. By default, the session numbers start at 1 and go up from there, but you can specify session 3 (for instance) right from the start by typing:

```
vncserver hostname:3
```

This highlights another benefit of VNC. Until you kill a VNC session, it retains its current state. That means you can disconnect from a session, reconnect later, and return right where you left off. In fact, you can even share a session so multiple users can access it. More on that later.

When you start the vncserver for the first time, you are prompted for a password to access the server. You can always change it later using the vncpasswd command. Once the server is activated, you can connect to it using the vncviewer command. The format is:

```
vncviewer host:session_number
```

To exit the viewer or send specific key sequences, press the F8 key, and then click Quit Viewer to close the session. You can also start a shared session so that others may use the same X window session with this version of the command:

```
vncviewer -shared host:session_number
```

When you start the vncserver, it creates a .vnc directory under your home directory (/root/.vnc). Several files are kept here, among them individual log files associated with each server you run and a .pid file to allow for removal of the server. By the way, you kill a vncserver process like this:

```
vncserver -kill :1
```

Remember that the :1 could be a :2 or :3, depending on the session you are trying to kill.

The other file I want you to look at is xstartup. If you do a cat on the file, you get something that looks like this:

```
#!/bin/sh
xrdb $HOME/.Xresources
xsetroot -solid grey
xterm -geometry 80x24+10+10 -ls -title "$VNCDESKTOP Desktop" &
# twm &
startkde &
```

The second-to-last line is commented out and a startkde line is added below, because VNC uses twm (the Tab Window Manager) as its default desktop. I chose to run KDE instead, and added the final line. If you prefer another window manager, change it here.

Just when you thought it couldn't get any better, the VNC viewer can be run from your favorite web browser as well through a small Java applet. From your Mozilla browser, use the URL http://server_name:580session_number/ to access the Java client. Be sure to substitute host and session_number with yours.

Let me clarify that a bit. I have a machine with a hostname of `gateway` (as in a gateway to my intranet) on my network. If I want to connect to `vncserver` session number 1 on that machine, my URL is `http://gateway:5801/`.

Java starts on your browser, and you are presented with a password prompt, the one you gave when you first started the server. Unlike the command-line viewer, you don't use function keys to cut and paste or disconnect from the session. Four small buttons remain at the top of the screen for you to use.

This is a small, fast client that responds very quickly. With the browser client, you can access your Linux or UNIX server from any PC with a Java-capable browser.

How about Windows? Earlier on, I mentioned that VNC offers a server for Windows as well. Using this product, you no longer have to spend hours on the phone walking a user through a problem with a Windows application—you simply take control. To do so, you need to install the Windows product that comes as a .zip file. The current version of the file is `vnc-3.3.3r2_x86_win32.zip`. This works with all Windows products. Have a peek at Figure 22-1. This is a Windows XP session running Mozilla that is being accessed from my Linux system via the Konqueror web browser inside a KDE session.

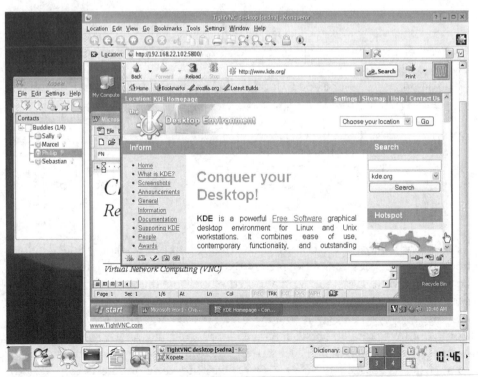

FIGURE 22-1   Controlling a Windows XP machine from Linux using VNC.

To get in on the action, extract the file into the directory of your choice (using your favorite Windows archive client, such as `pkzip` or WinZip). Two folders are created. One is `vncviewer`; it contains a single executable, vncviewer.exe, which can be run to access your Linux server or any VNC server without any special installation. You can put this file on a floppy disk and carry it around with you if you do not want to install it on every PC. The other directory is `winvnc`, which contains the full distribution, including the VNC server for Windows. To install VNC for Windows, simply run the setup.exe file in the folder.

Next, click the Start button, and then select Program Files > VNC > Administrative Tools. Click the Install Registry Key link, and then click Install WinVNC Service (depending on the VNC version you install, you may be offered this as a choice in the install). To run the server, either reboot or click Start WinVNC Service. You should see a little VNC icon appear in the tray of your Windows task bar (over by the clock on the right). Now, go back to your Linux machine and run `vncviewer` either from the command line or the browser by connecting to the host at service number 0. In other words, for me to connect to my PC called natika, I run either of the following two commands (the second actually being a URL and not a command):

```
# vncviewer natika:0
http://natika:5800/
```

The last thing I should mention is that you can also run a VNC viewer from Windows by selecting it in the VNC program group (click the Start button and select Program Files > VNC, and so on).

Note Unlike on the Linux server, you *cannot* run multiple sessions of VNC from Windows. You are not magically given a multiuser Windows system. This is strictly remote control.

KDE Remote Desktop Connection

As you can see, sometimes nothing works better than taking control of a remote desktop to do what needs to be done. Perhaps the best incentive is the office environment in which many of us work. Using desktop sharing, a system administrator could deal with individual desktop issues without leaving the comfort or convenience of the office. Do you need to show a user how to add an icon to the desktop? Connect to their desktops, and let them watch. Have you received a call asking for help interpreting an error message? Connect to the system, and ask the user to recreate the scenario while you watch. The possibilities are endless.

The problem with VNC, that excellent cross-platform remote-control package, is that it doesn't provide any means of controlling the main X display ($DISPLAY:0), so taking control of a user's desktop to fix a problem or to show them how to do something is out of the question.

KDE comes equipped with a solution to that problem with Desktop Sharing, a system that lets your users invite someone to either watch their desktop session or take control of it. Administrators can also set it up so that they can take control whenever necessary.

To configure your client PC for remote access, start by bringing up the KDE Control Center from your application starter menus (the big K in the lower-left corner). You also can start the Control Center by typing `kcontrol` at a shell prompt. When `kcontrol` starts, click on the Internet & Network icon in the left sidebar menu and select Desktop Sharing, as shown in Figure 22-2. As you can see, a three-tabbed window appears on the right side.

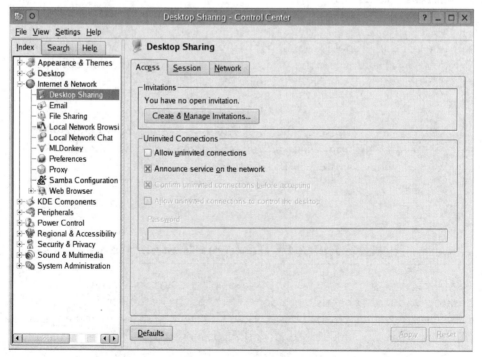

FIGURE 22-2   Configuring KDE Desktop Sharing from the Control Center.

The three tabs are Access, Session, and Network. Click the Network tab, and you'll have the opportunity to override the default of Assign Port Automatically. KDE Desktop Sharing's default port is 5900, but turning off this box enables you to assign a specific port number. The Session tab simply turns the background image on and off during a control session, thereby giving you slightly better performance. On to the Access tab. Invitations are the means by which access is granted to the desktop, but it also is possible to allow uninvited connections as well. I don't think I need to explain the security implications of this course of action. For this reason, allow me to tell you how to create and manage invitations. If you are the administrator of this site and the client machines are under your care, you may wish to allow uninvited connections. If you select this, you can take control of a remote workstation without user intervention. As long as the machine is up, you have access. Otherwise, the user will have to confirm your remote control session each time.

For individual connections, click, or have your users click, the button that says Create & Manage Invitations. The window that pops up offers you two important choices. You can create either a new personal invitation or a new email invitation. Let's start with a personal invitation (Figure 22-3).

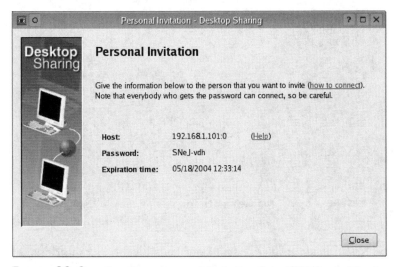

FIGURE 22-3   Creating a personal invitation for a KDE Control Session.

For security reasons, the invitation itself lasts for only an hour. If you don't do anything else, Desktop Sharing automagically comes up with a password and an expiration time for the session. The host address necessary for the connection is displayed also. Overriding either the password or the expiration time is not allowed. Make sure you pass on the information as it is shown to the person who will be connecting. When you have passed on the information (or written it down), click Close.

The other option is an email invitation, which is essentially the same, except that the connection details are sent via email rather than read over the phone. The only catch here is you are sending the means to access your system via email during that one hour period. If you choose this option, you'll receive a warning about plain-text email over the Internet and the wisdom of encrypting said email. Click Continue to get past the warning, and a Kmail message appears, ready for you to click Send. If no one answers the invitation, it disappears within an hour.

I've shown you how to do this via the KDE Control Center, but you also can manage invitations directly with the krfb command. The function is the same, but the front end dialog is a little different, as you can see in Figure 22-4.

FIGURE 22-4　Managing desktop sharing sessions using krfb.

Before moving on, click Close to get past all those invitations, and have another look at the second means of providing access: uninvited connections. If sending an email invitation presents interesting security concerns, then a wide-open, permanent invitation should ring additional bells. As I suggested, in an office environment it also may be the sanest method of giving yourself access. If you check on Allow Uninvited Connections, you still have to assign a password for connecting. Furthermore, you have the opportunity to confirm uninvited connections before accepting. You also can decide to give those uninvited connections the ability to control the desktop.

To connect to the desktop, you can use any VNC client (TightVNC, for example), but the slicker way is to install KDE Desktop Sharing on the controlling desktop also. You'll find the interface friendly and appealing. To start the client, either select it from the Internet menu under the big K or call the program directly from the command line using the `krdc` command. From the dialog that pops up, you can enter the host connection information as shown in Figure 22-5.

FIGURE 22-5   To connect to a client PC, use the krdc command.

After you create an open invitation with a confirm option, a remote client trying to connect generates a warning message asking whether you want to allow that connection (Figure 22-6). You can also specify whether that connection is allowed to control the keyboard and mouse or just watch.

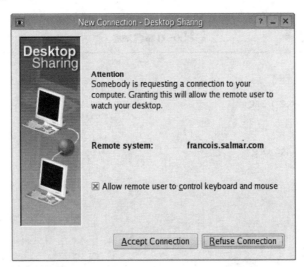

FIGURE 22-6   A request for Desktop Control.

Assuming that you haven't opened up your system to uninvited connections, the remote user still has to enter the password, at which point you'll see a nice blue eye staring at you from the system tray.

One of the great things about krdc is you can resize or scale the virtual desktop to almost any size. Size your window, then click on the magnifying glass icon.

rdesktop for Windows Control

Another remote-control package worth your consideration is called rdesktop, and it is very likely on your distribution CDs. Here's the idea: From time to time, you may have to work on a box running Windows 2000. If that box requires you to connect using Win2K's Terminal Server, you no longer need to shut down your Linux system to do your work.

Simply put, rdesktop is free Linux-based Windows (NT/2000) Terminal Server client, which means it uses RDP (remote desktop protocol). If you can't find it on your CDs, you can pick up your copy of the source at www.rdesktop.org. Running the program is as easy as typing rdesktop from the command line (or using your <Alt+F2> program launcher):

```
rdesktop -u Administrator -p PaSsWoRd 192.168.22.212
```

The -u parameter specifies a user account on the Windows server, while the -p option specifies the password. Have a look at Figure 22-7 for a screenshot of a KDE desktop running rdesktop to a remote Windows 2000 server.

Resources

rdesktop
www.rdesktop.org
TightVNC
www.tightvnc.org

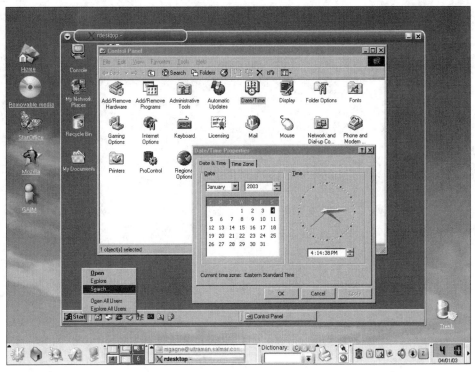

FIGURE 22-7   Windows terminal server access using rdesktop.

chapter
23

Security

When you set up your Linux system, you brought up a powerful, high-level, multitasking network operating system—one that was maybe a little too powerful. Depending on your installation and the choices you made, a large number of services may have started (`rlogind`, `inetd`, `httpd`, `innd`, `fingerd`, `timed`, `rhsd`, and others). Do you know what they all are? You should. As a system administrator, you've got enough things to worry about, such as that hung printer, but if your machine is exposed to the Internet, you should pay particular attention.

Security is a huge topic, one that could easily fill a few books. Covering it in complete detail is beyond the scope of this book. I can, however, provide you with basics that will give you a great start in making sure that your system is secure from unwanted access. In this chapter, I'll show you how to shore up simple defenses, build a firewall, and decide just what gets in and what stays out.

Remember, though, the parting lesson from Chapter 7, "Installing New Applications." Make sure you keep up to date with the latest patches and package updates. Crackers will use the latest distributed exploits (programs or techniques) to break through a well-known or recently uncovered security hole in your system. The good news is that you, as a security administrator, are just as capable of becoming aware of these exploits. Regular visits to your Linux distribution web site, such as Red Hat, SUSE, or Debian, can keep you on top of the latest patches to stop those exploits. While you're at it, find out about the exploits themselves by checking out the BugTraq forum or CERT (see the Resources section at the end of the chapter for URLs). Innovators or not, cracking a system is made so much easier if the door to your server is left wide open.

OpenSSH

Once upon a time, plain text communications was the norm. We used TELNET to connect to systems where we needed to get work done. Even today, there is still a tendency for people to use TELNET rather than more secure forms of communication. From a security perspective, however, plain-text communications have real dangers.

Anyone running a network sniffer program, such as Sniffit (`http://reptile.rug.ac.be/~coder/sniffit/sniffit.html`) can snoop on every packet sailing across your network. If you are logging in using TELNET, that person can see your username and password plain as day. For example, see if you can guess what password the user natika thinks is being safely tranmitted across the network in Figure 23-1. This should dissuade you from using TELNET for any kind of communication where security is even remotely important.

One way around this dilemma is to use the secure shell. OpenSSH is an open-source implementation of the secure shell protocol that comes with almost every major Linux distribution. You can run out to `www.openssh.org` to get the latest and greatest, but you probably already have it on your system. That said, keeping up to date with the latest version of OpenSSH is essential if you want to maintain security. So, if your version of OpenSSH is more than a few months old, you may want to consider checking for an update.

The secure shell is more than a simple way to keep your passwords to yourself. Logging securely certainly qualifies as the basics for OpenSSH, but there are some nifty features that should make you wonder why you would use anything else to communicate (well, almost).

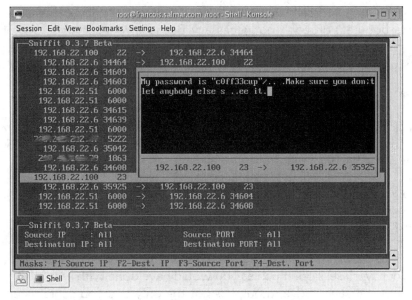

FIGURE 23-1   Sniffit and other such tools make it easy to find passwords.

OpenSSH has several components: a client and server, utilities for generating public and private encrypted keys for strong authentication, and a secure FTP server. Before you log in using a secure shell, you need to start a secure server, which usually happens at boot time through a script in /sbin/init.d or /etc/rc.d/init.d, depending on your system. Look there for a script called simply sshd. You also can start the sshd daemon by typing sshd at the shell.

To log in to the remote system named speedy, I then would use the command:

```
ssh speedy
```

By default, the sshd daemon (or server) runs on TCP port 22—check it out by doing a more or less on your /etc/services file—but you can specify a different port with the -p option. Say you wanted to run the server on port 2222, to make it a little more difficult for unwanted guests to probe your system. To change this, simply type:

```
sshd -p 2222
```

By the way, you can run multiple sshd dæmons on however many ports you like, but that's probably not necessary. Because your server is now running on port 2222, you also would use the -p option to connect to speedy, the same as you did for the server.

```
ssh -p 2222 -l inewton speedy
```

Yes, I did add another option. The -l option tells the system to log in using the user name inewton. By default, an ssh login uses whatever your current logged-in user name happens to be.

```
Warning: Permanently added 'speedy,192.168.22.3' (RSA) to the list
of known hosts.
marcel@speedy's password:
```

Simple enough. At this point, you would enter your password, log in, and start your work session, much as you would have done with TELNET—only safer. The message above, though, is not the only one you could receive. I'll cover some others in a moment. For now, I want you to look at the words list of known hosts. In your home directory ($HOME), you should find a directory called .ssh that contains a file called known_hosts. This is where the key information is stored; in the above case, it stored the RSA key. It looks something like this:

```
speedy,192.168.22.3 ssh-rsa
AAAAB3NzaC1yc2EAAAABIwAAAIEAw4MQ4ubLTHuQCW9rlksXLME9wnYYege1z/
K3J3caMpzkFy7DpJ1VQjIspf03wyHgdAbg3jaV6NBbN7y35UOLy2oqJ/vk3QISdgKc
a/OqH/
UpeesyXB0kMb0HMCX8LD8tJVaCzEtoi2BZNSAOZNheHx7znz80uTWUTA2cQkk7gs0=
```

Don't worry. I don't expect you do sit there and read it with anything other than curiosity. Remember this file, though, because from time to time, on connect, you may receive a message like this:

```
@@@@@@@@@@@@@@@@@@@@@@@@@@@@@@@@@@@@@@@@@
@    WARNING: REMOTE HOST IDENTIFICATION HAS CHANGED!    @
@@@@@@@@@@@@@@@@@@@@@@@@@@@@@@@@@@@@@@@@@
IT IS POSSIBLE THAT SOMEONE IS DOING SOMETHING NASTY!
Someone could be eavesdropping on you right now (man-in-the-
middle attack)!
```

```
    It is also possible that the RSA host key has just been
changed.
    The fingerprint for the RSA key sent by the remote host is
    76:3f:54:71:22:48:36:5b:c8:8c:42:e5:e7:db:60:60.
    Please contact your system administrator.
    Add correct host key in /home/mgagne/.ssh/known_hosts to get
rid of this message.
    Offending key in /home/mgagne/.ssh/known_hosts:119
    Password authentication is disabled to avoid man-in-the-middle
attacks.
    X11 forwarding is disabled to avoid man-in-the-middle attacks.
    Permission denied (publickey,password,keyboard-interactive).
```

Yes, it does sound nasty and it could very well be, but it may in fact also be harmless. As the message says, it is also possible that the RSA host key has just been changed. If you know and trust the system, you can edit your `~/.ssh/known_hosts` file and delete the line containing the offending key. The connect error message conveniently lets you know which line number you can jump to; in this case, it's line 119. If, like me, you tend to use `vi`, here's a cool trick for getting there quickly:

```
vi +119 ~/.ssh/known_hosts
```

The +119 takes you right to line 119. Once there, a quick `dd` gets rid of the offending line for you. If you would prefer something friendlier than `vi`, you could also use your `kate` editor as described in Chapter 10, "Becoming One with the Shell," but I digress.

I mentioned that on connect, you might see different messages. To refresh your memory, here's the message I received when connecting to the host speedy:

```
Warning: Permanently added 'speedy,192.168.22.3' (RSA) to the list
of known hosts.
marcel@speedy's password:
```

Another common message I could have received is:

```
The authenticity of host 'speedy (192.168.22.3)' can't be
established.
```

```
RSA key fingerprint is
83:9f:6b:3f:69:02:2a:94:c5:ef:5f:35:f9:42:71:17.
Are you sure you want to continue connecting (yes/no)?
```

The difference has to do with yet another configuration file. Both the `sshd` daemon and the `ssh` command itself have global configuration options that can be found in the `/etc/ssh` directory. If you built OpenSSH from source, you may find it in `/usr/local/etc/ssh` instead. The `sshd` daemon's configuration file is named `sshd_config`, and the `ssh` client's configuration file is named `ssh_config`. For the moment, I'm going to concentrate on the `ssh_config` file:

```
Host *
  ForwardX11 yes
```

As you might guess from the asterisk at the end of the `Host` paragraph, you can set up different parameters for different hosts. This is a global setting. X forwarding allows you to run graphical applications on a remote system from your command line, a great boon for remote administration. For instance, if you connected to a remote system this way, you could run the KDE Control Center (command name: `kcontrol`) with full graphical display on your workstation.

```
kcontrol &
```

Making things even nicer is that this program's communications are also encrypted along with your logins as is everything you do from here on in.

Controlling Access to Your System

Now that we have instituted secure communications and people can't spy on us when we enter passwords, things are a little more secure. Everything we have done up to this point is good for system security, but it is just the beginning. Although some nefarious cracker won't be able to sniff the passwords coming across the network, there is still the issue of somebody getting into the system in the first place.

This brings up the subject of security holes, which we try to deal with by keeping up to date with the latest patches and security fixes for our systems—a good first solution. The second solution has to do with controlling access. Controlling access can be done in stages, and I'll cover a few of these shortly, but just who is this mysterious cracker?

What Is a Script Kiddie?

Most people would like to think that crackers are super-genius whiz kids with an IQ of 250 sitting up late in their high-tech computer rooms, which were assembled from old toasters, telephones, and pop-can pull-tops. Well, here's a real shocker: It doesn't take any great brains whatsoever to break into a system, just the right set of tools.

The term *"script kiddie"* says it all. Using a script downloaded from a *warez* web site or a cracker newsgroup, script kiddies literally follow the script. They run the programs, scan your network, and when they find the right signature (an insecure version of BIND, the name service daemon, for instance), they follow the next step on the script. Usually, this means running a program that exploits that network program's particular weakness; for instance, they may cause a buffer overrun in a susceptible program.

A script kiddie is not necessarily a genius. A script kiddie is just persistent and has a lot of time on his or her hands. It's time to shut the script kiddie down.

The Basics: TCP Wrappers

The simplest means of controlling access—short of turning off your machine—is through a program called a *TCP wrapper*. Chances are good that you loaded it as part of your system installation. I covered TCP wrappers briefly in Chapter 20, "Thin Clients: The Server."

Using the wrapper, you can restrict access to some of those services I mentioned earlier. Best of all, the wrapper logs attempt to gain entry to your system, so you can track who is testing the locks on your virtual doors. If you do not need to have people logging in to your system using `telnet`, `ssh`, or `rlogin`, you should close the door to remote access by adding this line to your `/etc/hosts.deny` file:

```
ALL:ALL
```

The first `ALL` refers to all services. The second `ALL` refers to everybody. Nobody gets in. Now, you should probably let the people on your internal network have access. Pretend you've set up your LAN with the approved internal network addressing scheme as detailed in RFC 1918 (a document that describes this standard). Assume a Class C network at 192.168.1.0 for this example. You'll also add your local host (127.0.0.1) network. Here's the `hosts.allow` entry:

```
ALL: 127.0.0.1
ALL: 192.168.1.
```

Yes, that's right. There's a dot after the 1 and nothing else. Now everyone in the 192.168.1.whatever network can get in to your system. For the changes to take effect, you must now restart your `xinetd` process. One that should work for everyone is as follows (note that the quotes are back quotes):

```
kill -1 `cat /var/run/xinetd.pid`
```

On distributions that use the service command (Red Hat, Mandrake, and so on), you might try this instead:

```
service xinetd restart
```

Safe, right? Not exactly. The `hosts.deny` file controls access only to services controlled by `xinetd` and wrapped by `/usr/bin/tcpd`, your TCP wrapper. The wrapper looks at incoming network requests, compares them to what is in your `hosts.allow` and `hosts.deny` files, and makes a decision on what to allow through. You could be running services not covered by the wrapper, or you may not have had the wrapper configured and the cracker has already gotten through. How can you tell? How can you make your system even more secure?

An iptables Firewall

For industrial strength protection, your system needs a *firewall*. With modern Linux distributions, this is done with the Netfilter system, a kernel-level IP filtering system. Using Netfilter, you can define a set of rules that decides what happens to those packets as they enter or leave your system. Most people don't talk about Netfilter usually; they talk about *iptables*, the package, or command, that lets you administer Netfilter. The two terms are often spoken of interchangeably. For the balance of this discussion, I will be using the term "iptables."

Prior to iptables, Linux systems were using ipchains and some systems still ship with both systems of filtering (I covered ipchains in my first book). If you have a choice, I recommend that you choose iptables. The iptables package also installs an iptables service that loads the appropriate kernel modules: `ip_conntrack`, `ip_conntrack_ftp`, `iptable_nat`, `ip_nat_ftp`, `ipt_MASQUERADE`, and others. On such systems as Red Hat, Fedora, or Mandrake, you can use the service command to start it, as in:

```
service iptables start
```

The first thing you might want to do is see what sorts of rules are already in place. To do so, run the iptables command with the -L flag like this:

```
iptables -L
```

Note that you should be running the iptables command as the root user. Running the command, you may see output similar to this:

```
Chain INPUT (policy DROP)
target     prot opt source              destination
block      all  --  anywhere            anywhere

Chain FORWARD (policy DROP)
target     prot opt source              destination
block      all  --  anywhere            anywhere

Chain OUTPUT (policy ACCEPT)
target     prot opt source              destination
```

That was a fairly short sample of a much longer output. For now, I just want you to get a feel for the style and, just perhaps more importantly, the concept of chains. A *chain* is just a list of rules that defines what happens to packets as they make their way through your system. By default, the kernel has three chains built in:

- INPUT: packets coming in from the outside
- OUTPUT: packets from your system bound for the Internet
- FORWARD: packets being routed through your system, as is the case with masquerading

In addition to these three default chains, you, as the administrator, can define or name your own by using the -N flag:

```
iptables -N mychain
```

You might also have noticed in the command output that each chain had a policy beside it. You define that policy as well.

```
iptables -P INPUT DROP
iptables -P FORWARD DROP
iptables -P OUTPUT ACCEPT
```

This is probably a good start to a firewall. Allow all outgoing packets to leave the system (ACCEPT), but ignore any attempts to send packets in or to forward them through the system (DROP). In this example, the catch comes if you happen to be creating this firewall from outside. Logged in directly into the system, there is no problem, but as soon as you issue the first command from a remote host, your access is cut off. You could also be completely safe and set your default OUTPUT policy to DROP as well.

To clear or flush all the rules that may have been defined on the system, use the -F flag. To delete any user-defined chains, use the -X flag. If you are writing a firewall script, it makes sense to start by flushing all chains and deleting any user-defined chains.

```
iptables -F
iptables -X
```

Let's try something a little more complex. Pretend for a moment that you have an internal network address of 192.168.22.11 on eth0 (your first Ethernet card) and an outside address of 199.243.101.44 on eth1 (your second Ethernet card). One of the first rules you might want to institute is to allow full access to your internal LAN and its private network. Use the command:

```
iptables -A mychain -s 192.168.22.0/24 -i eth0 -j ACCEPT
```

The -A flag tells iptables to append the rule to the chain called mychain. You could name the chain almost anything you like, or you could choose a name that best fits the function of the rules you are trying to create. In this example, the -s flag describes the source of the traffic (my LAN), the -i identifies the *incoming* Ethernet interface, and the -j sets the policy to ACCEPT. It's also a good idea to make sure the loopback interface isn't subject to either incoming or outgoing rules.

```
iptables -P INPUT -i lo -j ACCEPT
iptables -P OUTPUT -o lo -j ACCEPT
```

We've added another interface selection with the -o flag, specifying outgoing traffic. So far so good. Now, let's say that this is a web server and that you would like to allow all access from the outside on port 80.

```
iptables -A mychain -p tcp --destination-port 80 -j ACCEPT
```

As you can see, this command has a couple of new flags. The -p allows you to narrow down the port 80 traffic to a specific protocol, in this case tcp (udp, icmp, and all are other possibilities). Finally, the --destination-port flag defines the port number itself.

Let's add a few more rules. This time, we will allow port 25 in for incoming email traffic and port 53 for DNS queries. Notice that port 53 is set to allow both tcp and udp traffic.

```
iptables -A mychain -p tcp --destination-port 25 -j ACCEPT
iptables -A mychain -p tcp --destination-port 53 -j ACCEPT
iptables -A mychain -p udp --destination-port 53 -j ACCEPT
```

There is one more rule I would like you to take a look at. It has to do with masquerading or network address translation.

```
iptables -t nat -A POSTROUTING -o eth1 -s 192.168.22.0/24 -j MAS-
QUERADE
```

What makes this interesting is that it seems to throw in a completely new chain called POSTROUTING. Plus, the -t flag is pointing to nat. This is a table definition with its own special chain called POSTROUTING. Finally, if it hasn't already been done with the system startup, we need to turn on IP forwarding for the masquerading to work.

```
echo "1" > /proc/sys/net/ipv4/ip_forward
```

I covered this a little differently back in Chapter 9, "Network and Internet Connections," when discussing the network file in /etc/sysconfig. Back there, it was a setting called FORWARD_IPV4.

Graphical Firewall Tools

Building a decent firewall doesn't have to be hugely complicated, but it isn't something you can do blindfolded. You have to make sure you get things just right and doing all this by editing text files may not be the easiest thing in the world. That's the reason why major vendors provide their own firewall configuration tools with the systems they sell. Most modern Linux distributions set up basic firewall rules for you when you installed the system, so something is likely already in place, but fine-tuning your firewall for limited access to certain useful services may be in order, and that's where the tools come into play.

For instance, SUSE provides firewall configuration through the YaST administration tool (program name: `yast`). When YaST starts, click Security and Users in the left side's bar, then select Firewall from the right side's menu of applications.

Mandrake users can get to their firewall configuration tool via the Mandrake Control Center (program name: `drakconf`). Choose Security from the menu then, when presented with the next menu, select Firewall.

As you can see, the first place to look for a graphical administration tool is probably your own distribution. That said, there are other options and those options cross distribution boundaries. In an environment where many different distributions exist, it may make more sense to rely on one of these tools.

Webmin

Of course, there is your old friend Webmin, which comes with a module for maintaining your Linux iptables firewall (in `/etc/sysconfig/iptables`). It even converts a running firewall for you if you are running it from your own script. To get to the Webmin module, click on the Networking tab and select Linux Firewall. You can also get to it directly by using this quick path, assuming your server is called your_server:

```
http://your_server:10000/firewall/
```

KMyFirewall

One very nice tool that I recommend is KMyFirewall (command name: kmyfirewall), which is built to fit nicely into your KDE desktop (Figure 23-2). You will probably have to download it from `http://kmyfirewall.sourceforge.net`. Source is available, but you can also find a number of contributed prebuilt packages as well.

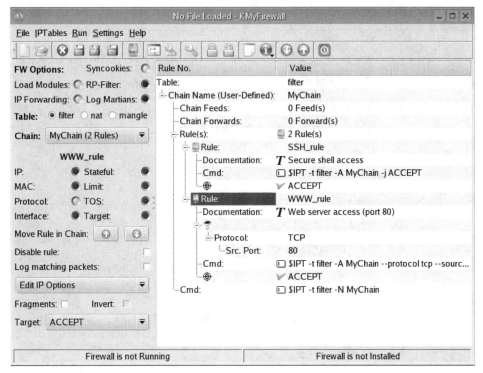

FIGURE 23-2   KMyFirewall is a great distribution-neutral firewall creation tool.

When KMyFirewall starts up, you will be asked for the root password, because you need to manipulate iptables as root. On the very first run, you have to accept a little disclaimer; it basically warns you that security is your responsibility and that although the program can help you in creating a firewall, it can't read your mind and will only do what you ask (more or less). Click Accept, and you are on your way. Finally, if this is the first time, KMyFirewall tries to guess your existing configuration. Next, you are presented with a settings dialog. Note that at the bottom of the screen, there is a button labeled Try Autoconfiguration. It essentially causes the program to act as though you were running it for the first time (as described above), so keep that in mind here.

From there, it's a point and click affair. Add a chain, then add rules to that chain, and so on.

Resources

BugTraq list (to subscribe, send mail to subscribe-bugtraq@securityfocus.com)

    www.securityfocus.com

CERT Advisory Mailing List

    www.cert.org/contact_cert/certmaillist.html

Linux Security HOWTO

    www.tldp.org/HOWTO/Security-HOWTO.html

KMyFirewall Home Page

    http://kmyfirewall.sourceforge.

RFC Editor (archives of RFC documentation)

    www.rfc-editor.org

Sniffit

    http://reptile.rug.ac.be/~coder/sniffit/sniffit.html

3

The Linux Business Desktop

24

Email Clients

These days, it seems that when we think about the Internet, we think about web browsers first. To those of us who have been on the Net for more years than we care to admit, that always seems a bit strange. The chief medium of information exchange on the Internet has always been electronic mail—email. Although the perception has changed, email is probably still the number one application in the connected world.

For a powerful, graphical email client, you need look no further than your KDE desktop. Its email package is called *Kmail*, and I'm going to tell you all about it. With the release of KDE 3.2, Kmail can still be run as a solo application, but it is also tightly integrated into the new and powerful Kontact groupware suite. Users coming from Outlook or similar clients will be familiar with the handy accessibility of multiple functions such as address books, calendars, to do lists, and so on. Keep reading, though; you'll soon be sending and receiving mail like a Linux pro.

I'm also going to talk about an alternative package called *Evolution*. Those of you who are coming from that other OS and who might be pining for the look and feel (and the integration) of Outlook are going to be pleasantly surprised. Evolution integrates many powerful features, including a contact manager and a well-connected organizer.

Be Prepared

Before we start, make sure you have handy your email username and password, as well as the SMTP and POP3 server addresses for sending and receiving your email. Your Internet service provider (ISP) or your company's systems administrator should have provided all of this information for you.

Kmail

On a default installation of the KDE desktop, the icon for Kmail is already sitting in your Kicker panel. Look for the icon with an envelope leaning against an orange *E*. You can also get to Kmail by clicking the big K, looking into the Internet submenu, and selecting Kmail from there.

Shell Out If you wish to start Kmail from the shell, just type its command, `kmail &`, at the shell prompt. Alternatively, you can press <Alt+F2> and type the command there.

The very first time you use Kmail, it starts up the groupware configuration system (Figure 24-1). The defaults are to enable groupware functions with the standard groupware server settings, specifically to run a Kolab server (www.kolab.org). If this is the case in your organization, you can click Next here. If, however, you have chosen not to run a Kolab server and the groupware functionality is not required or desired, simply click Cancel. I'm going to continue the next few paragraphs as though we are configuring for groupware functionality.

Note Kolab (think collaboration) was a project contracted by the German Bundesamt für Sicherheit in der Informationstechnik (BSI) (Federal Agency of IT-Security). The idea was to create a full-featured open source groupware package that could work with Linux clients as well as the very popular Outlook clients that continue to make up the majority of groupware clients. (You can think of it as a free Microsoft Exchange replacement if you like.) The project itself was called Kroupware but the resulting products were the Kolab server and KDE Kontact client (of which Kmail is one component). For more information, check out the Kolab web site at www.kolab.org or my own web site.

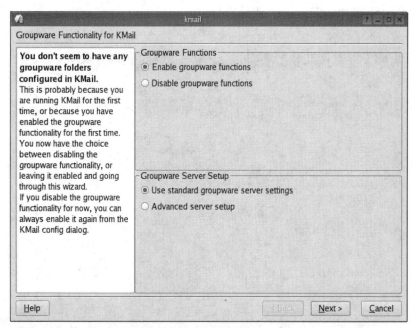

FIGURE 24-1   To groupware, or not to groupware.

Quick Tip You can return to all of the settings I cover here by clicking Settings on Kmail's menu bar and selecting Configure Kmail. In fact, you could just click Cancel here, and do all of this from a new Kmail session. This is good to know, because the configuration dialogs that I describe were handled entirely through Configure Kmail in KDE 3.1.

The next step is to create a default identity (Figure 24-2). I mention the word "default" because you can have multiple identities with Kmail, using different names and email addresses from the same package. You can add new identities later when Kmail is up and running. For now, enter your name and email address. You may also choose to add your business or organization name here. Click Next, and you are taken to the Kolab server configuration screen. Enter the login name and password (your systems administrator should have provided these) as well as the host name of the Kolab server. The interval at which the client will contact the server to check for mail is set at one minute. I find this a little short and usually tone it down to every five or ten minutes. The other defaults, such as storing the IMAP password in Kmail's configuration file, should probably be left alone.

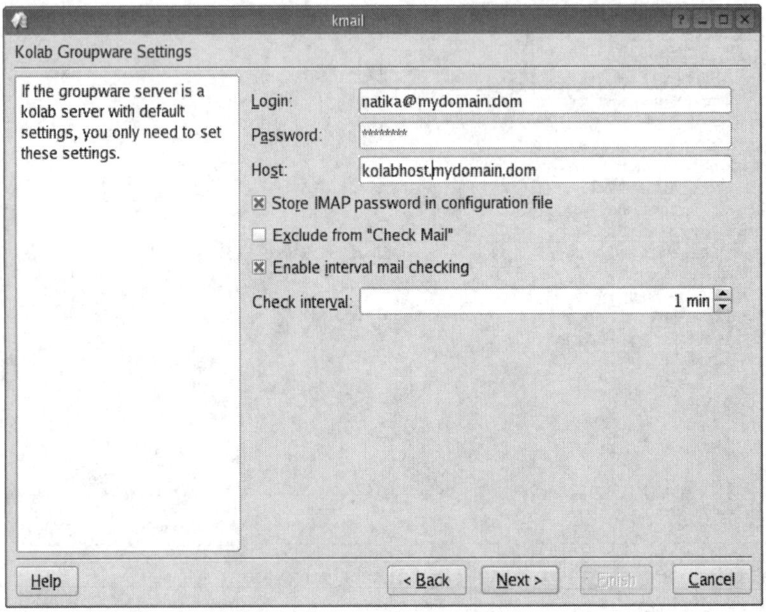

FIGURE 24-2   *Creating a default identity.*

When you click Next after this screen, Kmail attempts to contact the Kolab server. Because the SSL certificate for the server has not been registered with Kmail, you get a dialog box like the one in Figure 24-3. Confirm that you are indeed connecting to the correct server, and click Continue. When asked whether you wish to accept this certificate for the current session or forever, choose Forever.

FIGURE 24-3   Do you accept this certificate?

It is now time to choose your default language. The default is English. If that is okay, simply click Next. The next screen is the final screen in this setup. It contains a little message stating the groupware settings you chose and offers an opportunity to go back and make changes, or cancel entirely. If you are happy with your settings, click Finish and you are done with the groupware settings.

Things are a little bit different if you chose not to go the groupware route. When Kmail starts, click the Disable Groupware Functions radio button and click Next.

The Importance of Being Networked

Now that Kmail knows who you are and the kind of wittiness you like to provide at the end of your communication, you are no doubt anxious to send and receive some mail. For that you need a little network configuration. Click on the Network icon in the Configure Kmail dialog sidebar, to open two tabbed windows on the right side—one for sending and one for receiving (Figure 24-4). Because the Sending tab is selected by default, let's start with that one.

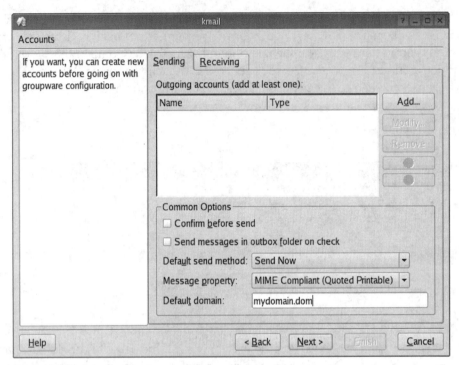

FIGURE 24-4   Configuring your network settings.

You can actually specify different transports here, as well as different hosts to use for outgoing mail. You are probably already aware that your Linux system isn't your run-of-the-mill operating system. Depending on your distribution's default install, it is quite capable of acting as its own mail server. In fact, notice that there is already one outgoing account setup: sendmail. This is your system's default mail transport, and depending on your network or your ISP, you may simply be able to leave this default. Unfortunately, that isn't likely. Most ISPs I know of that service home users *don't allow* sendmail traffic from their clients to pass through their servers. If you are sending mail, they would prefer that you use their servers. This means that you have to click Remove and get rid of the default outgoing account. Now click Add to create a new account. The dialog box shown in Figure 24-5 appears, asking you to specify a Transport.

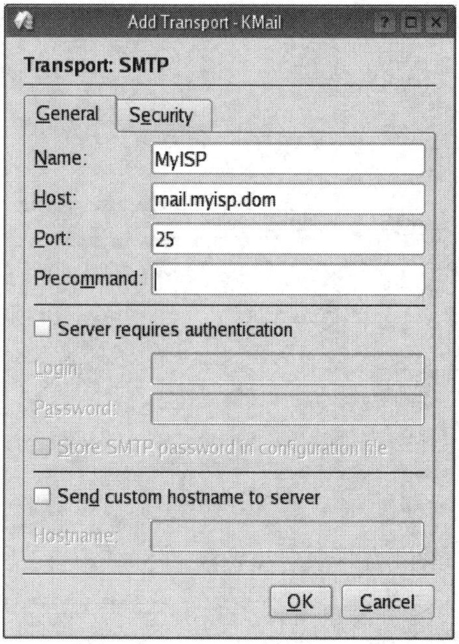

FIGURE 24-5   SMTP server configuration.

Choose SMTP. This brings up the Add Transport dialog, where you specify a name for the connection (choose anything with meaning to you, such as "My ISP"), the mail Host (which your ISP or office will provide), and a Port number. Although technically your ISP could run an SMTP host on something other than port 25 (the default), this will likely never happen. Accept the default of 25, click OK, and you are ready to send. We're halfway there.

Click on the Receiving tab to prepare Kmail for your incoming mail, then click on the Add button on the right. A small box appears, asking you for the type of account you want to set up. Your choices are Local Mailbox, POP3, IMAP, and Maildir Mailbox. Most ISPs are still using POP3 as the default mail delivery protocol, but double-check this to make sure. If you are setting up your PC in an office environment, you are likely going to use either IMAP or POP3. When you are happy with your choice, click OK, and you should be presented with the dialog box shown in Figure 24-6.

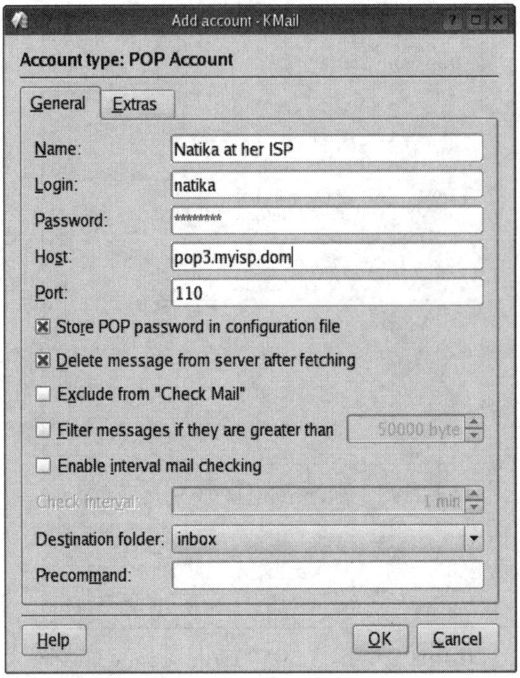

FIGURE 24-6   Setting up a POP3 mail account.

The Add Account dialog window appears, and this is where you configure your account. Please note that you can configure a number of different accounts, and all of them can be accessed through Kmail, just as you could configure many identities.

Start by filling in the Name field. Once again, this is just a name that makes sense to you, so it can be anything you like. The login, password, and host information will be provided by your ISP or system administrator. As with the SMTP port 25 discussions earlier, although it is *possible* that your ISP could use something other than port 110 for POP3 (or 143 for IMAP), I can pretty much *guarantee* that it won't happen. You can safely leave those settings as the default.

Before you go clicking OK in all this excitement, there are a couple of other options you should consider. Notice the check box on the window that says Store POP Password in Configuration File. Unless you want to be asked for your password each and every time you check your mail, it is probably a good idea to set that here. Also, specify that you want to delete the mail from server when you pick it up.

The last thing I want to point out is the Destination folder near the bottom of the window. Most people want their new mail to arrive in their inboxes. But for those of you who are going to configure multiple accounts and identities (there's a joke there somewhere), this is where you specify different folders for each of those accounts and personalities—uh, I mean *identities*.

Before we wrap on creating a POP3 (or IMAP) mail account, take a moment to have a look at the Extras tab. If your ISP or company uses encrypted mail downloads or an alternate method of authentication, you may need to set it here. When you have entered all the information, Click OK, then click Apply, then OK once more to leave the configuration settings.

That is all there is to it. If you are connected to your ISP or through your company LAN, you can start sending and receiving mail. If you configured an IMAP account, notice the folder with that account's name in your folder list. When you click on the plus sign beside the folder, Kmail connects to your IMAP server and shows you the rest of your folders. Take a look at Figure 24-7 for a look at a new Kmail window. Notice that some folders have been created for you on the left side; there's an inbox and an outbox. There's also sent-mail, trash, and drafts folders. These are local folders, and you'll find them in a directory called .Mail in your own home directory. If you enabled the groupware settings, you should also see a Kolab group with a default INBOX.

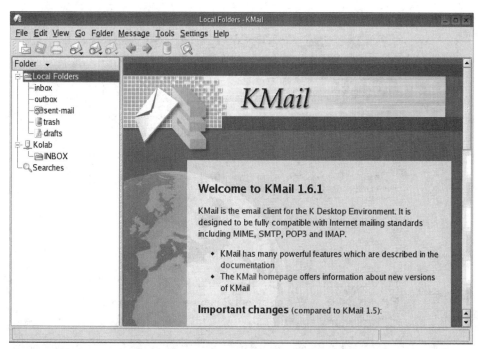

FIGURE 24-5   Kmail as it appears the first time after configuration.

Note Earlier I mentioned that you can modify all of the settings that you went through to get your email up and running by clicking Settings on the menu bar and selecting Configure Kmail. You get a dialog box with some familiar categories in a sidebar on the left: Identities, Network, Appearance, and so on. Make your changes to these categories in the main window on the right.

Now that everything is configured, it's time to send some mail.

Let's Communicate!

Sending messages is easy. Click on the New Message icon—the first one at the top left, just below the File menu. If you like the idea of keyboard shortcuts, press <Ctrl+N>, and you'll achieve the same result. The Kmail composer window (Figure 24-8) appears, and you can start typing your message.

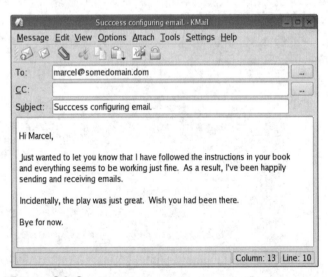

FIGURE 24-8   Writing an email message in the composer window.

I'm working on the premise that you have all sent email at some point; I'll let you take it from there. Fill in who the message is going to and the subject of your message, then start writing. When you are ready to send the message, click the Send Message icon (directly under the Message menu on the Kmail composer menu bar). For the keyboard wizards out there, try <Ctrl+Enter>.

Receiving Mail

To pick up your mail, click File on the menu bar and select Check mail. You can also use a <Ctrl+L> keyboard shortcut or the Check Mail In icon (Figure 24-9). It is usually fourth from the left in the icon bar.

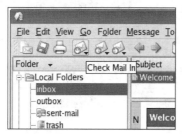

FIGURE 24-9 Checking for mail with a click.

Your Little Black Book

The ladies and gentlemen reading this book have by now wondered when I was going to talk about address books. After all, email implies some kind of social-izing, whether it be email or personal. When composing an email message (as in Figure 24-8), notice the button with the ellipsis at the end (...). Clicking this button brings up the address book from which you can select who you would like the message to go out to.

The only problem is that you probably don't have anything in the address book at this moment. Assuming you are starting from scratch, look in the icon bar at the top of either Kmail's main window or the composer window. You should see a little icon that looks like a book. You can also get to the address book by clicking on Tools on the menu bar and selecting Address Book. When KDE's address book opens up, click on File and select New Contact, or click the icon directly beneath the File menu. The keyboard wizards can press <Ctrl+N>. You will see the dialog box shown in Figure 24-10.

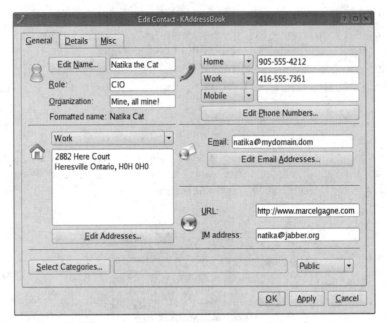

FIGURE 24-10   New contact address book information.

When the Entry Editor appears, add whatever information is appropriate for the contact. The person's name and email address are sufficient if these are all you need. When you are done entering information, click OK. You can add as many names as you want in one sitting. To save your address book as you go, click that little diskette icon in the tool bar. When you do close, Kmail saves your changes automatically.

Another way to add names to your address book, and by far the *easiest* way, is to take the address from a message you received. While you are viewing an email, right-click on the email address in the From field. When the small pop-up menu appears, click Add to Address Book, and you are done (Figure 24-11).

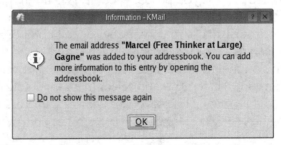

FIGURE 24-11   Right-click an address from Kmail to quickly add it.

Attached to You

As you sit there writing your letter to your old high-school friend, it occurs to you that it might be fun to include a recent picture of yourself. After all, you haven't seen each other in 20 years. To attach a file, click on the paper clip icon directly below the menu bar. If you have a Konqueror file manager window open, you can also drag an icon from Konqueror into your composer window. In fact, if you have an icon on your desktop, you can drag that into your composer as well, and Kmail attaches the images (or documents) automatically.

If you prefer the menu bar, click on Attach and select Attach File. The Attach File dialog window appears, giving you the opportunity to navigate your directories to find the appropriate file. Directly to the left of the navigation bar, an icon enables you to turn the preview mode on and off. This is handy when you are trying to find the right picture to attach. Figure 24-12 shows this dialog in use.

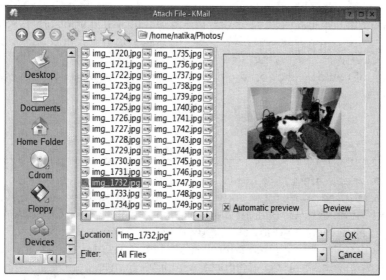

FIGURE 24-12   Browsing for an email attachment

Once you attach a file, it shows up in a separate attachments pane in your composer window. From there you can select those attachments and change your mind. Right-click on the attachment, and select Remove.

Send Now or Later

People who aren't online all the time may find that it makes more sense to queue messages, rather than to send them immediately. When the time is more convenient and you are online, you can send all queued messages. To do this, write your message as always. When you are ready, click Message on the menu bar and select Queue; Kmail transfers the messages to your outbox folder. You can also click the icon directly to the right of Kmail's Send icon (on the default KDE theme, it looks like a stack of pages). To actually *send* the messages, dial up to your ISP, click File on the menu bar, and select Send Queued. Note that this menu option is grayed out if there are no messages in your outbox.

Convenient timing affects more than just when you are online; it also affects when you can finish an email message you happen to be working on. Let's say that you are composing a rather long message to Aunt Sybil, who lives in Australia. After about an hour of typing, you realize that you were supposed to be at your brother's wedding. Looking at your watch, you note that you have only ten minutes to get to the wedding, and Aunt Sybil's email will certainly take another hour. Because you've already done all this work and you don't want to risk losing it, consider saving your email in your drafts folder.

From the composer window, click Message on the menu bar and select Save in Drafts Folder. When you are ready to resume your email (after the wedding, of course), click on the drafts folder and double-click on your email in process.

Evolution

For some people moving to Linux, saying goodbye to certain familiar applications is hard. One of the most commonly used email packages in the Windows world is Outlook and its cousin, Outlook Express. If you like Outlook, you will feel right at home on your new Linux desktop when you fire up *Evolution*. Check out Figure 24-13—seem familiar? In fact, Evolution looks and feels like Outlook but with some very important improvements.

Once again, it is likely that you will find Evolution on your distribution CD. Another way to get a copy is to head over to www.ximian.com, the site of the Evolution authors.

Upon starting Evolution for the first time, you are presented with the Evolution Setup Assistant to take you through the various preparatory steps. After you click Next through the introductory window, you are asked for your default identity. This is where you enter your full name and email address, along with other options, such as a default signature (Figure 24-14).

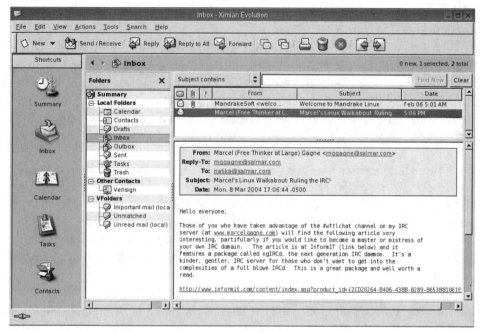

FIGURE 24-13   Evolution will make Microsoft Outlook users feel right at home.

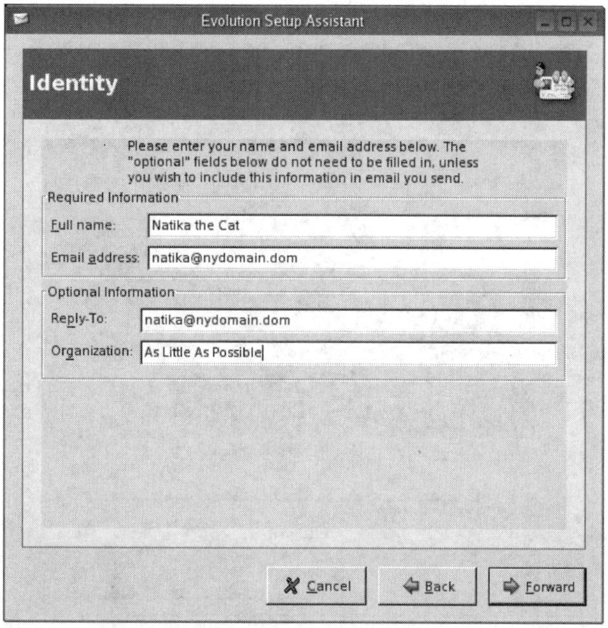

FIGURE 24-14   Evolution's Setup Assistant.

When you are done, click Next, and get ready to enter information for receiving mail. You start by selecting a server type. For most users, this is POP or IMAP (as with Kmail earlier). Enter the host name of the POP3 or IMAP host (as provided by your ISP), as well as your user name. If you don't want to enter your password each and every time Evolution checks for mail, click the Remember This Password check box. When you click Next, you get the opportunity to decide whether Evolution checks for mail automatically; the default is to check every ten minutes. Don't set this unless you are always connected. Click Next again, and you can configure your outgoing mail.

The default server type for sending is SMTP, and that is almost certainly what you will need. Enter the hostname as provided by your ISP (or system administrator), and click Next. The Account Management screen follows with your new email account listed as it will be displayed in Evolution. You could change this to be a name rather than an email address if you prefer. If this is your initial setup, leave the button labeled Make This My Default Account checked on, and click Next.

You are almost done. The final step is to select your time zone. Select an area on the map (preferably near to where you live) to narrow down your search. The map zooms in to the area you clicked, allowing you to fine-tune your selection (Figure 24-15). Make your final selection (you can use the drop-down box for help), click Next again, click Finish, and you are done.

FIGURE 24-15   Evolution's Setup Assistant zooms in to help in selecting your time zone.

Evolution starts up with a *summary* screen (Figure 24-16), showing you the weather for the area of your choice, your Tasks and Appointments lists for the day, as well as a summary of what is in your inbox and your outbox. Like the Outlook package in Windows, a set of icons runs down the left side, giving you access to your Calendar, Tasks, Contacts, and email.

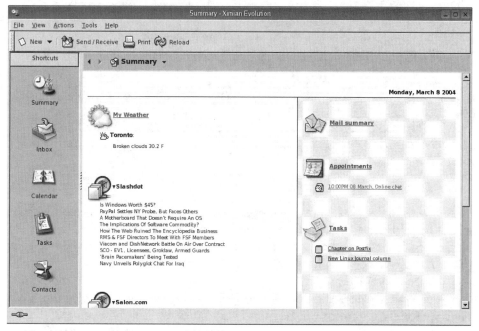

FIGURE 24-16 Evolution's summary screen.

Sending and Receiving Mail

To send a message, start by clicking on the Inbox icon (under the Shortcuts sidebar), then click the New Message button just below the menu bar (you can also click File on the menu bar and select New Message from there). Evolution's compose window appears (Figure 24-17).

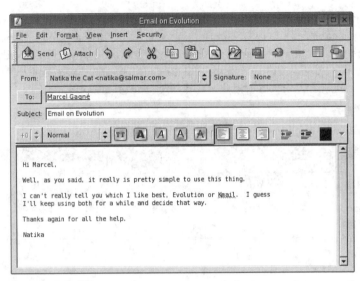

FIGURE 24-17   Sending a message with Evolution: the compose window.

As with Kmail, this is pretty standard stuff. Fill in the person's email address in the To field, enter a Subject, and type your message. When you have completed your message, click the Send button on the compose window (or click File on the compose window's menu bar, then select Send).

To pick up your email, make sure once again that you have the Inbox button selected, then click the Send/Receive button at the top of Evolution's main window (or click Actions on the menu bar and select Send/Receive).

The first time you pick up your mail, Evolution pauses and ask you for the password (Figure 24-18). You have an interesting choice to make here. Beside the words "Remember This Password" is a radio button that lets you lock in the information. If you choose not to record your password with Evolution, you will have to enter your password each time you check for mail.

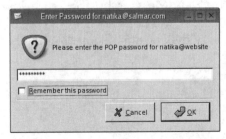

FIGURE 24-18   Remember the password?

Like Microsoft Outlook, Evolution is an integrated contact management, email, and scheduling system all in one. Aside from using the basic email functionality, you can also plan your day, set alarms, keep a contact list, and more. I'll discuss some of those capabilities in more detail when I cover ways to stay organized in the next chapter.

What to Use?

As to whether you use Kmail or Evolution (or some of the other options I'll mention in a moment), this is something you will have to experiment with to decide. Personal preference is a huge factor here. I, for one, do not particularly enjoy integrated clients such as Evolution. I want my email package to be an email package only; for scheduling, I may decide to use another tool. Others can't imagine using anything other than Evolution for reasons that are exactly opposite to the one I mentioned. It's your system and your choice. The best way to discover what you want is to try things out.

Other Options

In this chapter, I've paid a lot of attention to Kmail and introduced you to Evolution. By no means should you look at these as your only options. If you are used to working with Netscape or Mozilla mail in the Windows world, these very options are available with Linux, and they work exactly the same. Currently, there is a new addition to the Mozilla lineup for email. If you are looking for an email-only client, check out the new *Mozilla Thunderbird*.

Graphical clients aren't the only things available, either. Some people find that they prefer to work with text-only clients. After all, email is primarily about writing and reading words, and less about attached files. The average Linux distribution installs a handful of very nice, text-only email clients. Notable among these are *mutt* (`www.mutt.org`) and *pine* (`www.washington.edu/pine`). In both cases, check your distribution CDs first before you download.

Resources

Kmail

http://kmail.kde.org

Kolab

www.kolab.org

Mozilla Thunderbird

http://www.mozilla.org/products/thunderbird/

Ximian Evolution

www.ximian.com/products/evolution

25

Getting Organized

It is sometimes hard for me to fathom as I look at the piles of papers, books, cables, devices, and toys scattered across my desk, that computers have helped in getting us more organized. No, it's true. Work with me here.

Once upon a time, I used to make appointments, scribble down the information and hope that I could find it again later. Maybe it wasn't an appointment, but a dinner date or somebody's birthday. Either way, if I got lucky and managed to find my paper planner or scrap of paper in time, I might just make it to where I was supposed to be. My friends will tell you that I was always 20 minutes late. These days, I'm only five minutes late. The reason? My personal digital assistant. Currently, it is a Handspring Visor, but I have had others. There's nothing like an alarm going off to remind you that yes, you did have something planned.

I keep my PDA backed up and synced to my notebook computer on which I do my writing. My notebook also has a copy of the calendar with all its appointments on it in a great little piece of software called Korganizer. Now, if I happen to leave my PDA in another part of the house, there is a second piece of software ready to warn me when I'm supposed to return a phone call. My life is far from being perfectly organized, but trust me, it has improved dramatically. With the new Korganizer and its shared calendars, I'm aiming for being only two minutes late. Let me tell you about it.

Korganizer

Korganizer is included as part of your KDE desktop. It is a feature-packed time management system and electronic organizer that could become one of the most important tools on your desktop. Besides the obvious calendar and schedule capabilities, Korganizer features group scheduling, to-do lists, import and export of calendar data, such as holidays, sharing of free/busy lists, Exchange 2000 integration, and synchronization with PDAs to name just a few of its features.

Start Korganizer by clicking on the K menu and looking under Office Applications. You can also get to Korganizer by starting Kontact. It is one of the applications in the left bar. For now, I'm going to look at the package as a standalone application.

 Shell Out If you wish to start Korganizer from the shell, just type its command, `korganizer &`, at the shell prompt. Alternatively, you can press <Alt+F2> and type the command there.

When Korganizer starts up, you'll get a Tip of the Day window. As with other KDE components, you can choose to stop these by checking off the Show Tips on Startup box at the lower left. As I've mentioned before, until you are completely familiar with the application, you might want to leave these on. Once you've absorbed the information, click OK to close the tip.

Let's jump right in and have a look at the Korganizer window (Figure 25-1). You may want to adjust or maximize the display to suit your viewing preferences.

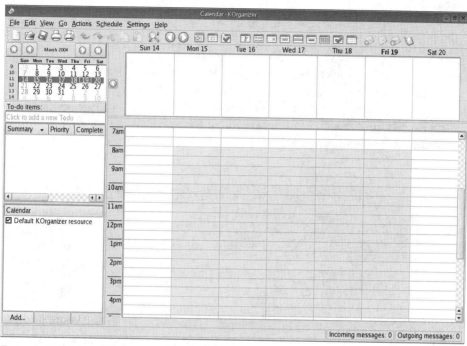

FIGURE 25-1   Starting off with a fresh Korganizer.

Looking along the top, you'll find the familiar menu bar, and directly below that is the icon bar. The icon bar, in this case, is highly geared to navigating the calendar. Pausing over each button with the mouse pointer brings up a tool tip identifying that button's function. With a single click, you can switch views from a single day, a seven-day week, a five-day work week, three days, or a full month. Buttons let you enter to-do items, appointments, or create journal entries. You can also switch views by clicking View on the menu bar and choosing the display you would like to see. If, after moving around in the calendar, you want to find yourself back at today, click Go on the menu bar and select Go to Today.

The left side of the screen provides a small calendar known as the *Date Navigator* that lets you jump quickly to any day, month, or year. Below that and in the middle is a list of to-do items. Before we start adding things to the calendar, have a look at the final window on the bottom left, the one labeled Calendar. When you started Korganizer, you loaded up the default calendar, which makes sense, because we are starting with a clean slate. Over on the right side, taking up most of the screen real estate, is the main window. This is where most of the action takes place.

Adding an Event

Let's just jump right in and add an appointment. Using the Date Navigator, choose an appropriate date. If you want your appointment to be on the same day, you can quickly jump to that day by clicking Go on the menu bar and selecting Go to Today. Start an appointment by double-clicking in a chosen time slot in the main window. Another way to start a new event is to click Actions on the menu bar, and select New Event. I'll choose 10:00 am for this example. You should now be looking at the Edit Event dialog (Figure 25-2).

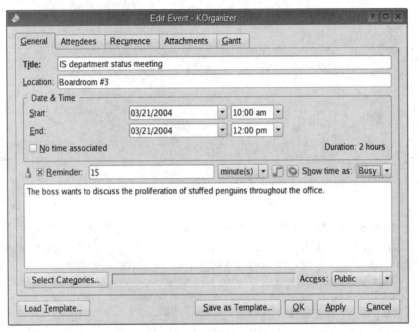

FIGURE 25-2   Creating a new event.

There is a lot we can do in terms of describing an event. The five tabs at the top hint at some of those possibilities. For the moment, let's keep this first example simple and stick to the information in the General tab. Enter a title for the event—say, IS department status meeting—and a location—call it Boardroom #3. You can change the default duration time of two hours by clicking on the drop-down box for the Start and End times. Speaking of start times, this is one meeting you don't want to miss, so click on the check box next to the bell icon and just to the left of Reminder. Usually, it's good to have something more than a one minute reminder, so change this to 15 minutes.

Take a look to the right of the reminder time, specifically the drop-down list that currently says minutes. You'll see two icons there. The first icon has a musical note on it; use it to set some kind of sound file to go off when the alarm pops up. You might not be at your desk, but still within hearing range, or perhaps you want to annoy your co-workers. Clicking this icon starts the Open File dialog from which you can select the appropriate .wav format file. You'll find sounds for various applications in numerous places on your system. Some sounds are included with the Korganizer application; look under `/usr/share/apps/korganizer/sounds`. The `alert.wav` file is particularly attention-getting. The second icon (directly to the right of the musical note) lets you set a program. Perhaps five minutes before the meeting is a great time to have the system automatically start a game of solitaire or patience (`/usr/bin/kpat`).

You're almost done entering your first event. That large box just below the reminder bell lets you enter more detailed notes on the event. Below the comment box and to the left, click on the button labeled Select Categories. Korganizer provides a handful of useful preset categories, but you can easily add more by clicking the Edit Categories button. Make your selection (or make several), then click OK.

FIGURE 25-3   You can assign categories to events.

You'll find yourself back at the Edit Event dialog. Click OK to close the dialog, and you are done! When the alarm time appears, you'll see a popup box similar to Figure 25-4. To acknowledge the alarm, click OK. You can also press the equivalent of the snooze button by setting a Suspend Duration time in minutes and clicking the Suspend button.

FIGURE 25-4   It's alarming! Time for your meeting.

We'll get back to looking at more complex events shortly. For now, let's take a look at entering a to-do item.

So Much To-Do

To-do items in Korganizer can be added in a similar fashion to events, but they do have some very different properties. To start a new to-do, click Action on the menu bar and select New To-Do. You can also start a new to-do by clicking the appropriate icon on Korganizer's icon bar—it looks like a small calendar with a red check mark inside and a little *new* starburst in the top-left corner. The Edit To-Do dialog appears (Figure 25-5).

Along the top of the Edit To-Do dialog, there are three tabs: General, Attendees, and Attachments. For the first part of this example, I'm going to concentrate on the General tab. Much of what you see here is quite similar to what you saw when entering an event. Start by giving your to-do or task a title, such as "Get driver's license renewed." Then, if necessary, enter a location, such as Vehicle licensing center.

Many times, a to-do item is just a list of things that need to get done by a certain due date, and sometimes the list just needs to get done *sometime*. If the item does have a due date, click the Due check box. For items that have a specific date associated with the start of your task, click Start and enter a start date and time. For instance, I might need to have my license sticker by April 30th, but I might want to start working on it a couple of weeks earlier than that. If the task in question has a specific time associated with it, click the Time Associated check box and enter that information as well.

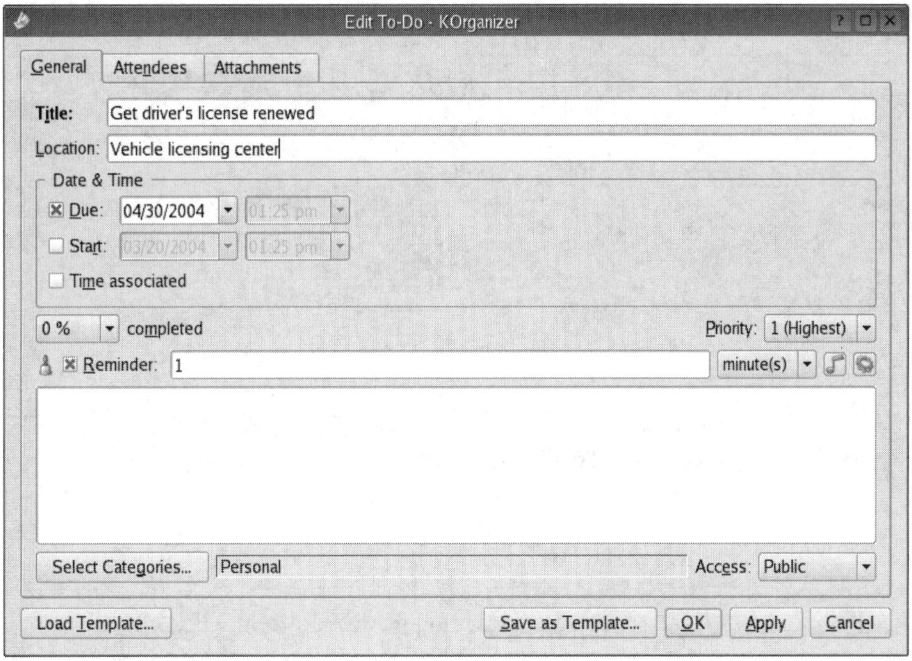

FIGURE 25-5   Entering a new to-do item.

Below the date and time information, there's a section regarding the status of the to-do item. Because tasks may be worked on over several days or weeks, you can update the to-do item from time to time by adjusting the percent completed value. Obviously, in the case of my license sticker, it is either done or it isn't. You might, however, want to track the progress of finishing a report for a customer. Furthermore, tasks and to-dos often have a priority associated with them. By default, everything has a priority of 3. Priorities can be adjusted from 5 at the low end to 1 for the highest priority.

Just a little over halfway down the page, below the Reminder settings, there's a large area for entering additional detail about the current task. As you did when entering information for an event, it is also possible to assign categories to the to-do items. When you have everything entered, click OK.

You'll notice that to-do items do not appear directly on the main calendar view. Instead, your new to-do items show up on the left side in the To-Do Items window. To get a more detailed view, click View on the menu bar and select To-Do List. The results are displayed in a nice, tabular format as in Figure 25-6. To return to the normal Korganizer view, click on View and select any of the day, week, or month display modes.

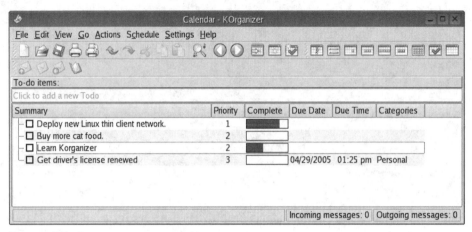

FIGURE 25-6   Viewing your list of to-do items.

 Quick Tip To enter a super-quick to-do item, click inside the box just above the to-do list on the left side of your Korganizer window. You'll see the words "Click to add a new Todo" in gray. Enter your few words of information and press <Enter>. Korganizer creates a to-do item without a specific date and with a priority of 3.

Printing Your Calendar

Paperless society aside, there are times when nothing beats hard copy. Printing the day's calendar is easy to do. Select the day you want to print (you might find it easier to switch to a one-day view for this), click File on the menu bar and select Print. Korganizer's Print dialog appears (Figure 25-7) with a list of options. Click the appropriate radio button to select a single day, a week, a month, or your to-do items. You have the opportunity here to select a different day or a range of days, depending on the type of report you want. Before you go and click that print button, select Print Week if you haven't already done so. A Type of View dialog appears on the Print window to let you select the style of printed page: Filofax style or timetable view. When you are happy with your settings, click Print.

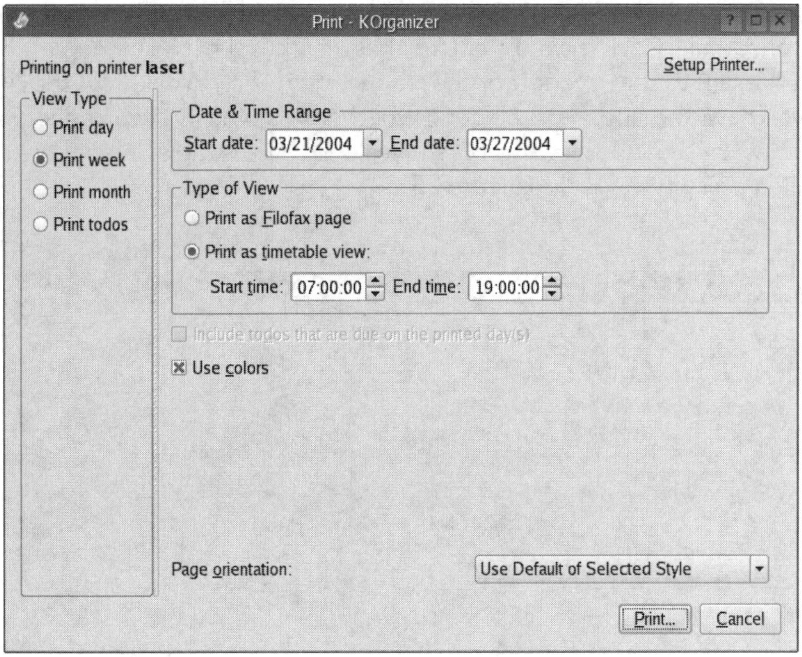

FIGURE 25-7   Getting ready to print your calendar.

Note that these are all single-page views (one day per page, one week per page, and so on). If you would like a preview before sending things to the printer (or if you want to see the difference between Filofax and timetable format), click File on the menu bar and select Print Preview instead. The dialog is much the same, but it has a Preview button instead of Print.

Wow! Déja-vu (Recurring Events)

If that Monday morning IS status meeting is something you have to attend every two weeks, it doesn't make sense to enter the event over and over. That's the whole point of recurrence, and it's the first advanced event configuration I want to look at. Double-click on the Monday meeting you created earlier, or create a new entry. When I had you enter your first event, I concentrated my attention on the General tab. There are four other tabs in the KDE 3.2 version of Korganizer: Attendees, Recurrence, Attachments, and Gantt.

To activate a recurring event, click on the Recurrence tab and start by clicking on the Enable Recurrence check box. Directly below the check box, you will

see the initial information relating to the event you created. Below that is the
Recurrence Rule. Click the radio button that matches the kind of recurrence you
want to assign to that event. For that IS meeting, click Weekly. To the right of
that, you have the option of selecting whether this weekly recurrence is every
week or every second, third, or fourth week. In this example, I've set the meeting up for every two weeks (Figure 25-8).

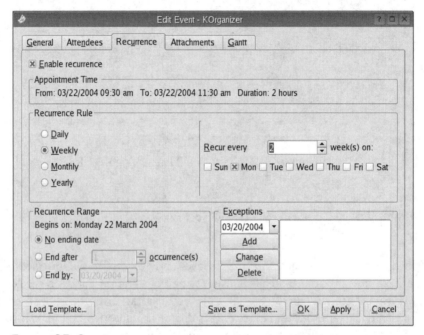

FIGURE 25-8   *Setting an event to recur every two weeks.*

Perhaps this meeting relates to a project that is currently under way, and,
therefore, the recurrence will end in another couple of months. That's the idea
behind the Recurrence Range (bottom left). Select a date for the termination
of the recurrence or specify a fixed number of occurrences.

Finally, look to the right. You'll see an area for entering exceptions to the rule
you are creating. (Perhaps you get a few of those weekly meetings off for good
behavior.) Click the drop-down box, and a small calendar similar to the Date
Navigator drops down. Select the date you want, and the calendar retracts.
Click Add, and you have your exceptions. When you are happy with your
changes, click OK.

Inviting Others to an Event

Meetings would not be a lot of fun if only one person attended. All right, maybe they would fun, but a one-person meeting is a contradiction. Let's create an event so that it isn't too lonely. Either double-click on an existing event or start a new one. After making sure you have the information you need in the General tab, click on the Attendees tab (Figure 25-9).

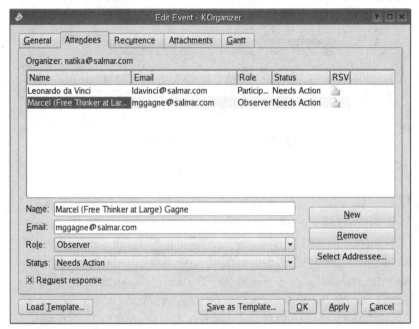

FIGURE 25-9   Adding and defining the role of attendees to an event.

In the beginning, there will be no entries on the page. There are two ways to enter information. The first is to click New, then enter a name in the Name field and an email address in the Email field. You can also choose from a list of names in your address book by clicking the Select Addresses button. A dialog box appears with a list of names currently in your address book. Select a name by clicking on it, then click the OK button to add it. That's all there is to it.

Below the Email field you'll see a drop-down box for Role. From this list, select what role the attendee will have in this event. You can select from Participant, Optional Participant, Observer, or Chair. Below the Role selection is the Status field for the attendee. Your choices here are Needs Action, Accepted, Declined, Tentative, Delegated, Completed, or In Process. In all likelihood, you'll want confirmation from those people invited to your meeting, so click the Request Response check box. A small Email icon appears to the right of the attendee's information. Should no response be necessary, a red X appears instead.

Now that you have an event scheduled, its recurrence information taken care of, and a list of attendees defined, you can click OK to close and save this entry. If, as in this case, there are attendees associated with the event, a dialog box pops up informing you of this and asking whether an email should be sent to those people (Figure 25-10). The correct answer here is probably Yes.

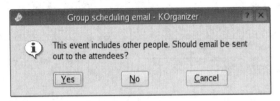

Figure 25-10   Should attendees be informed via email?

A Kmail message will be created with the list of attendees in the To: field. Review the message and click the Send icon (or press <Ctrl+Enter>).

What Happens When You Get Invited?

The invitation email goes out with an iCal attachment (the attachment has have a .ics extension). That means any iCal-compliant organizer software will be able to import the item (as I will discuss in just a moment). You can save the attachment to your folder or directory and import it manually.

Those running Kontact will find this just too easy. All you need to do is drag the message onto the Calendar icon in the Kontact sidebar. The Edit Event dialog (Figure 25-2) appears with all of the information already filled in. Review the information, and click OK to accept it into your own calendar.

Importing Calendars

Do you find that there's just not enough penciled in to your calendar? This little tip can help you out. Korganizer can import iCal format files to supplement the current list of information in the default calendar. This can be someone else's calendar (or your old iCal files), but as it turns out, there are a number of sites on the Internet that provide downloadable calendar files that cover local holidays, televisions schedules, historical events, concert tour dates, and a whole lot more. Using Konqueror, pay a visit to www.icalshare.com for plenty of choices. Given the truly impressive list of calendars on the site, you are bound to find something you *need*.

Importing a calendar is easy. Find something you like (a calendar of astronomical events, for instance), and save it to your home directory. Then, from Korganizer, click File, then Import, and select Merge Calendars. When the file selection dialog appears, navigate to where you downloaded your iCal file, then click <OK>. That's all there is to it.

> *Warning* This is only so scary, but the more calendars (iCal files) you import into your Korganizer, the more cluttered things start to appear. Keep that in mind as you populate your calendar with all sorts of interesting events.

Evolution

In the last chapter, I mentioned that Evolution was a great email client for those coming from the Windows world, particularly if they were used to working with Outlook. This is equally true when working with Evolution's calendar applications.

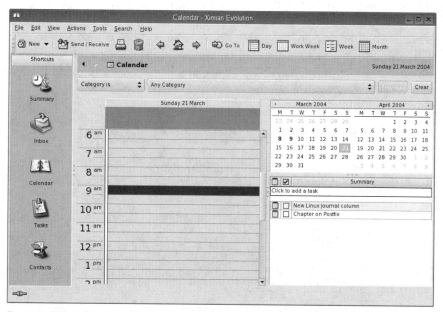

FIGURE 25-11 Evolution's calendar view.

Take a look along the top of the application, just below the menu bar. The icons to the left let you quickly create appointments, send and receive email, print, and so on. To the right, there are four calendar views: one day, a five-day work week, a full week, and a month. Clicking any of the view buttons changes the calendar view in the main window below.

The main window is broken up into three sections. In the center is your main calendar view. To its right, a small calendars show you the current month and the next month; to jump to a date, click it in these calendars. Still in the right-hand section, but below the calendars, is a quick summary of your to-do items. Finally, like the Outlook package in Windows, a set of icons runs down the left bar, providing you with quick access to Calendar, Tasks, Contacts, and email.

Quick Tip To select any number of days and create your own view, just highlight a sequence of days in the mini calendars to the right. The main calendar view will update with your selection.

Creating Appointments

Korganizer calls them "events," Evolution uses the term "appointments," but the idea is the same. To create a new appointment in Evolution with a single click, move your mouse pointer to the New button and click there (or use <Ctrl+N>). Notice that there is a down arrow beside the New button (Figure 25-12). Clicking on the arrow brings up a number of additional choices from creating a mail message to a contact in your address book. If you like, you can always take the multiclick route by clicking File on the menu bar, selecting New, then selecting Appointment.

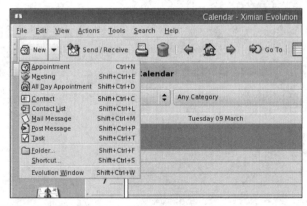

FIGURE 25-12   Evolution makes creating new items easy.

Another way to do this is to double-click on the time you want in the main calendar view. As soon as you do this, the new Appointment dialog appears (Figure 25-13). Start by entering your summary information, such as Meeting with board of directors, and a location, such as 2nd floor boardroom. A start time will have been entered as well as an end time, but you may have to fine-tune those. Clicking on the down arrow beside the date pops up a small calendar from which you can quickly pick the date. The drop-down list associated with the time is broken up in half-hour intervals.

Quick Tip Look to the right of the Start and End Time drop-down lists. See that little icon? Clicking it brings up a world map from which you can select the time zone in which the appointment will take place. Click on one of the dots, and the map zooms in to let you fine-tune your choice.

An appointment can also be set as an all-day event by clicking the All Day Event check box. Doing this blanks out the start and end times, but not the dates.

If this is an important appointment, you will likely want to be reminded of it. Click on the Reminder tab (Figure 25-13). The bottom half of this pane has a large area in which you can add all sorts of reminders. The default is a pop-up window with a message regarding the start of your appointment. Unless you change the settings, the message will appear 15 minutes before the appointment. At the end of the line of buttons, there is one labeled *Options*. This lets you change the default message to whatever else you might like. You can even specify a repeat for the alarm. Another way to look at it is: How often do you want to be nagged?

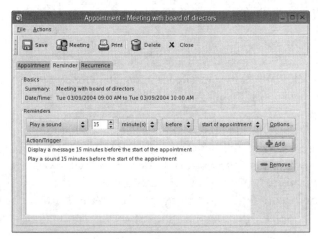

FIGURE 25-13   Evolution can remind you in many different ways.

To activate this alarm, all you have to do is click the Add button once. Now you get the idea. To create a different type of alarm, click on the Display a Message button (under the Reminders label) and change it to either Play a Sound or Run a Program. Click the Options button here again, and navigate your files to find the sound you want to play or the program you want to run. Click Add until you have all the reminders you want.

Let's Do That Again: Evolution Recurrence

Before we move on to making this more than a one-person appointment, let's look at recurrence. If the board meets every week or every month at the same place and time, it just makes sense to enter the appointment once and have the system do the rest for you. Click on the Recurrence tab.

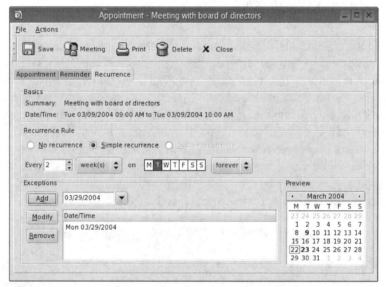

FIGURE 25-14   Setting recurrence information for an Evolution appointment.

Activate recurrence by clicking the Simple Recurrence radio button. Choose how often you want this appointment to occur and with what frequency, such as every two weeks on Monday. Directly below is the Exceptions dialog. Clicking on the down arrow to the right of the Add button pops up a small calendar. Select those days that don't apply to the standard recurrence, such as your holidays, and click Add. You can specify as many exceptions as you like. When you are happy with everything, click the Save button (top left). The new appointment will appear in your main calendar view.

The Makings of a Meeting

Turning an Evolution appointment into a meeting is simple. First, you need some people to invite. Then, you need to create another appointment or edit an existing one. You can do this by double-clicking on an appointment in your main calendar view. The Appointment dialog appears. Note the button near the top that says Meeting. Click that, and two new tabs appear in addition to the Appointment, Reminder, and Recurrence tabs. These new tabs are labeled Scheduling and Meeting (Figure 25-15).

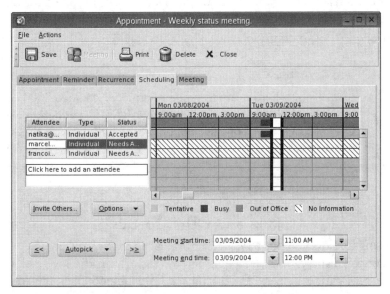

FIGURE 25-15   Scheduling a meeting with Free/Busy information.

Click on the Meeting tab. The first thing you should see (if you created this appointment) is that you are listed as the *Organizer* of the meeting. This is something you can override, but if you created the meeting, it probably makes sense to leave it as is. Below that is a large window with a field labeled Click Here to Add an Attendee. Click on this field, and a field opens in which you can add the person's email address. Under the Type heading, you can define whether that attendee represents an individual, or some other resource. Next, under the Role heading, select whether the individual will act as chair, a participant (required or not), a nonparticipant (an observer), or whether the person's role is unknown. Under the next heading, RSVP, decide whether or not the attendee should confirm their attendance. Finally, under Status, you may define whether the attendee has already accepted, declined, or whether their attendance is tentative.

Finally, we have the Scheduling tab. This is another way to select individuals, but one that allows you to check Free/Busy information. Near the bottom of this window, you'll see the word "Autopick" in a drop-down box. To the right and left are buttons with double-arrows on them. Click these and Evolution automatically selects the next block of time (either before or after your initial attempt) in which all invitees are free, based on their published Free/Busy information.

 Quick Tip If your office uses a Microsoft Exchange 2000 or 2003 server, Evolution can share Free/Busy calendar information with Outlook clients. All of this happens automagically with the Ximian Connector (`http://ximian.com/products/connector`).

Tasks and Other To-Dos

When using Evolution, your to-do items are called *tasks*. Looking at Evolution's main calendar display, you'll see a summary task list in the lower-right pane. Adding a new task is as easy as clicking the field labeled Click to Add a New Task. Type a brief description of your task, then press <Enter> when you are done. For a task-only list, click the Tasks icon in the Shortcuts sidebar. That will provide you with a much larger view and another quick entry field.

FIGURE 25-16   A more complex Task dialog.

Double-click on any field and a dialog appears offering you a much more detailed view of the task in question (Figure 25-16). The new window features two tabs labeled Basic and Details. These allow you to enter a description of the task, assign a completion date and time, and indicate priority and status information, such as whether the task has been started and its percentage of completion.

One last and fairly important feature is the ability to delegate this task to someone else. Click Action in the Task dialog's menu bar, and select Assign Task. The Assignment tab appears from which you can select an individual to carry out the task. When you have entered the information, a window pops up asking you whether the assigned task should be sent. The correct answer is, of course, Yes.

Other Tools

We've come a long way from the yellow sticky notes on your desktop to the modern, connected organizers of today. Or have we?

One of the really cool applications under the KDE desktop is *Knotes* (program name: `knotes`). This program lets you write electronic versions of those little yellow notes which you can then scatter across your desktop where they vie for your attention. Knotes docks nicely into your icon tray and remembers past notes and your changes. There's more than a paper replacement here though. You can email these notes, print them, or change the color. Furthermore, through Kontact and Kpilot, they will sync to your palm device as notes.

Another program worth your time is *KArm* (program name: `karm`). This is a small event timer. Let's say that you are on the phone with a customer and you want to track how long the call takes. Use KArm to start a new task, then click the Start Clock button. A timer will start keeping track of how much time you spend on that call. KArm also lets you create subtasks, pause timing, resume (so you can track multiple events through the course of a day), and, if necessary, print the results.

Resources

Kontact

http://kontact.kde.org

Korganizer

http://korganizer.kde.org

Kpilot

http://kpilot.kde.org

Ximian Evolution

http://ximian.com/products/evolution

26

Surfing the Net

When it comes to web browsers on the desktop, Linux users are faced with an embarrassment of riches, with plenty of alternatives to choose from. For those who are looking for a screaming-fast browsing experience and can do without the graphics, Linux offers a number of text-based browsers, which I'll talk about at the end of the chapter.

In the graphical world where most people spend their browsing time, the classic favorite, Netscape Navigator, has been replaced in favor of its powerful cousin Mozilla (`www.mozilla.org`). For those who may not be aware of the history or the connection, in 1998, Netscape released its source code under an open source license, and eager developers accepted the challenge. Mozilla was born. A few short years later, things are very different. The current incarnation of Netscape is based on Mozilla and not the other way around. Chances are that Mozilla is part of your distribution, and is most likely installed by default. Incidentally, Mozilla is also available for Windows, thus providing those users with some of the powerful advantages that Mozilla has over Internet Explorer.

Then, we have KDE's own browser, Konqueror. Besides being a great browser, Konqueror is also a powerful file manager. I should tell you that I do tend to move back and forth between browsers. In fact, I tend to be a two-browser guy, flipping back and forth between Mozilla and Konqueror (although I do tend to favor Konqueror these days). If you are running KDE, you won't need to download Konqueror. It's part of the whole KDE environment. Exploring Konqueror's web browser *persona* is where I will begin this chapter. Then, I'll move on to Mozilla. Compare the features and decide for yourself what will define *your* browsing experience.

Konqueror

To start surfing the Net with Konqueror, you need to connect to the Internet. (It's a good thing we covered that way back in Chapter 9.) Starting Konqueror as a browser is the same as starting Konqueror any other way. Most distributions, however, have an icon either on the desktop or on Kicker itself to start up Konqueror as a browser. The difference is that in the browser configuration, you can set a home page (more on that later).

Konqueror does pretty much everything you expect from a graphical web browser—and some things you don't. You can go forward and back, save bookmarks (click Bookmarks in the menu bar), download files, or print pages. Because I am assuming that you have all used a browser before, I'll concentrate on the things that I think you will want to know. To start surfing the Net, this is all you have to do: fire up Konqueror, enter your favorite web site's URL into the Location bar window, and press <Enter>. In a few seconds, your web site's page should appear.

 Quick Tip Notice the black arrow with an x through it to the immediate left of the Location label. Clicking it automatically clears the Location field. No need to select or backspace over the last URL.

Page Home for Me

Setting your home page is easy. Simply visit the site of your choice, drag the Konqueror browser window to the size you want, click Window in the menu bar, and select Save View Profile>Web Browsing. This brings up the Profile Management dialog (Figure 26-1), where you can save the page as your default Konqueror web view.

Notice the two check boxes at the bottom. Make sure that you click them both if you want to preserve the size of the browser window that you specified along with the link to your home page. Click Save, and you are done. Next time you fire up the Konqueror browser, you'll head straight to your home page.

FIGURE 26-1   Saving your Konqueror browsing profile.

What's the point of creating a profile just to set your home page? Profiles are interesting, because you can create custom Konqueror views as desktop icons. When you start any other browser, you have one home page. Sure, you could put links on your desktop that go to a specific site by right-clicking the desktop, choosing Create New, and selecting Link to Location (URL). But what if you want one browser to be a certain window size as well? What if you want the navigation panel on for some sites and off for others? Profiles let you do this.

Here's how it works. Start by creating a new profile; click Window on the menu bar and select Configure View Profiles. Enter a name where it says Enter Profile Name, then click on Save. Now click on Window one more time, select Load View Profile, and select the profile you just created. Surf over to the site of your choice, size the windows as you would like them to be, open (or don't) a navigation panel, and so on. When you are happy with your new *starting point*, click Window and click on Save View Profile YourProfileName.

Almost there. The last thing you need is a desktop icon that automagically loads this profile. The easiest way to do this is to click on the big K, open the Internet menu, and find Konqueror. Click and drag the Konqueror icon onto the desktop. You'll be asked whether you want to Copy, Move, or Link the program. Choose Copy, right-click on the new icon, and select Properties. As before, you can choose an icon that suits you, and you probably want to pick a name for the newly-created icon. The real work here is done on the Application tab (Figure 26-2). Notice that under Command, it says `konqueror --profile webbrowsing`. That represents the default profile. You want to replace the word "webbrowsing" with whatever you called your profile. A word of caution: If you used spaces in your profile name (I created one called My Daily News), you must surround the profile name with quotes. For example:

```
konqueror --profile "My Daily News"
```

Click OK to save your icon, and you are done.

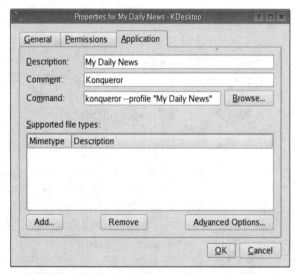

FIGURE 26-2   Creating a new browsing profile.

Cool Konqueror Tricks

I am going to show you a few things to try with Konqueror that you may find quite handy. You'll learn some great tricks, shortcuts, and otherwise fun things to do with your KDE browser.

Split Views

Remember all of the things that you learned when using Konqueror as a file manager? They still apply. For instance, you might remember that you could split your Konqueror window to provide multiple views. Let's say that you wanted to look at two web sites simultaneously, with the top half of the browser displaying one site and the bottom half displaying another. Try this: open Konqueror, and surf over to the site of your choice. Click on Window in the menu bar, and choose Split View (either Top/Bottom or Left/Right). You should have two copies of the same site open in two separate views. You can close either view by clicking on Window, then clicking on Remove Active View.

Like when you used Konqueror as a file manager, the active window has a little *green light* on in the bottom-left corner. Click that bar on either window to switch from one to the other. You can now enter a new address into the Location field to open a new web site.

Super-Speedy Searches

Ah, shameless alliteration…. Say you want to search on Linux media players in Google. Normally, you would enter `http://www.google.com`, wait for the site to load, type in *Linux media players*, and click to start the search. With Konqueror, a number of quick search shortcuts have been defined that make searching feel so much easier. To search Google for media players, you could simply type the following in the Location field:

```
gg: Linux media players
```

Konqueror automatically feeds the search terms to Google. You can do a rapid-fire search of the Google Usenet groups' archive as well. Pretend that you are having problems with an FTL3D VR card for your system. Type:

```
ggg: FTL3D VR card setup Linux
```

There are other great shortcuts. For instance, typing `fm:` enables you to search the Freshmeat software archives, and `rf: package_name` searches `RPMfind.net` for RPMs of your favorite software. Table 26-1 provides a list of others you may want to try.

TABLE 26-1   Web Search Shortcuts

Shortcut	Function
`av:`	Use the AltaVista search engine
`ggn:`	Search Google News
`hb:`	Search HotBot
`ly:`	Search Lycos
`sf:`	Look through SourceForge
`wi:`	Perform a WhatIs query

You can check all of these out for yourself by clicking on Configure Konqueror in the menu bar under Settings. When you choose Enhanced Browsing from the sidebar on the left, you get a nice long list of these shortcuts. One of my favorite shortcuts of all time is the online dictionary search. Use the `dict:` shortcut, and Konqueror searches through the *Merriam-Webster Dictionary*. Likewise, `ths:` enables you to look things up in the online thesaurus:

```
ths: thesaurus
```

(You know, there really is no synonym for the word "thesaurus.")

 Quick Tip You can add your own web search shortcuts. When looking through the shortcuts under Enhanced Browsing, select one, click Modify, and follow the example to create your own.

Go for the Big Screen

Nothing beats looking at the virtual world through a big screen. As much as I would like to, I can't increase the size of your monitor, but I can help you with the next best thing. When you are busy surfing the Internet and you want as much screen as possible, why not try Konqueror's full-screen mode?

At any time while you are viewing a page, you can click Window on the menu bar and select Full-Screen Mode. The title bar disappears, as do Kicker and all other border decorations. When the switch happens, pay attention to the icon bar (just below the menu bar). A *new icon* appears to the right of all the others. Clicking on it returns your Konqueror session to normal. You can also quickly toggle back and forth by pressing <Ctrl+Shift+F>.

Yum...Cookies

Not that kind of cookie. Cookies are simply small text files transmitted to your browser or system when you visit a web site. The original idea behind cookies was that a server would give you a cookie as a marker to indicate where you had previously visited. That cookie might store a username and password to access a particular web site or other information related to your visit, such as an online shopping cart. When you next visit the site, the server would ask your browser whether it had served you any cookies, and your browser would reply by sending the cookies from before. In this way, the web site would recognize you when you next visited, and certain useful defaults would be set up for you. Cookies can be very good.

The problem with cookies is that they can also be shared within larger domains, such as advertising rings. Using these shared cookies, advertisers can build a profile of your likes and dislikes, tailoring and targeting advertising to you specifically. Many people object to this method of building user profiles and consider the use of cookies to be quite unethical and an invasion of privacy. The dilemma then is to find a way to accept the cookies you want and reject the others. Konqueror lets you do just that.

Click on Settings, then select Configure Konqueror. From the side panel, click on Cookies. Under the Policy tab, make sure that you have cookies enabled with the check box. Then, using the check box below that, select Ask for Confirmation Before Accepting Cookies.

FIGURE 26-3   Do you accept or reject this cookie?

The first time a site offers you a cookie, a dialog box will appear, asking you whether you want to accept or reject that cookie. Best of all, it asks you whether you want to reject them now or always (Figure 26-3). Choose All Cookies from this Domain before you click Reject, and that ad site will never store another cookie on your computer.

Ban the Pop-Ups Forever!

Honestly, I can't think of a single person who likes to visit a web site, only to have that site throw up annoying pop-up window ads. Konqueror lets you turn off this "feature" that certain sites provide. Once again, click Settings>Configure Konqueror, and choose Java & Javascript from the sidebar. Select the JavaScript tab, and click whichever radio button suits your taste. (Figure 26-4).

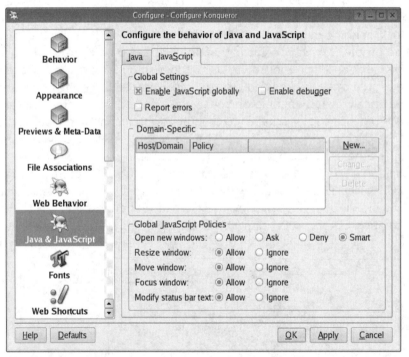

FIGURE 26-4   Configuring Konqueror to ban pop-up ads.

I've found that Smart is indeed pretty smart, and that it generally takes care of deciding whether to allow pop-ups. You can also decide to have Konqueror ask you each and every time a site tries to open a popup, or you can simply deny everything.

Keeping Tabs on the Web

Starting with KDE 3.1, Konqueror sports a great feature called *tabbed browsing* (Figure 26-5). Here's how it works.

Sometimes when you are viewing web sites, you want to keep a particular site open while moving to another place on the web. Normally, you would click File and select New Window. This is fine, except that if you keep doing this, you'll wind up with however many versions of a browser open on your desktop. Switching from one to the other involves doing a little digital juggling. Tabs make it possible to bring a nice, clean air of sanity to what could otherwise become a very cluttered taskbar (or desktop).

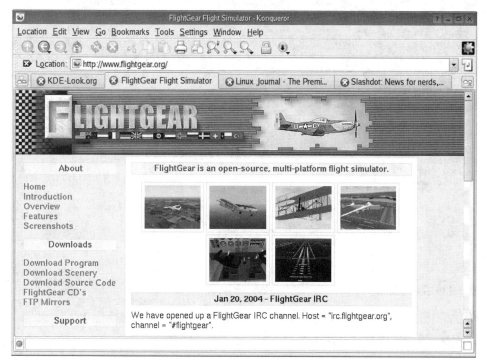

FIGURE 26-5   Konqueror does tabbed browsing.

To open new tabs, click Window on the menu bar and select New Tab or simply press <Ctrl+Shift+N>. You can also open a new tab from a link in the current web page by right-clicking on that link, then selecting Open in New Tab. Have a look at Figure 26-5 to see Konqueror's tabs in action.

Mozilla

To this day, I find myself switching back and forth between Mozilla (Figure 26-6) and Konqueror. The features I've mentioned for Konqueror make it an amazingly useful browser. In some ways, it is more like the Swiss Army knife of browsers. Mozilla, on the other hand, has the Netscape Navigator look and feel that I've grown accustomed to over the years in a much more mature and *flexible* package. It includes an email package and IRC client, is ideal for reading newsgroups, and comes with an HTML editor.

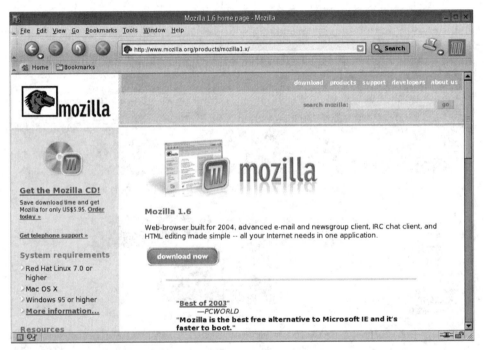

FIGURE 26-6   Mozilla is an excellent and capable browser.

To start Mozilla, click on Kicker's big K, select Internet, and choose Mozilla from the list. If Mozilla isn't installed, you can get the package at www.mozilla.org or simply get it off your distribution CDs. If you do head to the Mozilla web site, it probably makes sense to choose a stable release unless you are feeling particularly adventurous and want to experiment with the leading edge. Just remember that it can be wobbly on the edge.

Working from Home

When you first start Mozilla, it takes you to its home, the Mozilla welcome page. Getting to a web site and navigating Mozilla is much the same as it is in any other browser you have used, particularly if you were using Netscape (or Mozilla) with your old OS. In the Location bar, type the URL of the web site you want to visit, and away you go. If you would like to start each time on a personal home page, this is easily done.

Click on Edit in Mozilla's menu bar, and select Preferences. The Preferences window opens up with a left-side Category panel, from which you select which part of Mozilla you want to modify. By default, it opens up to the Navigator category; Navigator is the browser part of Mozilla (Figure 26-7). Over on the right, you'll find three radio buttons. Clicking the top button starts Mozilla on a blank page, and clicking in the middle lets you specify a home page. The third radio button tells Mozilla always to start up on the last page visited. Now looking below, you'll see a field for entering the URL of your desired home page—enter the URL there. When you are done, click OK.

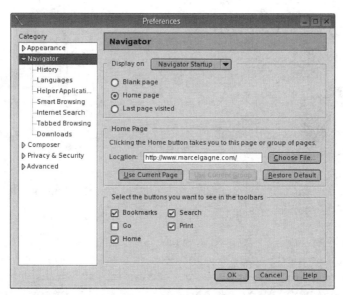

FIGURE 26-7   Setting your home page in Mozilla's Preferences menu.

Mozilla Does Tabs, Too

Before I tell you how tabs work in Mozilla, it seems only fair that I tell you that
Mozilla had tabbed browsing before Konqueror did (particularly because I gave
Konqueror first billing). The concept behind tabbed browsing in Mozilla is the
same, but the keystrokes are a little different.

Start by visiting a site of your choice. Now click on File, select New, and
choose Navigator Tab from the drop-down menu. You can also use the
<Ctrl+T> keyboard shortcut to do the same thing. Notice that Mozilla now
identifies your sites with tabs just below the location bar (Figure 26-8). Add a
third or a fourth if you like. Switching from site to site is just a matter of clicking the tabs on your single copy of Mozilla.

FIGURE 26-8   Mozilla showing off its tabs.

While in tab mode, you can right-click on a tab to bring up the tab menu.
From there you can close or reload the current tab (or all tabs) and even open
new tabs. Another way to close the active tab is to click on the X at the end of
the tab list.

Still Don't Like Pop-Up Ads?

I have to mention this again, because it is one of the things that make some of these Linux browsers so wonderful—the ability to stop unwanted pop-up window ads. Like Konqueror, Mozilla lets you do this easily.

Start by bringing up the Preferences menu again (click Edit on the menu bar and choose Preferences). From the category list (Figure 26-9), choose Privacy & Security and open the submenu (by clicking the little arrow directly to the left of the word "Privacy"). From that submenu, choose Popup Windows. The check box for Block Unrequested Popup Windows is off by default. Click it on, then click OK to close the Preferences menu.

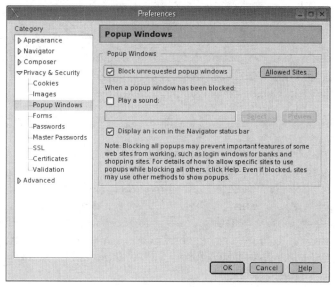

FIGURE 26-9   Configuring Mozilla to stop pop-up ads.

Cookie Control

Mozilla is also very versatile in its handling of cookies. Before you excitedly turn off all cookies, do remember that they can be useful, particularly with online services such as banks and e-commerce sites. That said, you may very much want to curb cookie traffic as much as possible.

From the Preferences menu, open up the Privacy & Security category submenu (Figure 26-10). Then, click on Cookies.

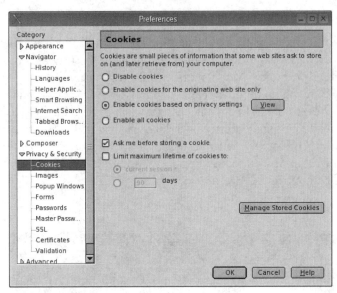

FIGURE 26-10   Back to Mozilla's Preferences menu to configure cookie policies.

Unless you really want to refuse all cookies, leave the Enable All Cookies Based on Privacy Settings radio button checked on. Then, make sure that you have the check box labeled Ask Me Before Storing a Cookie checked on. Click OK, and resume your surfing. When you visit a site that tries to set or modify a cookie, an alert pops up, alerting you to the cookie and asking you how to proceed. If you decide to deny a cookie and you never want to see another cookie from that site, check Use My Choice for All Cookies from This Site before clicking Deny (Figure 26-11).

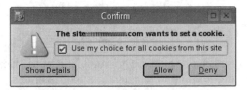

FIGURE 26-11   A pop-up enables you to allow or deny a cookie.

The Mozilla Sidebar

You have already seen the sidebar, because it is open by default when you use Mozilla for the first time. The sidebar is a quick way to get to your information, be they bookmarks, active searches, and so on. You can quickly activate the sidebar by pressing <F9> or by clicking View on the menu bar, then selecting Show/Hide>Sidebar. The sidebar will appear (or disappear).

The sidebar makes Net searches easy. At the top of the sidebar, you'll see a search field. Just type your search keywords in the Location bar, and press <Enter>. By default, Mozilla passes your search terms to Netscape's search engine. You can modify this default by going into the Preferences menu and choosing Internet Search under the Navigator category.

The sidebar is customizable, as well. While the sidebar is open, click on the Tabs drop-down list, select Customize Sidebar (Figure 26-12), and you can add, remove, or change the order of things as they appear.

FIGURE 26-12   *Customizing the Mozilla sidebar.*

Wrapping up

I started this chapter by telling you that Linux has many browsers available. On the GNOME side, we have *Epiphany*, which is based on Mozilla's rendering engine. If you installed support for both the KDE and GNOME desktops, you should have it already installed. *Epiphany* can be downloaded from `http://www.gnome.org/projects/epiphany`.

Another browser worth a look is *Opera*, an excellent, very fast, lightweight graphical browser that is distributed using an interesting model. The freeware version of the browser serves up small banner ads in the upper part of the browser as you use it; you can also purchase an ad-free version. To take Opera for a spin, head to the Opera web site at `www.opera.com` and pick up a copy.

I can't stop there. Most Linux distributions include several browsers, including some text-only browsers, such as Lynx and Links. If these aren't already installed on your system, they are most likely on your distribution CDs.

Shell Out When you feel like seeing the World Wide Web without its clutter of images, why not give Lynx or Links a try? Just open a Konsole shell and type:

```
lynx http://www.marcelgagne.com/
```

```
links http://www.marcelgagne.com/
```

You may be amazed at the speed and performance of a non-flashy web experience.

Resources

Epiphany
www.gnome.org/projects/epiphany

Konqueror
www.konqueror.org

Links
http://atrey.karlin.mff.cuni.cz/~clock/twibright/links

Lynx
http://lynx.isc.org

Mozilla
www.mozilla.org

Opera
www.opera.com

chapter
27

Word Processing (It Was a Dark and Stormy Night...)

Sorry, but I just had to use that famous opening from Edward George Bulwer-Lytton's <u>Paul Clifford</u> (written in 1830). Those famous words were made even more famous (infamous?) by Charles M. Schulz's Snoopy, that barn-storming, literary beagle. They just seem fitting, considering this chapter's topic: word processors.

Word processors run the gamut in terms of complexity, from simple programs that aren't much more than text editors to full-blown desktop publishing systems. Users coming from the Microsoft world are most likely to use OpenOffice Writer, part of the OpenOffice.org suite. I'm using version 1.1 to write this book.

OpenOffice.org is actually the free sibling of the commercial StarOffice suite. When Sun Microsystems decided to open the source to StarOffice, it became another boon for the open source community, not to mention the average user. OpenOffice became the free version of this powerful word processor, spreadsheet, and presentation graphics package, and StarOffice became the corporate choice. Both of these are full-featured office suites, and users familiar with Microsoft Office should feel right at home.

You might be wondering what differences exist between these two sibling suites. The great difference is the price. For anyone with a reasonably fast Internet connection or a helpful friend, OpenOffice is *free*. StarOffice, on the other hand, will cost you something for the boxed set. Included with StarOffice is documentation and support, as well as additional fonts and clipart. That said, you'll find that it is still *far less expensive* than the Windows alternative.

If you are following along and using the KDE desktop, you probably also have *KWord* at your disposal. Then, as I hinted, there are the others. We'll talk about a few of them at the end of this chapter.

OpenOffice.org Writer

Start Writer by clicking on the big K, scrolling up to the OpenOffice.org menu (in some distributions, check under the Office menu), and clicking on OpenOffice.org Writer. The first time you start Writer, the Address Data Source AutoPilot dialog box appears. The applications in OpenOffice.org can access information in your Netscape or Mozilla address book from an external LDAP server or from a number of other data sources, such as a database file. This information can then be used when you are creating mailing labels or distribution lists. If you don't have anything set up, don't worry. Simply click Cancel, and you are done.

 Shell Out To run OpenOffice.org Writer from the command line or via your <Alt+F2> shortcut, use the command `oowriter` (think OpenOffice.org Writer). Please note that some distributions may still use `swriter`, which is the StarOffice version of the command.

OpenOffice.org Writer starts up with a blank page, ready for you to release that inner creative genius. At the top of the screen, you'll find a menu bar where commands are organized based on their categories, including the friendly-sounding Help submenu (more on that shortly).

You should also see a selection box open on the screen for Paragraph Styles (Figure 27-1). This lets you quickly access and apply styles such as headings, text boxes, and so on to your paragraphs. The *Stylist* floats above your document at all times for rapid access. I'll tell you more about the Stylist later. For now, click the X in the corner to close it. You can always turn it on later by pressing <F11> or clicking Format on the menu bar and selecting Stylist.

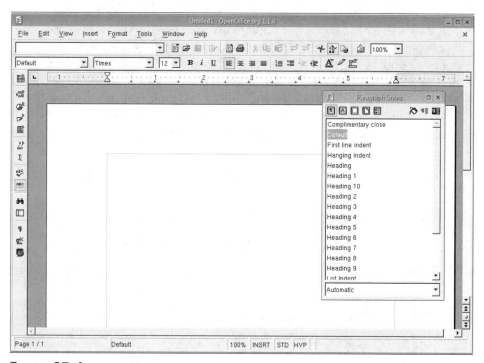

FIGURE 27-1   OpenOffice.org Writer on startup.

Write Now!

At this point, Writer is open, the Stylist is gone, and you are looking at a blank screen. Let's write something. As any writer will tell you, nothing is more *intimidating* than a blank page. Because I opened this chapter with the famous phrase, "It was a dark and stormy night," why don't we continue along that theme? That phrase is often pointed to as an example of bad writing, but the phrase in itself is only so bad. The paragraph that follows is even worse. Type this into your blank Writer page, as shown in Figure 27-2:

Paul Clifford, by Edward George Bulwer-Lytton

It was a dark and stormy night; the rain fell in torrents—except at occasional intervals, when it was checked by a violent gust of wind which swept up the streets (for it is in London that our scene lies), rattling along the house-tops, and fiercely agitating the scanty flame of the lamps that struggled against the darkness. Through one of the obscurest quarters of London, and among haunts little loved by the gentlemen of the police, a man, evidently of the lowest orders, was wending his solitary way. He stopped twice or thrice at different shops and houses of a description correspondent with the appearance of the quarter in which they were situated—and tended inquiry for some article or another which did not seem easily to be met with. All the answers he received were couched in the negative; and as he turned from each door he muttered to himself, in no very elegant phraseology, his disappointment and discontent.

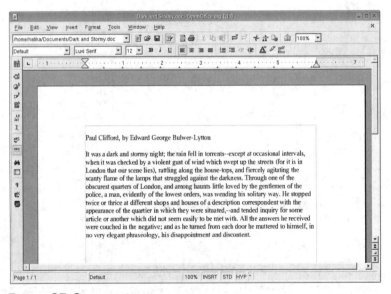

FIGURE 27-2   Your first document.

Okay, you can stop there. Isn't that wonderful stuff? If you feel the need to read more, I've got links to the story and the famous Bulwer-Lytton fiction contest at the end of this chapter.

The Hunt for Typos

For years, I've been including the tag line *This massagee wos nat speel or gramer-checkered* in the signature section of my emails. Given that I continue to use this line, I am obviously amused by it, but never running a spell check is far from good practice when your intention is to turn in a professional document.

OpenOffice.org Writer can do a spell check as you go without actually correcting errors. Click Tools on the menu bar, then Spellcheck, and select AutoSpellcheck. Words that don't appear in the dictionary show up with a squiggly red line underneath them, which you can then correct. Many people find this a useful feature, but some, like me, prefer to just check the whole document after writing.

To start a full document spell check, click Tools on the menu bar, then Spellcheck, and click on Check. You can also just press <F7> at any time to start a spell check.

What Language Is That?

OpenOffice.org supports many different languages, and depending on where you picked up your copy, it may be set for a different language than your own. To change the default language, click Tools on the menu bar, then Options, Language Settings, and Writing Aids.

The dialog box that appears (Figure 27-3) should have OpenOffice.org MySpell SpellChecker checked on. Click the Edit button next to it, and select your language of choice under the Default Languages for Documents drop-down box. When you're done, click OK to exit the various dialogs.

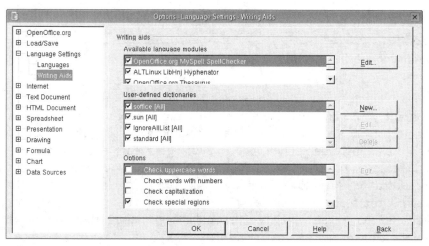

FIGURE 27-3   *Configuring writing tools.*

Saving Your Work

Now that you have a document (Figure 27-2), you need to save it. Click File on the menu bar, and select Save or Save As. When the Save As window appears (Figure 27-4), select a folder, type in a filename, and click Save. When you save, you can also specify the file type to be OpenOffice.org's default format (.sxw), RTF, straight text, or Microsoft Word format.

If you want to create a new directory under your home directory, you can do it here as well. Click the icon that looks like a folder with a star beside it (near the right corner), then enter your new directory name in the Create New Folder pop-up window.

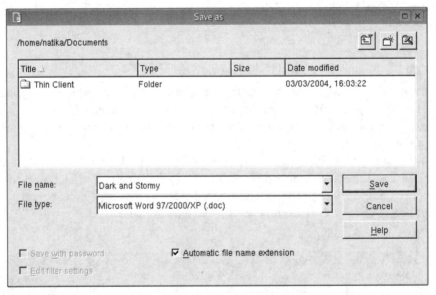

FIGURE 27-4   It is always good to save your work.

Should you decide to close OpenOffice.org Writer at this point, you can always return to your document at a later time by clicking File on the menu bar and selecting Open. The Open File dialog appears, and you can browse your directories to select the file you want. You can specify a file type via a fairly substantial drop-down list of available formats. This gives you a chance to narrow the search to include only text documents, spreadsheets, or presentations. You can also specify a particular document extension, only *.doc files, for example, or a particular pattern.

Printing Your Document

Invariably, the whole point of typing something in a word processor might be to produce a printed document. When you are through with your document, click File on the menu bar and select Print.

The Print dialog (Figure 27-5) has several options. The easiest thing to do after selecting your printer is just to click OK. The print job is directed to your printer of choice, and, in a few seconds, you'll have a nice, crisp version of your document. You can select a page range, increase the number of copies (one to all of your friends), or modify the printer properties (paper size, landscape print, and so on).

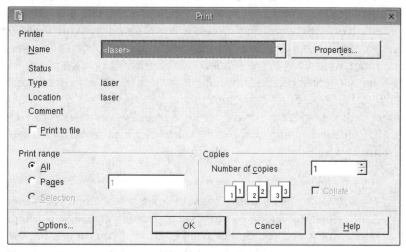

FIGURE 27-5   Printing your Writer document.

You can also print to a file. This is particularly interesting in that you can filter that print job so that the result is a PDF file, readable with Adobe Acrobat Reader or Linux's own *xpdf*.

To print a PDF file, select the PDF Converter from the printer selection list. Click the Print to File check box, and the Save As dialog appears (as in Figure 27–4). Choose a file name (make sure you add the .pdf extension), select PDF from the File Type drop-down menu, and click Save. When the Print dialog returns, click OK to create your PDF document.

Toolbars of Every Kind

Now that you are feeling comfortable with your new word processor, it's time for a quick tour of the various toolbars, icons, and menus in Writer.

The icon bar directly below the menu bar is called the *Function bar*, and it contains icons for opening and creating documents, cutting and pasting, printing, and others. The Function bar is common to all of the OpenOffice.org applications (Writer, Calc, Impress, and so on). On the left side of that Function bar is a combo box, a blank field where you can directly enter the path to a document you want to edit.

Below the Function bar is the *Object bar*. It provides common editing options, such as font selection, bold, italics, centering, and so on. Select words or phrases in your document with the mouse (hold, click, and drag across the desired text), then click B for bold or I for italics. This bar changes from application to application, depending on what type of formatting is most needed.

At the bottom of the editing screen is the *Status bar*, which displays the current page number, current template, zoom percentage, insert (or overwrite) mode, selection mode, hyperlink mode, and the current save status of the document (if the document has been modified and not saved, an asterisk appears).

Finally, off to the left is the *Main toolbar*; it provides a quick method of inserting objects into the document, doing a search and replace, or running a spell check. Pause over each of the icons with your mouse cursor to see a tool tip describing the functions of the individual icons.

Quick Tip   After using OpenOffice.org a few times, you'll eventually get a pop-up asking you to register your software. This is completely voluntary, and you do not need to do it. If you do register, you can contribute by letting the OpenOffice.org team know about bugs, features you'd like, and so on. Unless you request a future reminder, this is the last time you will see this screen.

Help!

Under the Help heading on the menu bar, you'll find plenty of information. By default, tooltips are activated: When you pause your mouse cursor over an item, a small description appears. Click Help, and you'll see Tips checked on. Just below the word "Tips," there is something else you might find useful—Extended Tips. Turning this on gives you slightly more detailed tool tips.

If you are looking for help on a specific topic, choose Contents to open up the OpenOffice Help screen. The various tabs at the top-left of the Help screen let you search for topics by application by using the Contents tab, alphabetically by using the Index tab, and by keyword by using the Find tab. You can even set bookmarks under the Bookmarks tab for those topics you regularly access.

To Word, or Not to Word?

Ah, that is the question indeed. OpenOffice.org's default document format is XML (eXtensible Markup Language), an open standard for document formats (although it is saved with an .sxw extension). The main reason for sticking with OpenOffice.org's native format is one of support and portability. XML is an emerging standard, and many applications in development either support XML or plan to.

Alternatively, the main reason for sticking with Word format is, quite frankly, that Word is everywhere. The sheer number of Word installations is the very reason that OpenOffice.org was designed to support the Microsoft Office format as thoroughly as it does. That said, if you do want to switch to XML format, Writer provides an easy way to do that. Rather than converting documents one by one, the Document Converter speeds up the process by allowing you to run all of the documents in a specific directory in one pass. It also works in both directions, meaning that you can convert from Word to OpenOffice.org format and vice versa. The conversion creates a new file, but leaves the original as it is.

From the menu bar, select File, move your mouse to AutoPilot, then select Document Converter from the submenu. To convert your Microsoft Office documents (you can do the Excel and PowerPoint documents at the same time), click Microsoft Office in the menu, then check off the types of documents you want. The next screen asks you whether you want both documents and templates or just one or the other. You then type in the name of the directory you want to import from and save to it (this can be the same directory). After you've entered your information and gone to the next screen, the program confirms your choices and gives you a final chance to change your mind. Click Convert to continue. As the converter does its job, it lists the various files that it encounters and keeps track of the process.

When the job is done, you'll have a number of files with an .sxw extension in your directory. If you change your mind, don't worry. Your original files are still there, so you've lost nothing.

If working with Word documents in Word format is important, then read on. Ah, heck. Even if it isn't, you should read on.

Personalizing Your Environment

Every application you use comes with defaults that may or may not reflect the way you want to work, and Writer is no different.

Click Tools on the menu bar and select Options. There are a lot of options here, including OpenOffice.org, Load/Save, Language Settings, Internet, Text Documents, HTML Document, SpreadSheet, Presentation, Drawing, Formula, Chart, and Data Sources. You've no doubt already noticed that although we are working with Writer here, the various components can be configured in this mode as well. Because there are so many options, I certainly can't cover them all, and besides, I don't want to bore you. Instead, I'll mention a few things that I think are important and let you discover the rest.

The main OpenOffice.org dialog covers a lot of general options regarding the look and feel of the applications. Take a moment to look at the Paths settings. If you keep your documents in a specific directory, you'll want to set that here. Under Type, choose My Documents, click Edit, then enter the new path to your directory of choice.

The Load/Save settings menu (Figure 27-6) is very important. If you are going to move documents back and forth constantly between systems running Microsoft Word and your own, you'll want to pay special attention here. Click the plus sign to the left of it, then click Microsoft Office.

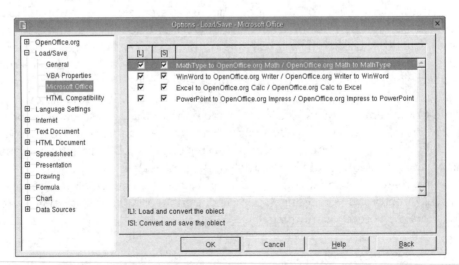

FIGURE 27-6   Load/Save defaults for Microsoft documents.

Click the Convert on Save (and load) check boxes on, and your OpenOffice.org Writer documents will be saved in Word format by default while your Calc sheets will wind up in Excel format. We're almost there. Although the conversion is pretty automatic here, when you try to resave a document that you have been working on, Writer may still disturb you with the occasional pop-up message informing you of the *minuses* of saving in Word format.

You can get around this with one other change. In the same menu section, click General. Notice where it says Standard File Format (Figure 27-7). For Document Type, select Text, and click Microsoft Word in the Always Save As drop-down list to the right. While you are here (assuming you are making these changes, of course), you probably want to change the Always Save As format for Spreadsheet to be Microsoft Excel.

Click OK, and you are done.

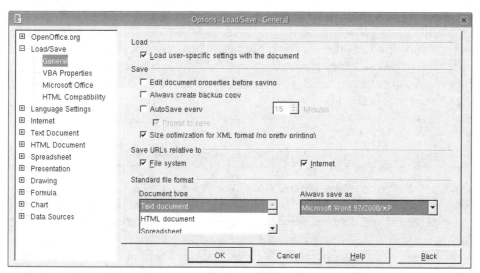

FIGURE 27-7   Defining the standard file format to be Microsoft Word.

Note I'm not saying that Microsoft's document format is in any way superior—it isn't—but if you have to move back and forth all the time, you don't want to be bothered with doing a Save As every time.

In the *Text Document* category (in the left sidebar menu), the changes relate specifically to the Writer application. Whenever you start a new document, OpenOffice.org assigns a default font when you start typing. This may not be your ideal choice, and you don't have to accept it. Sure, you can change the font when you are writing, but why do this with every document when you can change it once? Under Text Documents, click Basic Fonts, and you'll have the opportunity to change the default fonts your system uses.

When you are done with the Options menu, click OK to return to the OpenOffice.org application.

Screen Fonts

Fonts aren't limited to your documents. They also define how those menu options in the menu bar look. This is also true for those little tool tips. The default menu font is Andale Sans UI, and quite honestly, I'm not particularly fond of it, so I changed it the first time I ran OpenOffice.org.

To change it, click Tools from the menu bar and select Options. From the OpenOffice.org category, select Font Replacement. On the left side, choose Andale Sans UI from the list (or type it in), then select a replacement on the right side. (I use Helvetica for my system.) Add the font by clicking on the green checkmark, make sure to click Always, and you are done. As you can see, doing the change isn't really a big deal.

Running on AutoPilot

OpenOffice.org comes with a number of templates that are available throughout the suite. The AutoPilot feature helps you choose and walk through the setup of some basic documents. The easiest way to understand what AutoPilot can do for you is to dive right in and try it.

On the menu bar, click File, and move your mouse over to AutoPilot. You'll see a number of document types here, from letters to faxes to presentations. Choose Letter as an example. When the AutoPilot starts up (Figure 27-8), it offers you two kinds of letters—business and personal—then asks for a style—classic, modern, or decorative. As you progress through the various steps, you are asked to enter some basic information related to the type of document that you chose. For a letter, this would involve a sender and recipient name and address. You can also add graphics to the document, decide on its position, change the margins, and so on.

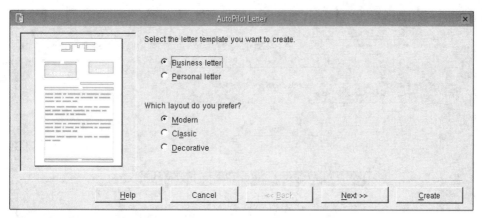

FIGURE 27-8   Writing on AutoPilot.

Navigating Style

Near the beginning of this chapter, I told you about the Stylist, that floating window (labeled Paragraph Styles) sitting above your document. Now, I'd like to give you some idea of how useful this little tool can be in formatting your documents. If you've banished the Stylist, bring it back by clicking its icon or pressing <F11>.

Whenever you start a new document, it loads with a default style. That style is actually a collection of formatting presets that define how various paragraphs will look. These include headings, lists, text boxes, and so on. All you have to do is select a paragraph, double-click on a style, and your paragraph's look—including font style and size—is magically updated. As an example of how to use this, try the following.

Start by reloading your dark and stormy document, then highlight your title text to select it. At the bottom of your stylist, it says Automatic. With your title highlighted, double-click on Heading 1. The heading changes to a large, bold, sans serif font. Now click the arrow at the bottom of the list, and change from Automatic to Chapter Styles. Double-click on Title, and your title is suddenly centered with the appropriate font applied (Figure 27-9).

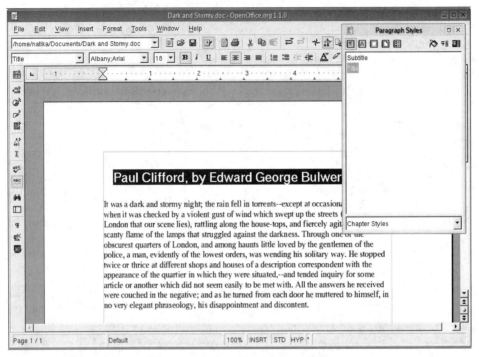

FIGURE 27-9   *Styles make paragraph formatting easy and consistent.*

The Stylist is pretty smart, really. Look back to the bottom of the list at those categories: HTML Styles, Custom Styles, and so on. Depending on the document type that you are working on, the Stylist comes up with a pretty sane list for that Automatic selection. If you call up an HTML document, HTML formatting shows up in the Automatic list.

Navigating the Rivers of Text

The second floating window is called the *Navigator*. This is a great tool for the power user or anyone who is creating long, complex documents. When you start up the Navigator by clicking Edit, then Navigator (or by pressing <F5>), you see a window listing the various elements in your document (Figure 27-10). These are organized in terms of headings, tables, graphics, and so on.

FIGURE 27-10   The Navigator.

What makes this a great tool is that you can use it to navigate a document quickly. Let's say that, as in this chapter, you have a number of section headings. Click on the plus sign beside the word "Headings," and a treed list of all the headings in the document is displayed. Double-click on a heading, and you instantly jump to that point in the document. The same goes for graphics, tables, and other such elements in your document.

Speaking of Document Elements. . .

Take a look over at the far right corner of the Function bar. See the little icon that looks like a picture hanging on a wall? That's the *Gallery* of graphics and sounds, decorative elements that you can insert in your document. When you click the picture (or select Gallery from Tools on the menu bar), the gallery opens up with a sidebar on the left, listing the various themes.

Wander through the collection until you see something that suits your document, then simply drag it into your document, just as I did with that globe at the end of this paragraph. To banish the gallery, just click the icon again.

While you were using the Gallery, did you notice the words "New Theme" at the top of the category sidebar? Click those words (which is really a button), and you'll be able to create a new category of images, clipart, or sounds. If you've got a directory of images you've collected, enter the path to that directory, pick a name for the collection, and you are done. Next time you bring up the Gallery, you can select from your own custom collection.

Direct PDF Exports

With release 1.1 of OpenOffice, several refinements were added. One of these was a one-button export to PDF. With this handy little feature, you can create documents to be viewed with Adobe's Acrobat Reader and a few very nice Linux-based viewers as well). When you use PDF (Portable Document Format), others will see your documents as you intended them to look. What's more, the inclusion of this feature as part of OpenOffice.org means that you don't have to spend anything extra on expensive tools to do the same job.

Here's how you use it. In your Function bar, look for the printer icon next to the cut and paste group of icons. Directly to the left of the printer icon is a little document-shaped icon with a red banner at the bottom proclaiming PDF. Pause the mouse cursor over it, and the tool tip will let you know that you are in the right place. When your document is ready and polished in all it glory, click the Export to PDF button. You can also click File, then select Export as PDF from the menu if you prefer. In either case, the Export dialog appears (Figure 27-11).

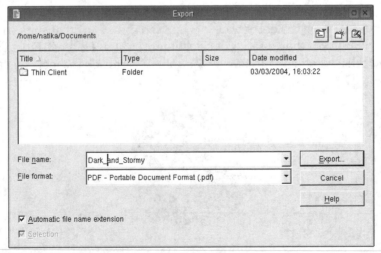

FIGURE 27-11   Exporting to PDF is a one-button affair.

More! Give Me More!

OpenOffice.org comes with a limited number of templates, graphics, and icons. That's one of the advantages of its commercial (non-free) cousin, StarOffice from Sun Microsystems. For now, if you find yourself in need of more templates than you already have or a richer gallery, take careful note of the OO Extras web site (www.ooextras.org). It may be the answer to your prayers. In addition to supplying individual macros, icons, and templates, the goal of this web site (created by Travis Bauer) is to provide downloadable packages to enhance OpenOffice.org's suite.

Quick Tip If you enter a URL to a web site in that combo box, you can actually open, view, and edit the web page! Yes, Writer is an HTML editor as well.

For those of you who are familiar with using your word processor as an HTML editor, this can be an extremely useful feature. Be warned, however, that the resulting code can be a little wordy and not altogether pleasant when working with other HTML editors.

Quick Tip In writing this book, I occasionally switched among a handful of fonts. If you find yourself in that situation, here's a way to speed up the process. After selecting a word or phrase to change, click on the font selection list, type a portion of a font name, or scroll down the list to choose what you want. Note that if you press <Enter> to select a font, you have to go through the whole selection process again next time. If you click on the font name with your mouse, however, that font will appear at the top of the list of recently used fonts. This makes for faster access.

Other Options

I've concentrated on OpenOffice.org Writer, because it is perhaps the real contender to Microsoft Office and the one that most people moving to Linux from the Microsoft Office world are likely to want to use. That's not to say that this is your only choice. For instance, the KDE suite comes with its own word processor, *KWord*, which is part of the KOffice suite. KWord is a frame-based word processing package. People who are used to working with desktop publishing packages such as FrameMaker will find this a familiar environment, just as those coming from Microsoft Word will experience somewhat of a learning curve. What KWord does is enable you to create extremely precise documents where the layout of text and graphics must be accurate.

Another excellent word processor worth your consideration is *Abiword*.

You can probably find Abiword on your distribution CDs, but you can always get the latest version on the Abisource web site (`www.abisource.com`). Abiword's main strengths are its size and performance. This is a lightweight application that performs well even on slower machines. It starts up fast and is excellent at what it does.

What KWord and Abiword have going against them, at least at the time of this writing, are compatibility issues with Microsoft Word documents. Both read the documents fairly well, but they do not export quite as well. As time goes on and development in import and export filters continues, this may not be an issue for long.

Resources

Abiword

www.abisource.com

Bulwer-Lytton Fiction Contest

www.bulwer-lytton.com

KDE's KWord

http://koffice.kde.org/kword

OpenOffice.org

www.openoffice.org

Sun Microsystems' StarOffice

http://wwws.sun.com/software/star/staroffice

28

Spreadsheets: Tables You Can Count On

A spreadsheet, for those who might be curious, allows you to organize data onto a table comprised of rows and columns. The intersection of a row and a column is called a cell, and each cell can be given specific attributes, such as a value or a formula. In the case of a formula, changes in the data of other cells can automatically update the results. This makes a spreadsheet ideal for financial applications. Change the interest rate in the appropriate cell, and the monthly payment changes without you having to do anything else.

The *idea* of a computerized spreadsheet probably existed before 1978, but it was in that year that Daniel Bricklin, a Harvard Business School student, came up with the first *real* spreadsheet program. He called his program a *visible calculator*, then later enlisted Bob Frankston of MIT (Bricklin names him as co-creator) to help him develop the program further. This program would come to be known as *VisiCalc*. Some argue that with VisiCalc, the first so-called *killer app* was born.

Now that we have the definitions and history out of the way, let's get back to your Linux system and have a look at OpenOffice.org's very own spreadsheet program. It is called *Calc*—an appropriate name, given what spreadsheets tend to be used for.

Starting a New Spreadsheet and Entering Data

There are a few ways to start a new spreadsheet. If you are already working in OpenOffice.org Writer (as I am right now), you can click File on the menu bar, move your mouse to the New submenu, and select Spreadsheet from the drop-down list. Another way is to click the application starter (the big K) and select Calc from the OpenOffice.org or Office menu. When Calc starts up, you'll see a blank sheet of cells, as in Figure 28-1.

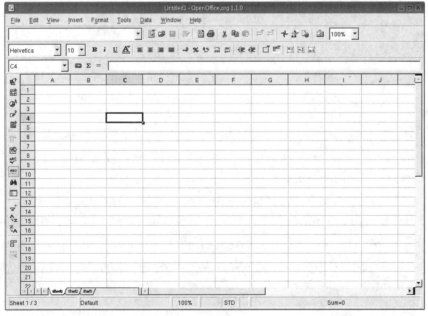

FIGURE 28-1   Starting with a clean sheet.

Directly below the menu bar is the Function bar. As with Writer, the icons here give you access to the common functions found throughout OpenOffice.org, such as cut, paste, open, save, and so on. Below the Function bar is the Object bar. Some features here are similar to those in Writer, such as font style and size, but others are specific to formatting content in a spreadsheet—percentage, decimal places, frame border, and so on.

Finally, below the Object bar you'll find the Formula bar. The first field here displays the current cell, but you can also enter a cell number here to jump to another cell. You can move around from cell to cell by using your cursor keys, <Tab> or <Shift+Tab>, or simply by clicking on a particular cell. The current cell you are working on has a bold black outline around it.

Basic Math

Let's try something simple, shall we? If you haven't already done so, open a new spreadsheet. In cell A1, type Course Average. Select the text in the field, change the font style or size (by clicking on the font selector in the Object bar), then press <Enter>. As you can see, the text is larger than the field. No problem. Place your mouse cursor on the line between the A and B cells, directly below the Formula bar. Click and hold, then stretch the A cell to fit the text. You can do the same for the height of any given row of cells by clicking on the line between the row numbers (over to the left) and stretching these to an appropriate size.

Now move to cell A3, and type in a hypothetical number somewhere in the range of 1 to 100 to represent a course mark. Press <Enter> or cursor down to move to the next cell. Enter seven course marks so that cells A3 through A9 are filled. In my example, I entered 95, 67, 100, 89, 84, 79, and 93. (It seems to me that the 67 is an aberration.)

Now, we are going to enter a formula in cell A11 to provide an average of all seven-course scores. In cell A11, enter the following text:

=(A3+A4+A5+A6+A7+A8+A9)/7

When you press <Enter>, the text you entered will disappear and instead, you'll see an average for your course scores (Figure 28-2).

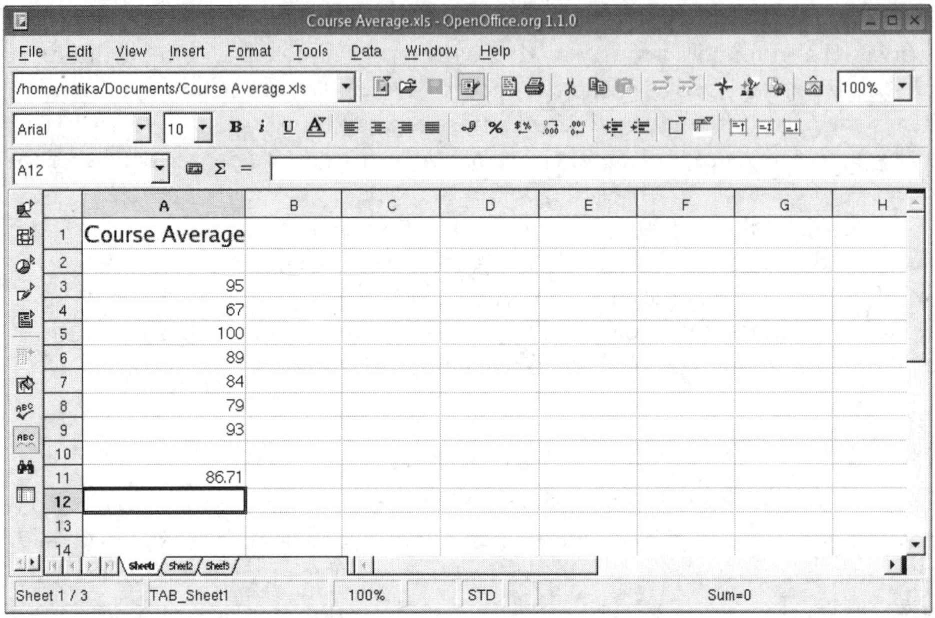

FIGURE 28-2   Setting up a simple table to determine class averages.

An average of 86.71 isn't a bad score (it is an A, after all), but if that 67 really was an aberration, you can easily go back to that cell, type in a different number, and press <Enter>. When you do so, the average automagically changes for you.

Calculating an average is a simple enough formula, but if I were to add 70 rows, the resulting formula could get *ugly*. The beauty of spreadsheets is that they include formulas to make this whole process somewhat cleaner. For instance, I can specify a range of cells by putting a colon in between the first and last cells (A3:A9) and using a built-in function to return the average of that range. My new, improved, and cleaner formula looks like this.

=AVERAGE (A3:A9)

Incidentally, you can also select the cell and enter the information in the input line on the Formula bar. I mention the Formula bar for a couple of reasons. One is that you can obviously enter the information in the field, as well as in the cell itself.

The second reason has to do with those little icons to the left of the input field. If you click into that input field, you'll notice that a little green checkmark and a red X appear. Click the green check to accept any changes you make to the formula and the red X to cancel the changes. Now look to the icon furthest on the left. If you hold your mouse over it, it should pop up a little tool tip that says AutoPilot: Functions. Try it. Go back to cell A11, then click your mouse into the input field on the Formula bar. Now click onto the AutoPilot Functions icon; you can also click Insert on the menu bar and select Function. You'll get a window similar to the one in Figure 28-3.

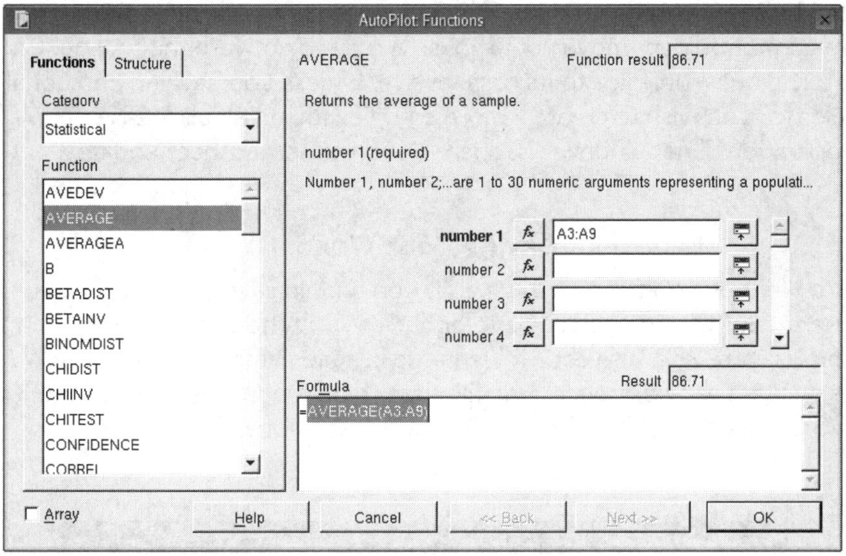

FIGURE 28-3   Using the AutoPilot to generate a function.

On the left side, you'll see a list of functions with their descriptions off to the right. For the function called AVERAGE, the description is "Returns the average of a sample." Because this is what we want, click the Next button at the bottom of the window. When the next screen appears, look at the window labeled Formula at the bottom of the screen. You'll see that the formula is starting to be built. At this point, it says =AVERAGE() and nothing else.

Near the middle of the screen on the right side are four data fields labeled number 1 through number 4. The first field is required, whereas the others are optional. You could at this point enter A3:A9, click Next, and be done. Alternatively, you could click the button to the right of the number field (the tool tip will say Shrink) to shrink the AutoPilot to a small bar floating above your spreadsheet (Figure 28-4).

FIGURE 28-4   The AutoPilot Formula bar.

On your spreadsheet, select a group of fields by clicking on the first field and dragging the mouse to include all seven fields. When you let go of the mouse, the field range is entered for you. On the left side of the shrunken AutoPilot bar is a maximize button; move your mouse over it to activate the tool tip. Click it to return your AutoPilot to its original size. Unless you have an additional set of fields (or you wish to create a more complex formula), click OK to complete this operation. The window disappears, and the spreadsheet updates.

Saving Your Work

Before we move on to something else, you should save your work. Click File on the menu bar, and select Save or Save As. When the Save As window appears (Figure 28-5), select a folder, type in a file name, and click Save. When you save, you can also specify the file type to be OpenOffice.org's default format (StarCalc), DIF, DBASE, or Microsoft Excel format.

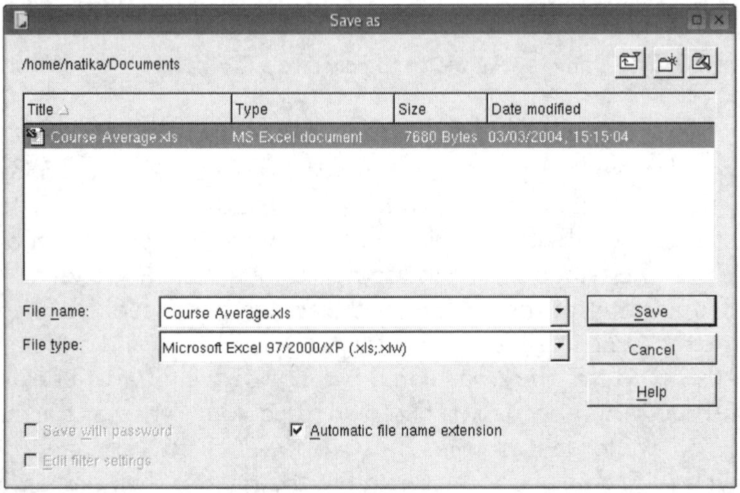

FIGURE 28-5   Don't forget to save your work.

Should you decide to close OpenOffice.org Calc at this point, you could always go back to the document by clicking File on the menu bar and selecting Open.

Complex Charts and Graphs

This time, I'll show you how you can transform the data that you enter into your spreadsheets into a slick little chart. These charts can be linear, pie, bar, and a number of other choices. They can also be two- or three-dimensional, with various effects applied for that professional look.

To start, create another spreadsheet. We'll call this one Quarterly Sales Reports. With it, we will track the performance of a hypothetical company

In cell A1, write the title (Quarterly Sales Reports), and in cell A2, write the description of the data (in thousands of dollars). Now, fill in the following headings in the specified cells:

A4: Period
A6: Q1
A7: Q2
A8: Q3
A9: Q4

Finally, enter some headings for the years. In cell B4, enter 1998, 1999 in cell C4, and continue on in row 4 right up to 2002. You should have five years running across row 4, with four quarters listed.

Time to have some virtual fun. For each period, enter a fictitious sales figure or a real one if you are serious about this. For example, the data for 1999, Q2 would be entered in cell C7, and the sales figure for 2001, Q3 would be in cell E8. If you are still with me, finish entering the data, and we'll do a few things.

Magical Totals

Let's start with a quick and easy total of each column.

If you used the same layout as I did, you should have a 1998 column that ends at B9. Click on cell B11. Now look at the icon in the middle of the sheet area and the input line on the Formula bar. It looks like the Greek letter Epsilon. Hold your mouse pointer over it, and you'll see a tool tip that says Sum. Are you excited yet? Click the icon, and the formula to sum up the totals of that line,

=SUM(B6:B10), automatically appears (Figure 28-6). All you need to do to finalize the totals is click the green checkmark that appears next to the input line.

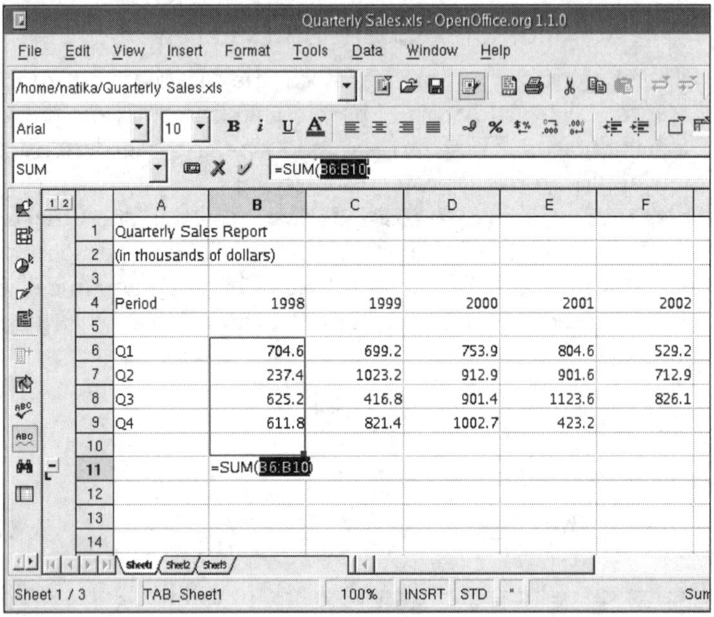

FIGURE 28-6   Select a series of cells, and Calc automatically generates totals for you.

Because a sum calculation is the most common function used, it is kept handy. You can now do the same thing for each of the other yearly columns to get your totals. Click on the sum icon, then click your beginning column and drag the mouse to include the cells you want. Click the green checkmark, and move on to the next yearly column.

Nice, Colorful, Impressive, and Dynamic Graphs

Creating a chart from the data you just entered is pretty easy. Start by selecting the cells that represent the information you want to see on your finished chart, including the headings. You can start with one corner of the chart and simply drag your mouse across to select all that you want.

Warning If there are some empty cells in your table, you should deselect them. Hold down the <Ctrl> key and click on those cells. For the example, I would deselect that empty row 5.

When all of the cells you want are selected, click Insert on the menu bar, and select Chart. The first window that appears (Figure 28-7) gives you the opportunity of assigning certain rows and columns as labels. This is perfect, because we have the quarter numbers running down the left side and the year labels running across the top. Check these on.

Before you move on, notice the drop-down list labeled Chart Results in Worksheet. By default, Calc creates three tabbed pages for every new worksheet, even though you are working on only one at this time. If you leave things as they are, your chart will be embedded into your current page, although you can always move it to different locations. You have a choice at this point to have the chart appear on a separate page (those tabs at the bottom of your worksheet). I'm going to leave our example chart on the first page. Make your selection, then click Next.

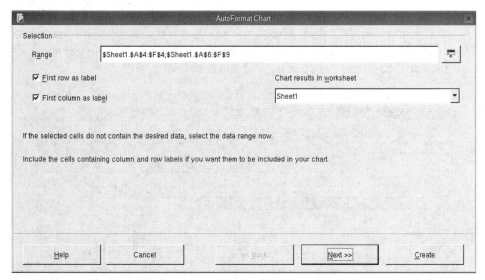

FIGURE 28-7   The AutoFormat Chart dialog.

In the next window (Figure 28-8), you can choose from chart types (bar, pie, and so on) and see a preview, enabling you to determine which of the various chart options best shows off your data. If you want to see the labels in your preview window, click on the check box for Show Text Elements in Preview.

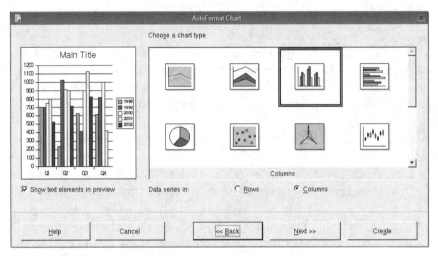

FIGURE 28-8   Lots of chart types to choose from.

You can continue to click Next for some additional fine-tuning on formatting (the last screen lets you change the title), but this is all of the data you actually need to create your chart. When you are done, click the Create button. Your chart appears on your page (Figure 28-9).

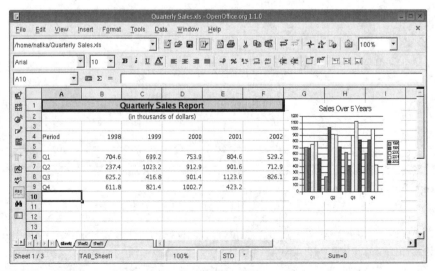

FIGURE 28-9   Just like that, your chart appears alongside your table.

To lock the chart in place, click anywhere else on the worksheet. You may want to change the chart's title as well. Double-click on the title, then make your changes. I'm going to call mine "Sales Over 5 Years." If the chart is in the wrong place, click on it, then drag it to where you want it to be. If it is too big, grab one of the corners and resize it.

What's cool about this chart is that it is dynamically linked to the data on the page. Change the data in a cell, press <Enter>, and the chart automatically updates!

Final Touches

If you select (highlight) the title text in cell A1 and click the centering icon, the text position doesn't change. That's because A1 is already filled to capacity, and the text is essentially already centered. To get the effect you want, click on cell A1, hold the mouse button down, and drag to select all of the cells up to F1. Now, click Format on the menu bar, select Merge Cells, and click Define. All six cells merge into one; now you can select the text and center it.

For more extensive formatting of cells, including borders, color, and so on, right-click on the cell, and select Format. The Cell Attribute window (Figure 28-10) appears, from which you can add a variety of formatting effects. Try this with your title cell.

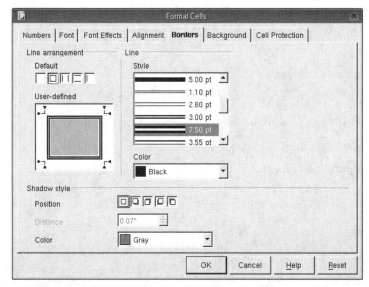

FIGURE 28-10   Adding borders and fill to a cell.

A Beautiful Thing!

When you are through with your worksheet, it is time to print. Click File on the menu bar and select Print. Select your printer, click OK, and you'll have a product to impress even the most jaded bean counter. While you are busy impressing people, keep in mind that you can also export this spreadsheet to PDF with a single click, just as you did with Writer files in the last chapter.

Alternatives

Because OpenOffice.org is such an obvious and excellent replacement for Microsoft Office (including Word, Excel, and PowerPoint), it's easy to forget that there are other alternatives. One of the great things I keep coming back to when I talk and write about Linux is the fact that we do have alternatives, some costing no more than the time it takes to download and install them.

When it comes to spreadsheet programs, your Linux distribution CDs likely came with a few. In addition to OpenOffice.org's Calc, the primary candidates are Gnumeric and KSpread.

Both Gnumeric and KSpread are certainly worth a look, and I've found Gnumeric to be particularly good when it comes to working with Excel spreadsheets.

Resources

Gnumeric

www.gnome.org/projects/gnumeric

KSpread

www.koffice.org/kspread

OpenOffice.org's Calc

www.openoffice.org

29

Presentation Graphics: For Those Who Need No Introduction!

Once upon a time, even a simple business presentation could be quite a costly affair. The person putting together a presentation first used a word processor—maybe even pen and ink—then transferred all of this to a business graphics presentation tool. Alternatively, a special design service might be hired to take that next step, but eventually, the whole thing was sent to yet another service that would create 35mm slides from the finished paper presentation.

On the day of the big meeting, the old carousel slide projector came out, and the slides were painstakingly loaded onto the circular slide holder. Then the lights dimmed, and the show began. If luck was with you, the slides were all in the right order, and the projector did not jam up.

These days, we use tools that streamline this process, allowing us to create presentations, insert and manipulate graphical elements, then play the whole thing directly from a notebook computer. The projector simply plugs into the computer's video port. There are many software packages to do the job under Linux. The most popular is called *Impress*, and it is part of the OpenOffice.org suite. For those of you coming from the Microsoft world, Impress is very much like PowerPoint. In fact, Impress can easily import and export PowerPoint files.

Getting Ready to Impress

After working with OpenOffice.org's Writer and Calc, you should feel right at home using Impress. Working with menus, inserting text, spell checking, and customizing your environment all work in exactly the same way. The editing screen itself is probably more like Calc than Writer in some ways. The Impress work area has tabbed pages so you can easily jump from one part of the presentation to the other. Each page is referred to as a *slide* in a nod to the history of business presentations and those 35mm slides.

To start Impress, click on your application starter (the big K), select OpenOffice.org (or Office), and click on OpenOffice.org Impress in the submenu. You can also start a new presentation from any other OpenOffice.org application, such as Writer or Calc. Just click File on the menu bar, select New, and choose Presentation from the submenu.

When you start up Impress for the first time, you see a blank page all ready for your creative spirits to make it come alive (Figure 29-1). You may find that a small dialog box floats above the page. This is the presentation box, and it contains a number of quick access tools for working with slides. You may leave it alone or close it for now. It's easy enough to bring back. The last icon on the tool bar just above the ruler toggles it on and off.

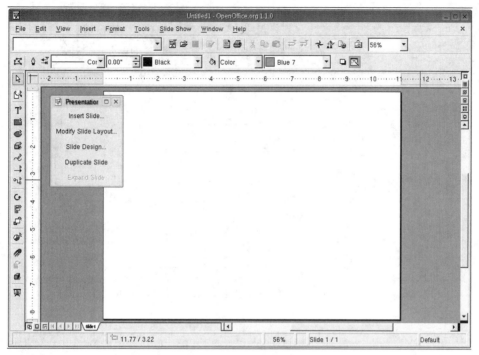

FIGURE 29-1　Starting from scratch with OpenOffice.org's Impress.

Let's work through a new presentation together. Choose File>New, then select Presentation to start the presentation AutoPilot, which presents you with a number of choices. You can start with an empty presentation (Figure 29-2), work from a template, or open an existing presentation. Incidentally, the AutoPilot was the default entry point for Impress in version 1.0 of OpenOffice.org.

 Quick Tip At the time of this writing, OpenOffice.org shipped with only a couple of Impress templates. As I've mentioned before, one of the differences between OpenOffice.org 1.1 and its commercial sibling StarOffice 7.0 is that StarOffice 7.0 comes with a number of templates. That said, you can still download some free templates for OpenOffice.org from www.ooextras.org.

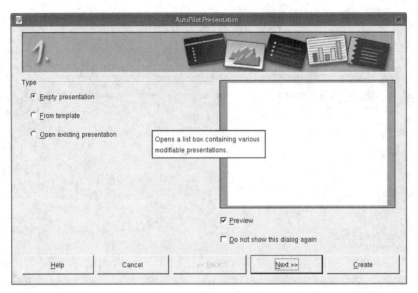

FIGURE 29-2   Starting a new presentation with the AutoPilot.

The AutoPilot enables you to select from existing presentations as well as templates. For the moment, I'm going to stick with the very basics. Leave Empty Presentation selected, and click Next. Essentially, this starts you off with a blank slide. Step 2 (Figure 29-3) gives you the opportunity to select a slide design. You may find a few options for slide design here; these are your templates. Choose <Original>. Before you click Next, pause and look at the options for output medium. By default, Impress creates presentations designed for the screen or a projector connected to your PC.

Step 3 (Figure 29-4) lets you define the default means for slide transition. You've all seen these presentations; slides dissolve into each other or fly in from the side or drop like a trap door closing. At this stage of the game, pick one of the effects from the drop-down box labeled Effect, then choose the transition's speed. The preview window on the right side shows you what each effect looks like when you select it.

Directly below the slide transition selection, you select the presentation type. Your choices are Default and Automatic. By default, slide transitions occur after you press a key, whether it be <Enter> or <Spacebar> (you can define this). To run presentations without any intervention from the presenter, you would select Automatic and define the amount of time between slides or even between presentations. For now, however, accept the default setting here, and click Create to start building your presentation.

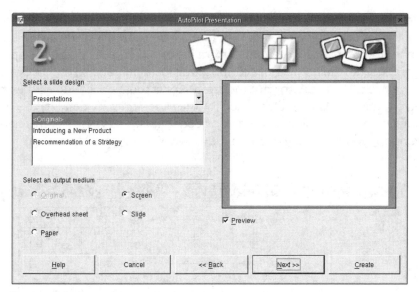

FIGURE 29-3   Impress defaults to creating presentations designed for the screen.

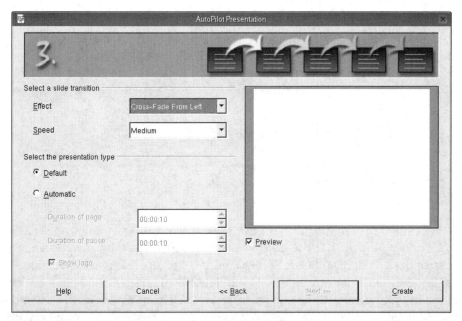

FIGURE 29-4   Selecting slide transition effects.

You now have everything you need to start working on your presentation. A Modify Slide dialog box appears (Figure 29-5) with small preview images of a number of potential slide layouts. From here, you can decide on the appearance of the slide, the number of columns, title locations, and so on. If you pause over one of the images with your mouse cursor, a tool tip tells you a little about the layout format. There's also space for the slide's title. By default, the title is Slide, followed by the slide's number in sequence. If you don't like this naming convention, you can easily override it by changing it in the Name field.

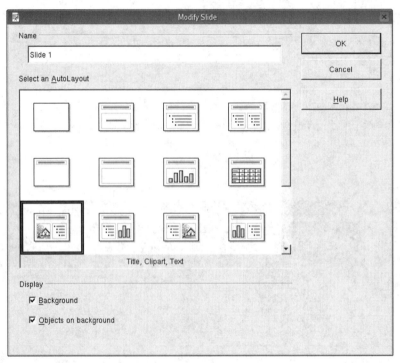

FIGURE 29-5   *Selecting your slide layout.*

Follow along with me: Choose the Title, Clipart, Text layout, and click OK to continue. Notice that the editing window has a startling resemblance to those of both Writer and Calc. The menu bar sits just below the title bar, and the function bar is directly below. The object bar also has a number of options unique to working in the Impress environment. On the left side of the page, the main toolbar provides quick access to objects, drawing functions, 3D effects, and so on (Figure 29-6).

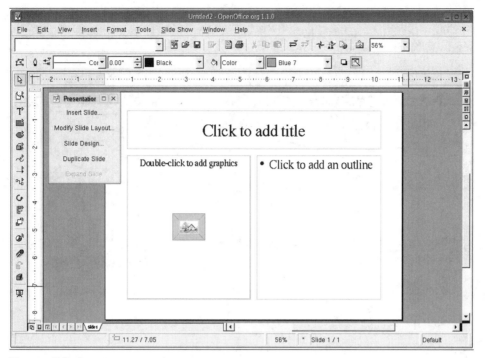

FIGURE 29-6   *Starting with a slide template.*

You can also click the last button in the list to start your slide show. There won't be much to see at this point, but you can click it at any time to see how your presentation is coming along. Another way to start the show is to click Slide Show on the menu bar and select the first option.

To start editing your slide, click (or double-click for images) the section you want to change. Make your changes by typing into that area. For example, you might enter the phrase "Introducing Linux!" for the title. When you are happy with your changes, click outside of the frame area. Over on the right, in the frame that says Click to Add an Outline, insert these bulleted points:

- What is Linux?
- Is Linux really free?
- What can it do?
- Advantages?
- Disadvantages?

As you might have noticed, this outline serves as talking points that mirror the first chapter of this book. Now, over on the left side, double-click on the frame (as instructed on the default slide) and insert a graphic. The Insert Graphics dialog appears (Figure 29-7), allowing you to navigate your folders and look for the perfect image.

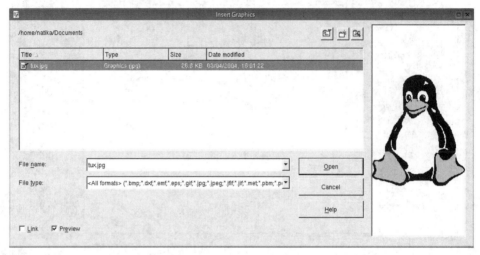

FIGURE 29-7   Inserting a graphic into the presentation.

You can use any image you like here. For my image, I used Konqueror to surf over to Larry Ewing's web site (`www.isc.tamu.edu/~lewing/linux`), where I picked up my Tux graphic from the source. (I'll tell you more about Tux at the end of this chapter.) You may choose another image if you prefer. With your image selected, click Open, and it will replace the default text in the left frame.

Quick Tip Another option is to single-click the default image and press <Delete>. Then you can click Tools on the menu bar, select Gallery, and drag one of the included images onto your slide.

That's it. Your first slide is done! You might want to pause here and save your work before you move on. (Masterpieces must be protected.) Click File on the menu bar, select Save As, then enter a filename for your presentation. I used Linux_Intro as my title. Now click Save, and we'll continue building this presentation.

Inserting Slides

You might have already noticed the floating menu labeled Presentation. You can use it to add another slide easily. If you choose this road, the Modify Slide dialog you used earlier (Figure 29-5) reappears.

If you are just as happy to continue with the *same* slide design, I can show you a *really fast* way to add slides. Look at the tabs down at the bottom of the screen. Each slide has a corresponding tab. Simply click in the blank, gray area to the right of the last tab, and another blank slide (with its own tab) automagically appears.

For the time being, click Insert Slide from the floating menu, and select the one called Title, Text (Figure 29-8).

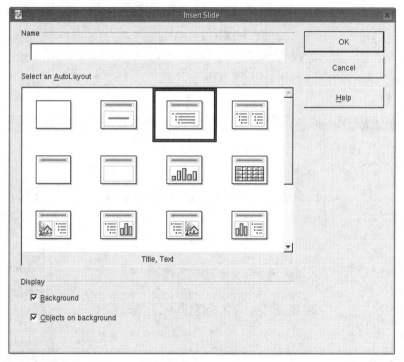

FIGURE 29-8   The second slide.

We'll switch from two text frames to just one. Click OK, and a tab appears, showing you Slide 2. Because there need to be five points after the introductory slide, add a quick four slides by clicking the gray area next to Slide 2. You should now have tabs labeled Slide 1 through Slide 6.

Okay, click on the tab for Slide 2, then click the top frame where it says Click to Add Title. Enter the first bullet point from Slide 1, then repeat the process for the next four slides, inserting the appropriate bullet point for the title of each.

Quick Tip You can give those tab labels more useful names by right-clicking on them and selecting Rename Slide.

As to what to enter in the text area of each slide, I leave that to your imagination or your memory of Chapter 1. When you have finished entering all of the information you want, save your work. I'm going to show you how to dress up those plain white slides.

Adding Color

Right-click on your slide (not on the text), and select Slide from the pop-up menu. Now click on Page Setup (Figure 29-9).

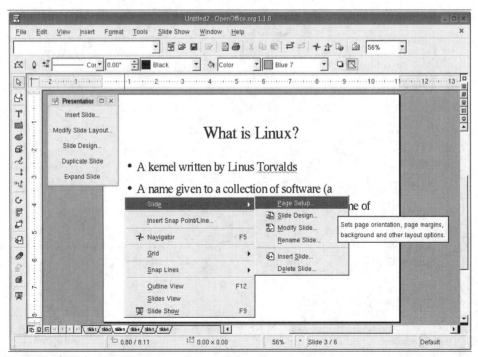

FIGURE 29-9   Modifying the page (slide) setup.

Now you see a window with two tabs: Page and Background. Click on the Background tab. Notice the five radio buttons (Figure 29-10). Each provides an option for background selection—plain white, colors, gradients, hatching, bitmaps. Click them to see the choices that they offer.

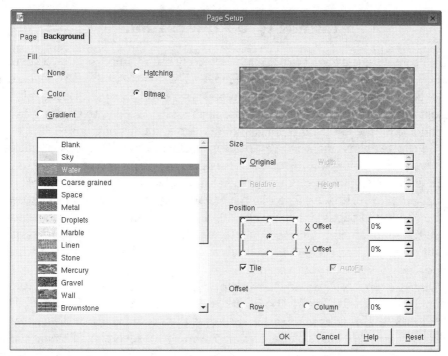

FIGURE 29-10   Impress background selection.

For example, you might choose the Linear blue/white gradient (a very business-looking background) or perhaps the Water bitmap. The choice is yours. When you click OK, you are asked whether you want the background setting to be for all slides. For now, click Yes.

You've done a lot of work, so save your work. It's time to see the fruits of your labors. Click Slide Show on the menu bar and select Slide show. You can also use the <Ctrl+F2> keyboard shortcut. The slides will transition with a touch of the <Spacebar>.

Printing Your Presentation

As with the other OpenOffice.org applications, print your presentation by clicking File on the menu bar and selecting Print—you can also click the small printer icon in the function bar.. The standard OpenOffice.org print dialog will appear from which you can select your printer of choice.

Instant Web Presentations

Here's something you are going to find incredibly useful. Impress lets you export your existing presentation to HTML format. The beauty of this is that you can make your presentation available to anyone with a web browser. Best of all, the export functionality takes care of all the details associated with creating a web site, including the handling of links and forward and back buttons.

To create an instant web presentation in OpenOffice 1.1, here is what you do. Make sure that your current Impress presentation is open and that your work is saved. Click File on the menu bar and select Export. The Export dialog appears (in version 1.0, the File Save dialog appeared instead). Because all of the generated pages will appear in the directory you choose, it might make sense to create an empty directory into which to save your files before entering a filename. That filename, by the way, is the HTML title page, normally called `index.html`. If you would like a different name, choose it here, minus the `.html` extension (perhaps, Linux_Intro), and click Export (or click Save in OpenOffice.org 1.0). The HTML Export dialog now appears (Figure 29-11).

To create a new design, make sure that the New Design radio button is clicked on, and click Next. You are given the choice of several publication types. The default choice (and probably a very good one) is Standard HTML format. You can also decide to create an HTML publication with frames, if you prefer. If you want to be totally in control of what your audience sees, you can elect to create an automatic slide show (using HTM refresh times of whatever you choose) or a WebCast. When you have made your choice, click Next.

In the next window (Figure 29-12), you must decide the *resolution of the images* created for your web publication. The default is to use JPG images at 75% quality. You can elect to set this all the way up to 100% for the best quality possible, but be aware that the higher the quality, the larger the images and the slower the download time will be. If this presentation is meant to be viewed on your personal office network, it probably doesn't matter.

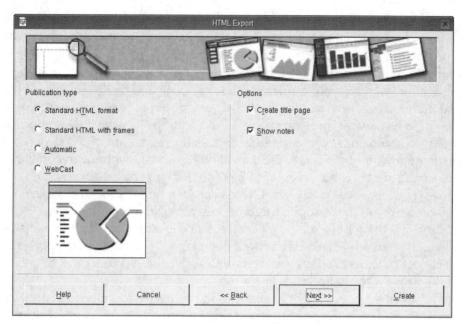

FIGURE 29-11   The HTML Export dialog in Impress.

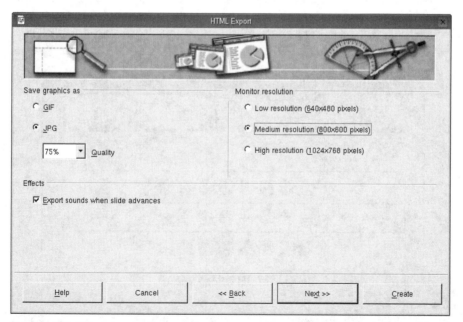

FIGURE 29-12   Select your image resolution and type.

You are also asked to choose the *monitor resolution*. This is an excellent question that is probably worth more than a few seconds of configuration. At some point in your history of surfing, you must have come across a web site where the web page is larger than your browser window. To view the page, you needed to move your horizontal slide bar back and forth just to read the text. Although we are used to scrolling up and down to read text, left to right scrolling is somewhat more annoying. If you want to be as inclusive as possible for your audience, use 640×480 for monitor resolution. That said, most personal computer monitors these days handle 800×600 without any problem. The same isn't true, however, of 1024×768 displays (however common). Is there a right answer? Probably not. Consider your target audience, make your decision based on those considerations, then click Next.

One last thing before moving on. Notice the check box under the label Effects. I'm not a big fan of web pages that play sounds when I do things. You can choose to export sounds whenever slides advance. The best way to decide what you like is to try both. It's all for fun, anyhow.

On the next window that appears, fill in *title page information* for the web presentation. This is the presentation title, your email address, and a link back to your own web site, if you wish. Click Next, and you'll then have the opportunity to decide on the graphics you wish to use for the forward and back buttons. If you don't want to use graphical buttons, you don't have to. In fact, the default is to use Text only, so to use a particular button style, make sure you uncheck the check box (Figure 29-13), select your button style, and click Next.

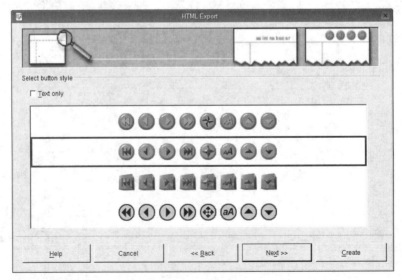

FIGURE 29-13   Pick a button style, any button style.

We are almost there. The final window lets you decide on the *color scheme* for the presentation. The default is simply to use the colors from the original Impress publication, but you can override this, as well as the color for hyperlinks and the web page background. Make your choices and click Create. One last window appears, asking you to name the HTML design. This is a freeform text field. Enter a brief description, and click Save.

The process of exporting your presentation may take a few seconds or a few minutes, depending on the speed of your machine and the complexity of your presentation. To view the presentation, open your browser and point to the title page. That's all there is to it.

How About A Little Flash? Shocking!

Before we wrap up, let's revisit that Export dialog one more time. Click File from the menu, and select Export. When the Export dialog appears, have another look at the File format selection box, just below the Filename field. The default is to export to an HTML document, but there are other options. For one, you have a PDF export—the one button export is common to Impress as well.

Notice, too, that you also have a Macromedia Flash export capability. Isn't that interesting? Enter a filename for your presentation (no need to add the .swf extention). With a single click of the Export button, you can save your presentation to Macromedia's Flash format. Now, your presentation is viewable from any browser with a Macromedia Flash or Shockwave plugin. The advantage of this over the HTML export is that all your animated slide transitions are preserved. Visitors to your site can view the presentation as it was intended.

So What's with the Penguin?

Having made you run off to Larry Ewing's site for a copy of Tux, I suppose I should take a moment to answer one of the most frequently asked questions in the Linux world. After all, every time you look at a Linux book, boxed set, or web site, you stand a good chance of coming face to face with a fat, smiling penguin. You may well be wondering what Linux has to do with this penguin (Figure 29-14). Well, for starters, his name is *Tux*, and he is the Linux mascot. The most famous version of Tux, and there are many, is Larry Ewing's design.

FIGURE 29-14   Tux, the Linux mascot.

The story behind Tux is the stuff of legend now and, like most legends, a little hard to pin down. Linus Torvalds was asked what he envisioned for a mascot. The answer from Linus was, "You should be imagining a slightly overweight penguin (*), sitting down after having gorged itself, and having just burped. It's sitting there with a beatific smile—the world is a good place to be when you have just eaten a few gallons of raw fish and you can feel another 'burp' coming."

There is also another story in which Linus claims he was attacked by a killer penguin at the Canberra zoo, where he contracted "penguinitis," a disease whose main symptom is that you "stay awake at nights just thinking about penguins and feeling great love towards them."

That's the thing about legends. They tend to get strange over time.

> Some people have told me they don't think a fat penguin really embodies the grace of Linux, which just tells me they have never seen an angry penguin charging at them in excess of 100mph. They'd be a lot more careful about what they say if they had.
>
> —Linus Torvalds

Extra! Extra!

Before we move away from the classic office applications, I would like to take another moment to address the issue of templates. Although StarOffice, the nonfree commercial sibling of OpenOffice.org, comes with a number of templates for word processing, spreadsheets, and presentation graphics, OpenOffice.org is still quite *light* in this area. As I mentioned earlier, the Impress package has no included templates at all.

The *OO Extras* web site (`http://ooextras.sourceforge.net`) was born to resolve this issue.

Travis Bauer has put together a great site with a number of community-created and -distributed templates for the OpenOffice.org suite. The site is laid out so that you can look for things specific to your application of choice, and screenshots are provided so that you can get a preview of what the document will look like. Because OO Extras has become an international affair, these extras come in different languages, as well.

A visit to OO Extras is well worth your time. Perhaps in time, you too will contribute to this growing body of work.

Resources

Larry Ewing's "Tux" (The Official Linux Penguin)

www.isc.tamu.edu/~lewing/linux

Linux Logo Links at Linux.org

www.linux.org/info/logos.html

OO Extras

http://ooextras.sourceforge.net

30

Office Graphics and Art (Just Call Me Leonardo)

Oddly enough, applications allowing users to work with graphics are among some of the most highly developed in the world. To see the truth in this rather bold statement, turn your eyes to Hollywood. Such blockbusters as "Titanic," "Star Trek: Nemesis," "Shrek," and others use Linux and Linux clusters to create the complex special effects.

In terms of graphical design and photo editing, your Linux system comes with one of the most powerful, flexible, and easy-to-use packages there is—regardless of what OS you are running. It's called the GIMP, and I'll be introducing you to its features a little later in this chapter.

Then we have digital cameras. In the world of your old OS, you needed special software to work with your particular camera. In the Linux world, you can do it all with a single interface. In fact, if you've come this far in this book, you probably already know almost everything thing you need to work with your camera.

Finally, I'll cover another of piece of graphical magic making when I show you how to use a scanner with your Linux system, from capturing your old photos to capturing and interpreting text.

Ready? Then smile!

Working with a Digital Camera

Behind the fancy graphical front end that takes photos from your camera and lets you work with them on your Linux system is a little package called *gPhoto2*. This package is actually a back end used by various other graphical programs, including, as you will see shortly, Konqueror.

A number of digital cameras are supported through gPhoto2; 433 of them as I write this chapter. To discover whether your camera is supported directly, shell out and type:

```
gphoto2 --list-cameras
```

You should see output similar to the following shortened list:

```
Number of supported cameras: 433
Supported cameras:
 "AEG Snap 300"
 "Agfa CL18"
 "Agfa ePhoto 1280"
 "Apple QuickTake 200"
 "Apple QuickTake 200"
 "Argus DC-100"
 "Barbie"
 "Canon PowerShot A20"
 "Canon PowerShot S10"
 "Canon PowerShot S100"
 "Chinon ES-1000"
 "DE300 Canon Inc."
 "Digitaldream DIGITAL 2000"
 "Epson PhotoPC 500"
 "Epson PhotoPC 550"
```

If your camera is not listed, don't despair. A visit to the gPhoto web site (`http://gphoto.sourceforge.net`) for an updated version of the software may be all you need.

Picture-Perfect Konqueror

Getting images from your USB digital camera is not at all difficult. Connect your camera to your Linux system via the USB cable. Every camera is a little different, but all have some kind of switch or setting to turn them on and allow transfer to the PC. Mine has a little jagged line with arrows at either side to represent a connection. Check your camera's manual for details.

Depending on your Linux distribution, a camera icon may appear on your desktop when you plug in the camera. When you click on that icon, Konqueror opens and your camera's internal directories are there for you to see. If such an icon doesn't magically appear, it's time for your old friend, Konqueror, to come to the rescue.

If it isn't already open, bring up Konqueror's navigation sidebar by pressing <F9>. Type `camera:/` in the Konqueror location field, and press <Enter>. You should see your digital camera listed in Konqueror's main window. The USB-connected camera on my system shows up as Canon PowerShot S10 (Figure 30-1). Click on that icon, and you'll see folders corresponding to the way your camera stores its images. Just navigate down those directories until you get to your photo directories.

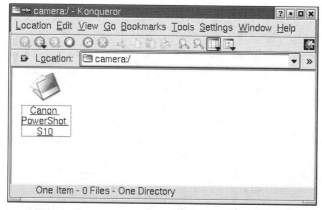

FIGURE 30-1   Konqueror is the easiest way to get pictures from your USB camera.

Quick Tip If you want a preview of your images, click View on Konqueror's menu bar, select Preview from the menu bar, and check off Images in the drop-down list. You should now see little thumbnail images (Figure 30-2) corresponding to the images on your camera.

FIGURE 30-2   Pictures appear as thumbnails in Konqueror.

To move or copy your photos into a folder, select the images you wish (or press <Ctrl+A> for all the images) and drag them into a folder in the navigation window on the left side. That is all there is to it.

Note If you are looking for something more full-featured when it comes to working with your camera, consider taking a look at Digikam (http://digikam.sourceforge.net). This package features a super-friendly interface through which you can sort and organize your photos into albums. Digikam offers numerous features from simple editing to tight integration with other KDE apps so you can scan with Kooka (which I'll cover shortly), email images, drag and drop with Konqueror, and much more.

Scanning

In smaller offices, scanners can be far more than a way to create digital copies of photographs or images. People use them as a photocopier or a means of sending a fax as well. Your Linux system *talks* to your scanner using a package called *SANE* (Scanner Access Now Easy). In all likelihood, it is installed on your system already. If not, look for two packages: `sane-backends` and `sane-frontends`.

There are many scanner options available, from old-fashioned parallel port devices to SCSI-connected scanners. These days, most people choose a USB scanner for its low price and easy connection to the system. As with all devices, a visit to the USB devices for Linux web site (`http://www.qbik.ch/usb/devices/`) will save you time and money by helping you select a device that is well-suited to run under Linux. Assuming your scanner is supported under Linux, getting it recognized is sometimes just a matter of plugging it in. In some cases, you may have to do a little configuration. I'm going to use an Epson USB scanner as an example to give you an idea of what might be required. On one of my systems, the scanner was instantly and automatically configured as soon as I plugged it in. On another, I had to do a little work. Here's what you would do.

Start by plugging in your scanner and, if necessary, turning it on; some scanners are on as soon as you plug them in. Any recent Linux distribution should do a very nice job of automatically noticing your scanner and loading the appropriate driver. Depending on your system, your USB scanner will be represented by the filename `/dev/scanner0` or `/dev/usb/scanner0`. You may want to check for the existence of this file; to do so, open a shell and type:

```
ls -l /dev/scanner0
```

or

```
ls -l /dev/usb/scanner0
```

Another way to check for the existence of your scanner is to use the command:

```
sane-find-scanner
```

This command is part of the SANE package. In response to it, you'll get several lines of text and information. Look for lines that begin with the word "found," such as:

```
found USB scanner (vendor=0x04b8, product=0x0110) at
/dev/usb/scanner0
```

Before you can use your USB scanner, you may have to do a little setup work. Luckily, this is pretty simple, and *you have to do it only once*. For starters, it is possible that you *may* have to create the device file for your scanner manually. If the file isn't there, open a shell and switch to the root user with the command:

```
su - root
```

Then use these commands to create the USB scanner device file and make it usable by all users:

```
mknod /dev/usbscanner0 c 180 48
chmod 666 /dev/usbscanner0
```

You are almost there. Still running as root, change directory to /etc/sane.d and do an ls in that directory. You'll see a number of files ending in .conf and prefixed by a scanner brand name. In the case of my Epson scanner, I had to edit the /etc/sane.d/epson.conf file and change the following line:

```
#usb /dev/usb/scanner0
```

That # character at the beginning denotes a comment. *Removing* that character makes the line *real*. Once you make the change, save and exit your file, then type the following to load up the scanner module:

```
modprobe scanner
```

Type exit to leave the root shell, then exit again to close Konsole.

Sharing a Scanner on Your Network

Let's take a little side trip here before we actually get into scanning tools. If you have an employee dedicated to doing graphical design work, I can pretty much guarantee they have their own scanner at their side. Others may need only occasional access to a scanner. With the *saned* package (you may have to install this one), it is possible to make a scanner available to other users on other workstations. Setting this up is extremely easy. The first step is to make sure that saned is installed.

On the server side, you need to edit the /etc/sane.d/saned.conf file. This is just a text list of clients that are allowed to use the local scanner device. Clients can be listed as a host name, an IP address, or a range of IPs in CIDR notation (discussed in Chapter 9, "Networks and Internet Connections"). Here's a sample.

```
clientpc1.mydomain.dom
192.168.22.0/24
```

Each client needs an entry in their `/etc/sane.d/net.conf` file indicating the address of the server. Again, this is a simple text file with host or IP information for the server.

```
scan_server.mydomain.dom
192.168.22.155
```

Now, let's take a look at the tools to use a scanner.

Scanning under KDE: Kooka

A number of scanning programs exist for Linux, and most are front ends to SANE. One such front end is included with your Linux system: *Kooka*, which is part of KDE.

Kooka is both a scan and optical character recognition (OCR) program. What this means is that you can use it to scan a document of text and export that text back into a word processing package of some sort for further editing.

You'll find Kooka under the main Multimedia or Graphics menu, but you can also start the program from the shell or with your quicklauncher <Alt+F2>. The actual program name is `kooka`. When you start the program, you will see a dialog box similar to that in Figure 30-3. Kooka looks for available scanners and offers you a choice. If you have only one scanner on your system (as is usually the case), check the box labeled Do Not Ask on Startup Again, Always Use this Device before clicking OK.

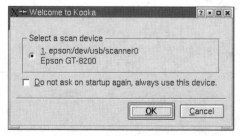

FIGURE 30-3   Kooka autodetects your connected scanner.

Once you are past this point, Kooka's main window appears (Figure 30-4). It is made up of three primary areas, or *frames*. The two horizontal frames to the left consist of a navigation window up top and a Scanner Setting window at the bottom. The large right side is the scan window itself. Along the top, you'll see a familiar-looking menu and icon bar. You can resize the main window to suit your tastes (and monitor size), as well as the individual frames.

Let's start by having a look at the navigation window and its two tabs here: Gallery and Preview. Ignore the Preview tab for now and click on the Gallery tab. Now, look directly beneath those tabs. Notice a directory and file browser with a default directory called Kooka Gallery. You can create additional folders below this by right-clicking on the directory and selecting Create Directory. As with all such dialogs, you can create directories inside of directories to organize your files efficiently. Scanned files will be saved in these directories.

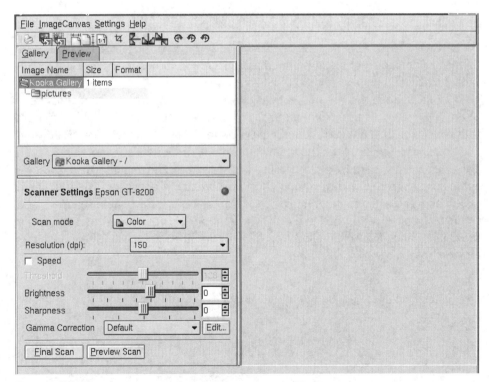

FIGURE 30-4   Kooka's main screen and work area.

Before scanning your first image, look down at the bottom-left window, where you make your scanner settings. What you see there will vary, depending on the model and type of scanner you are running. On my system, I used an Epson GT-8200. You can adjust scan mode (black and white, grayscale, or color), as well as resolution. Keep in mind that although higher resolution generally means higher quality, it also means a *much larger file* in terms of storage space. For web page purposes, 75 to 100dpi is probably ideal.

On my scanner, I can also adjust the brightness, sharpness, and gamma correction. The correct settings are somewhat of a trial-and-error affair. More than one scan may be necessary to decide what works and looks best.

Note These settings are scanner-specific, and different scanners may have different settings.

Find a photograph or picture you like, and put it on the scanner. Click the Preview Scan button in the Scanner Settings window. After the scan is complete, you can preview the results by clicking on the Preview tab in the top-left window.

In the image preview window, you can select the scan size to define the actual dimensions of the scanned file. If you want only a small portion of the photo, you can also drag the dotted lines in the preview window (with the mouse) to encompass only the part you wish to save. When you are happy with the preview, click Final Scan in the settings window.

When the scan is complete, the Kooka Save Assistant appears (Figure 30-5). It displays the various image formats available, along with a description to help you decide which format you wish to use. For instance, JPEG is described as a "high compression, quality losing format for color pictures with many different colors." If you are always saving in the same format, you can elect to click the check box labeled Don't Ask Again for the Save Format If It Is Defined. Should you change your mind, click Settings on the menu bar, and select Configure Kooka. Under Image Saving, you can elect to bring back the Save Assistant.

FIGURE 30-5   The Save Assistant helps you choose the file format.

After you click OK, your scanned picture appears in the scan window to the right (Figure 30-6). You can select view options, such as Scale to Width, Set Zoom, or Rotate Image Clockwise by right-clicking on the image. Switch back to the Gallery view by clicking the tab on the right side; scanned images now appear with sequentially assigned names.

FIGURE 30-6   The final scan.

Saving Your Work

In a strange way, your images are already saved. In your home directory, you'll find another directory called .kde, which contains your KDE configuration files, Kmail address books, Konqueror bookmarks, and other files. As it turns out, your scanned images are already saved there, although technically, they are still work files. If you want to have a look, check out .kde/share/apps/ScanImages in your home directory. If you created new directories in your Gallery, you'll see them as well.

To *officially* save your work in Kooka, right-click on one of your scanned images in the Gallery frame (top left), and select Save Image. You are presented with the standard KDE save dialog. Choose a directory and a name for your image, and click Save (Figure 30-7).

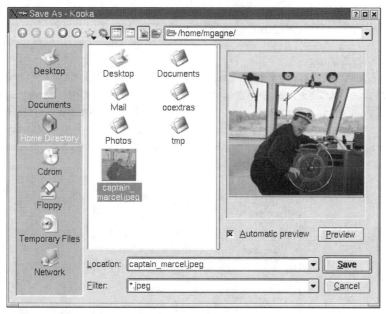

FIGURE 30-7 *Now it is time to save your images.*

You can now take that image, fire up the GIMP, and modify it at will.

The GIMP? I'll cover that very soon. I still have a little scanning magic to share with you.

Optical Character Recognition

Before I wrap up this discussion of Kooka, let me tell you about one other very cool thing the program does. Say you have an old document page that you want to transcribe. The obvious first choice is to sit it in front of you, open up a word processor, and start typing. Your second option is to pop that page on your scanner, use Kooka to scan it, then run it through OCR.

Here's how you do it. Because most people won't be using OCR, most distributions don't install the supporting software by default. Visit `jocr.sourceforge.net` (that is not a typo) or check your distribution CDs for a package called *gocr* and install it. Kooka uses it to do OCR.

Start by scanning your page as you would any image. Binary scan mode is probably fine for straight text but this is one case where *the higher the resolution, the better your chances* are of an accurate OCR. When you are happy with the preview, click Final Scan, and you should see your page in the right window. Now click ImageCanvas on the menu bar, and select OCR Image. Alternatively, you can click the second icon from the left in the icon bar—it does the same thing.

A window labeled Optical Character Recognition pops up (Figure 30-8), which allows you to specify a handful of settings to tune the character recognition software. Remember; OCR is not perfect by any means, but with some tweaking, you can achieve fairly high levels of accuracy. For your first scan, simply leave it at the defaults and click Start OCR. The whole process of character recognition may take a few seconds, so be patient.

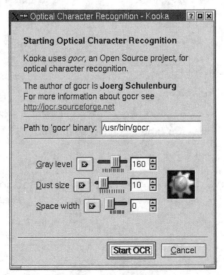

FIGURE 30-8   OCR settings.

Upon completion, a window appears showing you the results of the OCR process (Figure 30-9).

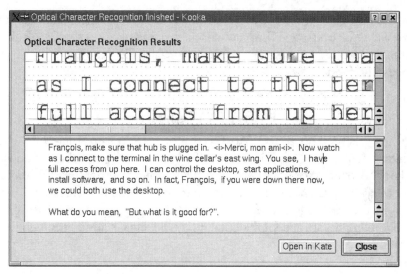

FIGURE 30-9   Kooka OCR results window.

If you want to save the results, click Open in Kate, which starts KDE's multipurpose text editor. Once in the editor, click File from the menu bar, select Save As, and you'll be able to save the document in whatever directory you wish. You then can edit further with OpenOffice.org Writer or whatever word processor suits your needs.

Welcome to the GIMP

The GIMP is one of the programs that has helped create an identity for Linux. Of course, there are plenty of programs out there, as I'm sure I have demonstrated by this point in the book, but the GIMP is special in some ways. The Linux community has used it to create images, buttons, desktop themes, window decorations, and more. Even the Linux mascot, Tux the Penguin, as created by Larry Ewing (the mascot's best-known incarnation) was a product of the GIMP.

The GIMP is an amazingly powerful piece of software. With a little bit of work, a lot of fun, and a hint of experimentation, anyone can use the GIMP to turn out a fantastic piece of professional-quality art. You doubt my words?

Then follow along with me, and in just a few minutes, you'll have created a slick-looking logo for your web page or your desktop. That said, with time, you can also learn to wield the GIMP with the power of a Hollywood special-effects master.

Ladies and gentlemen, start your GIMP. Click on the application starter (the big K), scroll up to the Graphics submenu, and click on the GIMP. You can also use your program quickstart by pressing <Alt+F2> and entering gimp into the command field.

The First Time

If you are starting up the GIMP for the very first time, the GIMP User Installation dialog appears (Figure 30-10). It asks you a number of questions regarding the location of your personal GIMP directory (defaults to a directory called .gimp-version.no under your personal home directory), how much memory you wish to allocate for the GIMP to do its work, and so on. For the most part, you can just accept the defaults by clicking Continue through the various screens.

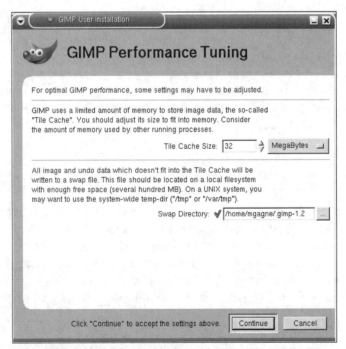

FIGURE 30-10 When you start the GIMP for the first time, you'll need to adjust a few settings.

Immediately after the performance tuning screen, you'll be asked for your monitor's resolution. If you plan on doing particularly fine work and you would like the GIMP to display images in their natural sizes, you should adjust your monitor's resolution. If you know the resolution, you can enter it manually, or accept the default of 72dpi.

Your final option for absolute accuracy is to click on the Calibrate button. When a ruler appears on your screen (Figure 30-11), measure it with a physical ruler and enter the actual size into the fields provided. When you are happy, click OK. This method can yield very different results from the defaults. My settings came in at 84.848 pixels per inch for the X axis (horizontal) and 85.106 pixels per inch for the Y axis (vertical).

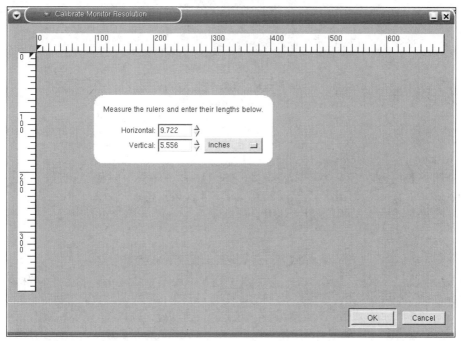

FIGURE 30-11   Fine-tuning the GIMP to match your monitor resolution.

Once you have entered all of this information, the GIMP proper starts up. You will probably get a number of panels aside from the GIMP's main screen. You will also likely get the GIMP Tip of the Day. As with all such tips, you can elect not to have one appear each time the program starts. Uncheck the Show Tip Next Time Gimp Starts button before you hit Close, and you won't be bothered with them again. As for those additional windows (Layers, Tools Options, and Brush Selection), closing them before you close the GIMP ensures they don't come up by default.

The most important of those windows is the GIMP toolbox (Figure 30-12). Let us take a few moments to get familiar with it.

FIGURE 30-12
The GIMP toolbox.

Along the top and directly below the title bar is a familiar-looking menu bar labeled, quite simply, File, Xtns, and Help. Clicking on these shows you additional submenus. Below the menu bar is a grid of icons, each with an image representing one of the GIMP's tools. I will cover all of these things shortly, but first let's take the GIMP out for a spin.

Easy Logos with the GIMP

The nitty-gritty can wait. I think we should do something fun with the GIMP right now. I'm going to show you how to create a very cool-looking corporate or personal logo with just a few keystrokes. If you don't have the GIMP open yet, start the program now. From the main toolbox menu bar, select Xtns, scroll down to Script-Fu, and another menu will cascade from it.

Quick Tip Notice that the menus have a dashed line at the top. These are menu tear-offs, and you have seen them before when working with the KDE menus. By clicking on the dashed line, you can detach the menu and put it somewhere on your desktop for convenient access to functions you use all the time. In fact, all of the menus, including submenus, can be detached.

From the Script-Fu menu, move your mouse to Logos. You should see a whole list of logo types, 3D Outline, Cool Metal, Starscape, and more. For this exercise, choose Cool Metal.

Every logo has different settings, so the one you see in Figure 30-13 is specific to Cool Metal. Particle Trace, for example, has a completely different set of parameters. To create your Cool Metal logo, start by changing the Text field to something other than the logo style's name. I typed *Linux rocks!* for mine. The font size is set to 100 pixels; leave it at that for now.

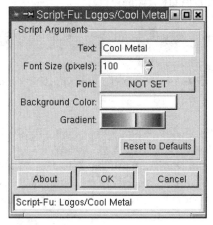

FIGURE 30-13   *Script-Fu logo settings.*

You haven't yet set the font, so click the NOT SET button and pick a font style and size from the list that pops up. The Font Select window shows you the various fonts available on your system and lets you try different font types, styles, and sizes. A preview window gives you an idea of what the font looks like (Figure 30-14). If you want, you can even change the text in the preview window from the default of abcdefghijk ABCDEFGHIJK to your own words, so that you can really see what it will look like.

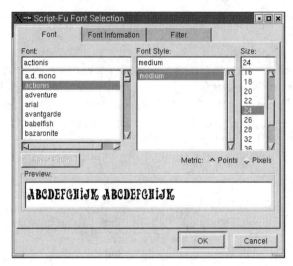

FIGURE 30-14   Script-Fu font selection dialog.

As I wrote this part of the book, I was working on a Mandrake test system and chose a font called actionis (actually, I used several distributions during the course of this book). You may choose whatever you like. When you have decided on a font, click OK. Then click OK again, this time in the Script-Fu:Logos/Cool Metal window. The result should be something similar to my own logo in Figure 30-15.

FIGURE 30-15   Just like that! A professional-looking logo.

If you don't like the results, close the image by clicking the close button in the corner (usually an X unless you have changed your desktop theme or style).

A warning box pops up, telling you that changes have been made and that perhaps you might want to save your work (more on that in a moment). Click Close, and it goes away. Then start over with another logo. You might try changing the background color or the gradient this time. You might even want to try a different type of logo altogether.

Saving and Opening Your Work

Now it is time to preserve your masterpiece. To save your work, right-click anywhere on the generated logo, select File from the pop-up menu, then click Save As. From the Save Image dialog box that appears, double-click on the directory you wish to save in.

Before you type in a filename, pay some attention to the Save Options. The default is indicated as By Extension. What this means is that I can save an image as JPG format simply by typing a filename such as mylogo.jpg (Figure 30-16) or as PNG format by typing mylogo.png. Most will do this, but you can also select from a number of supported file types (and there are many) by clicking the By Extension button and selecting your file type.

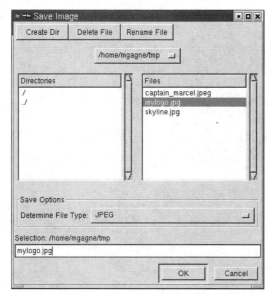

FIGURE 30-16   Now it is time to save your work.

After you enter your filename and select a file type, click OK—you're done.

Opening a file is similar. From the GIMP toolbox menu bar, select Open (or use the <Ctrl+O> shortcut) to bring up the Load Image dialog. The difference between this and the Save Image dialog is that when you click on a filename, you can also click on Generate Preview to display a small thumbnail preview in the Load Image dialog.

Printing Your Masterpiece

You've created a masterpiece. You are infinitely proud of it, and you want to share it with your friends, who, alas, are not connected to the Internet. It's time to print your image and send it to them the old-fashioned, snail-mail way.

Okay, perhaps you aren't feeling quite that sharing, but there are times when you'll want to print the results of your work. Simply right-click on your image, move your mouse over to the File menu, and select Print. A printing dialog box appears (Figure 30-17), from which you can specify a number of print options, including, of course, which printer you would like to use.

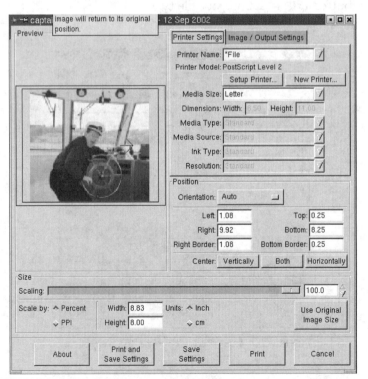

FIGURE 30-17   Time to print your masterpiece.

Quick Tip Some distributions include the GIMP's printing functionality as a separate package, perhaps because images are usually imported into other applications, such as word processors. That package is called *gimpprint* and it may have to be installed separately.

Tools, Tools, and More Tools

Now that we've had some fun and created some *true art*, it's time to find out what all of those icons in the GIMP toolbox do. First, however, look at those two boxes at the bottom of the toolbox, because what they offer affects what the icons do.

The block on the right is the color menu (Figure 30-18). It gives you quick and easy access to foreground and background colors. The black and white squares on the left can be changed to other colors by double-clicking on one or the other. If you click on the arrow between the two, you switch between foreground and background colors.

FIGURE 30-18   Color menu.

The box to the right is a quick dialog menu and really consists of three tools: a brush selector, a pattern selector, and a gradient selector. Click on any of them to bring up the list of choices each provides (Figure 30-19).

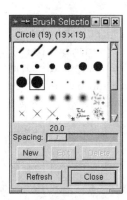

FIGURE 30-19   Brush selection.

If you select a different gradient, pattern, or brush from the resulting menus, you'll see them change on the dialog menu at the bottom of the GIMP toolbox as well. This gives you a quick visual feedback on which brush, pattern, or gradient is active at the moment.

Now, on to the Tool Icons

Start by moving your mouse over the various icons, pausing over each one to read the tool tips describing their associated tools. If you double-click on any of these icons, a new window appears, providing you with that tool's options (Figure 30-20).

FIGURE 30-20   Tool Options dialog.

So what are all those icons for? An excellent question. Let's look at them again, one row at a time, starting with—you guessed it—the first row (Figure 30-21).

 **FIGURE 30-21**   First icon group.

The first icon, represented by a dotted rectangle, lets you select a *rectangular* area. Just hold down the left mouse button at whatever point you choose for a starting corner, and drag it across your image. A dotted line indicates the area you've selected. If you hold down the <Shift> key at the same time as the left mouse button, your selections always will be perfect squares.

 Quick Tip To undo changes, press <Ctrl+Z>.

The dotted circle icon next to it is much the same, except that it selects *circular* or *elliptical* areas. As with the rectangular select, you can hold down the <Shift> key along with the left mouse button to select only perfect circles.

Next, we have the *Lasso* tool. This is another selection tool, but this one lets you select irregular or hand-drawn regions. Hold down the left mouse button, and *draw* your selection around the object.

 Quick Tip When you have selected an area on an image, you can right-click, move your mouse cursor over the Edit menu, and select Cut or Copy. You can then paste your selection back to another part of the image.

Next comes the *Magic Wand*. This is a strange tool to get used to. It selects an area by analyzing the colored pixels wherever you click. Holding down the <Shift> key lets you select multiple areas. This is a very useful tool, but it is also a little tricky. Double-click on the icon to change the sensitivity.

Finally, we finish the first row with the *Bezier* tool, which, to be honest, takes some getting used to. Once you get used to it, however, you'll be impressed with the flexibility it affords you in selecting both straight and curved areas. Click a point outside the area you want to select, and it creates an anchor point. Click again a little further along your outline, and you get new anchor points with a straight line connecting to the original. Click and drag an existing anchor point, and a *bar* appears with control boxes on either end. You can then grab those control points and drag or rotate them to modify the straight line between the points. Once you have joined the final point, click inside the outlined region to complete your selection. You'll see an animated dotted line, as with the other selection tools.

That wraps it up for the first row of tools. It's time to look at the next set (Figure 30-22).

 **FIGURE 30-22**   Second icon group.

We've still got one last selection tool to look at, the *Intelligent Scissors*. These will remind you somewhat of the Bezier tool, in that you select an area by clicking around it. What this tool does that the other does not is follow curved lines around an object. It does so by concentrating on areas of similar contrast or color. Simply click around the perimeter of the area you wish to select and watch the lines magically draw themselves. When you join the last dot, click inside the area to select it.

The second icon on the second row looks like a cross with arrows pointing in all directions. This is the *Move* tool. It is really quite simple. Click the tool, then grab the selected area on the screen and move it to where you want. If you haven't selected an area, you can move the entire image in the window.

The *Magnifying Glass* does exactly what you expect it to. Click an area of the screen to zoom in. Double-click the icon to reverse the zoom. This doesn't actually scale the image, it just changes your view of things. Zoom is usually used to make working on a small area of the image easier.

On to the knife icon: the *Crop* tool. I use the Crop tool all the time when I am trying to get a small part of a larger image. In fact, I used it to separate the rows of icons from the GIMP toolbox image I captured. Click on a part of the screen, drag it to encompass the area you want to keep, and click Crop when asked to confirm. You can also fine-tune the settings (X and Y position, and so on) at this time.

The final item on this row is the *Transform* tool, and it is really quite interesting. By default, this is a rotation tool. Click on an image or a selection, and a grid appears over your image or the selection. Grab a point on the grid, drag the mouse, and the grid rotates. When you have it in a position you like, click Rotate on the pop-up window that appears. The image locks into place. But that's not all: Double-click on the Transform tool's icon, and three additional capabilities appear: scaling, shearing, and perspective.

On to row three and Figure 30-23.

 **FIGURE 30-23**   Third icon row.

The first box is the *Flip* tool. By default, it flips the image horizontally. Double-click the icon to bring up the menu, and you can change it to flip vertically.

The next icon is the *Text* tool. That's what the big T signifies. Click on your image, and the font selection box you used for your logo appears. Select a font, type in your text in the Preview section, and click OK. Where the text appears on the screen, the Move tool is activated, enabling you to place the text accurately. The color of the text will be your current foreground color.

The third icon looks like an eyedropper. This is the *Color Picker*. Choosing an exact color can be difficult (if you need to get the tone just right), but if the color you want is on your existing image, click on that spot, and you've got it (your default active color will change).

Closely related to this is the fourth button on the third row, the paint can. This is the *Fill* tool. It can fill a selected area not only with a chosen color but with a pattern as well. To choose between color and pattern fill, double-click on the icon to bring up its menu.

The last item on this line is the *Gradient Fill* tool. Start by selecting an area on your image, then switch to this tool. Now click on a spot inside your selected area, and drag with the tool. The current gradient style will fill that area. This is one of those things you almost need to try in order to understand what I mean.

And now...row 4 (Figure 30-24)!

 **FIGURE 30-24**   Fourth row icons.

The first icon looks like a *pencil*. In fact, this and the next three buttons all work with a brush selection (the bottom right box). This pencil, as with a real pencil, is used to draw lines with sharply defined edges. Try drawing on your image with the different types to get an idea of what each brush type offers.

 Quick Tip Would you like a blank canvas right about now? Click File on the GIMP toolbox menu bar and select New.

The next icon is the *Paintbrush* tool. The difference between it and the pencil is that the brush has softer, less starkly defined edges to the strokes. Double-click the icon to bring up the Paintbrush's menu, and try both the Fade Out and Gradient options for something different.

If the next icon looks like an *eraser*, that's no accident. The shape of the Eraser tool is also controlled by the current brush type, size, and style. Here's something kind of fun to try. Double-click on the icon to bring up its menu, then change the Opacity to something around 50%. Then start erasing again.

Now it's on to the *Airbrush* tool. Just like with a real airbrush, you can change the pressure to achieve different results. Hold it down longer in one spot, and you'll get a darker application of color.

Finally, we have the *Clone tool* (the icon looks a bit like a rubber stamp). Sheep? No problem! We can even clone humans. Okay, that's a bit over the top. Where the clone tool comes in handy is during touch-ups of photographs. Open an image, hold down the <Ctrl> key, and press the left mouse button over a portion of the image. When the tool changes to a crosshair, let go of both the mouse button and the <Ctrl> key. This is your starting area for cloning. Now move to another part of the screen, click, and start moving your mouse button (the shape of the area uncovered is controlled by the brush type). As you paint at this new location, you'll notice that you are re-creating that portion of the image where you indicated with the <Ctrl+mouse-click> combination. Start with someone's head or body, and you can have twins on the screen.

And now, the last row of icons (Figure 30-25)!

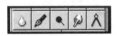 **FIGURE 30-25**   The final group.

The droplet you see on the first item represents the *Convolver* tool. Use it to blur or sharpen parts of an image. You switch between the two operations by double-clicking the icon and selecting the operation you want. Change the rate to make the effect more pronounced.

Next we arrive at another drawing tool, the pen, or *Ink* tool. Double-clicking the icon brings up a menu that lets you select the tip style and shape as well as the virtual tilt of the pen. The idea is to mimic the effect of writing with a fountain pen.

The *Dodge and Burn* tool looks like a stick-pin, but those who have worked in a darkroom might recognize it for something different—a stick with an opaque circle on the end of it. It is used to adjust the brightness or shade of various parts of an image (a photograph might have been partly overexposed).

On to the finger, or the *Smudge* tool. Pretend that you are painting. You press your finger on the wet paint and move it around. The Smudge tool has exactly the same effect on your virtual canvas.

Finally, we round up tools with the calipers, or *Measuring* tool. This doesn't actually change anything on your image but reports. Click a starting point on the image, then drag the mouse pointer to another part of the image. Now look at the bottom of your image window. You'll see the distance in pixels from your starting location to where you let go of the mouse pointer. The angle of the line will also be displayed.

Touching Up Photographs

I've mentioned the idea of touching up photographs on a few occasions while I discussed the tools. The GIMP is a wonderful tool for this and more than just a little fun. One of the most common functions I use is changing the light levels on photographs, automagically and instantly. After all, light levels are rarely perfect unless you are a professional photographer and paying attention to every shot. Here's what I do.

Right-click on the image to bring up the GIMP menu. Now move to the Image submenu, move over to Colors, and select Levels. You should see a window like the one in Figure 30-26. Notice the Auto button? That's where the magic is. I've found that more often than not, you can get a nice, dependable reset of levels just by clicking it.

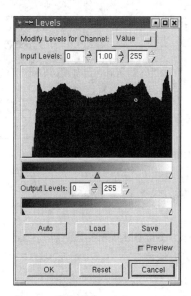

FIGURE 30-26   Adjusting levels with the GIMP.

Yes, you can modify contrast, brightness, or color, but there are also the silly and *just plain fun* things you can do.

For instance, open an image in the GIMP, perhaps one you scanned in earlier. If you don't have something handy, grab an image from a web site. This is just something to play with. Now right-click on the image, and choose Filters by moving your mouse to that part of the menu. A submenu opens with even more options. You might want to detach this menu; you'll certainly want to play with what is there.

Try FlareFX under the Light Effects menu. If you've ever taken a flash picture through a window, you'll recognize this effect. Then try Emboss under the Distorts submenu. The effect is that of a metal-embossed picture (Figure 30-27).

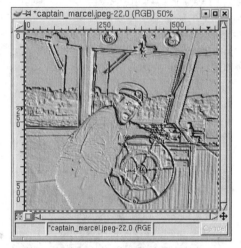

FIGURE 30-27   The Emboss filter.

Take some time to try the various filter options. When you are finished there, right-click on a fresh image and select the Script-Fu menu. There are other interesting effects available here, as well, such as Clothify under the Alchemy submenu. Your image will look as though it had been transferred to a piece of cloth.

So What Is Script-Fu?

Although it sounds like a strange form of martial arts, Script-Fu is, in fact, a scripting language that is part of the GIMP. With it, you can create scripts that automate a number of repetitive tasks to create desirable effects. When you created your logo, you might have noticed that a number of things were happening during the process. Try another logo and watch carefully what is happening. These steps are part of a Script-Fu script.

The GIMP comes with a number of Script-Fu scripts, and these are used for much more than just creating logos. Click Xtns on the GIMP toolbox, and scroll down to the Script-Fu menu. In addition to logos, you'll see options for creating buttons (for web pages), custom brushes, patterns, and more. Play. Experiment. Don't be afraid.

Open an image, right-click on it, and scroll down to the Script-Fu part of the menu. Another menu drops down with such selections as Alchemy, Decore, Render, and so on. These are all pre-created effects that would ordinarily require many repetitious steps. Script-Fu is very much like a command script, where one command follows another. In this case, the commands just happen to be graphical transformations.

Becoming a GIMP Guru

You can make some pretty cool images with the GIMP with just a little knowl-edge, but with time and further exploration, you can take that cool to the level of amazing. Make no mistake, the GIMP is a professional-grade tool, and cov-ering it in detail would fill a book of its own.

Consider a visit to the GIMP home page at `www.gimp.org` for the latest developments, software, and links to other GIMP documents.

Resources

Digikam
http://digikam.sourceforge.net

The GIMP
www.gimp.org

gocr
http://jocr.sourceforge.net

gPhoto
http://gphoto.sourceforge.net

Linux–USB Device Overview
http://www.qbik.ch/usb/devices/

31

Instant Messaging

The Internet was born on communication; email specifically was the tool that drove its development into the globe-spanning network that it is today. That's the reason why email is so important. It's also the reason why we hate spammers. These days, however, a new kind of communication has evolved—call it "mini-email." The one-liner. The short and sweet message. The instant message. The Net-connected society has grown to love these quick, always-on means of sending each other information.

Instant messaging (IM) is no longer strictly the playground of teenagers or friends and family looking to keep in touch across the networked world. It is rapidly becoming a serious tool for business as well. In some environments, IM is being added to the list of business-critical applications. Nothing beats being in constant touch with employees and team members, even if those people are scattered in offices around the globe. It's also a perfect means of communication for people on the move. Plug in, get online, and you are immediately available, wherever you are.

If your enterprise is ready to wade into the IM waters, you will soon discover that IM is a many-headed beast with protocols galore. There is MSN, Yahoo, Jabber, and a raft of others. You could run a client of each, but manipulating every package with its various idiosyncrasies may be more than some people are willing to put up with. The real solution is an IM client that supports all those formats so that you can chat with people regardless of which IM provider they have chosen. In this chapter, I'm going to show you two excellent packages.

What is Jabber?

Glad you asked. Jabber is an instant messaging protocol. In that respect, it is similar to those used by other providers such as the aforementioned AOL, Yahoo!, or MSN. Unlike these other messaging systems, Jabber is open source and open protocol. It's XML architecture uses the industry standard extensible messaging and presence protocol, or XMPP. As of this writing, Jabber/XMPP is also the only full-featured IM protocol ratified by the IETF (Internet Engineering Task Force).

There are several reasons aside from the two I just mentioned (open source and open protocol). The Jabber protocol doesn't belong to any one in particular, so there is no company driving its destiny, although companies are using Jabber. Jabber uses a decentralized approach, so the system is more robust. In fact, anyone can run a Jabber server. This is a boon to companies that may want to run a private, secure instant-messaging network.

Whether you choose to run Jabber, Yahoo, MSN, or something else, the ideal instant messaging client is a multiprotocol client, one that lets you talk to all of these services without having to run a client for Jabber, one for AOL, one for Yahoo, one for...well, you get the idea. In this chapter, I'm going to cover two superb Linux instant messaging clients. Both provide not only great multiprotocol support, but IRC as well.

I'll start with KDE's Kopete.

Kopete

Making its debut as part of KDE 3.2, Kopete is a powerful, multiprotocol instant-messaging system. It supports a plug-in based architecture, making it possible to extend the package with a variety of additional features. Some of the existing features include history, translation tools, text effects, cryptography, and more. Because it is part of KDE, it fits nicely into the desktop and docks into the system tray when not in use. It uses both sound notifications and passive text alerts that let you continue working.

You'll find Kopete under your Internet submenu in the program launcher. It's program name is kopete, which means you can launch it from the shell or with your <Alt+F2> keyboard shortcut. When Kopete starts for the first time, the Configure window pops up along with the main (currently empty) Kopete window (Figure 31-1).

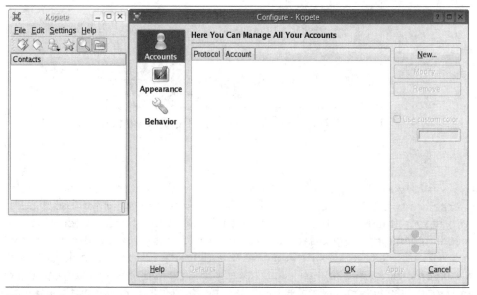

FIGURE 31-1   First time out with Kopete.

Time to create a new account: In the Configure Kopete dialog, make sure Accounts is selected in the left bar (this is the default), and click the New button on the right. The Add Account wizard appears. Click Next past the introductory screen to the protocol selection screen (Figure 31-2). You'll be presented with a list of the protocols supported by Kopete. These are AIM, ICQ, IRC, Jabber, MSN, SMS (telephone text messaging), and Yahoo.

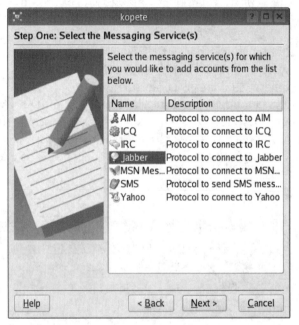

FIGURE 31-2   *Selecting a protocol for a new IM account.*

When you click Next, the Account Information setup window appears. There are two tabs here, one for Basic Setup and the other for Connection information (Figure 31-3). Let's start with the Basic tab. For a Jabber ID, enter a screen name that appeals to you. Keep in mind that you may have to try this more than once to make sure you get something unique (or you could just start with something unique). To avoid having to enter your password each and every time you connect, make sure that the Remember Password check box is checked on. Then, directly below, enter your password.

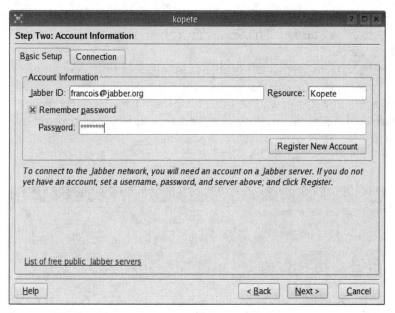

FIGURE 31-3   Registering a new Jabber account.

Quick Tip In my example, I used a screenname@jabber.org ID on the main Jabber public server. There are others, however, which may be closer to you or that offer additional services. You can find out about them right on the current Account setup page under the Basic Setup tab. Notice the blue highlighted words "List of free public Jabber servers." When you click this link, Konqueror launches and take you to Jabber.org's list of available, open, public servers where you can sign up for an account.

It's time to click the Connection tab (Figure 31-4). This one is pretty simple, but you should watch out for a couple of things—the most important deals with the server itself. In the Quick Tip, I mentioned that there are other Jabber servers out there. In fact, your own office may choose to run a Jabber server. That's one of the beauties of this open protocol. Consequently, unless you are registering with the central Jabber server, make sure you enter the correct name in the Server field. Just above that, there's a check box for Connect Automatically at Startup. This is strictly a personal preference, but it is a feature I find handy.

The other items on this tab deal with whether or not secure authentication is used, whether your company goes through a proxy (including whether it requires authentication), and so on. These vary based on the server you register with and with the security requirements in your own company. Home users generally don't need to worry about this.

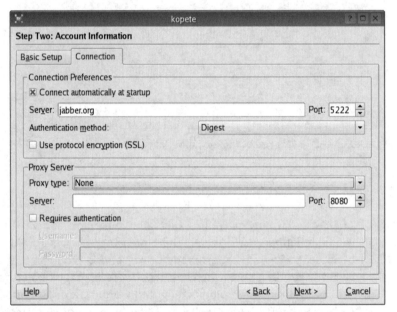

FIGURE 31-4   *Setting up basic account connection information.*

After entering all of your information, go back to the Basic Setup tab and click Register New Account. If you haven't yet seen the KDE Wallet Manager pop up, you may find yourself introduced now. KWallet is a password management tool for KDE that makes it easy to maintain and remember your many passwords. If KWallet has already been configured on your system, you'll have the opportunity to save this new username and password in your system wallet. When the wallet is accessed for the first time since a login, a KDE Wallet Service pop-up appears and asks for your master password.

A successful account registration at this point should mean that you can now connect using the account you just created. In the main Kopete window (Figure 31-5), you should see a little light bulb icon in the bottom-right corner of the main Kopete window. Click on the icon, and a menu of options associated with that account appears, including Go Online. Click Go Online. The light bulb icon will flicker and come on when the connection is established.

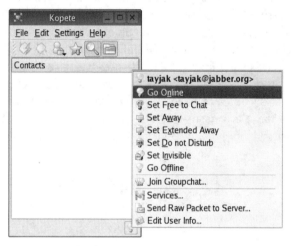

FIGURE 31-5   Kopete's account connection menu.

Quick Tip The account icons vary depending on the service you choose. MSN accounts have a butterfly, Yahoo has a Y with a smiley, ICQ has a flower, and so on.

Adding Kopete Contacts

Before you can chat with anyone, you need to add contacts to your Kopete account or they need to add you. Click File on the menu bar, and select Add Contact. You can also click the appropriate icon. Because Kopete is actually a KDE application, there are some interesting benefits. One of these has to do with adding contacts (sometimes referred to as buddies). When the Contact Addition Wizard appears, it asks you whether you want to use the KDE address book to enter this contact. This means that you can search for someone already in your address book or create a new entry for them as you add them to your Kopete contact list. You'll find a check box for this option at the bottom of this first window. If you don't want to use the address book, just uncheck it.

After you click Next to continue, you are asked to enter the Display Name and Group. At the top of the screen, enter a display name for the person you want to add. This isn't their account name or screen name, but what you want it to look like in your contact list, for example, Elizabeth in sales. Below that field is a list of group names. By default, there is only a Top-Level group, but you can choose to create a new one here, such as Sales, Customers, and so on by clicking the Create New Group button. Make sure that you check on the group you want to use, and click Next. The next screen is where you enter the actual Jabber account information, as in userid@jabber.org. Click Next, then Finish on the final screen, and you have added your contact. After you accept your new contact, they receive a message asking for confirmation, after which they appear in your main Kopete window (Figure 31-6).

FIGURE 31-6   Kopete with active contact list.

To start a chat, double-click on the contact name and type a message in the bottom part of the chat window (Figure 31-7). If someone contacts you for a chat, a passive alert appears near the Kopete icon in the system tray (bottom left of your desktop). Click View to answer the call or Ignore to pass.

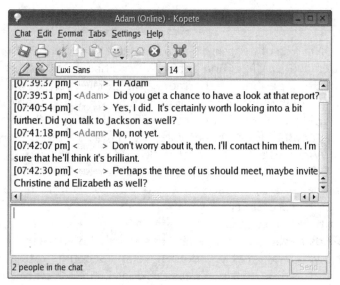

FIGURE 31-7   Holding a Kopete conversation.

Quick Tip By default, you can press the Send button every time you want to send a message or use press <Ctrl+Enter>. If you would like to remap this to be just <Enter>, click Settings on the menu bar of a chat window and select Configure Shortcuts. Scroll down until you see Send Message. Next, change the sequence by clicking the Custom radio button, then click on the <Ctrl+Return> button. A new window appears in which you can clear the current shortcut by clicking the button with the black X next to the word Shortcut, then pressing <Enter>. Finally, click OK to save.

Now that I've got you chatting with Kopete, I'm going to move on to another great instant messaging client called GAIM. Before we go, take a moment to go through some of the other Kopete settings. Just click Settings on the menu bar, and select Configure Kopete or Configure Plugins. You'll find options to configure the chat window, set tabbed messaging windows, configure history, encryption, and much more. It's worth checking out, and it can greatly enhance your Kopete experience.

Instant Messaging with GAIM

On the GNOME side of things, I'd like to introduce you to another great instant messaging package. GAIM is one of the best multiprotocol instant-messaging systems out there, period. Furthermore, this is one you can share with the people you know who are still running Windows—they'll thank you for the favor. With GAIM, they will no longer need a client for Yahoo, another for MSN, and yet another for AOL because GAIM (gaim.sourceforge.net) is available for Windows as well. It even looks and works the same.

To start GAIM, look under your Internet or Networking menu. The actual command name is gaim, in case you would rather start it from the shell or via the <Alt+F2> run program dialog.

The first time you start up GAIM (Figure 31–8), you get a simple window with text fields for Screen Name and Password. The Screen Name field is blank, letting you know that you don't have any accounts set up. Obviously, before you start using instant messaging through GAIM, you are going to need at least one account.

FIGURE 31-8   First time out with GAIM.

Look below the text fields and you'll see three buttons labeled Accounts, Preferences, and Sign On. Click on the Accounts button to open the Accounts window (Figure 31–9). At this stage of the game, there is nothing in it.

FIGURE 31-9   Time to add instant messaging accounts in GAIM's Accounts dialog.

Click Add, and the Add Account window appears. Halfway down that window, you should see a drop-down list labeled Protocol. By default, it says AIM/ICQ. Click on the Protocol button for a number of other possibilities, including AIM/ICQ, Gadu-Gadu, IRC, Jabber, MSN, Napster, TOC, Yahoo, and Zephyr (Figure 31-10).

FIGURE 31-10   GAIM supports a number of different IM protocols.

Select Jabber from the list, and watch as the window changes from AIM/ICQ to reflect the requirements of setting up a Jabber account (Figure 31-11).

FIGURE 31-11   Creating a Jabber account.

Enter your screen name (this doesn't have to be your real name), password (don't use an important password), and alias. To get a free account with Jabber.org, you can leave Server Name as is. In addition, you safely can leave Resource Name as Gaim. Unless you want to be asked for your password each time you log in, click the Remember Password check box. In much the same way, if you would like your GAIM client to log in to Jabber automatically every time you start up the client, click on the Auto-login check box as well.

When you are happy with the information you have entered, click the Register button. The Jabber.org server should respond with a Register New Jabber Account confirmation window that gives you the opportunity to add some additional information, such as an email address. Just click the Register button to confirm, and you are good to go. Your Accounts window should now show your new account (Figure 31-12).

Quick Tip The Jabber.org server provides space and resources for people to get free instant messaging accounts, and you may choose to take advantage of this service. Some companies, however, use their own instant messaging server for security and audit reasons. In this case, you would change Server to be something other than jabber.org, such as chat.yourcompany.dom.

FIGURE 31-12   The Accounts dialog reflects the newly added account.

You can either sign on here (by clicking the Online check box), or click Close and sign on from the main GAIM window. On your first time in, you'll get a welcome message from the Jabber.org server. You can close this window or visit the site for additional information.

Now that you have your very own Jabber instant-messaging account, you need some people to talk to. There are online chats that you can join by clicking Buddies on the menu bar and selecting Join A Chat. You can also use the keyboard shortcut by pressing <Ctrl+C> instead. To add friends to your Buddy List, select Add A Buddy from the menu. Your friends will have to give your their screen names, of course.

After you add your buddies to the list, they get messages letting them know that you want to add them. When they see the pop-up (Figure 31-13), they should click Accept, at which point, you can begin conversations with them.

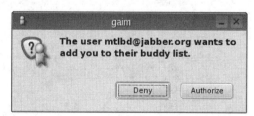

FIGURE 31-13   Accept your new buddy?

This accepting of buddies has to happen at both sides of the connection. They accept you, after which you accept them. Think of it as saying "I do" but to a more casual, dare I say, virtual relationship.

After all of this accepting takes place, your buddies appear in your buddy list (Figure 31-14). The icons beside their names indicate whether your friends are on.

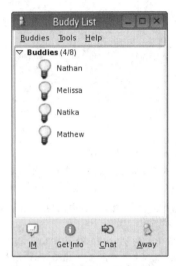

FIGURE 31-14   An active buddy list.

If they are, double-click on their names and start chatting (Figure 31-15). Enter text in the bottom part of the chat window and press <Enter>, or click the Send button to send your message. It is that easy.

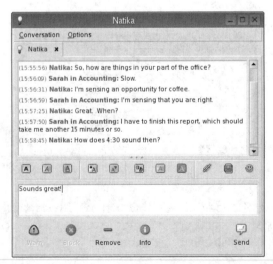

FIGURE 31-15   Chatting with colleagues in GAIM.

What about Windows Users?

One of the really great things about this particular chat client is that it supports so many different protocols up front. You don't need a separate client for Jabber and one for Yahoo and another for MSN and…well, you get the idea. The second nice thing is that the GAIM team also makes a Windows version of the program. For that very reason, you may want to point your friends who are running Windows over to the GAIM web site (`gaim.sourceforge.net`) so they too can cut the clutter and take advantage of this great little piece of software.

Resources

GAIM Instant Messaging

http://gaim.sourceforge.net

Jabber Software Foundation

www.jabber.org

Kopete

http://kopete.kde.org

32

Video Conferencing

Do you remember (2001: A Space Odyssey)?

Now that we are well and truly in the twenty-first century, I can't help but think about all of the promises that that particular vision of the future held, and it makes me a little sad. We have a space station, but it's not quite the movie's majestic wheel in space. There's certainly no lunar base nor orbital hotel, but at least we have webcams, video phones, and video conferencing.

The prevalent use for the webcam is on a web site, providing glimpses into the life of the individual running the site. Some sites provide a camera to reassure us that they are indeed working. Others are there to let parents observe their children playing at day care. The software that captures these images is sometimes called a *frame grabber*.

Note To achieve the highest level of success with the tools discussed in this chapter, I highly recommend making sure you have a recent kernel. This is particularly true, because a number of inexpensive webcams are USB devices and some use pretty bleeding-edge drivers. The more recent the kernel, the more likely these devices will be supported. While writing this chapter, I used two webcams, one based on the CPiA chipset and the other using a ov511 module.

GnomeMeeting

Video communication is now a possibility with Damien Sandras' GnomeMeeting. GnomeMeeting is an H323 video conferencing that provides VOIP (Voice Over IP) telephony so you can place video as well as just straight audio calls using your Internet connection. In keeping with my introduction, thinking of GnomeMeeting as a video telephone is a great analogy.

GnomeMeeting will even work with Microsoft's Netmeeting, so you can talk to your friends running that company's OS. Finally, don't let the name fool you. GnomeMeeting works extremely well with KDE and docks nicely into the panel.

Most modern Linux distributions come with GnomeMeeting, and the required libraries (`pwlib` and `openh323`) on their CD, although not necessarily installed. The `www.gnomemeeting.org` site does have packages for the major distributions (RPMs and debs), as well as source. Certainly look there first. You will need to install `pwlib`, because `openh323` depends on it. On both my Mandrake and Red Hat systems, I installed it using the RPMs. I should point out that although you can build GnomeMeeting from source, the `openh323` libraries can be difficult, not to mention lengthy. If you can use the binaries for this one, I would recommend it.

When starting GnomeMeeting for the first time, you are presented with the First Time Configuration Druid. Part of this process involves registering with the directory of GnomeMeeting users (Figure 32-1)—think of it as a large online telephone directory. You can opt not to be listed by clicking the check box at the bottom of the Druid's registration box. When you are happy with the information you are presenting, click the Forward button to continue. You then are asked to specify the type of connection you are using.

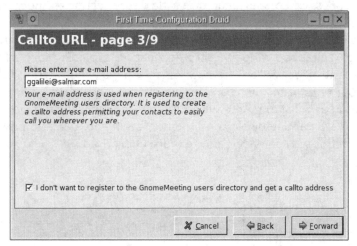

FIGURE 32-1   Registering your name with the GnomeMeeting directory.

Click Apply on the final screen, and GnomeMeeting fires up. You can configure several options with the package by clicking Edit on the menu bar and selecting Preferences. You also can rerun the Druid at any time. The first preference I set was under the Video Devices section. When GnomeMeeting starts up, I like the video preview to be on and the video size set to large.

To place a call to another PC on my local LAN, I type `callto://192.168.22.2` in the GnomeMeeting Location field, which is right below the menu bar. A little pop-up window appears on the second PC warning you of an incoming connection. If you accept the connection, the two clients are able to communicate.

FIGURE 32-2   Answering an incoming call.

Notice the button bar to the left in Figure 32-3. You can turn your video or audio on and off, and you can bring up a chat window for text message exchange. If you have a microphone, GnomeMeeting will make use of that as well. In fact, GnomeMeeting will work under a number of different configurations. You can run video only, audio only, text only, or any combination of the three modes. Of course, it can be a little disconcerting to know that somebody out there can see you, but you can't see them.

When you run GnomeMeeting, make sure you turn on the control panel. It opens up to a tabbed window in the application, providing support for audio and video controls as well as a history window. This window shows the status of calls, your registration with on-line directories, and other information; you can turn it on or off at any time without affecting the transmission.

Figure 32-3 handily displays a GnomeMeeting conversation in progress. Note that in this session, video and text are being used.

FIGURE 32-3   A GnomeMeeting conversation using video and text.

On the 2001 space station, the call was a long-distance one: from space to a little girl on Earth. While chatting inside our offices is fine, what about the outside world? Who are you going to call? The official telephone directory, which

I mentioned earlier while covering the setup for GnomeMeeting, is available at `ils.seconix.com`. To browse the directory and find other users, you must also be registered. Start GnomeMeeting and click on the directory icon to the left. You can also click Tools on the menu bar and select Address Book (Figure 32-4). A window will appear from which you can search for another party—simple...almost.

FIGURE 32-4   Looking up a user with the ILS online directory.

You see, if you are running GnomeMeeting on your corporate or home LAN, you should have no problems. The same holds true if you are running it from a single machine connected to the Internet; odds are this will work without a hitch. The catch comes when you try to work from behind a firewall using masquerading or NAT (Network Address Translation). If you are running an IP tables firewall (as discussed in Chapter 23, "Security"), you need to allow routing of port 1720 to your internal client.

At this stage of the game, you can get into some reasonably complex firewall issues. For starters, your client is *hiding* behind a firewall that is protecting its true IP address from the outside. This is great for security, but it makes it hard for people to contact you. Some networks that already do VOIP will be using a gatekeeper (such as the free GNU Gatekeeper) or a router that does H.323 forwarding. Others have to get more creative, but luckily, recent versions of GnomeMeeting make this easier.

Click Edit on the GnomeMeeting menu bar and select Preferences. From the sidebar on the left, select NAT settings. A window will appear like the one in Figure 32-5.

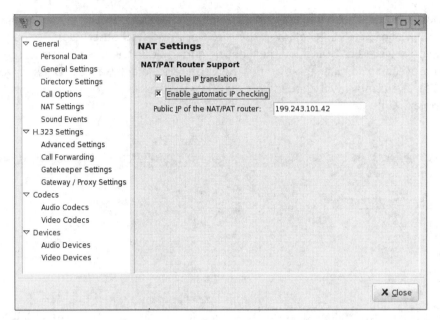

FIGURE 32-5   Changing NAT settings in GnomeMeeting's preferences dialog.

Over on the right, there are two check boxes. The first is labeled Enable IP translation. If you are running behind a firewall or router using NAT, enter your public IP address in the field below (labeled Public IP of the NAT/PAT router). To take advantage of this feature, you need to be registered with the ILS server's address book (which I talked about earlier). The second check box is related to the first. It enables IP checking from the directory server at ils.seconix.com.

The Road Ahead

GnomeMeeting is already a mature, well-engineered project and a great addition to the VOIP communication landscape, but it is also an active project with a great deal of energy behind it. The GnomeMeeting web site provides regular updates to the software, help, and other resources for VOIP. It's also a great place to check out what's coming in future releases. The future may be now, but it's also still out there.

Resources

GnomeMeeting

www.gnomemeeting.org

GNU Gatekeeper

www.gnugk.org

OpenH323

www.openh323.org

appendix

A

The GNU General Public License

This is a copy of the GNU General Public License. If you wish to see the original, visit the Free Software Foundation web site. The direct link to the license is www.gnu.org/copyleft/gpl.htm.

On that web site, you may also want to check out the comparative list of license types (both commercial and noncommercial) and how they compare to the GNU GPL. Most interesting here is the definition of whether a license qualifies as free and whether it is compatible with the GPL. To compare, go straight to www.gnu.org/philosophy/license-list.html.

Now, without further adieu, here is the GNU GPL.

GNU GENERAL PUBLIC LICENSE

Version 2, June 1991

Copyright (C) 1989, 1991 Free Software Foundation, Inc.

59 Temple Place, Suite 330, Boston, MA 02111-1307 USA

Everyone is permitted to copy and distribute verbatim copies of this license document, but changing it is not allowed.

Preamble

The licenses for most software are designed to take away your freedom to share and change it. By contrast, the GNU General Public License is intended to guarantee your freedom to share and change free software—to make sure the software is free for all its users. This General Public License applies to most of the Free Software Foundation's software and to any other program whose authors commit to using it. (Some other Free Software Foundation software is covered by the GNU Library General Public License instead.) You can apply it to your programs, too.

When we speak of free software, we are referring to freedom, not price. Our General Public Licenses are designed to make sure that you have the freedom to distribute copies of free software (and charge for this service if you wish), that you receive source code or can get it if you want it, that you can change the software or use pieces of it in new free programs; and that you know you can do these things.

To protect your rights, we need to make restrictions that forbid anyone to deny you these rights or to ask you to surrender the rights. These restrictions translate to certain responsibilities for you if you distribute copies of the software, or if you modify it.

For example, if you distribute copies of such a program, whether gratis or for a fee, you must give the recipients all the rights that you have. You must make sure that they, too, receive or can get the source code. And you must show them these terms so they know their rights.

We protect your rights with two steps: (1) copyright the software, and (2) offer you this license which gives you legal permission to copy, distribute and/or modify the software.

Also, for each author's protection and ours, we want to make certain that everyone understands that there is no warranty for this free software. If the software is modified by someone else and passed on, we want its recipients to know that what they have is not the original, so that any problems introduced by others will not reflect on the original authors' reputations.

Finally, any free program is threatened constantly by software patents. We wish to avoid the danger that redistributors of a free program will individually obtain patent licenses, in effect making the program proprietary. To prevent this, we have made it clear that any patent must be licensed for everyone's free use or not licensed at all.

The precise terms and conditions for copying, distribution and modification follow.

GNU GENERAL PUBLIC LICENSE
TERMS AND CONDITIONS FOR COPYING, DISTRIBUTION AND MODIFICATION

0. This License applies to any program or other work which contains a notice placed by the copyright holder saying it may be distributed under the terms of this General Public License. The "Program," below, refers to any such program or work, and a "work based on the Program" means either the Program or any derivative work under copyright law: that is to say, a work containing the Program or a portion of it, either verbatim or with modifications and/or translated into another language. (Hereinafter, translation is included without limitation in the term "modification.") Each licensee is addressed as "you."

Activities other than copying, distribution and modification are not covered by this License; they are outside its scope. The act of running the Program is not restricted, and the output from the Program is covered only if its contents constitute a work based on the Program (independent of having been made by running the Program). Whether that is true depends on what the Program does.

1. You may copy and distribute verbatim copies of the Program's source code as you receive it, in any medium, provided that you conspicuously and appropriately publish on each copy an appropriate copyright notice and disclaimer of warranty; keep intact all the notices that refer to this License and to the absence of any warranty; and give any other recipients of the Program a copy of this License along with the Program.

You may charge a fee for the physical act of transferring a copy, and you may at your option offer warranty protection in exchange for a fee.

2. You may modify your copy or copies of the Program or any portion of it, thus forming a work based on the Program, and copy and distribute such modifications or work under the terms of Section 1 above, provided that you also meet all of these conditions:

a) You must cause the modified files to carry prominent notices stating that you changed the files and the date of any change.

b) You must cause any work that you distribute or publish, that in whole or in part contains or is derived from the Program or any part thereof, to be licensed as a whole at no charge to all third parties under the terms of this License.

c) If the modified program normally reads commands interactively when run, you must cause it, when started running for such interactive use in the most ordinary way, to print or display an announcement including an appropriate copyright notice and a notice that there is no warranty (or else, saying that you provide a warranty) and that users may redistribute the program under these conditions, and telling the user how to view a copy of this License. (Exception: if the Program itself is interactive but does not normally print such an announcement, your work based on the Program is not required to print an announcement.)

These requirements apply to the modified work as a whole. If identifiable sections of that work are not derived from the Program, and can be reasonably considered independent and separate works in themselves, then this License, and its terms, do not apply to those sections when you distribute them as separate works. But when you distribute the same sections as part of a whole which is a work based on the Program, the distribution of the whole must be on the terms of this License, whose permissions for other licensees extend to the entire whole, and thus to each and every part regardless of who wrote it.

Thus, it is not the intent of this section to claim rights or contest your rights to work written entirely by you; rather, the intent is to exercise the right to control the distribution of derivative or collective works based on the Program.

In addition, mere aggregation of another work not based on the Program with the Program (or with a work based on the Program) on a volume of a storage or distribution medium does not bring the other work under the scope of this License.

3. You may copy and distribute the Program (or a work based on it, under Section 2) in object code or executable form under the terms of Sections 1 and 2 above provided that you also do one of the following:

a) Accompany it with the complete corresponding machine-readable source code, which must be distributed under the terms of Sections 1 and 2 above on a medium customarily used for software interchange; or,

b) Accompany it with a written offer, valid for at least three years, to give any third party, for a charge no more than your cost of physically performing source distribution, a complete machine-readable copy of the corresponding source code, to be distributed under the terms of Sections 1 and 2 above on a medium customarily used for software interchange; or,

c) Accompany it with the information you received as to the offer to distribute corresponding source code. (This alternative is allowed only for noncommercial distribution and only if you received the program in object code or executable form with such an offer, in accord with Subsection b above.)

The source code for a work means the preferred form of the work for making modifications to it. For an executable work, complete source code means all the source code for all modules it contains, plus any associated interface definition files, plus the scripts used to control compilation and installation of the executable. However, as a special exception, the source code distributed need not include anything that is normally distributed (in either source or binary form) with the major components (compiler, kernel, and so on) of the operating system on which the executable runs, unless that component itself accompanies the executable.

If distribution of executable or object code is made by offering access to copy from a designated place, then offering equivalent access to copy the source code from the same place counts as distribution of the source code, even though third parties are not compelled to copy the source along with the object code.

4. You may not copy, modify, sublicense, or distribute the Program except as expressly provided under this License. Any attempt otherwise to copy, modify, sublicense or distribute the Program is void, and will automatically terminate your rights under this License. However, parties who have received copies, or rights, from you under this License will not have their licenses terminated so long as such parties remain in full compliance.

5. You are not required to accept this License, since you have not signed it. However, nothing else grants you permission to modify or distribute the Program or its derivative works. These actions are prohibited by law if you do not accept this License. Therefore, by modifying or distributing the Program (or any work based on the Program), you indicate your acceptance of this License to do so, and all its terms and conditions for copying, distributing or modifying the Program or works based on it.

6. Each time you redistribute the Program (or any work based on the Program), the recipient automatically receives a license from the original licensor to copy, distribute or modify the Program subject to these terms and conditions. You may not impose any further restrictions on the recipients' exercise of the rights granted herein. You are not responsible for enforcing compliance by third parties to this License.

7. If, as a consequence of a court judgment or allegation of patent infringement or for any other reason (not limited to patent issues), conditions are imposed on you (whether by court order, agreement or otherwise) that contradict the conditions of this License, they do not excuse you from the conditions of this License. If you cannot distribute so as to satisfy simultaneously your obligations under this License and any other pertinent obligations, then as a consequence you may not distribute the Program at all. For example, if a patent license would not permit royalty-free redistribution of the Program by all those who receive copies directly or indirectly through you, then the only

way you could satisfy both it and this License would be to refrain entirely from distribution of the Program.

If any portion of this section is held invalid or unenforceable under any particular circumstance, the balance of the section is intended to apply and the section as a whole is intended to apply in other circumstances.

It is not the purpose of this section to induce you to infringe any patents or other property right claims or to contest validity of any such claims; this section has the sole purpose of protecting the integrity of the free software distribution system, which is implemented by public license practices. Many people have made generous contributions to the wide range of software distributed through that system in reliance on consistent application of that system; it is up to the author/donor to decide if he or she is willing to distribute software through any other system and a licensee cannot impose that choice.

This section is intended to make thoroughly clear what is believed to be a consequence of the rest of this License.

8. If the distribution and/or use of the Program is restricted in certain countries either by patents or by copyrighted interfaces, the original copyright holder who places the Program under this License may add an explicit geographical distribution limitation excluding those countries, so that distribution is permitted only in or among countries not thus excluded. In such case, this License incorporates the limitation as if written in the body of this License.

9. The Free Software Foundation may publish revised and/or new versions of the General Public License from time to time. Such new versions will be similar in spirit to the present version, but may differ in detail to address new problems or concerns.

Each version is given a distinguishing version number. If the Program specifies a version number of this License which applies to it and "any later version," you have the option of following the terms and conditions either of that version or of any later version published by the Free Software Foundation. If the Program does not specify a version number of this License, you may choose any version ever published by the Free Software Foundation.

10. If you wish to incorporate parts of the Program into other free programs whose distribution conditions are different, write to the author to ask for permission. For software which is copyrighted by the Free Software Foundation, write to the Free Software Foundation; we sometimes make exceptions for this. Our decision will be guided by the two goals of preserving the free status of all derivatives of our free software and of promoting the sharing and reuse of software generally.

NO WARRANTY

11. BECAUSE THE PROGRAM IS LICENSED FREE OF CHARGE, THERE IS NO WARRANTY FOR THE PROGRAM, TO THE EXTENT PERMITTED BY APPLICABLE LAW. EXCEPT WHEN OTHERWISE STATED IN WRITING THE COPYRIGHT HOLDERS AND/OR OTHER PARTIES PROVIDE THE PROGRAM "AS IS" WITHOUT WARRANTY OF ANY KIND, EITHER EXPRESSED OR IMPLIED, INCLUDING, BUT NOT LIMITED TO, THE IMPLIED WARRANTIES OF MERCHANTABILITY AND FITNESS FOR A PARTICULAR PURPOSE. THE ENTIRE RISK AS TO THE QUALITY AND PERFORMANCE OF THE PROGRAM IS WITH YOU. SHOULD THE PROGRAM PROVE DEFECTIVE, YOU ASSUME THE COST OF ALL NECESSARY SERVICING, REPAIR OR CORRECTION.

12. IN NO EVENT UNLESS REQUIRED BY APPLICABLE LAW OR AGREED TO IN WRITING WILL ANY COPYRIGHT HOLDER, OR ANY OTHER PARTY WHO MAY MODIFY AND/OR REDISTRIBUTE THE PROGRAM AS PERMITTED ABOVE, BE LIABLE TO YOU FOR DAMAGES, INCLUDING ANY GENERAL, SPECIAL, INCIDENTAL OR CONSEQUENTIAL DAMAGES ARISING OUT OF THE USE OR INABILITY TO USE THE PROGRAM (INCLUDING BUT NOT LIMITED TO LOSS OF DATA OR DATA BEING RENDERED INACCURATE OR LOSSES SUSTAINED BY YOU OR THIRD PARTIES OR A FAILURE OF THE PROGRAM TO OPERATE WITH ANY OTHER PROGRAMS), EVEN IF SUCH HOLDER OR OTHER PARTY HAS BEEN ADVISED OF THE POSSIBILITY OF SUCH DAMAGES.

END OF TERMS AND CONDITIONS

How to Apply These Terms to Your New Programs

If you develop a new program, and you want it to be of the greatest possible use to the public, the best way to achieve this is to make it free software which everyone can redistribute and change under these terms.

To do so, attach the following notices to the program. It is safest to attach them to the start of each source file to most effectively convey the exclusion of warranty; and each file should have at least the "copyright" line and a pointer to where the full notice is found.

<one line to give the program's name and a brief idea of what it does.>
Copyright (C) <year> <name of author>

This program is free software; you can redistribute it and/or modify it under the terms of the GNU General Public License as published by the Free Software Foundation; either version 2 of the License, or (at your option) any later version.

This program is distributed in the hope that it will be useful, but WITHOUT ANY WARRANTY; without even the implied warranty of MERCHANTABILITY or FITNESS FOR A PARTICULAR PURPOSE. See the GNU General Public License for more details.

You should have received a copy of the GNU General Public License along with this program; if not, write to the Free Software Foundation, Inc., 59 Temple Place, Suite 330, Boston, MA 02111-1307 USA

Also add information on how to contact you by electronic and paper mail.

If the program is interactive, make it output a short notice like this when it starts in an interactive mode:

Gnomovision version 69, Copyright (C) year name of author

Gnomovision comes with ABSOLUTELY NO WARRANTY; for details type 'show w'. This is free software, and you are welcome to redistribute it under certain conditions; type 'show c' for details.

The hypothetical commands 'show w' and 'show c' should show the appropriate parts of the General Public License. Of course, the commands you use may be called something other than 'show w' and 'show c'; they could even be mouse-clicks or menu items—whatever suits your program.

You should also get your employer (if you work as a programmer) or your school, if any, to sign a "copyright disclaimer" for the program, if necessary. Here is a sample; alter the names:

Yoyodyne, Inc., hereby disclaims all copyright interest in the program

'Gnomovision' (which makes passes at compilers) written by James Hacker.

<signature of Ty Coon>, 1 April 1989

Ty Coon, President of Vice

This General Public License does not permit incorporating your program into proprietary programs. If your program is a subroutine library, you may consider it more useful to permit linking proprietary applications with the library. If this is what you want to do, use the GNU Library General Public License instead of this License.

B

Automation and Scripting

I've joked for years that system administrators are notoriously lazy people. They will work impossibly long hours late into the night with the sole intention of automating a process so they never have to do the work again. That is precisely the kind of system administrator I have always been—which means I pay for my laziness by constantly working to find ways to not work. I am not alone in thinking this way. Larry Wall, the perl guru, claims that laziness is one of the three great virtues of a programmer. I say "administrator." He says "programmer."

As support for this claim regarding the virtue of laziness, I did a quick search on a popular Internet search engine recently using the words "laziness," "system," and "administrator," and I got over 6,900 hits. Robert A. Heinlein wrote a story about a man too lazy to fail. In fact, in *Time Enough for Love*, one of his characters, Lazarus Long, claims that "progress is made by lazy men looking for easier ways to do things." Suffice it to say that in the computer world, laziness (combined with a little cleverness) can be exceedingly useful to both administrators and their clients.

I am going to show you how to let your system do some of the repetitious, simple, yet time-consuming tasks for you. If you are ready to share the load with your Linux system, then here we go.

cron: Punching Linux's Clock

One of the basic processes running on your system is a utility called cron. The actual program is called crond (the cron daemon), and cron is a little program that does a great deal. Every UNIX system has some form of cron as part of the system scheduler. On my Red Hat Linux system (and on most distributions), cron is actually Vixie cron written by Paul Vixie. Slackware's cron is a little different; it uses Matthew Dillon's dcron package instead.

So, how, you ask, will change it your life? What will it do for you? It enables you to run repetitive tasks at the time and date specified by a user in a file called a crontab. Entries in the crontab run with the user's ID and privileges and are stored as the username (this is their name from the /etc/passwd file). For instance, root's crontab is called root. Every minute, cron wakes up and checks to see if any jobs need to be run. These jobs can be just about anything you can put into a script file: doing backups, cleaning up log files, removing core files, emailing you a daily Linux quote from the fortune program, and so on. This version of cron also checks to see if any of the directories and files it monitors have been changed. If so, it rereads those files and adds them to its to-do list again. The plus is that you do not have to restart cron.

The location of the crontab varies slightly from system to system. There are also cron jobs that exist on the system, more or less for the system alone. Have a look in your /var/spool/cron directory. On my Red Hat system, the various user crontabs are all there. On a Debian system, there is a further subdirectory called crontabs under which the user crontabs live.

The times at which the commands in `cron.daily`, `cron.weekly`, and others get executed are in the `/etc/crontab` file. Here's what mine looks like:

```
SHELL=/bin/bash
PATH=/sbin:/bin:/usr/sbin:/usr/bin
MAILTO=root
HOME=/
# run-parts
01 * * * * root run-parts /etc/cron.hourly
02 4 * * * root run-parts /etc/cron.daily
22 4 * * 0 root run-parts /etc/cron.weekly
42 4 1 * * root run-parts /etc/cron.monthly
```

Now that I have that out of the way, here is a `crontab` entry for the root user:

```
30 2 * * * /usr/local/.Admin/backup.system 1>/dev/null 2>/dev/null
```

Look at the last entry in the previous `crontab` snippet. The command is `/usr/local/.Admin/backup.system`, and its standard input and output is being redirected to `/dev/null`. Using the field definitions as explained previously, you can see that the command runs at 2:30 am every day of every week of every month. The * (asterisk) means always.

There are six fields in a `crontab` entry:

- Minute, which is always between 0 and 59
- Hour, which runs from 0 to 23
- Day of the month, which is from 1 to 31
- Month, which is from 1 to 12
- Day of the week, which is listed numerically, with 0 being Sunday
- Command string, which is what you wanted to automate in the first place

If you want something to run several times in a day, you don't need a line for each entry. For instance, a process set to run every 15 minutes could be written like this:

```
0,15,30,45 * * * * /path/to/my_15_minute/process
```

You can also indicate sequential periods without multiple lines. Let's take the same process as before, but this time I want it to run Monday through Friday at the same 15-minute intervals. I could enter the day field as 1,2,3,4,5. This could get tedious, not to mention ugly; however, I tried the same thing for something that ran from the first of the month through to the fifteenth of the month. Try this instead:

```
0,15,30,45 * * 1-15 * /path/to/my_15_minute/process
```

Testing Your Job

A good way to test a `cron` job is to schedule your job for five minutes from now (or whatever) and watch the results. In addition, `cron` sends messages indicating any output information to the user's mailbox, which is particularly useful when you are redirecting `stdin` and `stdout` to `/dev/null`.

Editing the crontab

The proper way to edit a `crontab` is to use the command `crontab -e`. This puts you into the `vi` editor, where you can make your changes. When you write your changes, `crontab` verifies (to some degree) the sanity of your changes and informs you if you have done something really strange. For those of you who are less than fond of `vi`, you can specify another editor by using the `EDITOR` environment variable, as in:

```
export EDITOR=pico
```

You can also edit another user's `crontab`, assuming you are root, by using this version of the command:

```
crontab -u user_name -e
```

The -u flag defines the alternate user.

Could I See an Example?

I know that you are just dying to go out and automate something with `cron`—but what? Here's a thought. Every system builds up a collection of old junk files that no one ever looks at again. Every system accumulates core files, those discards of a program gone bad or interrupted less than gracefully. Let's look at some ways to automate the process of discovery, starting with a look at find, which was introduced in Chapter 10, "Working with the Shell."

Here's a little one-line refresher that looks for anything greater than 500K (1,024 512-byte blocks) that hasn't been modified (the -mtime parameter) or accessed (the -atime parameter) in the last 12 months. The -ls parameter simply means that find should list what it finds.

```
find /data -size 1024 \( -mtime +365 -o -atime +365 \) -ls
```

> *Note* Remember not to ignore those backslashes in front of the parentheses; these are shell escape characters that need to be there.

The previous example is fairly simple, but you can use it as the basis of something a bit more complex. How about a job that runs every night, logs what it finds, and emails the result to you at another machine?

```
#!/bin/bash
#
# Locate files and report to me.
# Marcel Gagne
#
search_log=/tmp/foundfiles
rm -f $search_log
touch $search_log
#
echo "---------------------------- " >> $search_log
echo "Looking for big old files . . . " >> $search_log
echo "---------------------------- " >> $search_log
#
find /data1 -size +2048 \( -mtime +180 -o -atime +180 \)  \
    -ls -exec file {} \; >> $search_log
#
echo "---------------------------- " >> $search_log
echo "Looking SUID / GUID files . . . " >> $search_log
echo "---------------------------- " >> $search_log
#
find / -type f \( -perm -2000 -o -perm -4000 \) -ls >> $search_log
#
echo "------------------------------------------- " >>
```

```
$search_log
echo "Looking for core files or old editor files . . . " >>
$search_log
echo "------------------------------------------------- " >>
$search_log
#
find / \( -name core -o -name "*~" \) -print >> $search_log
#
echo "------------------------------- " >> $search_log
echo "All done!" >> $search_log
mail -s "Big and old file report" myuser@anothersys.com < $search_log
```

I could have modified the search for core files so that it deleted them as it found them, but in this example, I want a complete report so that I can decide what gets deleted after I have had a chance to study the report and be sure. If you would like the core files automatically deleted as a result of the search, try this version of the find command:

```
find / -name core -exec rm -f {} \;
```

This simply seeks out and destroys any and all core files from your system. Note once again that the backslash with the semicolon is required at the end of the find command. The -exec option tells find that a command string will follow. The double braces ({}) at the end of the line tells find to substitute all it found and pass it to the command string, which in this case is rm -f.

 Warning Normally, I might worry about letting the system simply delete what it finds (even if I am the one who told it to do so), but core files are an exception and I am using rm -f rather than rm -rf, which does a recursive delete of whatever it finds. Consequently, the only real fear I might have—that the core directory under /proc might accidentally be deleted—is addressed. It will remain safe, as this script/command will leave it untouched.

Call the script seekanddestroy (or whatever else you might like), and save it in your /usr/local/.Admin directory. Using chmod +x, let's make the script executable and then create a cron job to run it. How about every morning at 3:00?

```
0 3 * * * /usr/local/.Admin/seekanddestroy
```

Running Jobs with at

The truly great thing about `cron` isn't strictly that you can run scripts that automate otherwise tedious processes, but that you can have the system do it when you are not there. Ah, if only you could get your employer to pay you for doing work while you are away from the office.

Another way to run jobs is with the `at` command. You could, of course, do the same thing by letting `cron` handle it with a `crontab` entry. The reason for using `at` is that it enables you to do some pretty free-form stuff. For instance, say I am leaving on vacation next Tuesday. It is now Thursday, and I want to create a vacation notification for anybody sending me email while I am gone. The trouble is that although I remember to do this now, I might not remember on Monday. I could go through the trouble of creating a `cron` job, or just have `at` execute the command for me when the time comes.

```
at 6 pm Monday -f /path_to/file_that_updates_vacation_program
```

As you can see, `at` understands English-like definitions of time and dates, which makes defining when you want something to happen pretty easy. The `-f` parameter tells `at` to read the necessary commands from a script file. At any time, you can find out what jobs you have queued for the `at` command to execute with the `atq` command. By the way, `atq` is synonymous with `at -l`. The following is a sample of the command and its output. The 12 at the beginning reflects the job number for the `at` queue.

```
# atq
12   2000-09-26   18:00 a
```

If you don't want to bother with writing a script file, you can do the whole thing from the command line, as follows:

```
at noon today
at> /usr/games/fortune -l linuxcookie | mail -s "Read this"
me@here.dom
at> ^D
```

If I type the command as above, specifying only a date and time, the `at` command enters a dialogue with an `at>` prompt where I enter my commands.

The command prompt repeats with each line I enter. To signal completion of my commands, I press <Ctrl+D>. To give you an idea of the flexibility of Linux shell scripting, here is another way to do it:

```
at noon today << MY_COMMANDS
/usr/games/fortune -l linuxcookie | mail -s "Linux info"
me@here.dom
MY_COMMANDS
```

Finally, if it turns out that you are only kidding and you do not really want to run the job, you can delete it with the atrm command. Using the output from the previous atq example, you can remove job 12 from the queue like this:

```
atrm 12
```

A Question of Permissions

I suppose I should have told you about this earlier. Those of you who followed the golden rule of never running from the root account (unless absolutely necessary) probably found yourselves denied from doing any of this. The at command simply says:

```
You do not have permission to use at.
```

End of story. Meanwhile, cron is a tad more vocal:

```
You (mgagne) are not allowed to use this program (crontab).
See crontab(1) for more information.
```

Access to the at command is controlled by the /etc/at.allow and /etc/at.deny files. The cron command access is controlled by the (you guessed it) /etc/cron.allow and /etc/cron.deny files. These are simply text files with a list of users allowed access to either at or cron. If you want to give everyone access, simply leave an empty at.deny or cron.deny file in place, because these represent a list of who *isn't* allowed access. To limit access to a select few, you can simply create an at.allow or cron.allow file, because this is a text list of the *privileged* users of the at or cron command. In the latter case, make sure you at least include the root user in that list.

An Introduction to Writing Shell Scripts

One of my favorite lines is "I am not a programmer," which isn't to say that I don't know how to program or that I haven't wrestled with a number of different programming languages over the years. Names like COBOL, FORTRAN, BASIC, C, C++, Ada, perl, and the dreaded assembler all come to mind as a reminder. I have been known to write programs, and I am likely to do so again. It just doesn't happen to be the sort of thing that excites me. Administration excites me. So do network design, security, systems integration, and the great bugaboo, technical support (I love puzzles).

I'm like the chef who likes to put a number of ingredients together to create a new culinary masterpiece. Like that chef, I rely on others to provide me with the ingredients to do my work. Consequently, I have a deep admiration for professional (and amateur) programmers who can take a complex project and devote weeks or even months to bring out the tools that people like me rely on.

That said, as an administrator, you will need to program on some level. A single tool is rarely the answer to a single problem, but sometimes, assembling the right blend of tools will provide the exact solution you seek. Putting those tools together requires programming. The average Linux distribution comes with a plethora of programming and program development environments. Luckily, the average administrator can satisfy all of his or her programming needs with a couple of very neat languages.

One of those languages is something you are already using.

Shells as Far as the Eye Can See

The shell is the most basic of environments for working with your Linux system. Whatever you may think of working in a text environment, I guarantee that once you have fully experienced the power of simple text, you will be forever convinced. Text is compact. Text is fast. System administration over a network is best experienced at the shell level. Those forced to resort to graphical tools over a slow modem connection are also quickly converted.

What many people do not realize is that the shell is actually a programming language. There are many shells. The most common in the Linux world is called bash, the Bourne Again Shell. Other shells you may find on your Linux system include sh, the classic Bourne shell (I have yet to find a major Linux or

UNIX distribution that did not include it), `pdksh` (the public domain Korn shell), and that old programmer's favorite, `csh` (the C shell).

The list of shells I've given you so far is but a small subset. There's `ash` (stands for a shell), `tcsh` (an enhanced C shell), and `zsh` (the Z shell). Like walking along the beach and building a collection of interesting and unique shell specimens, a little tour through your favorite software repository, such as Freshmeat (`www.freshmeat.net`), will show you that people are constantly playing with and designing shells. Far from being an exhaustive list of the shells that exist for Linux, my list is merely a collection of the more popular ones. Certainly, all of these are likely to be on your distribution CD.

Programs written using these shells are collectively called *shell scripts*. Covering all of these in detail would constitute another book (or perhaps several books), so I won't even pretend to attempt it. I do, however, want to get you comfortable with the idea of writing small, useful scripts to do your job as an administrator of your Linux domain, no matter how small or large. To that end, I will concentrate on `bash`. Then, I'll cover some of the other scripting languages out there to see how they might best help you do your job.

It's Commands All the Way Down

A shell script can be just a collection of commands saved in a file. Too easy?

Say that throughout the day, I regularly check the time and date, print the disk-free information, and check how long my system has been running with `uptime`. I can open a blank file with my favorite editor and type each command on its own line like this:

```
date
df
uptime
```

If I save these lines as `check3` (a completely arbitrary name), I then can execute them as a script by typing:

```
bash check3
```

That's it. The shell, `bash`, executes the three commands in that file and exits. The simplest shell script imaginable is the command itself. For instance, while writing this book, I would occasionally capture a snapshot of a particular window using the `import` command. Often, I would capture images from another desktop, a notebook computer that sat beside the main workstation on which I did my writing. The reason for the two was that I could build and rebuild the notebook while leaving my workstation untouched. To capture the images on the notebook, I used this command:

```
import -border -frame -colorspace GRAY -display
testsys:0image_name.tif
```

To simplify my life and save several hundred keystrokes in the course of my work, I created this `alias` command:

```
alias grabwin0='import -border -frame -colorspace GRAY -display\
testsys:0'
```

I also used a `grabwin` alias for the local system. This reduced my typing to `grabwin0 filename.tif` for each capture. Another way to save keystrokes would have been to type the command into a file called `grabwin`, save it in `/usr/local/bin`, and make it executable. Rather than an alias, I would have had a shell script. Here are the steps:

```
vi /usr/local/bin/grabwin
[Note: Here you type the command in and save your work.]
chmod +x /usr/local/bin/grabwin
```

But wait—how do I pass the filename that I want to save? If I just run this script by typing `/usr/local/bin/grabwin my_file.tif`, it doesn't create the filename at all. That's because the script isn't using the information being passed to it. This brings us to the subject of parameters.

Passing Parameters

Here's a really simple way to experience how the shell interprets parameters passed to it. Write this little script and call it `paramtest`:

```
#!/bin/bash
# This script demonstrates positional parameters
#
echo "This is parameter 0 : $0"
echo "This is parameter 1 : $1"
echo "This is parameter 2 : $2"
echo "This is parameter 3 : $3"
echo "Here are all the parameters : $*"
```

Make it executable with:

```
chmod +x paramtest
```

Now, execute it like this:

```
./paramtest this is a shell script
```

This is the output you will see:

```
This is parameter 0 :  ./paramtest
This is parameter 1 :  this
This is parameter 2 :  is
This is parameter 3 :  a
Here are all the parameters : this is a shell script
```

The first thing you should notice is that the script name (or the command, if you prefer) is parameter $0. Parameters $1, $2, and $3 are the first three words passed to the script. Notice also that the last two words, "shell script," have simply been absorbed by the script. These would have been represented by $4 and $5, which you did not ask to have echoed to the screen. How about the last line? As you can see, the entire list of parameters (not counting the program name) is echoed back.

A First Look at Variables

The $0, $1, $2, and so on, are *variables*. In other words, they can represent different values depending on what parameters are passed to your script. The $* variable is a special one: It represents all the parameters passed to the shell. Like the $0, $1, and other number variables, this is one is built into the shell itself. You do not have to define it.

So, going back to the grabwin example, I could modify the script by simply adding a $1 to the end of the command. Then, passing a filename would work. Here's the right script now:

```
import -border -frame -colorspace GRAY -display testsys:0 $1
```

To make the script more intelligent, I could add a check for a parameter using the if construct. The following is my updated script. I am also going to specify that I always want to use the bash shell for execution.

```
#!/bin/bash
# This script will capture a window on system testsys
if [ $# -eq 0 ]
then
    echo "grabwin : You must specify a filename"
    exit 0
else
    import -border -frame -colorspace GRAY -display testsys:0 $1
fi
```

Lots of stuff here. The script checks to see if there are any parameters at all. If the count of parameters (that's what the variable $# means) is zero, it prints an error message and exits. If I remembered to pass it a filename, I get a much nicer, "job well done" kind of message.

```
$ grabwin eterm.tif
Capture of eterm.tif completed.
```

More on Variables

When you are programming with the shell, you deal with variables on different levels. You have the *built-in variables* you saw earlier, and you can *assign* variables. For instance, without writing a script, type this line at your shell (command-line) prompt:

```
hours=24
```

Then type this:

```
echo "There are $hours hours in a typical day"
```

The system responds with this:

```
There are 24 hours in a typical day.
```

You access that variable by putting a dollar sign ($) in front of it. If you just enter the echo line in a shell script (without the hours=24 line), made that script executable, and ran it, you would get this:

```
There are    in a typical day.
```

The shell script did not pick up the $hours variable. For the shell script to know about the variable named hours, you need to export it. There are two ways to do this. You can assign the variable as you did, and then type the command export hours. Or, you can put the whole thing on one line and save yourself some keystrokes, as in:

```
export hours="24"
```

Running the script now displays a much more intelligent message about how many hours are really in a day.

Aside from user-assigned variables, the script can make use of *environment variables*. These are variables set for you at login time by the system. Some of these are sometimes overwritten by the .bash_profile file in the user's home directory or the global /etc/profile. A common one to see modified is the PATH variable, which lists the possible search paths for executables. Check your own $HOME/.bash_profile file for the references to PATH.

```
PATH=$PATH:$HOME/bin:/usr/local/bin
export USERNAME BASH_ENV PATH
```

As you can see, you can modify an environment variable by referencing it in your assignment. The second line above exports PATH and a number of other variables so that they are available to you in any shell and any environment in which you might work. To have a look at your environment variables, type the env command.

Special Characters

Certain characters mean very specific things to the shell. Table B-1 lists a sampling of what you will encounter.

TABLE B-1   Characters with Special Meaning to the Shell

Character	Description
$	Highlights the beginning of a variable's name
#	Comments a line
?	Matches a character
*	Matches any number of characters
.	Sources or tells the shell to execute the filename that follows
"	Defines a string
'	Defines even special characters as part of a string
`	Executes what is inside the ticks
\	Escapes the character that follows
[ ]	Lists a range of characters inside the brackets

The dollar sign ($) is one that you have already seen. It indicates the beginning of a variable name. You've also see the comment character (#), and in the next section, I will discuss some of its special properties. And way back in Chapter 10, "Working with the Shell," I talked about the question mark (?) and the asterisk (*). So, let's now look at some of these others.

First and foremost, I want to talk about the backslash (\). When a backslash is put in front of a special character, it stops the shell from interpreting that special character. Here's a simple and, I think, effective demonstration. At your shell prompt, type this command:

```
$ echo *
```

Did you get a listing of every file in your directory separated by spaces? That's what I thought. Try it again, but this time put a backslash in front of the asterisk.

```
$ echo \*
```

Notice that the shell now echoes a single asterisk. Anytime you want to use a special character like those in the shell, but you don't want them treated in any way special, front them with the backslash, which I suppose is a kind of special treatment itself.

You Can Quote Me on That

Ah, quotes. I have lots of favorites. One of them is "I want to live forever or die trying," which is something Spider Robinson said but I wish I had. Sorry, different kind of quote.

Of course, I should be talking about what quotes mean to the shell. Double quotes ("") tell the shell to interpret what is inside them as a string. This is the way you define variables or echo text back to the terminal:

```
my_variable="This is a double quote \" inside my double quotes."
```

You'll notice that I put a double quote inside my double quotes, but escaped the character with a backslash. If I were to type echo $my_ variable, this is what I would get:

```
This is a double quote " inside my double quotes.
```

Single quotes (') would seem to do the same thing as double quotes on the surface, but they do have another important function. Let's set a couple of variables and build a little shell script.

```
$ os_name="Linux"
$ os_desc="way cool"
$ echo "$os_name is $os_desc."
Linux is way cool.
```

That's more or less what you would expect here. Now, let's put single quotes around that echo command and see the difference:

```
$ echo '$os_name is $os_desc.'
$ os_name is $os_desc.
```

Hmm…it would seem that single quotes stop the shell from interpreting dollar signs as indicators of variable names. Now, how about those back ticks? Back ticks (`), or back quotes, are special in that they execute what is inside them. For instance, if you had a shell script that echoed:

    The current date and time information is . . .

and you wanted to have that something or other filled in, you would want the output of the date command. Here's one way of doing this:

```
the_date=`date`
echo "The current date and time information is $the_date."
```

An easier way to do this is to put the back-quoted date command inside the echo line itself:

```
echo "The current date and time information is `date`."
```

Really Programming the Shell

One of the things I mentioned was that the shell is a real programming language. This is entirely true. You have access to constructs like if... then...else, while and for loops, case statements, and more. Just to give you an idea, here's a little script that runs the fabled Fibonacci sequence (named after famed thirteenth-century Italian mathematician, Leonardo Pisano, also known as Fibonacci).

```
# Run a Fibonacci sequence through 10 iterations
#
last_number=1
previous_number=1
fib_iterations=0
echo "The sequence starts with 1 and 1"
until [ $fib_iterations -ge 10 ]
do
        new_number=`expr $previous_number + $last_number`
        echo "The sum of $previous_number and $last_number is
$new_number"
        previous_number=$last_number
        last_number=$new_number
        fib_iterations=`expr $fib_iterations + 1`
done
#
echo "The sequence ends here after $fib_iterations."
```

Let's try something with a little more system administration potential. We know that Linux is a multiuser system, but letting people log in time and again when they already have sessions open may not be what you want. You may be running a hungry database application that costs you on resources (or licenses) each time somebody logs in. How can you stop users from logging in multiple times? In the following example, you'll create a file called user.allow that you'll put in a hypothetical script directory called /usr/local/.Admin. This is one I actually tend to use. The script is simple. If you list a user ID in this plain-text file with a space and a number, that user is allowed to log in however many times the number specifies.

```
marcel 3
tux 2
natika 4
```

In that example, marcel is allowed three logins, tux is allowed two, and natika is allowed a grand total of four. All other users, by default, are allowed only one login at a time. To make sure that everyone executes this script on login, add this line to the /etc/profile file:

```
.  /usr/local/.Admin/logtest
```

Notice the period at the beginning of the line that tells the shell to source, or execute, the filename that follows. Before you get too comfortable with this wonderful idea, you'll also want to make sure that the root user can log in as many times as needed. I think you've got it all, so let's have a look at the logtest script.

```
# Test for multiple logins and refuse login if beyond configuration
#
if [ "$LOGNAME" != "root" ]
then
        no_logins=`finger | grep $LOGNAME | wc -l`
        no_allowed=`grep $LOGNAME /usr/local/.Admin/user.allow |
cut -f2 -d" "`
        echo "No logins is $no_logins, while allowed is $no_allowed."
        if [ -z $no_allowed ]
        then
                let no_allowed=1
        fi
        echo "There are... $no_logins login processes under your name."
        echo "You are allowed $no_allowed login(s)."
        if [ $no_logins -gt $no_allowed ]
        then
                echo "You have exceeded your allowable limit."
                echo "Please try again later."
                sleep 5
                exit 0
        fi
else
        echo "You are SuperUser and can log in all you want!"
fi
```

Notice the -z test in the line that runs if [-z $no_allowed]. This tests the variable $no_allowed to see whether it is zero length or not. If it is zero (in other words, the UID was not listed in the user.allow exceptions file), you default that number to one.

> *Note* Your shell supports a number of tests on variables and file types. For example, you can test to see if a string length is zero sized (as you did in the example with the -z), if a file is executable (-x), or if a file even exists (-e). There are a number of such tests built in to be used with files or variables. To see what kind of tests the shell supports, type man test.

So, if you try to log in as marcel for the fourth time, you get this message:

```
There are...        4 login processes under your name.
You are allowed 3 login(s).
You have exceeded your allowable limit.
Please try again later.
```

At this point, you get logged out and have to start getting used to the idea of being somewhat less greedy.

Specifying the Shell

If you look through some of your start-up scripts in the /etc/rc.d/init.d directory, or perhaps the /etc/init.d directory, you'll notice that they start with a rather interesting little construct. Here are the first five lines of my inetd start-up script:

```
[root@testsys /root]# head -5 /etc/rc.d/init.d/inet
#! /bin/sh
#
# inet           Start TCP/IP networking services. This script
#                starts the Internet Network Daemon.
#
```

See that #!/bin/sh line at the beginning? This hash-bang, #!/path_ to_shell construct is a means of forcing a specific type of shell for execution of a script. Say that you created a shell script that used C shell-specific structures to do its work. Letting bash do the execution is certainly not going to yield the results you are looking for. Then, there are system functions, such as the at command, that execute all of their commands with /bin/sh. What if you created your script to use some bash commands that the basic sh doesn't understand?

The solution is simple. Just put this line at the top of your shell script:

```
#!/bin/bash
```

Now, even if the shell that runs it is /bin/sh, it will switch to /bin/bash for execution of the script. This is also used to define other scripting environments. Perl scripts have this line at the beginning:

```
#!/usr/bin/perl
```

Keep in mind that the path to the perl interpreter may vary from system to system.

Resources

BASH Programming HOWTO

www.tldp.org/HOWTO/Bash-Prog-Intro-HOWTO.html

Freshmeat

www.freshmeat.net

Index

About the CD-ROM

The CD-ROM included with *Moving to the Linux Business Desktop* contains the following:

WFTL Edition Knoppix: this is a Debian-based distribution that runs entirely from your PC's CD-ROM drive (though much slower than if you actually *install* Linux). That's right. You can run Linux on your personal computer system without having to change your system or uninstall Windows®. This CD is full of great software, some of which is covered in this book. You'll have access to email applications, web browsers, word processors, spreadsheets, games, and more. In fact, you should be able to follow along with this book and do many, *though not all*, of the things covered without having to install Linux at all.

 Note The version of Knoppix included with this book is *not* the official version, but one that has been slightly modified by your humble author. I wish to express my admiration and thanks to Klaus Knopper, the creator of Knoppix, for his fine work, but any questions regarding the included disk should be directed to myself. Visit http://www.marcelgagne.com.

Minimum Suggested Requirements and Instructions

For best performance, your system should have at least a 350 Mhz Pentium class CPU with at least 128 Megabytes of RAM. WFTL Edition Knoppix supports a wide variety of graphics cards, monitors, sound cards, network cards, and other hardware. The odds are pretty good that the WFTL Edition Knoppix CD will work with your system if the minimum requirements are met.

Using the CD should be as simple as shutting down Windows® and doing a reboot. Make sure your PC is set to boot from the CD. WFTL Edition Knoppix boots up to a nice, graphical screen with a simple `boot:` prompt from which you can simply press <Enter> and let the CD do the rest; this is an amazingly simple *install*. As the system comes up, you'll see a number of prompts as hardware is detected and your environment is created. This can take a few minutes, so please be patient.

Additional details on your WFTL Edition Knoppix CD can be found in Chapter 1 of this book in the section titled, "About the CD."

License Agreement

Nearly all of the software on the CD is licensed under the GPL or other OSI approved licenses, but there are some exceptions (see `http://www.gnu.org/copyleft/gpl.html` or the Appendix for a copy of the GPL). While you are free to copy and redistribute this CD, use of the software accompanying *Moving to the Linux Business Desktop* is subject to the terms of the License Agreement and Limited Warranty found in Appendix A.

CD *website* and excerpts from *Linux System Administration: A User's Guide* are copyright Marcel Gagné and Addison-Wesley Professional.

Technical Support

Addison-Wesley does not offer technical support for any of the programs on the CD-ROM. However, if the CD-ROM is damaged, you may obtain a replacement copy by sending an email that describes the problem to: disc_exchange@prenhall.com.